BOOK

The Philip E. Lilienthal imprint
honors special books
in commemoration of a man whose work
at University of California Press from 1954 to 1979
was marked by dedication to young authors
and to high standards in the field of Asian Studies.
Friends, family, authors, and foundations have together
endowed the Lilienthal Fund, which enables UC Press
to publish under this imprint selected books
in a way that reflects the taste and judgment
of a great and beloved editor.

The publisher and the University of California Press Foundation gratefully acknowledge the generous support of the Philip E. Lilienthal Imprint in Asian Studies, established by a major gift from Sally Lilienthal.

Along the Silk Roads in Mongol Eurasia

Along the Silk Roads in Mongol Eurasia

Generals, Merchants, Intellectuals

EDITED BY

Michal Biran, Jonathan Brack, and Francesca Fiaschetti

UNIVERSITY OF CALIFORNIA PRESS

University of California Press
Oakland, California

Library of Congress Cataloging-in-Publication Data

Names: Biran, Michal, editor. | Brack, Jonathan, editor. | Fiaschetti, Francesca, editor.
Title: Along the Silk Roads in Mongol Eurasia : generals, merchants, and intellectuals / Michal Biran, Jonathan Brack, Francesca Fiaschetti.
Description: Oakland, California : University of California Press, [2020] | Includes bibliographical references and index.
Identifiers: LCCN 2019057899 (print) | LCCN 2019057900 (ebook) | ISBN 9780520298743 (cloth) | ISBN 9780520298750 (paperback) | ISBN 9780520970786 (ebook)
Subjects: LCSH: Intellectuals—Mongolia—13th century—Biography. | Intellectuals—Mongolia—14th century—Biography. | Mongols—History, Military—13th century—Biography. | Mongols—History, Military—14th century—Biography. | Merchants—Mongolia—13th century—Biography. | Merchants—Mongolia—14th century—Biography.
Classification: LCC DS798.66.A2 A46 2020 (print) | LCC DS798.66.A2 (ebook) | DDC 950/.2—dc23
LC record available at https://lccn.loc.gov/2019057899
LC ebook record available at https://lccn.loc.gov/2019057900

Manufactured in the United States of America

25 24 23 22 21 20 19 20
10 9 8 7 6 5 4 3 2 1

This volume is dedicated to the memory of
Thomas T. Allsen (1940–2019)

Contents

Illustrations

MAPS

FIGURES

TABLES

Acknowledgments

The present volume originated in the Jerusalem ERC-funded project *Mobility Empire and Cross-Cultural Contacts in Mongol Eurasia* (ERC Grant Agreement n. 312397, under the European Union's Seventh Framework Programme [FP/2007–13]), to which most authors in this volume are connected as former members or friends. Two of the chapters (one by Mukai and Fiaschetti and another by Hodong Kim, kindly translated by Wonhee Cho) have already been published, in Chinese and Korean respectively. We thank the authors for agreeing to having their articles translated and adapted for the volume.

We would also like to thank Ido Wachtel and Amit Niv, who produced most of the maps for this volume, as well as the anonymous reviewers at the various stages, who helped broaden our biographies' selection and sharpen our arguments. At the California University Press, thanks are due to our editor, Eric Schmidt, for his enthusiastic encouragement since this volume's inception, and to Austin Lin, who kindly answered our myriad technical questions.

Michal Biran, Jonathan Brack, Francesca Fiaschetti
Jerusalem-Ulaanbaatar, August 2019

Notes on Dates and Transliterations

Dates are generally given according to the Gregorian calendar. *Hijri* and Chinese dates are given only when they have a special relevance.

Chinese names and terms have been transliterated according to the Pinyin system.

Arabic words, titles, and names have been transliterated according to the system used in the *International Journal of Middle Eastern Studies.* The transliteration of words and names of Persian origin have followed in most cases the Arabic transliteration (e.g., Juwaynī, not Juvaynī, nāmah, not nāme). Common words and place names such as sultan, mamluk, amir, Shiraz, and Baghdad, appear in the text without diacritical points. Well-known place names (e.g., Jerusalem or Damascus) appear in their common English form.

Russian has been transliterated according to the system of the Library of Congress.

Names and terms of Mongolian origin have been transliterated according to Antoine Mostaert's scheme (modified by F.W. Cleaves), except for the following deviations: č has been rendered as ch; š as sh; γ as gh; and ǰ as j. Kh has been rendered q, except for the word khan (instead of qan) and its derivatives. We retained, however, the form qa'an. In general some Mongol terms appear in their Turkicized form, in accordance with their more common appearance in the sources (e.g., yarligh, not jarligh). When this occurs, both forms are indicated in the index.

Introduction

MICHAL BIRAN, JONATHAN BRACK, AND
FRANCESCA FIASCHETTI

In the thirteenth and fourteenth centuries, Chinggis Khan and his heirs established and ruled the largest contiguous empire in world history, an empire that, at its height, extended from Korea to Hungary, and from Iraq, Tibet, and Burma to Siberia. Ruling over roughly two-thirds of the Old World and profoundly impacting also regions beyond its reach, the Mongol Empire created remarkable mobility across Eurasia, with people, ideas, and artifacts traversing vast geographical distances and cultural boundaries. The exchange of goods, people, germs, and more had far-reaching consequences for the Eurasian political, cultural, and economic dynamics. Introducing new commercial, diplomatic, and intellectual networks, but also revitalizing ancient ones, the Mongol Empire significantly advanced the integration of the Old World.

At the center of these transformations were the Silk Roads, the various trade routes—continental and maritime—that connected East Asia mainly to the Islamic world and Europe, and flourished under Mongol rule. Although the term "Silk Road" was introduced only in the late nineteenth century,[1] the various roads that crisscrossed the Old World, from east to west and north to south, were used, in changing constellations and volumes of traffic, already in prehistorical times.[2]

The Mongol era marked a new stage in the history of the Silk Roads, due not only to the growth in volume and scope of the traffic that they channeled. Prior to the Mongol conquests, trade on the Silk Roads was mainly relay trade. Merchants did not travel themselves the entire distance from eastern to western Eurasia; rather, trade was carried out in shorter circuits, eventually linking East Asia and the Islamic world or Europe. Under the Mongols, however, for the first time in history, individual merchants and travelers could, and did, travel the entire distance themselves, from Europe to China and vice versa. The prominent presence of European merchants along the Silk Roads was another innovation of the Mongol period, though Muslim trade networks remained dominant in most of Mongol-ruled Eurasia. In addition to the rise in the number of travelers, their diversity was equally if not more remarkable; in addition to diplomats, soldiers, and merchants, experts in various fields—medicine, astronomy, entertainment, religion, and military affairs, to name just a few—also spanned the continent. Moreover, a considerable group of those who traversed the Silk Roads did so as "commodities" themselves, ranging from captives and slaves to highly skilled personnel who were delivered as tribute. All were forced to relocate across Eurasia.

The chapters in this volume seek to illustrate life along the Mongol Silk Roads by focusing on the stories of male and female individuals of three elite groups from across Mongol Eurasia: military commanders, merchants, and intellectuals. These people came from diverse backgrounds and ethnic groups. They included Mongols, Chinese, Muslims, Qipchaqs, and Europeans. Their personal experiences elucidate aspects of Eurasian cross-cultural contact and physical and social mobility, beginning with the formative years of Chinggis Khan (r. 1206–27) and ending with the empire's collapse during the second half of the fourteenth century.

BACKGROUND: THE MONGOL EMPIRE

The "Mongol moment" in world history (1206–1368) is commonly divided into two: first, the era of the United Mongol Empire (1206–60)—when an ever-expanding polity ruled the newly conquered lands from its center in Mongolia; second, the period of "the Mongol Commonwealth," during which the empire dissolved into four regional empires. Known as khanates or *ulus*es,[3] these four Mongol polities were centered in China, Iran, Central Asia, and the Volga region, and were headed by contending branches of Chinggis Khan's descendants. With the dissolution of the United Empire, the Great Khan's capital shifted from Mongolia to North China, eventually settling in Beijing. Despite the numerous, often bloody, disputes between the four Mongol polities, they retained a strong sense of Chinggisid unity. In the mid-fourteenth

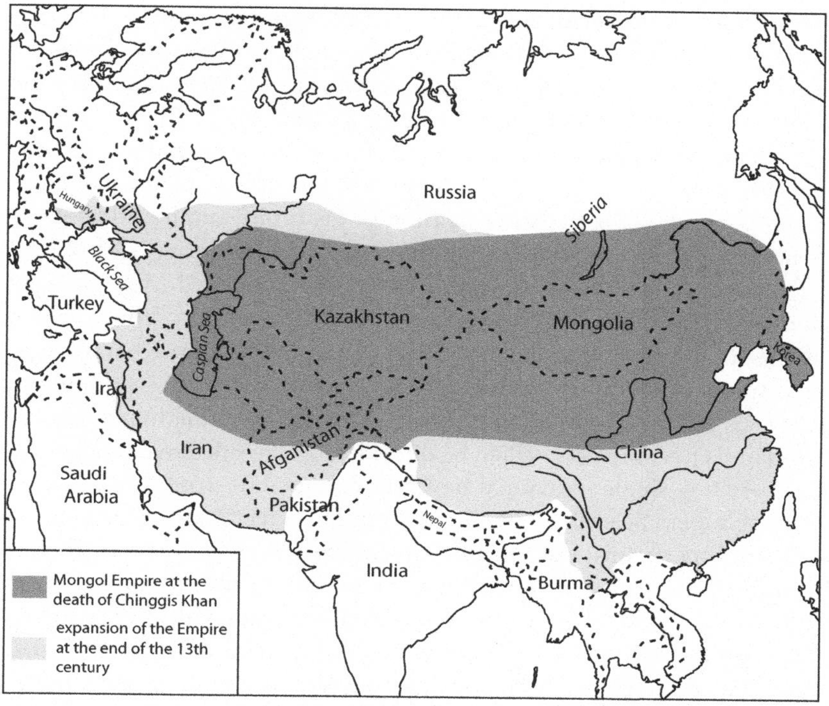

MAP 0.1. Mongol Eurasia (1206–1368) (after Biran 2007, 12–13).

century, all four empires were embroiled in political crises that led to the collapse of the Mongol states in Iran (1336) and China (1368), and considerably weakened the two remaining Steppe khanates. The fall of the Great Khan's state in China is generally considered the end of the "Mongol moment" in world history, although Chinggis Khan's descendants continued to rule in the western Steppe, Muslim Central Asia, and India, until the eighteenth and nineteenth centuries. Moreover, the memory of the empire and its political structures continued to influence patterns of imperial formation and rule across Eurasia well into the early-modern period.

THE UNITED MONGOL EMPIRE (*YEKE MONGGHOL ULUS*, 1206–59)

Most of the empire's territorial expansion, as well as the formation of its institutions and ideology of world domination, took place during the period of the United Empire. After two decades of bloody internecine wars, Temüjin united the Mongolian tribes and in 1206 was enthroned as Chinggis Khan (literally: universal ruler or harsh ruler). He spent the next few years (1204–9) organizing his nascent state. Relying on the precedents established by the earlier Inner Asian nomadic empires, notably the Turkic Empire of the sixth to eighth centuries, Chinggis Khan borrowed, for the consolidation of his future empire, ideological concepts, a writing system, and military and administrative institutions.

Following its incubation period, the newly organized Mongol army had to be put into action soon to prevent its soldiers from turning against each other, provide booty, and maintain Chinggis Khan's image as a successful military leader. Hence, principally from 1209 onward, Chinggis Khan led his armies outside Mongolia, gradually expanding from raids to conquests. When he died in 1227, he ruled over the largest territory any single individual had ever conquered—from north China to the Caspian Sea. One turning point in his career was his victories in Central Asia, against the Muslim Khwārazmshāh, who in the early thirteenth century ruled a vast, though recently assembled, empire, from Iran to the Jaxartes River (present-day Uzbekistan's eastern border). Through his military achievements in Central Asia during the 1220s, Chinggis Khan gained both considerable territory and human capital, including highly qualified nomadic warriors. These conquests also added a new set of Muslim precedents and talent to his administrative and imperial toolkit. The extraordinary success of his western campaign convinced Chinggis Khan himself and everyone around him that he was indeed destined to rule the earth.[4]

How were Chinggis Khan and his heirs able to conquer and rule such a large swath of land, and moreover, to accomplish this in such a short period? Several external factors contributed to the Chinggisids' success: the political fragmentation of Eurasia in the centuries leading to his rise; the emergence of post-nomadic states along the Eurasian Steppe, in eastern, central, and western Asia, which provided the Mongols with guiding models for ruling nonnomadic populations; and finally, nearly two decades (1211–25) of extremely high levels of rainfall in Inner Asia providing the vegetation and fodder needed for the quick and massive expansion of the Mongols' nomadic military apparatus, which heavily relied on horses and husbandry.[5]

The main reason for the Mongols' success, however, was none of the above. It was, above all, Chinggis Khan's own policies, notably the efficient mobilization of resources—human, material, and spiritual—and his pragmatic willingness to learn from others both in military and civil matters.[6] The reorganization of the army was one of the major steps Chinggis Khan took toward securing his rule in Mongolia and the empire's expansion. Military technological innovations or the usage of gunpowder-based artillery appear to have played a minor role, if any at all, in their success. In terms of armament and tactics, the Mongol armies largely kept to the traditional methods of Steppe warfare.[7] Rather, it was their superior leadership, discipline, and strategic planning that made the Mongols exceptionally successful, and enabled them to mobilize the Steppe's chief military resource—the mounted archers (and at later stages, sedentary soldiers from the conquered lands as well).

Chinggis Khan retained the typical Inner Asian decimal units (10, 100, 1,000, 10,000), but abolished the tribal division of the military. The new units included individuals from different tribes; they were led, not by tribal chieftains, but by Chinggis Khan's own *nökör*s (personal retainers). Selected according to merit and loyalty, the empire's new *nökör* elite provided the Chinggisids with a highly professional and reliable military elite. However, the heads of several tribal lineages were allowed to retain a segment of their troops. Their loyalty to the Chinggisids was also secured through marriages with the Chinggisid family. Although some tribal identities proved to be more enduring—or were cleverly resurrected—the Chinggisids never faced a serious tribal threat after this reorganization. The Mongols incorporated large numbers of submitted soldiers into their armies, dividing them among the decimal units.

The army's allegiance was further buttressed with draconian disciplinary measures on the one hand, and generous distribution of the booty on the other. Both the distribution of plunder and the troops' discipline were sanctioned by the famous *Jasaq* (Turkish: *Yasa*)—the continually evolving law code ascribed to Chinggis Khan. The implementation of the *Jasaq* was supervised by his newly appointed judges (*jarghuchi*s).

Chinggis Khan moreover adopted the Inner Asian institution of the supratribal royal guard (*keshig*). A combination of crack troops, police force, and a personal retinue, the *keshig* became the "nursery" of the empire's new military and administrative elite.[8] The composite army was constantly at war, securing conquest and booty and wreaking havoc.

Another important factor in the Mongols' success was the unprecedented devastation their armies left behind, and the violent massacres they carried out during their conquests, which have shaped the Mongols' image ever since. However, the violence they unleashed was not driven by wanton cruelty. Rather, as a strategic ploy, destruction and violence were enacted both as a means of psychological warfare and a brutal but effective way of compensating for the Mongols' numerical inferiority. The Mongols established a wide belt of destruction around their territories which functioned as a buffer zone preventing future incursions, and facilitated their further expansion, as well as increased available pasture. The Mongols substantially reduced the devastation in the later stages of the conquests (e.g., South China in the 1260s to 1270s). Further, some areas were restored shortly after the conquest, even becoming flourishing sedentary centers of the empire.[9]

Another major reason for the Mongol success was their willingness to learn from others—subjects, neighbors, and visitors—and their skill in doing so. This was particularly apparent in the military field (e.g., the use of siege engineers from both China and the Muslim world, or the establishment of the Mongol navy). Yet, the Mongols were on the lookout for talent and innovation in other fields as well: administration, medicine, astronomy, and entertainment, to name but a few. As early as 1204, Chinggis Khan adopted the Uighur script for writing Mongolian, thereby creating a literate staff. Thereafter, the Mongols drew extensively on their experienced subjects to administer the conquered territories and operate their courts. As with their military successes, the resourceful mobilization of talent and skills greatly contributed to the Mongols' effective administration. Their policy of religious pluralism and the respect and privileges they conferred upon religious and intellectual elites further enabled them to co-opt their subjects. Their active promotion of trade secured the support of the merchants, who were also often recruited to the imperial administration.

The Mongols' success in itself was the final factor that led to their further success. After heading out of Mongolia, Chinggis Khan did not suffer one single humiliating defeat, and his later victories were easier and quicker than his initial attacks on China. His record of conquest remained unblemished throughout his campaigns. Each victory further motivated his soldiers and discouraged his rivals. His military successes bolstered Chinggis Khan's public image as a charismatic ruler, preordained by Heaven (Tengri, the Mongols' supreme sky god) to conquer the world. Under his heirs, the mission of world conquest became the collective destiny of his entire clan. The Chinggisids' spate of victories continued throughout the United Empire. When the Mongols began to experience defeat (e.g., in 1258 in Vietnam, or in 1260 in Palestine), these downfalls were still dwarfed by the empire's previous achievements.[10]

Chinggis Khan also tried to avoid one of main weaknesses of nomadic empires, namely royal succession. Several overlapping and contradictory succession principles were employed in Steppe societies, creating the potential for bitter succession struggles after the demise of each khan. Both linear (father to son) and lateral (from brother to brother) succession were common, and principles of seniority and direct progeny (patrilineal and matrilineal) played a role as well. Moreover, the contenders' skills and success on the battlefield had significant, perhaps even primary, importance in deciding the successor. To avoid his succession turning into a bloody struggle, Chinggis Khan appointed his third son, Ögödei (r. 1229–41), as heir. Selected for his generosity and good temperament, which helped keep the empire together, Ögödei proved to be a fine choice. He not only continued his father's military expansion; under his reign, the empire's administration, policies, and ideology were further developed and systemized.

Assuming the title qa'an or great khan, Ögödei thus established his own position as superior to his brothers', who bore only the title khan. He founded the Mongol capital, Qaraqorum ("Black Sands") in the Orkhon valley in central Mongolia, the sacred territory of the Turks and Uighurs, and systematized the *jam* (Turk. *yam*), the mounted postal courier system. Post stations were established at stages, one day's journey apart (about every 33 to 45 kilometers), and provided animals, fodder, and couriers for authorized travelers. Travelers on the *jam* were therefore able to cover large distances, about 350 to 400 kilometers a day. The *jam* enabled the effective and quick transmission of imperial orders from the court, and the delivery of information from the far ends of the empire to the ruler. And it further secured the routes for ambassadors and for the merchants who had a special relationship with the Mongol elite.[11]

Ögödei also shaped the central administration of the empire, separating military and administrative authorities, employing professional administrators from the conquered regions, and regulating revenue collection and military recruitment. The Mongol ideology of world conquest was further elaborated and openly proclaimed, fueling a new wave of expansion. In 1234, the Mongols annihilated Chinggis Khan's bitter enemy, the Jin dynasty (1115–1234), and in 1237–41 they wrought havoc in Europe, devastating south Russia and the Ukraine, and reaching as far as Germany before retreating to the plains of Hungary. After Jalāl al-Dīn Khwārazmshāh's death in 1231, the small Mongol contingent that had been pursuing the Muslim ruler went on to subdue Georgia and Armenia, and even advanced into Anatolia during the interregnum between Ögödei's death (1241) and the succession of Ögödei's eldest son, Güyük (r. 1246–48). During these five years, when the empire was ruled by Ögödei's widow, Töregene (d. 1246), most of the empire's expansion came to a halt. Güyük too died before achieving further major conquests. This situation, however, changed under his cousin and successor, Möngke (r. 1251–59), the son of Chinggis Khan's younger son, Tolui.

Möngke rose to power after a bloody coup, also known as the Toluid revolution,[12] in which Tolui's sons replaced the Ögödeids as the ruling family line. Möngke's accession was secured by massive purges among the Ögödeid and Chaghadaid branches and their supporters,[13] as well as by administrative reforms that advanced the empire's centralization. Using censuses, Möngke was able to mobilize the resources of his vast realm to advance the empire's expansion. He appointed his brothers to lead new campaigns: Qubilai (r. 1260–94) was sent to China, and Hülegü (r. 1260–65) to the Middle East. Hülegü first subdued the Assassins, the Shīʿī Nizārī Ismāʿīlī sect. Based in the fortress of Alamūt in the mountains of northern Iran, the Ismāʿīlīs were infamous for the clandestine assassinations of their enemies.

In early 1258, Hülegü's forces stormed Baghdad, the seat of the ʿAbbasid Caliphate, putting an end to the more than half a millennium-old Muslim caliphate. While Hülegü was campaigning in the Middle East, his brother Möngke was fighting against the Chinese Song dynasty (r. 960–1279) in southwest China. In 1253–4, another sibling, Qubilai, conquered the kingdom of Dali, in today's Yunnan province in China. Qubilai then continued to fight the Song forces on the Yangtze River, where, in the summer of 1259, he learned of Möngke's death.

The process of empire building, briefly sketched above, involved the extensive mobilization of human and material resources throughout Mongol territories and farther afield. This was due, first, to demographic considerations. The Mongols, who by Chinggis Khan's time numbered less than a million people, were able to create their huge empire only by fully mobilizing all resources, human and material, from the regions under their control. Moreover, mobility was central to the nomadic Mongols' culture and way of life, and thus it was natural for them to use it for imperial needs. Since the Chinggisids regarded skilled individuals as a form of booty to be distributed across the empire and among the family, myriad people were transferred across Eurasia to provide for the empire's military, administrative, and cultural needs.

The military was the main catalyst for the mobilization of individuals. The Mongols appropriated the defeated nomadic and sedentary

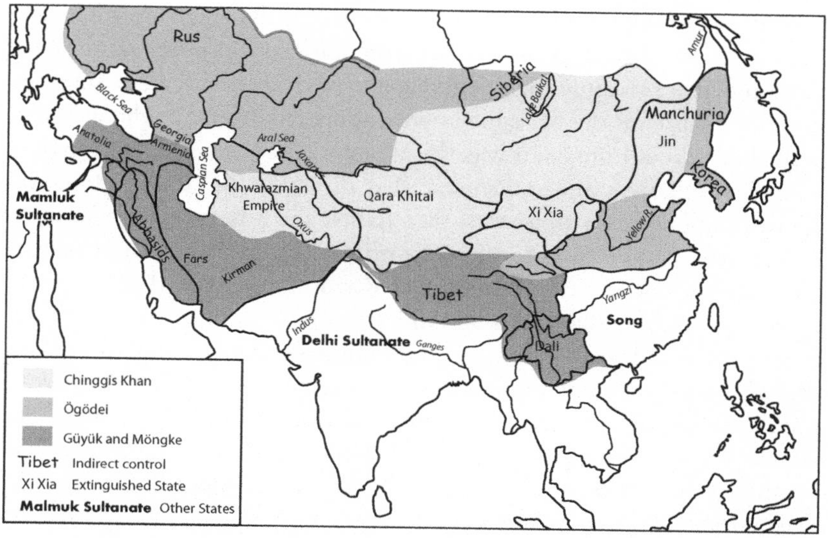

MAP 0.2. Conquests of the United Empire (1206–59).

populations, and organized them into decimal units, sent to wage war across the continent. Their formidable army further instigated the mass flight of people, as throngs of refugees from all classes and professions fled the approaching storm. The Mongol campaigns further resulted in myriads of captives flooding the empire's slave markets, and in defections of both individuals and collectives, though mostly after 1260. The empire transferred thousands of farmers and artisans to repopulate and revive devastated areas. The Mongols looked for experts in fields such as administration, military technology, trade, religion, craftsmanship, science, and entertainment. The recruitment of these professionals was systematized as early as the late 1230s, with the establishment of the census, classifying people according to their vocational skills. After the dissolution of the United Empire, the four khanates competed for and exchanged specialists in order to optimize their wealth and enhance their royal reputation.

Cross-Eurasian mobility, however, was not just a matter of coercion under Mongol rule. The rulers' reputation for rewarding loyal retainers, their encouragement of trade, their pluralistic attitude toward the religions of their subjects, and their preference for ruling through foreigners, namely employing nonlocal administrators, all assisted in attracting many gifted individuals to Chinggisid service.

The wide-ranging mobility of experts across the empire further promoted cross-cultural exchanges on a previously unprecedented level. Although it was mainly the cultural elements of their sedentary subjects, and not aspects of the Mongols' own culture, that were exchanged and trafficked across Eurasia, it was the Mongol elite who initiated the bulk of these exchanges and influenced their direction and extent. Imperial agents, ranging from diplomats, merchants, and administrators, to artisans, soldiers, and hostages, were the prime conveyers of cultures, ideas, and materials across the Mongol Silk Roads. Moreover, these imperial agents prioritized the exchange and transmission of the cultural elements of the sedentary subjects that were particularly compatible with the Mongols' cultural preferences. These included medical expertise (i.e., healing), astronomy, and divination (the reading of heaven), and geography and cartography (through which military intelligence was acquired). Functioning as cultural "filters," the Mongols' affinities and needs determined, to a large extent, the flow of people, ideas, and artifacts across Eurasia.[14]

The Mongols also cultivated economic ties that extended far beyond the empire's confines. They inherited, invigorated, and extended the various trade routes along the Silk Roads, as well as sundry means for resource extraction and exchange, including plunder, asset redistribution, taxation or tribute, and gifting. Not only did the Mongols provide security and transportation infrastructure, but they were active participants in Eurasian trade, both as investors and consumers.

Trade had long been essential to nomads, since their resources could not cover all their needs. In addition, nomadic political culture required leaders to redistribute wealth (e.g., silk), which was often produced or assembled by their sedentary neighbors or subjects, among their followers. Chinggis Khan was certainly aware of the benefits of commerce, which was the premise behind his expansion into Central Asia. And Muslim and Uighur merchants were among his earliest supporters. As the empire grew, systemic plunder was the major source of luxury goods. Redistributed among the Mongol elite, the khans and princes often chose to invest these considerable fortunes in international trade. Consequently, they entrusted their capital to commercial agents, *ortaq*s (partners), most of whom were Muslims and Uighurs.

The *ortaq* was a trader (or trading company) acting on behalf of, or financed by, a Mongol or other notable, in return for a share in the profits. The revenues were often spent on lavish consumption that typified the nouveaux riches, but was also meant to showcase the ruler's prestige and power. The establishment of Qaraqorum further induced trade, for the resources of Mongolia could hardly support such an imperial center. The Chinggisids were ready to generously pay to enjoy the best the sedentary world could offer, all the while remaining on the Steppe. Many traders eagerly exploited these opportunities, benefiting from the safe roads and access to imperial post stations. International trade, both in luxury and bulk goods, therefore resumed soon after the conquests, and trade along the overland Silk Roads picked up once again during the United Empire.[15]

"THE MONGOL COMMONWEALTH": POST-1260 POLITIES

The succession struggle that erupted immediately upon Möngke's demise, from which Qubilai Qa'an (r. 1260–94) emerged victorious, led to the empire's dissolution. The process was accelerated by the empire's sheer size, which made its management increasingly challenging. Moreover, the empire's growth beyond the ecological borders of the Steppe rendered more difficult the additional military expansion, which had served to keep the *ulus*es together. Eventually the United Empire was replaced by four big *ulus*es or khanates.

The Khanate of the Great Khan (in Mongolian *Qa'an ulus*), later known as the Yuan dynasty (1271–1368), ruled over China, Mongolia, Tibet, Korea, and Manchuria, and enjoyed a nominal, though not uncontested, primacy over its counterparts. The Ilkhanate (1260–1335), literally "the empire of the submissive khans" (in Mongolian *Ulus Hülegü,* after its founder, Hülegü), ruled in modern Iran, Iraq, Azerbaijan, Turkmenistan, parts of Anatolia, and the Caucasus. The Golden Horde (1260–1480), in Mongolian *Ulus Jochi,* after Chinggis Khan's firstborn son, governed the northwestern Eurasian Steppe, from the eastern border of Hungary to Siberia, as well as the Russian principalities. The Chaghadaid Khanate (in Mongolian *Ulus Chaghadai,* after Chinggis Khan's second son Chaghadai) held power in Central Asia, from eastern Xinjiang (China) to Uzbekistan, until Tamerlane's rise to power in 1370, and over eastern Central Asia through the late seventeenth century. Until the early fourteenth the Chaghadaids shared rule in Central Asia with their cousins, the Ögödeids. Ögödei's grandson, Qaidu (r. 1271–1301), resurrected the Ögödeids' power after it was curbed under Möngke. Qaidu refused to acknowledge the authority of the Great Khan in China, and throughout his reign, raided the Yuan and the Ilkhanate, often with

Chaghadaid support. Further conflicts involved Jochid and Chaghadaid claims to Azerbaijan and Khurasan, both territories that had been conquered before Hülegü's western campaign, but were subsequently incorporated into the nascent Ilkhanate.

Despite these ongoing disputes, the four polities retained a strong sense of Chinggisid unity, seeing themselves as "brotherly states." The four khanates, moreover, shared the same Mongol institutions (e.g., the *keshig, Jasaq, jam, jarghuchi, darughachi*, and the *ordo* [the Mongol court]), which existed alongside regional variants and local institutions.[16] In 1304, the Chinggisid polities negotiated a peace treaty, which, however, resulted in another decade of internal strife in Central Asia and led to the final annihilation of the Ögödeid *ulus*. Two decades later, in the early 1320s, the four polities finally acknowledged the superiority of the Great Khan in China, although by this point, it was no more than nominal authority. This peaceful stage in the "Mongol Commonwealth" did not last long. The fourteenth-century global climatic cooling and the related natural disasters, which had multiplied by the mid-fourteenth century, dealt a strong blow to both nomadic and sedentary economies. The mid-fourteenth century witnessed the collapse of the Ilkhanate in Iran and Yuan China, and the considerable weakening of the two Steppe khanates. The mid-fourteenth century thereby marked the end of the "Mongol moment" in world history.

The post-1260 period also saw growing rapprochement between the Mongols and local societies in each polity. This gradual process was driven by practical considerations—to gain legitimation and the cooperation of local elites, and to achieve more effective rule overall. It was also motivated by the increased assimilation of the Mongols, especially their rank-and-file, within the native populations, whose size greatly exceeded that of their conquerors. The Mongols' assimilation was further expressed in their embracing of the universal world religions—Buddhism in China, and Islam in the rest of the Mongol khanates, as well as in the Mongols' adoption of sedentary imperial models, mainly in China and Iran, where such models existed. However, in a typical nomadic amalgamation, the various legitimizing and spatial concepts—Chinggisid, religious, local, and others—all coexisted in the Mongol states; they were never deemed mutually exclusive.

The post-1260 Mongol polities continued to cling to the Chinggisid ideology of world conquest. However, after 1260, its implementation became far more challenging. Inter-Mongol conflicts prevented the mobilization of the vast imperial resources that had characterized the

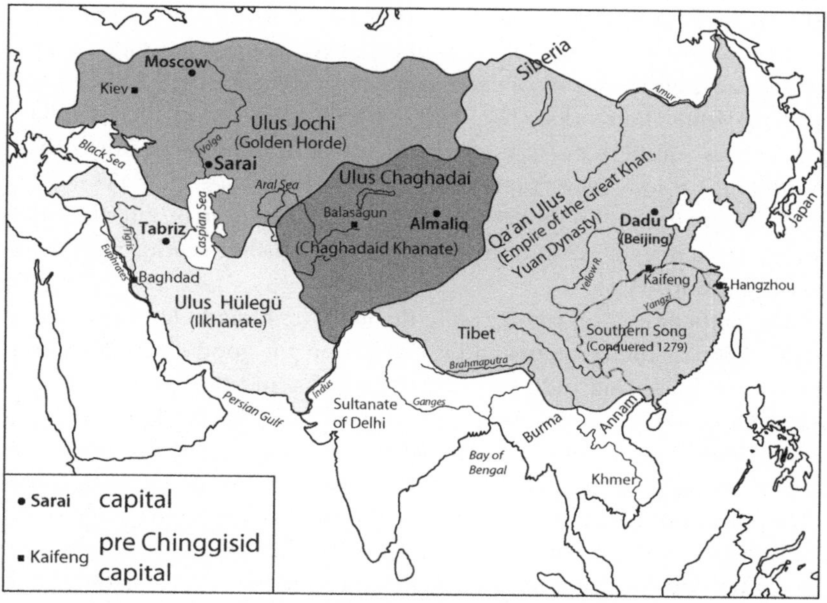

MAP 0.3. "The Mongol Commonwealth": The Four *Uluses*, ca. 1290.

earlier campaigns. The khanates were forced to channel their troops to defend their borders against rival *uluses*, rather than concentrate their efforts on their expansion. Furthermore, by 1260, the empire had reached the ecological border of Steppe nomadism on all its frontiers. Further expansion therefore demanded military organization, warfare techniques, and equipment that significantly differed from their earlier light cavalry campaigns. Through the mobilization of Chinese and Korean infantry and sailors, and the assistance of Iranian siege engineers, the Mongols managed to break the ecological border into South China, where their gains were by far the greatest in terms of both the economy and legitimation.[17] Yet, they were less successful on other frontiers.[18] Thus, from the late 1270s, Mongol expansion largely came to a halt.

However, the deceleration in the Mongol expansion after the empire's dissolution corresponded with an acceleration in the expansion of trade activities along the Mongol Silk Roads. With taxation replacing booty as the main source of revenue, the Mongol governments promoted local and international commerce, which provided taxes, markets, profits, and prestige. The khanates competed for commercial specialists, laid down infrastructure for transcontinental travel, and played a significant role in facilitating transcivilizational (East-West) and transecological (North-South) exchanges. The conquest of the Song in southern China was decisive also in terms of expanding the continental Silk Roads trade into maritime networks. The Yuan subsequently controlled China's prosperous southern ports, and when conflict in Central Asia disturbed continental trade, they employed the maritime routes. China's ports, notably Quanzhou (in modern Fujian), became centers of international trade, attracting merchants from India, the Muslim world, Southeast Asia, and Europe.

The main axes of exchange were through the Indian Ocean: between South China—the terminus and relay station for goods from East and Southeast Asia—and India; and between India and the Persian Gulf or the Red Sea. From there, the cargos continued, either by land, to Iran, Iraq, Anatolia, and Europe (both eastern and western); via the maritime routes, through Egypt and the Mediterranean, to Europe; or from Aden to the shores of East Africa. Shorter sea routes catered to the lively slave trade between the Golden Horde's ports on the Black Sea and Egypt, involving Muslim, Italian, and Byzantine traders. The maritime and overland routes were closely interlinked. The Black Sea ports serviced luxury goods arriving from the east over continental routes. And caravans headed inland from the Indian coast during the seasons when sailing was deemed dangerous. This thriving proto-global exchange reached its height in the 1320s to 1330s; further, it survived the fall of the Ilkhanate (1335), with its routes shifting from Iran to the Golden Horde. However, the Yuan collapse (1368) on the heels of the Black Death in Europe and the Middle East, which also coincided with further upheavals in the Golden Horde, severely curtailed the Mongols' international system of trade.[19]

GENERALS, MERCHANTS, AND INTELLECTUALS ON THE MOVE

This book illustrates life along the Silk Roads by focusing on the stories of individuals from three elite groups—military commanders, merchants, and intellectuals. Their personal experiences elucidate aspects of cross-cultural contact and physical and social mobility during the thirteenth to fourteenth centuries in Mongol Eurasia. Our division of these individuals into the three groups may seem arbitrary at times: their careers often overlap with more than one category, so they could have just as easily been assigned to other groups, such as administrators and diplomats.

Thus, the Muslim merchant Ja'far Khwāja (fl.1201–21?), whose career Qiu studies in chapter 7 of this volume, began his career as a merchant, but also guided the Mongol troops to attack the Jin capital (modern-day Beijing) and eventually governed the city for the Mongols. As governor, he conversed with Daoist priests and Confucian scholars, among others, regardless of his Muslim identity. Other figures, and in general, many new elite members, were polymaths and thus versed in several disciplines. The Muslim Ilkhanid vizier Rashīd al-Dīn (ca. 1247–1318), whom Brack examines in chapter 11, is a telling example: he was a prolific historian and theologian, a court physician and a cook, with a special interest in agriculture and agronomy, all in addition to his role as chief minister of the realm. Whereas the capable women examined in this volume became prominent mainly due to their noble genealogies and marriage links to the Chinggisid house, the men discussed therein all joined the new elite based on their divergent sets of skills.

The life stories that this volume displays further evince different types of migrations in Mongol Eurasia. These included temporary and permanent relocation; coerced, impelled, and voluntary migrations; individual and collective mobility; as well as refugee, labor-, and study-related migrations. Their movements were induced mainly by political factors under the United Empire, and by economic factors in the "Commonwealth" period; they were further stimulated by marriage, diplomatic missions, administrative appointments, and the search for knowledge.

Military commanders were central to the empire's establishment and expansion. Often tasked with leading their own military campaigns, Mongol and non-Mongol generals frequently enjoyed great autonomy in their operations and later, in their regional rule, as Yildiz shows in chapter 2, on the Mongol general Baiju (d. 1260) and his campaigns in the Middle East and Anatolia. Aside from their military skills, commanders were also valued for their uncompromising loyalty to the Chinggisids. Their loyalty was secured through recruitment into the royal guard (*keshig*), where future generals often shared their training with future emperors, or through marriages into the royal household.[20] As succession struggles afflicted the empire and its successor states, loyalty to specific Chinggisid scions proved to be decisive in shaping the generals' fate. Like Baiju, they might find themselves in the crosshairs of dynastic struggles that would ultimately lead to their discharge or execution. Alternatively, as Shurany demonstrates in chapter 6, a study of the Qipchaq Yuan general Tuqtuqa (1237–97) and his offspring, military commanders could become deeply involved in the selection process of the new qa'an, and use the loyalty of their troops to back a favored candidate.

The military was a major catalyst and conduit for the mobilization of individuals, groups, and technologies across Eurasia,[21] in addition to social mobility and integration. Skilled soldiers, captives, defectors, and refugees of various ethnicities were regularly incorporated into the military machine. Some rose to prominent positions and even passed their posts to their offspring, establishing "minor dynasties." Such was the case of the Qipchaq general Tuqtuqa, whose father had surrendered to the Mongol forces in their European campaign in the 1230s, and who, together with his offspring, established local roots in Chinese society. The Mongol khans valued nonnative generals, deeming them more trustworthy than the often-hostile conquered local elites, or the volatile Mongol elite. The practice of recruiting foreigners and captives, however, was not limited to the Mongols. As chapter 5, by Mazor, demonstrates, Mongol captives and defectors themselves served as valued military assets in the armies of the Mongols' enemies. Furthermore, as both Mazor and Hodous (chapter 1) show, ethnic solidarity was not always the determining factor when a conflict of loyalties arose.

Skilled local generals, however, too reached prominence, as did the Chinese generals Guo Kan (1217–77) (and his forefathers) and Yang Tingbi (fl. 1270s to 1280s) . Both generals, moreover, commanded Mongol forces far beyond their local realms. Commanders were further valued for their technological expertise and their versatility in providing services, not just military, but also administrative, diplomatic, and other types.

The mobilization of the military was, furthermore, a conduit for the transfer and assimilation of military technologies, especially those of naval and siege warfare. Through their skill sets and expertise, the generals themselves had a role in facilitating these technological exchanges. Thus, Guo Kan, as discussed by Hodous, led Chinese mangonel engineers in the Mongol campaigns in Baghdad and further westward, thereby contributing to the transfer of battlefield technologies across Eurasia.

The roles of the commanders' personal initiative and creative response when encountering new challenges—environmental, political, and other—come to the fore especially in the Chinese general Yang Tingbi's case. As Mukai and Fiaschetti demonstrate in chapter 4, Yang employed his skills in navigation, mediation, and diplomacy in his effort toward gaining the Yuan dynasty a foothold in the flourishing ports on the shores of the Indian Ocean. To advance the Yuan maritime expansion, he collaborated with local elites in India.

Finally, as Biran shows in chapter 3, in the Mongol Empire, women too could play an active role in the military sphere, usually by providing support and logistics, but in rare cases, even as generals. Biran investigates here one extraordinary example, the Central Asian warrior princess Qutulun (d. 1307), who led her own troops and was renowned for outmatching her male peers on the battlefield.

Merchants were the true go-betweens of the Mongol Silk Roads, linking together local, transregional, and continental routes of travel and trade. Merchants' knowledge of Eurasian terrains, languages, and accounting methods made them especially useful as imperial agents, from Chinggis Khan's time onward, as manifested in the career of Jaʿfar Khwāja, described above.

In chapter 9, Gill examines the Mongols' commercial partnerships (*ortaq*), mentioned in several other chapters as well. He analyzes the global trade of the Ṭībīs, a Baghdadi family of pearl merchants, whose trade networks reached China, India, Africa, and the Middle East; and describes the plethora of exchange mechanisms the Ṭībīs employed, from family networks, tribute, and taxation to the valuable *ortaq* partnership with the Mongol court. Chapter 10, by Kovács, also focuses on the Mongols' active involvement in trade highlighting the role of Mongol elite women, in this case Taydula (d. 1361), the widow of the Golden Horde Khan Özbek (r. 1313–41), in creating partnerships and promoting trade and interreligious exchange in the Black Sea region. The Black Sea trade and its connections to both Venice and Qaraqorum under the United Empire are also reviewed in chapter 8, by Giebfried, who focuses on the life and journey of the Flemish crusader ambassador Baldwin of Hainaut (fl. 1260).

Together, the chapters in this section further attest to the mainly northeastward shift of the Silk Roads' land routes under the Mongols. This transition was made first to include the Mongol capital of Qaraqorum, and later due to the establishment of the new Mongol capitals (Beijing, Tabriz, Sarai, Almaliq), which were all closer to the northern Steppe than the former capitals (Baghdad, Hangzhou, Kiev, Balāsāghūn).[22] The Mongols also impacted the southern maritime routes. As the two chapters by Gill and Mukai-Fiaschetti demonstrate, the "Mongol Commonwealth" witnessed an increased interest in extending Yuan and Ilkhanid reach into maritime trade networks in the Indian Ocean, and a corresponding rise in the volume of travelers and commodities even reaching Southeast Asia. Connecting the maritime with the continental routes, the Mongols created a protoglobal trade system across the Old World. Other individual travelers, such as itinerant and immigrant scholars, also benefited from this interlinking of maritime and continental routes.

Like merchants, *intellectuals* in Mongol service too had a significant role as mediators of cross-cultural and scientific exchange. Experts in medicine, astrology, history, and languages, among others—fields that strongly catered to the Mongols' own cultural preferences—were often employed in the empire's civil administration. Furthermore, as Kim shows in chapter 13 on the Western Asian Christian ʿĪsa Kelemechi ("Jesus the Interpreter," 1227–1308), who served the Yuan court in China together with his sons, intellectuals, especially polymaths such as ʿĪsa, were often sent as envoys on behalf of the khan, due to their knowledge of numerous tongues and their skills as cultural brokers.

The Mongols particularly valued astronomy, astrology, and other forms of divination ("futurology") and sought to employ such experts to assist them in their military, governmental and personal decisions. Adding to their service experts in both Chinese and Islamic astronomy, the Mongols aimed to collect and register an abundance of divergent, even conflicting, expert opinions. Isahaya's chapter 12, on Fu Mengzhi, a Chinese Daoist physician and amateur astronomer at Hülegü's court in Iran, shows how Fu's encounters with Muslim astronomers expose both the remarkable horizons that Mongol rule opened for scientific exchange across Asia, and the obstacles that stood in the way of the transfer of knowledge and cross-cultural commensurability.

Or Amir's chapter 15, on the fourteenth-century itinerant Central Asian Muslim scholar Jalāl al-Dīn al-Akhawī, and De Nicola's chapter 14, on Pādshāh Khatun (1256–95), show that elite patronage—for example, through the establishment of institutions to support scholars such as hospices or colleges—was one of the main mechanisms that enabled and further increased the mobility of intellectuals. Amir's chapter also illustrates how scholars traveled remarkable distances in the pursuit of knowledge. He draws attention to the networks of Hanafi-Muslim scholars. Benefiting from the new opportunities generated by Turco-Mongol patronage, these scholars reached far beyond Mongol-ruled domains, linking together both the well-established and emergent Muslim centers of learning and scholarship.

De Nicola's chapter focuses on the unique case of the Muslim queen Pādshāh Khatun, who despite marrying two infidel Mongol rulers, not only patronized Muslim culture but also contributed to it herself. Finally, Brack's chapter 11, on Rashīd al-Dīn, proves that intellectuals, even those who did not travel themselves across Eurasia, played a major role in documenting these cross-ecumenical exchanges. Highlighting the function of the Ilkhanid court as an arena of interreligious communication and debate, Brack shows that even when Rashīd al-Dīn's attitude toward the newcomers—in this case, the Buddhist monks—was ambiguous or hostile, his works still played a vital role in recording these interactions, translating and transmitting the new knowledge to his Muslim audience, and challenging it without entirely dismissing it.

SOURCES

Just as the individuals covered in this volume represent the remarkable diversity of the Mongol Empire, so do the textual sources used to uncover their stories. First, we should note the linguistic diversity of the sources at hand for the study of the empire, from Mongolian and Chinese to Persian, Arabic, Latin, Russian, Armenian, Georgian, and more. Further, our sources appear in various formats and repositories. They include Persian chronicles, Arabic biographical dictionaries, Chinese stele inscriptions and gazetteers (*difangzhi,* local chronicles), Mongolian royal edicts translated into Russian, Italian trade documents, Latin travelogues, and more. The diverse modes of writing on individuals, which were informed by the cultural world of the authors, are also addressed throughout the volume. For example, while the lion's share of the *Yuanshi,* the official history of the Mongol Yuan dynasty in China, compiled in 1369–70, is devoted to exemplary biographies (*liezhuan*), most of the information provided concerns the official posts they held and their advancement in the military or bureaucratic ranks, leaving other details of their lives undocumented.[23] Lists of appointments are also prominent in Chinese private biographical writing, often commissioned by the offspring of the biography's subject. These are richer in anecdotes, but since their goal was to praise their subjects, they must be taken with a grain of salt.[24] Medieval Arabic biographical dictionaries, on the other hand, might provide us with lively anecdotes about the individuals we study; however, these stories, often exaggerated or altogether fictive, are included for their literary appeal and entertainment value.[25] Furthermore, such biographies often focus on the Muslim subject's religious piety or the impressive list of teachers with whom he studied, leaving little room for other significant details.[26]

Most of the sources used in this volume, and for the study of the Mongol Empire in general, were not penned by the Mongols themselves, but by their subjects and neighbors. Since these Chinese, Muslim, or Christian authors were each bounded in the concepts and premises of their own civilization as well as local historiographical traditions, their perspectives can also blur our understanding of the Mongols. Still, we are able to reconstruct the Mongols' own voice, not only by employing the few available indigenous Mongolian sources,[27] but also by further juxtaposing and comparing sources from different parts of the empire, as many of the chapters here do. Several chapters also raise historiographical concerns, which are unavoidable for those studying the history of the empire.

The personal stories in this volume bring to the fore new information for the study of the Mongol Empire from a diverse body of primary sources, and provide important insights into the social and cultural history of a period unique for its rapid and far-reaching transformations. The chapters shed new light on the political, military, economic, and cultural history of the Mongol Silk Roads, illuminating issues such as acculturation (of the Mongols and their subjects), imperial administration, ethnicity, gender, diplomacy, and religious and scientific exchange. Read together or separately, they offer a compelling starting point for any discussion of the Mongol Empire's impact on China, the Muslim world, and the West, as well as vividly illustrating the scale, diversity, and implications of the multifaceted mobility and cross-cultural exchange along the Mongol Silk Roads.

NOTES

1. The term Silk Road was first coined in 1877 by the German geographer Baron Ferdinand von Richthofen, who, in the 1860 to 1870s, compiled an atlas of China. He applied the name Silk Road to the route connecting China and Europe, with the idea of employing it for a planned railroad as well (Hansen 2015, 6–8). Von Richthofen himself included several possible routes under the umbrella term of the "Silk Road" and thus, even before the term was broadened to include both continental and maritime roads, the "Silk Road" never represented one single route. The plural "Silk Roads," therefore, is more appropriate.

2. For the Silk Roads before the Mongol era: de la Vaissière 2014; Hansen 2015; Frankopan 2015, 1–157.

3. In Mongolian, *ulus* originally meant the people subject to a certain lord; later the term also became equivalent to the nation and the state (as it still does in modern Mongolian today).

4. Biran 2007, 47–73.

5. Pederson et al. 2014.

6. Biran 2007, 69–73.

7. May 2012, 130–57; Biran, forthcoming; cf. Haw 2013.

8. Biran 2007, 41–43; Biran 2015; Biran forthcoming; May 2007.

9. Biran 2015; May 2007.

10. Biran 2007, 69–73; Biran forthcoming.

11. For the *jam:* e.g., Silverstein 2007, 141–64; Allsen 2011; Shim 2014; Vér 2019.

12. May 2018, 144–80.

13. Chaghadai was Chinggis Khan's third son from his chief wife.

14. Allsen 2001; Biran 2015.

15. Allsen 1997; Allsen 2019; Biran 2015.

16. Kim 2009; Biran forthcoming.

17. Rossabi 1988, 76–95; Davis 2009.

18. The Ilkhans fought the Mamluks in Syria up to the early fourteenth century without durable success. Their inability to conquer Syria from the Mamluks ultimately led to the signing of a peace treaty in 1323 (Amitai 2005; Amitai 2013, 15–36). The Chaghadaids and the Golden Horde abandoned the conquest campaigns altogether and reverted to raiding north India or Eastern Europe respectively. Jackson 1999, 218–37; Biran 2009; Vásáry 2009. In China, beyond the Mongol conquest of the Southern Song in 1279, further campaigns met only partial success (in Burma and Vietnam in the 1280s through the 1290s), or were completely disastrous (Japan in 1274 and 1281 and Java in 1292): Rossabi 1988, 99–103, 207–20.

19. Biran 2015; Biran forthcoming.

20. May 2007, 37–72.

21. Allsen 2015.

22. Biran 2004.

23. For the compilation of Chinese dynastic histories like the *Yuanshi:* Twitchett 1992; for Yuan sources: Wilkinson 2012, esp. 775–87.

24. The privately recorded inscriptions include interred tomb inscriptions (*muzhiming*) stele inscriptions (*shendaobei;* literally, "spirit-way stele") or epitaphs. For a recent survey of these materials and their relation to the *liezhuan* section of the *Yuanshi:* Humble 2017, esp. 19–83.

25. Little 1970, 102–6, 112–13.

26. On Arabic biographical literature: Gibb 1962; Khalidi 1973; Robinson 2003, 55–82; al-Qadi 2006. For Muslim sources on the Mongols: Jackson 2017: 14–45.

27. These include, notably, *The Secret History of the Mongols,* the only indigenous contemporary literary source for the rise of Chinggis Khan, together with Mongol edicts, letters, documents, inscriptions, seals, and coins. For *The Secret History:* de Rachewiltz 2006; Atwood 2004, 492–93; Atwood 2007.

BIBLIOGRAPHY

Allsen, Thomas T. 1997. *Commodity and Exchange in the Mongol Empire: A Cultural History of Islamic Textiles.* Cambridge: Cambridge University Press.

———. 2001. *Culture and Conquest in Mongol Eurasia.* Cambridge: Cambridge University Press.

———. 2011. "Imperial Posts, West, East, and North: A Review Article: Adam J. Silverstein, *Postal Systems in the Pre-Modern Islamic World*." *Archivum Eurasiae Medii Aevi* 17: 237–76.

———. 2015. "Population Movements in Mongol Eurasia." In *Nomads as Agents of Cultural Change: The Mongols and Their Eurasian Predecessors*, ed. Reuven Amitai and Michal Biran, 119–51. Honolulu: University of Hawai'i Press.

———. 2019. *The Steppe and the Sea: Pearls in the Mongol Empire*. Philadelphia: University of Pennsylvania Press.

Amitai, Reuven. 2005. "The Resolution of the Mongol-Mamluk War." In *Mongols, Turks, and Others: Eurasian Nomads and the Sedentary World*, ed. Reuven Amitai and Michal Biran, 359–90. Leiden: Brill.

———. 2013. *Holy War and Rapprochement. Studies in the Relations between the Mamluk Sultanate and the Mongol Ilkhanate (1260–1335)*. Turnhout: Brepols.

Atwood, Christopher P. 2004. *Encyclopedia of Mongolia and the Mongol Empire*. New York: Facts on File.

———. 2007. "The Date of the 'Secret History of the Mongols' Reconsidered." *Journal of Sung-Yuan Studies* 37: 1–48.

Biran, Michal. 2004. "The Mongol Transformation: From the Steppe to Eurasian Empire." *Medieval Encounters* 10: 338–61.

———. 2007. *Chinggis Khan*. Oxford: OneWorld.

———. 2009. "Central Asia from the Conquest of Chinggis Khan to the Rise of Tamerlane: The Ögödeied and Chaghadaid Realms." In *The Cambridge History of Inner Asia*. Vol. 2. *The Chinggisid Age*, ed. Peter B. Golden, Nicola Di Cosmo and Allan Frank, 46–66. Cambridge: Cambridge University Press.

———. 2015. "The Mongol Empire and the Inter-Civilizational Exchange." In *The Cambridge History of the World*. Vol. 5. *Expanding Webs of Exchange and Conflict, 500 C.E.–1500 C.E.*, ed. Benjamin Kedar and Merry Wiesner-Hanks, 534–58. Cambridge: Cambridge University Press.

———. Forthcoming. "Mongol Imperial Space: From Universalism to Glocalization." In *Universality and Its Limits: Spatial Dimensions of Eurasian Empires*, ed. Yuri Pines, Michal Biran, and Jörg Rüpke. Cambridge: Cambridge University Press.

Davis, Richard L. 2009. "The Reign of Tu-tsung (1264–1274) and His Successors to 1279." In *The Cambridge History of China*. Vol. 5, part I. *The Sung Dynasty and Its Precursors*, ed. Denis Twitchett and Paul Jakov Smith, 913–62. Cambridge: Cambridge University Press.

de Rachewiltz, Igor. 2006. *The Secret History of the Mongols: A Mongolian Epic Chronicle of the Thirteenth Century*. Leiden: Brill.

Frankopan, Peter. 2015. *The Silk Roads: A New History of the World*. London: Bloomsbury.

Gibb, Hamilton A. R. 1962. "*Islamic Biographical Literature*." In *Historians of the Middle East*, ed. Bernard Lewis and Peter. M. Holt, 54–58. London: Oxford University Press.

Hansen, Valerie. 2015. *The Silk Road. A New History*. Oxford: Oxford University Press.

Haw, Stefan, 2013. "The Mongol Empire: The First Gunpower Empire?" *Journal of the Royal Asiatic Society* 23: 449–61.

Humble, Geoffrey F. 2017. "Biographical Rhetorics: Narrative and Power in *Yuanshi* Biography." PhD diss., University of Birmingham.

Jackson, Peter. 1999. *The Delhi Sultanate: A Political and Military History*. Cambridge: Cambridge University Press.

———. 2017. *The Mongols and the Islamic World: From Conquest to Conversion*. New Haven, CT: Yale University Press.

Khalidi, Tarif. 1973. "Islamic Biographical Dictionaries: A Preliminary Assessment." *Muslim World* 63: 53–65.

Kim Hodong. 2009. "The Unity of the Mongol Empire and Continental Exchanges over Eurasia." *Journal of Central Eurasian Studies* 1: 15–42.

Little, Donald P. 1970. *An Introduction to Mamluk Historiography*. Wiesbaden, Germany: Franz Steiner.

May, Timothy. 2007. *The Mongol Art of War*. London: Pen and Sword Publications.

———. 2012. *The Mongol Conquest in World History*. London: Reaction-Globalities.

———. 2018. *The Mongol Empire*. Edinburgh: Edinburgh University Press.

Pederson, Neil, et al. 2014. "Pluvials, Droughts, the Mongol Empire, and Modern Mongolia." *Proceedings of the National Academy of Sciences* 111.12: 4375–79.

al-Qadi, Waddad. 2006. "Biographical Dictionaries as the Scholars' Alternative History of the Muslim Community." In *Organizing Knowledge: Encyclopaedic Activities in the Pre-Eighteenth Century Islamic World*, ed. Gerhard Endress, 23–75. Leiden: Brill.

Robinson, Chase. 2003. *Islamic Historiography*. Cambridge: Cambridge University Press.

Rossabi, Morris. 1988. *Khubilai Khan: His Life and Times*. Berkeley: University of California Press.

Shim, Hosung. 2014. "The Postal Roads of the Great Khans in Central Asia under the Mongol-Yuan Empire." *Journal of Song-Yuan Studies* 44: 405–69.

Silverstein, Adam. J. 2007. *Postal Systems in the Pre-Modern Islamic World*. Cambridge: Cambridge University Press.

Twitchett, Denis. 1992. *The Writing of Official History under the T'ang*. Cambridge: Cambridge University Press.

de la Vaissière, Étienne. 2014. "Trans-Asian Trade, or the Silk Road Deconstructed (Antiquity, Middle Ages)." In *The Cambridge History of Capitalism*, eds. Larry Neal and Jeffery G. Williamson, 1: 101–24. Cambridge: Cambridge University Press.

Vásáry, István. 2009. "The Jochid Realm: The Western Steppe." In *The Cambridge History of Inner Asia: The Chinggisid Age*, ed. Nicola Di Cosmo, Peter B. Golden, and Allan J. Frank, 67–86. Cambridge: Cambridge University Press.

Vér, Márton. 2019. *Old Uyghur Documents Concerning the Postal System of the Mongol Empire.* Berliner Turfantexte XLIII. Berlin: Berliner Branderburgische Akademie der Wissenschaften.

Wilkinson, Endymion, 2012. *Chinese History: A New Manual.* 3rd ed. Cambridge, MA: Harvard University Asia Center.

PART ONE

Generals

CHAPTER 1

Guo Kan

Military Exchanges between China and the Middle East

FLORENCE HODOUS

Guo Kan (1217–77) was a Chinese general who took part in the Mongol campaigns in Central and Western Asia and participated in the Mongol conquest of Baghdad in 1258. He led the mangonel engineers, Chinese specialists in siege warfare, who were instrumental in the Mongol armies' success. While legendary feats and victories over Muslim and Christian kingdoms in the Middle East are further ascribed to Guo Kan, the general appears to have returned to China after the Mongol victory in Baghdad. Back home, he served in a military capacity under Qubilai Qa'an (r. 1260–94), founder of the Yuan dynasty. Guo Kan's journey offers the opportunity to explore not only the transfer of military experts and warfare technologies across Mongol Eurasia but also speaks to the role that material artifacts played in Chinese imaginations of the Middle East and Europe, as well as to the expansion of Chinese knowledge on their geography and politics.

A WORTHY DESCENDANT

Our sole source on Guo Kan is his biography in the *Yuanshi* or the *History of the Yuan Dynasty*.[1] There are no references to him in the Persian sources, making it impossible to corroborate details about Guo Kan's military feats in the Islamic world. Still, we can draw an outline of Guo Kan's life and career and compare it with other sources on the Mongols' campaigns.[2] Since Guo Kan's *Yuanshi* biography was compiled years

FIGURE 1.1. *Guo Ziyi Receiving the Homage of the Uighurs*, Li Gonglin (eleventh century). Collection of the National Palace Museum, Taipei.

after his death, it is also valuable for exploring how later Chinese authors envisioned their relationship with and involvement in the Mongol westward expansion.

As his biography in the *Yuanshi* points out already at its opening, Guo Kan was a descendant of Guo Ziyi (697–781), a famous general of China's Tang dynasty (618–907). In addition to quelling the An Lushan rebellion (755–63),[3] Ziyi took part in several campaigns against the Tibetans and the Uighurs.[4] Two traditional enemies (and occasionally allies) of the Tang dynasty, the Tibetans and the Uighurs would both later submit to the Mongols. Guo Kan's next known ancestors are his grandfather, Guo Baoyu, and his father, Dehai, both of whom were also generals mainly active in the Chinese western frontiers in Central Asia and further west (see fig. 1.1).

Although six centuries lapsed between the Tang general Ziyi and Guo Kan's grandfather Guo Baoyu, the latter was likewise born and raised in Ziyi's hometown Huazhou (in today's Shaanxi province). Unlike Ziyi, however, Guo Baoyu seems to have been a rather minor *mingghan* commander (head of a unit of a thousand) under the Jin dynasty (1115–1234), in charge of defending Dingzhou (nowadays southwestern Hebei). As soon as Chinggis Khan's general Muqali

(1170–1223) and his forces advanced to northern China, Guo Baoyu defected, enlisting with the new Mongol overlords.[5]

Muqali then took the defector Baoyu to see Chinggis Khan, whom Baoyu impressed with his practical and bold advice. Receiving the post of general command officer of artillerymen,[6] he accompanied Muqali on his campaign to subdue the Jin dynasty. More importantly for his future as well as for the prospects of his descendants, he managed to forge a close personal relationship with Chinggis Khan. His biography gives a vivid account of Baoyu's injury during Chinggis Khan's campaign against the Qara-Khitai (1124–1218) and Muḥammad Khwārazmshāh (r. 1200–20) in Central Asia: "Baoyu was hit in the chest with an arrow, so the Emperor [Chinggis Khan] ordered to cut open the belly of a cow and place him inside it, and in a short while he recovered."[7] The biography goes on to claim prodigious feats for him. It recounts how Baoyu quickly returned to battle after his injury and accepted the submission of the city of Beshbaliq (in north Xinjiang), before crossing the Jaxartes river to take Samarqand (modern-day Uzbekistan), and then crossing the Oxus River to advance until Merv (modern-day Turkmenistan).[8]

Baoyu is furthermore presented as instrumental in bringing Chinese inventions to the battlefield. The biography mentions that at the Oxus, he used *huojian,* literally "fire arrows," against the enemy ships. Scholars have debated how to identify these "fire arrows." By then, the Mongols had already encountered gunpowder weapons, particularly in the form of explosive gunpowder bombs, in their wars against the Jin in northern China. The presence of Chinese engineers such as Guo Kan in the Mongol armies conquering the West has led to the speculation that the Mongols may have imported such weapons into Western Asia.[9] However, there is insufficient evidence to support this conclusion. It is more likely that the fire-arrows Baoyu introduced were not rockets, but arrows carrying incendiary charges.[10] They may well have been an innovation from China, albeit falling short of being true gunpowder weapons.

In any case, in 1220–23, Guo Baoyu participated together with his son Dehai in the famous campaign of Chinggis Khan's generals Jebe (d. 1223) and Sübe'etei (1175–1248), which circled the Caspian Sea and returned back to Mongolia via Russia and the Qipchaq Steppe. Dehai's biography follows his father's in the same chapter of the *Yuanshi,* and though the section on Dehai is very short, it nevertheless records that he quelled the rebellions of a Tibetan and an Uighur commander, just as his ancestor the Tang general Ziyi had fought centuries earlier with Tibetans and Uighurs. Dehai further contributed to the campaign against the Jin dynasty until his death from a battle wound in 1234.[11] Baoyu and his son, though not quite as famous or central to their dynasty, nevertheless exceeded the accomplishments of Ziyi in terms of their geographical reach; and Dehai's son Guo Kan was to do even more.

GUO KAN THE ARTILLERYMAN (*CHAQMAQ*)

Guo Kan was seventeen years old when his father died. Through the mediation of his father and grandfather, he was already well regarded by major figures of the Yuan dynasty, and the great general Shi Tianze (1202–75) himself hosted him in his house and educated him. At the age of twenty, he was appointed commander of a hundred, and accompanied Sübe'etei, and later Tianze himself, on campaign, rising to leader of a thousand.

Like his grandfather, he participated in a campaign to the west, this time the campaign led by Chinggis Khan's grandson Hülegü (1218–65), brother of the reigning Qa'an Möngke (r. 1251–59). Hülegü's campaign set out in 1253 and culminated in the establishment of the Ilkhanate and direct Mongol rule in the realm of greater Iran. The material contribution of Chinese personnel to the siege warfare on this campaign has been well documented.[12] According to the *Yuanshi:* "In the year *guichou* [1253] the army [i.e., the vanguard commanded by Kitbuqa (d. 1260)] reached the realm of *Munaixi* [the realm of the so-called Assassins].[13] . . . Guo Kan defeated the army of fifty thousand soldiers, took 128 cities, and decapitated its commander *Hududa'er* [= Qududar?] *Wuzhu suantan* [sultan].[14] *Suantan* in Chinese means *wang* [king]."[15]

The Western Regions (*Xiyu*) was the Chinese name for any place west of China proper. It could imply any geographical location from today's Xinjiang and Qinghai through Central Asia and the Muslim world and up to Europe. This section refers to the Mongol attack on the so-called Assassins or the Nizārī Ismāʿīlīs, a Shīʿī Muslim sect that caused considerable fear among their co-religionists and others through their occasional murderous attacks on their political rivals. Based in a series of mountain fortresses in northern Persia and Syria, they had carved out a state for themselves. Hülegü was sent to subdue these fortresses and later ordered their destruction.

The text describes how in 1256 Guo Kan "arrived at Qidubu [Girdkūh]. The fortress was situated on the top of (Yan) [Dan]han [Damghān] mountain." One of the famous mountain redoubts of the

Assassins, Girdkūh was also one of the last Ismāʿīlī fortresses to surrender to the Mongols. It held out for nearly two decades, from when it was first put under siege by Kitbuqa's vanguard in 1253, until 1270. The ruins of Girdkūh remain to this day, not far from Damghān in northern Iran.[16] The account, however, conflates the siege of Girdkūh, by which Guo Kan would have passed as part of Hülegü's army in 1256, with the attack on another Ismāʿīlī castle, Maymūndiz, which surrendered in 1256.[17] "[The fortress] was only accessible by suspended ladders (*xianti*), and these were guarded by the most valiant troops. [Hülegü] surrounded it, but it could not be taken. [Guo] Kan attacked by means of catapults on mounts, when the general [Huo]zhe Nashi'er [Khwāja Naṣīr] opened the gate and surrendered. Hülegü sent Guo Kan to Sultan *Wuluwunai* [= Rukn],[18] to summon him to come and submit."[19] Although the suspended ladders mentioned here seem to refer to the mountain's defenses, the term *xianti* was well known in Chinese sources as referring to a type of mobile ladder.[20] This choice is perhaps an indication of the overall attempt of the author to use terms that the Chinese would have readily understood. The account suggests, in any case, that Guo Kan's "catapults on mounts" (*jiapao*) were crucial to the victory. The text also correctly names Rukn al-Dīn Khūrshāh (r. 1255–57), the leader of the Assassins who came down from the fortress of Maymūndiz to submit to the Mongols, and Naṣīr al-Dīn Ṭūsī (1201–74), the influential scholar and theologian who took refuge with the Assassins. The latter was instrumental in urging Rukn al-Dīn to submit (see fig. 1.2).[21]

Next, in the first month of 1257, Guo Kan reached Wuli'er (Kalar),[22] where after a battle, a certain Sultan Haiya submitted to him.[23] He proceeded to another mountain redoubt, Alading (Alamūt),[24] dispersed an army of thirty thousand soldiers, and allegedly received the submission of Sultan Mazanda'er. The presentation of Mazandaran, a region of Iran near the Caspian Sea, as a sultan (ruler) surely indicates confusion on the part of the biography's compilers. Yet, it also demonstrates the careful literary composition of the text, which is chiefly concerned with glorifying Guo Kan and the Mongol conquests that took place around the time of the beginning of the Yuan dynasty. Thus, every single place name is followed by the name of a sultan who allegedly submitted to the general, and all foreign names are fitted into this schema.

The biography then turns to Hülegü's conquest of the ʿAbbasid caliphate and the city of Baghdad. Here we find a few quite accurate historical details on the Mongol subjugation of Baghdad. One should

FIGURE 1.2. The Assassins' stronghold, Girdkūh, in northern Iran. Photo by Sonja-Beatrice Wiebe.

note that the city was separated by the Tigris River into eastern and western districts:[25]

> There was the great state of the Xirong [Western barbarians],[26] eight thousand *li* [distant], where father and son had succeeded each other for forty-two generations and its victorious troops numbered a hundred thousand. [When Guo] Kan arrived, he defeated seventy thousand of its troops, and massacred its western city. Then he defeated its eastern city. . . . Between the two cities was a great river [the Tigris]. [Guo] Kan made in advance a floating bridge to cut off escape. The city was defeated, and sultan Halifa [the ʿAbbasid caliph] got into a boat, [but] looking at the river [he saw that] there was the floating bridge cutting him off, so he went himself to the gate of the army [encampment] to surrender. His [the caliph's] general Zhouda'er [Taoda'er, al-Dawādār] fled, and [Guo] Kan pursued him. When sunset arrived, the entire army wanted to stop and camp, but [Guo] Kan would not listen, and went over ten *li* further, then stopped. In the night there was heavy rain, and in the place where they had first desired to stop, the water reached several feet deep. The next day, [Guo Kan] captured Zhouda'er and decapitated him and he captured over three hundred cities.[27]

First, forty-two generations is nearly an accurate representation for the number of caliphs in the ʿAbbasid dynasty (thirty-nine), and the capture of the western and eastern parts of the city also accords with other records. Moreover, the caliph's chancellor, or *dawādār*,[28] indeed attempted to flee by boat.[29] This is a slightly garbled, but surprisingly well-informed version of the events, presenting Guo Kan as the man of action who caught the Dawādār.

TANGIBLE TREASURES FROM THE WEST

Booty was an important part of the Mongol military machine. It is said that Chinggis Khan's initial attraction to the empire of China was for its riches. And the Mongol armies were continually transporting booty—whether in the form of precious objects, bullion, or even talented individuals and groups (such as artisans) back to Mongolia, where they could confirm and boost the status of their owners.

Guo Kan's biography also provides a colorful description of Baghdad's exquisite riches, and furthermore claims that Guo Kan retrieved and carried back home some of these lavish items including a lute and a coral lampstand. Adding little-known details to the well-rehearsed story of the Mongol capture of Baghdad, the biographer writes: "Then [Guo Kan] defeated [Baghdad's] eastern city, which had a palace hall entirely made of heavy sandalwood; it caught fire and burnt down, and the smell [of the fire] could be smelled for a hundred *li*. He obtained [as booty] a seventy-two-string lute, and a five-foot coral lampstand."[30]

The reference to sandalwood introduces the topic of the unparalleled riches of this realm just conquered by the Mongols. Sandalwood was an expensive and desired resource across Eurasia at the time, known for retaining its fragrance for decades, and is still considered among the most expensive woods. A heavily traded Eurasian commodity, it was a symbol that was shared across Asia's societies, and thus, might also function as a medium through which the author of the text easily represented the city of Baghdad as both exotic and familiar.[31]

The seventy-two-string lute and the coral lampstand, on the other hand, were physically transported to China according to the text. The "lute" may have been an Arabic *qanūn*. First attested in the fourteenth century, the *qanūn* is closely related to the Persian *santūr,* but usually has seventy-two strings.[32] That it is plucked with the fingers would explain how the instrument in the text came to be described as a *pipa* or lute. "Today, a thirty-six-stringed instrument known as the *kalong* [perhaps derived from *qanūn*] is played in southern and eastern Xinjiang—in fact, along the route that Guo Kan may well have taken on his return journey from the Middle East."[33]

As for the coral lampstand, it would have been very impressive indeed at five feet or 1.7 meters.[34] As a material not readily available in China, coral had been associated from ancient times with the Western Regions, including Persia, and was connected with extravagance as well

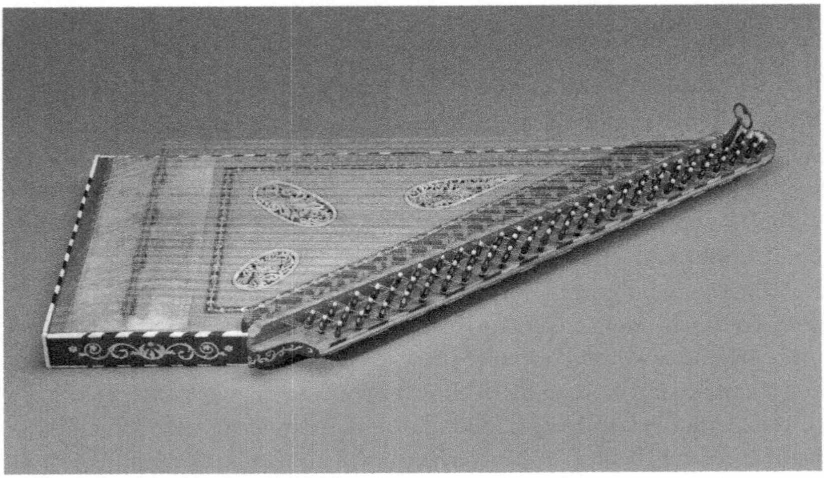

FIGURE 1.3. This *qanūn* (nineteenth-century Turkish) with seventy-two strings in twenty-four courses, may be similar to the lute Guo Kan brought from Baghdad. The Crosby Brown Collection of Musical Instruments, 1889.

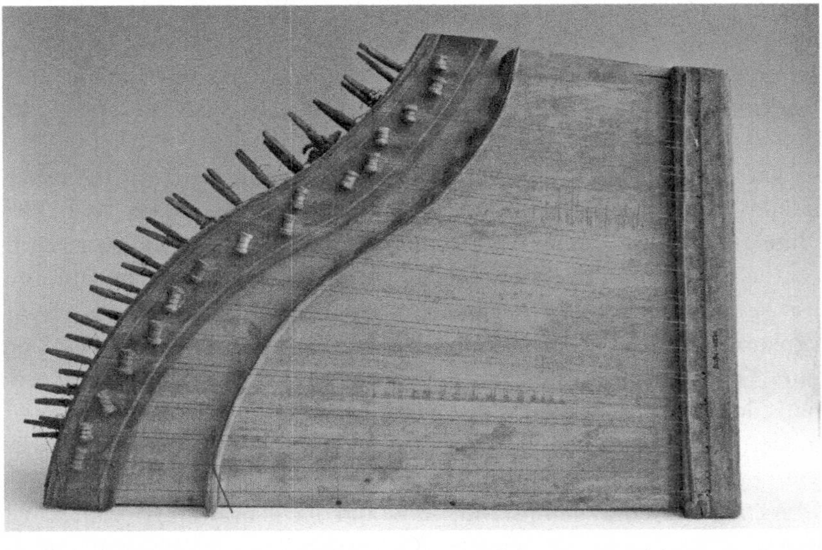

FIGURE 1.4. The Uighur *kalun* (Ch. *kalong*) is a modern variation of the *qanūn*. It remains an important instrument in the Uighur musical tradition. Aksu Museum, Xinjiang.

as perceived as an ideal item for tribute payments to China.[35] The word *shanhu* (Chinese: coral) itself possibly derives from Persian,[36] in which case, both the word and the material are testaments to long-standing Eurasian interconnectedness.

During the sack of Baghdad, the caliph's treasures were looted, as were many other residences in the city, while other parts of Baghdad were burned to the ground. Interestingly, Naṣīr al-Dīn Ṭūsī, who after the fall of Maymūndiz joined Hülegü's retinue and became his astronomer and councilor, notes that looted objects were immediately distributed among members of the army, which might explain how these objects came into Guo Kan's hands. While one function of booty was to impress those back home, another was to keep one's own followers satisfied, which could be best achieved by prompt and generous sharing of the spoils. Thus, Ṭūsī writes: "[Hülegü] went to examine the caliph's residence and walked in every direction. The caliph [who had already been taken captive] was fetched and ordered presents to be offered. Whatever he brought the King at once distributed amongst his suite and the emirs, military leaders and [all] those present."[37]

IMAGINARY CONQUESTS IN THE WEST

The biography continues with further exploits in the West. It claims that the Mongols—this time under the leadership of Guo Kan himself—defeated the "sultans" of Mecca, Egypt, and "the Franks." Even if we suppose that these claims echo some actual, albeit more limited, conquests of the Mongols, they clearly belong to the more legendary lore. Though the Mongols wished to conquer Egypt and raided Syria, they never came near Mecca. And while "the Franks" may refer to Antioch or some other Frankish principality, the text more significantly tells us something broader about the Chinese attitude toward "the West."

> Again [Guo Kan] went three thousand *li* to the west up to [Tian]fang [Mecca]. Its general Zhushi[38] sent a letter requesting to submit. [. . .] Sultan Ba'er [Baybars?] submitted [to him]. . . . Going yet further west by four thousand *li*, [Guo Kan] reached Mixi'er [Egypt]. . . . Ke'nai [Ketu = Qutuz] sultan was greatly alarmed and said: "This general, [sent by] the Eastern Heaven (*dongtian*)[39] is a holy man (*shenren*)."[40] Then he submitted [to Guo Kan].
>
> In 1258, Hülegü ordered [Guo] Kan to go to the west crossing the sea and take Fulang. . . . Wudu sultan said: "The holy man I dreamt of yesterday is [this] general." Immediately he came to submit.[41]

"Tianfang" and "Mixi'er," the terms used for Mecca and Egypt respectively, as well as the term "Fulang" for "the Franks," were well established in Chinese history writing by this time.[42] Sultan Ketu seems to refer to the Mamluk Sultan Qutuz (r. 1259–60),[43] while Ba'er might be a reference to Baybars (r. 1260–77), who succeeded Qutuz as the Mamluk sultan in Egypt and Syria, or to a Meccan authority.[44] The source seems to be entirely uninformed about the Mongol defeat at the hands of the Mamluk forces in 1260 at the battle of ʿAyn Jālūt (in modern-day north Israel), which stopped them from conquering Syria or any lands beyond.

What these sections in the biography, however, lack in historical accuracy, they make up for in drama, for Guo Kan is presented not only as a general, but also as a holy man. The account regarding Arabia sets the scene by painting his foes as untrustworthy,[45] and the rulers of Egypt and the Franks both defined Guo Kan as a holy man (*shenren*).[46] The sudden emphasis on Guo Kan's spiritual power in the biography could be an attempt to paint these supposed conquests as predestined or justified. Or, if we consider the biography a carefully crafted text, they could represent the superiority of Guo Kan's spiritual power, or that of the "East," over the "Western" (Muslim and Christian) spiritual forces.[47]

This section of the biography also describes some more military tactics of Guo Kan. In Egypt, it shows him evading the Egyptian sultan's troops by using arrows as gags, silently moving his army to a different location.[48] The technique of using arrows as gags is mentioned in several other places in the *Yuanshi,* and continues the theme of Guo Kan's campaigns being aided by his background in Chinese military tactics.

ON THE WAY BACK

After his exploits in "the West," the biography continues with a series of locations which theoretically add up to a return journey. As it happens, these locations may have less to do with his actual journey than with the order of places mentioned in a closely related source, the *Record of an Embassy to the West,* or *Xishiji.* The work chronicles the travels of the tax collector and medical expert Chang De, who was sent by Möngke Qa'an to Hülegü in Iran in 1259.[49] It is written in the style of a travelogue, initially (like Guo Kan's biography itself) cataloging stages in Chang De's journey, later mentioning a series of "exotic" places while acquainting the reader with their products and customs. The locations mentioned in Guo Kan's biography appear in exactly the same order as those in the *Record.*[50]

Thus, the biography next turns to Shiraz (in southern Iran), where Guo Kan is said to have defeated enemies and attained the surrender of "the sultan, Huansigan Adabi [Atabeg]."[51] This detail reflects near-accurate knowledge of the location as the rulers of Shiraz were not sultans but carried the lesser title of *atabegs*. Moreover, "Huansigan" ("*Aosi*" in the *Xishiji*) would seem to refer to Abish Khatun, the female ruler of the province between 1264 and 1287.[52]

Next, in a land called Bintie, a sultan by the name of Jiaye is said to have surrendered to Guo Kan.[53] The next location, Wulin, presumably refers to Rūm or Anatolia, and the ʿAlāʾ al-Dīn who is said to have submitted may refer to ʿAlāʾ al-Dīn Kayqubād II (r. 1249–57).[54] Next, Guo Kan is said to have arrived in Qiliwan (Kirmān), where "Sultan Hudumading" came to submit. Hudumading likely refers to the ruler of Kirmān Quṭb al-Dīn, who died in 1257.[55]

Coming to the end of Guo Kan's adventures in the west, the biography says that, returning to report his victories, he arrived in 1259 at the fortress at Diaoyu mountain (near Chongqing in Sichuan, southwest China), which Möngke was besieging, but hearing of Möngke's death, "returned to Deng [nowadays Henan province], started a military farm (*tuntian*), and secured the border." It is at this point that the biography claims that "the Western Regions were pacified" thanks to Guo Kan's feats.[56]

A NEW START

These last statements perhaps more than any other give a clue as to Guo Kan's true stature. For a general who had seen extraordinary success in the "Western Regions," it was probably disappointing to simply retire to a military farm in Deng while awaiting developments after Möngke's death. But the compilers of the biography were much more likely to have accurate information about his career in China. Moreover, after his return, he is described as merely a chiliarch, only later attaining the rank of myriarch. Thus, while undoubtedly a competent general and specialist in siegework as described, he is unlikely to have been a major player in the Mongols' armies.[57]

After his return to China, Guo Kan allegedly provided Qubilai with advice on the best way to conquer the Song in southern China. He then became assistant judicial proceedings officer,[58] and the next year, having been recommended by his former patron Shi Tianze, was quelling "rebellions" and penetrating deeper into Song territory, even capturing battleships.[59] This again shows Guo Kan's (and the Mongol armies') quick adaptation to new realities, as they acquired naval skills to defeat the Song.

When Shi Tianze, though a prominent general, statesman, and close associate of Qubilai Qa'an, fell from grace with the rise of Qubilai's Central Asian financial advisors in the mid-1260s, Guo Kan fell likewise. This indicates, again, that Guo Kan's position was possibly not as exalted as depicted in the description of his Western journey. In fact, he never came out of the shadow of his patron Shi Tianze. He is recorded as having protested the detention of an envoy to the Song, and having suggested the establishment of military colonies, a subject he should know something about after his experience at Deng. He suppressed rebellions, including by a Daoist master and a Buddhist monk, and toward the very end of his life was promoted to myriarch. Finally, "when Jiangnan [the economic and political center of South China] was pacified, he moved to Ninghaizhou [nowadays Shandong province], resided there for a year, and died."[60] The biography maintains the fiction of his exalted status, ascribing to him the pacification of Jiangnan (southern China) as he had been credited earlier with the pacification of "the West."

CONCLUSION

This biography of Guo Kan testifies to a general who descended from a family, which allied itself with Chinggis Khan early on. He was skilled in military matters, including siege technology and artillery, and brought his Chinese knowledge to the Mongol western campaign against the Assassins and Baghdad. He was probably familiar with the technique of using arrows as gags, though the instance in which he is said to have done this is rather fictional, and was later also involved in naval warfare.

Although Guo Kan's biography itself was put together in the very early years of the Ming dynasty, one of its most significant aspects is that it reflects how Chinese knowledge of Western Asia advanced under the Yuan. The knowledge it shows is remarkably accurate in some sections, for example, when describing the fall of Baghdad. The sandalwood in the caliph's palace and the looted artifacts—the lute and the coral lampstand—that he supposedly carried back to China were shared symbols of Eurasian riches. Yet, they also indicate the role of such items in depicting the West in the Chinese imagination as both exotic and familiar. The later section in the biography regarding Arabia, Egypt, and "the Franks," further shows how the West could become the setting for augmenting Guo Kan's military prowess and fame. Although the biography exhibits at this point little real interest in accurate knowledge of these foreign sites or the people, nevertheless, that the names of cities and rulers reflect real figures and sites is impressive as is. It anchors Chinese imaginations in actual places and historical figures, even if the events described are clearly fictitious. The glorification of the general points toward a biography, the majority of which was probably composed on the basis of another source, the *Record of an Embassy to the West.* The final part of the biography, which describes Guo Kan's career after his return to China, may have been based on official records of the Yuan dynasty. In all, it presents a general who confronted the armies of Central Asia, as his ancestor Ziyi and his grandfather Baoyu had done, but whose reach to Western Asia, even if only to Baghdad (and not Europe and Egypt as the biography claims), as well as his success and legacy, far outstripped theirs.

NOTES

1. Traditionally, in China, each dynasty would write the official history of the dynasty or dynasties that preceded it, and use this history to support their claim to rightful succession. The *Yuanshi* (Song 1976) was compiled under the subsequent Ming dynasty (1368–1644), and completed in 1370. A full translation of the biography of Guo Kan is found in Hodous 2018.

2. The main other Chinese source on Hülegü's western campaign is the *Xishiji* (Record of an Embassy to the West), which records the 1259 travels of Chang De, Möngke's emissary to Hülegü. See also Isahaya's chapter in this volume.

3. An Lushan (d. 757) was an important Tang general whose rebellion against the dynasty is considered the major dividing line in Tang history and the history of imperial China in general. The rebellion greatly weakened the Tang, thereby paving the road to a series of military, social, and intellectual changes that came to fruition under their successors, the Song dynasty (960–1279).

4. By the Tang period, the Uighurs held a large empire in Mongolia (744–840). After the dissolution of their empire they migrated westward, and on the eve of the Mongol conquest they were mostly concentrated in Gaochang, near present-day Turfan in eastern Xinjiang, China. Allsen 2015, 128–29; Rudelson 1998, 6–7.

5. De Rachewiltz 1966. Muqali led the Mongols' campaign in north China after Chinggis Khan went to the west in 1218.

6. *Chaoma* (Turk. *chaqmaq*) means "to launch [a projectile]." Brockelmann 1928, 50.

7. Song 1976, 149: 3521. The account reflects an actual medical procedure that was applied during this period to treat shock on the battlefield: the pressure of the animal on the body within it would restore the blood flow. Pressure trousers are used for a similar purpose in treating trauma injuries nowadays: May 2015.

8. Ch. *Bieshibali;* Huzhang refers to Khujand so Huzhang river must be the Jaxartes River, which flows through Khujand.

9. Thus, Allsen maintains that "the term *huojian* . . . originally denoted an incendiary arrow but by the 12th century the term had come to mean a rocket, a true gunpowder weapon." Allsen 2002, 277; also Haw 2013; cf. Raphael 2009; May 2012.

10. May 2012, 146–49; Allsen 2002, 274–77.

11. "The Tubo [Tibetan] commander Nilun and the Uighur [Huihe] commander Abiding rebelled, [but] again he defeated and beheaded them." Song 1976, 149: 3522.

12. Allsen 2002, 278; Needham and Ronan 1995, 250.

13. Bretschneider 1910, 1: 115, n. 289, 133. Probably a transcription of *mulāḥida,* heretics, a term used to denote the Assassins.

14. Dazhe Naxi'er in the *Xishiji,* in what is likely a transcription mistake.

15. Song 1976, 149: 3522–23.

16. Daftary 2001.

17. Jamal 2002, 47–48.

18. Chen 2017, 125.

19. Song 1976, 149: 3523–24.

20. The term *xuanti* is found already in the History of the fourth-century Jin Dynasty (*Jinshu*) written during the Tang (Fang Xuanling 1974, 128: 3184). Allsen 2002, 278.

21. On Ṭūsī: Isahaya's contribution in this volume.

22. Chen Dezhi 2015, 94, argues on the basis of a route from Nishapur to Alamūt that this city must be Kalar (today's Kelardasht, in Mazandaran). In the *Xishiji,* it appears as *Qili'er.*

23. Bretschneider (1910, 1:136) suggests that Haiya may stand for the Muslim name Ghiyāth.

24. Referring to 'Alā' al-Dīn Muḥammad, who ruled there (1221–55).

25. Song 1976, 149:3523–24.

26. *Baoda* [Baghdad] in the *Xishiji.*

27. Song 1976, 149: 3524.

28. Literally: bearer of the inkstand (Pers. *dawātdār),* the *dawādār* was one of the caliph's leading officials: Bosworth 1996.

29. Boyle 1961, 158; Park 2012, 224–25 n. 15.

30. Song 1976, 149: 3524.

31. Jackson 2005, 313.

32. Gifford 2001, 33–34; Touma 2003, 121.

33. Zeng 2003, 191–93; Ma 2003, 76; on musical exchange: Biran 2016, 133–54.

34. Farquhar 1990, 443.

35. Ptak 1990, 69–70; Kumar 2005, 61–62.

36. For the origins of this word: Chmielewski 1961, 83–86.

37. Boyle 1961, 159.

38. I was unable to identify this individual.

39. *Dongtian* is an unusual expression. It appears only three times in the *Yuanshi* and a handful of times in other dynastic histories. Literally it means "the Eastern Heaven/Sky," though it seems to function here as a generic reference to the "eastern regions."

40. Song 1976, 149: 3524.
41. Song 1976, 149: 3524–25.
42. *Tianfang*—"the heavenly square"—more specifically refers to the Ka'ba, while Egypt is identified by its Arabic name *Miṣr.* Zhang 1985, 74.
43. Chen Dezhi 2015, 101.
44. *Ba'er* may be a truncated version of the title *peiyanba'er* (prophet, from the Persian *payāmbar*) found in the *Record of the Embassy to the West,* a manuscript which is closely related to that of the biography. If so, then *Ba'er* would correctly refer to a descendant of the prophet, as were the local rulers of Mecca.
45. As Zhushi had asked to submit but eventually rebelled and had to be quelled. Song 1976.
46. Song 1976, 149: 3524–25.
47. This is remarkably different from the *Record of the Embassy to the West,* which mentions "Western" culture and customs more positively.
48. Song 1976, 149: 3524.
49. On him, see Isahaya's contribution in this volume.
50. For a comparison of the two: Hodous 2018.
51. Song 1976, 149: 3525.
52. The character *huan* 換 is probably a corruption of *ao* 襖. Chen Dezhi 2015, 103.
53. Song 1976, 149: 3525. Although Bintie is mentioned in the *Record,* in this source it is correctly identified as a type of fine steel from Persia or Kashmir, and not a region. Chen Dezhi 2015, 104.
54. Melville 2009, 55.
55. Bretschneider 1910, 1: 147 n. 398.
56. Song 1976, 149: 3525.
57. Also, from this point on, the biography contains no more parallels with the *Xishiji.*
58. The Assistant Judicial Proceedings Officer (*fuliwen*) was in charge of dealing with legal cases at the provincial level. Farquhar 1990, 369, 372, 379, 382, 385, 387, 391, 394, 397, 399.
59. Song 1976, 149: 3525.
60. Song 1976, 149: 3525.

BIBLIOGRAPHY

Allsen, Thomas. 2002. "The Circulation of Military Technology in the Mongolian Empire." In *Warfare in Inner Asian History (500–1800),* ed. Nicola Di Cosmo, 265–93. Leiden: Brill.

———. 2015. "Population Movements in Mongol Eurasia." In *Nomads as Agents of Cultural Change,* ed. Reuven Amitai and Michal Biran, 119–51. Honolulu: University of Hawai'i Press.

Biran, Michal. 2016. "Music in the Conquest of Baghdad: Safi al-Din Urmawi and the Ilkhanids Circle of Musicians." In *The Mongols' Middle East,* ed. Bruno de Nicola and Charles Melville, 133–54. Leiden: Brill.

Bosworth, C. Edmund. 1996. S.v. "Dawātdār." *Encyclopædia Iranica* 7: 136.

Boyle, John Andrew. 1961. "The Death of the Last Abbasid Caliph: A Contemporary Muslim Account." *Journal of Semitic Studies* 6: 145–61.

Bretschneider, Emil. 1910. *Mediaeval Researches from Eastern Asiatic Sources: Fragments towards the Knowledge of the Geography and History of Central and Western Asia from the 13th to the 17th Century*. London: Trübner.

Brockelmann, 1928. *Mitteltürkischer Wortschatz nach Maḥmūd al-Kāš;tarīs Dīvān lugāt at-Turk*. Leipzig: Harrassowitz.

Chen Dezhi 陳得芝. 2015. "Liu Yu Chang De Xishiji jiaozhu 劉郁《〔常德〕西使記》校注 [Liu Yu's 'Chang De's Record of an Embassy to the West', Collated and Annotated]." *Zhonghua wenshi luncong* 中華文史論叢 113.1: 67–108.

Chen Li-wei. 2017. "The Mountain Without the Old Man: Xishiji on Ismailis." In *Proceedings of the 2nd International Ismaili Studies Conference: "Mapping A Pluralist Space in Ismaili Studies,"* ed. Karim H. Karim, 123–33. Ottawa: Carleton Centre for the Study of Islam.

Chmielewski, Janusz. 1961. "Two Early Loan-words in Chinese." *Rocznik Orientalistyczny* 24: 65–86.

Daftary, Farhad. 2001. S.v. "Gerdkūh." *Encyclopaedia Iranica* 10: 499.

de Rachewiltz, Igor. 1966. "Personnel and Personalities in North China in the Early Mongol Period." *Journal of the Economic and Social History of the Orient* 9: 88–144.

Fang Xuanling 房玄齡. 1974. *Jinshu* 晉書. Beijing: Zhonghua shuju.

Farquhar, David M. 1990. *The Government of China under Mongolian Rule: A Reference Guide*. Stuttgart: Franz Steiner.

Franke, Herbert. 1978. *From Tribal Chieftain to Universal Emperor and God: The Legitimation of the Yüan Dynasty*. Munich: Verlag der Bayerischen Akademie der Wissenschaften.

Gifford, Paul. 2001, *The Hammered Dulcimer: A History*. Lanham, MD: Scarecrow Press.

Haw, Stephen G. 2013. "The Mongol Empire—the First Gunpowder Empire?" *Journal of the Royal Asiatic Society* 23: 441–69.

Hodous, Florence. 2018. "Record of an Embassy to the West and Biography of the Guo Family: Views of 'the West' in 13th and 14th Century China." *Xishiji he Guo Kan zhuan—shisan, shisi shiji Zhongguo zenme kan Xiyu* 西使記和郭侃傳—十三十四世紀中國怎麼看西域 [in English]. Postdoctoral thesis. Beijing, Renmin University.

Jackson, Peter. 2005. *The Mongols and the West, 1221–1410*. Harlow, Essex: Pearson Longman.

Jamal, Nadia Eboo. 2002. *Surviving the Mongols: The Continuity of Ismaili Tradition in Iran*. London: Tauris.

Juwaynī, ʿAṭā Malik ibn Muḥammad. 1912. *Taʾrīkh-i Jahāngushā*. Ed. Mīrzā Muḥammad Qazwīnī. 3 vols. London: Luzac.

———. 1997. *Genghis Khan: The History of the World-Conqueror*. Tr. John Andrew Boyle. 2 vols. Manchester: Manchester University Press.

Kumar, Yukteshwar. 2005. *A History of Sino-Indian Relations: 1st Century A.D. to 7th Century A.D.* New Delhi: APH Publishing.

Ma Jianchun 馬建春. 2003. "Yuandai de huihui leqi yu ledian 元代的回回樂器与樂曲 [Musical Compositions and Musical Instruments of the *Huihui* in the Yuan Period]." *Huizu yanjiu* 回族研究 [Researches on the Hui] 50.2: 74–76.

May, Timothy. 2012. *The Mongol Conquests in World History*. London: Reaktion Books.

———. 2015. "Spitting Blood: Medieval Mongol Medical Practices." In *Wounds and Wound Repair in Medieval Culture*, ed. Larissa Tracey and Kelly DeVries, 175–93. Leiden: Brill.

Melville, Charles. 2009. "Anatolia under the Mongols." *The Cambridge History of Turkey*, ed. Kate Fleet, 1: 51–101. Cambridge: Cambridge University Press

Needham, Joseph, and Colin A. Ronan. 1995. *The Shorter Science and Civilisation in China*. Cambridge: Cambridge University Press.

Park, Hyunhee. 2012. *Mapping the Chinese and Islamic Worlds: Cross-Cultural Exchange in Pre-modern Asia*. Cambridge: Cambridge University Press.

Ptak, Roderich. 1990. "Notes on the Word *Shanhu* and Chinese Coral Imports from Maritime Asia, c.1250–1600." *Archipel* 39: 65–80.

Raphael, Kate. 2009. "Mongol Siege Warfare on the Banks of the Euphrates and the Question of Gunpowder (1260–1312)." *Journal of the Royal Asiatic Society* 19: 355–70.

Rudelson, Justin J. 1998. *Oasis Identities—Uyghur Nationalism along China's Silk Road*. New York: Columbia University Press.

Sarkozi, Alice. 1993. "Mandate of Heaven: Heavenly Support of the Mongol Ruler." In *Altaica Berolinensia: The Concept of Sovereignty in the Altaic World*, ed. Barbara Kellner-Heinkele, 215–21. Wiesbaden, Germany: Harrassowitz.

Song Lian 宋濂. 1976. *Yuan shi* 元史. Beijing: Zhonghua shuju.

Touma, Habib Hassan. 2003. *The Music of the Arabs*. New expanded ed. Tr. Laurie Schwarts. Portland, OR: Amadeus Press.

Zeng Gongliang 曾公亮 and Ding Du丁度. 1988. "*Wujing zongyao* 武經總要 [Complete Essentials for the Military Classics]." In *Zhongguo bingshu jicheng* 中國 兵書集成 [Collection of Chinese Military Writings], vols. 3–5. Ed. *Zhongguo bingshu jicheng* Editing Committee. Beijing: Jiefangjun chubanshe and Liaoshen shushe.

Zeng Jinshou. 2003. "Chinas Musik und Musikerziehung im kulturellen Austausch mit den Nachbarlaendern und dem Westen." PhD diss., University of Bremen.

Zhang Wenchun 張文淳. 1985. "Aiji diming youlai chutan 埃及地名由來初探 (一) [A Preliminary Discussion of the Place Name for Egypt (first part)]." *Xiya Feizhou* 西亚非洲 [Western Asia and Africa] 3: 74–76.

CHAPTER 2

Baiju

The Mongol Conqueror at the Crossfire of Dynastic Struggle

SARA NUR YILDIZ

In 1258, Hülegü (r. 1260–65), Chinggis Khan's grandson, ordered the execution of the ʿAbbasid caliph al-Mustaʿṣim (r. 1242–58), together with his sons and attendants, in a village outside of Baghdad where the Mongol khan was encamped.[1] The ignoble end of the ʿAbbasid caliphate at the hands of the Mongols, along with their conquest of Baghdad, ushered in a new era of Mongol rule in Western Asia under the Ilkhanate (1260–1335), the regional Mongol state founded by Hülegü, centered in western Iran and Iraq. During the campaign, Hülegü had been particularly dependent upon Baiju, or Baiju Noyan (fl. 1230s to 1260),[2] whose activities since the 1230s made him the most experienced and knowledgeable Mongol commander in the western territories (comprising today's Iran, Iraq, northern Mesopotamia, Anatolia, and the Caucasus).

Baiju's career encapsulates the tensions arising between the military and the administration during the rapid expansion of the Mongol imperial domains. The ad hoc predatory behavior of military commanders often clashed with the aims of Mongol civilian administrators in charge of implementing bureaucratic rule over subjugated sedentary populations and restoring agricultural lands and cities following the violent conquest. Baiju was the rapacious and implacable Mongol commander par excellence, hated and feared by local populations, Christian and Muslim, implementing the Mongol military strategy of terror as an effective way to subjugate sedentary populations. Baiju is primarily known as the conqueror of Anatolia. In 1243, he rendered the Seljuks of Anatolia, the Armenian kingdom of Cilicia, and the city of Mosul under the rule of Sultan Badr al-Dīn Lu'lu' (r. 1233–59) as tributary states, and in 1256 placed Seljuk Anatolia under Hülegü's direct authority. In addition to being the twice-conqueror of Anatolia, Baiju conducted raids and campaigns throughout neighboring regions, going as far as Baghdad. Together with Chormaqan, the first Mongol commander-in-chief of the western territories, and his superior, Baiju was responsible for imposing Mongol rule in the western regions of the empire. Finally, Baiju played a major role in bringing about the fall of Baghdad in 1258.

For exactly whom Baiju imposed Mongol rule needs clarification, for his military operations in the western periphery occurred in the context of disputes over political authority among the royal family. Following the death of Ögödei Qa'an (r. 1229–41), Mongol authority, in particular, that over the conquests in the western territories, was contested by rival members of the Chinggisid dynasty. Before Güyük Qa'an (r. 1246–48) was elected as his father's successor, imperial authority was wielded by the regent, Töregene Khatun (r. 1241–46), who was Ögödei's widow and Güyük's mother. Following Güyük's brief reign, his widow likewise ruled as regent until 1251. Batu Khan (r. 1227–ca. 1255), founder of the Mongol state centered in the Volga region and known as the Golden Horde, however, opposed Töregene's regency and her son Güyük's election as qa'an. As the senior male member of the Chinggisid ruling family, Batu challenged their authority over the western territories, which lay contiguous to his own appanage, spanning the Qipchaq Steppe and Khwārazm. Batu Khan thus imposed his authority over Baiju, claiming jurisdiction over the latter's conquests, including the Seljuk realm of Anatolia.[3] Following Batu's death, however, Baiju found himself in changed political circumstances. He was now under the authority of Hülegü, the brother of the new Qa'an Mönkge (r. 1251–59), who had replaced the Ögödeids. Moreover, Hülegü was the implacable enemy of Batu's descendants. It was thus in the name of Hülegü that Baiju waged his second campaign of conquest against the Seljuks in 1256.

Over the course of his long career as the chief commander of the western territories, Baiju had survived the bitter infighting among the royal family. Yet, soon after the military campaigns against Baghdad and Syria, Hülegü had Baiju executed. Operating in the distant western frontier, Baiju had become accustomed to autonomy. Hülegü, it seems, suspected his loyalty and accused him of acting independently of imperial authority.

The Mongol occupation of the Anatolian interior steppeland by Baiju's armies had long-term repercussions. The displacement of Turkmen pastoralists from the plateau resulted in large-scale disruptions in their economic, social, and political life. Forced off their pastures on the eastern and central Anatolian plateau, the transhumant Turkmen took refuge in the mountain ranges flanking the interior on all sides or crowded into the western alluvial lowlands bordering the Byzantine march to the west. The displacement of the Turkmen from the interior in turn spawned the creation of the Turkish principalities, or *beylik*s, in the late thirteenth and early fourteenth centuries, including the nascent Ottoman state, along the peripheries of Mongol-dominated Anatolia.[4]

BAIJU'S EARLY CAREER UNDER CHORMAQAN: THE IMPERIAL PERIOD, 1230S TO 1248

Of the Mongol Besüd clan,[5] Baiju was a kinsman of Chinggis Khan's seasoned commander Jebe (d. 1223). Jebe was one of the earliest Mongol commanders to pass through Western Asia with a contingent of troops, sweeping through Azerbaijan and the Transcaucasus in 1220–21 in pursuit of Muḥammad Khwārazmshāh (d. 1220). Like Chormaqan, his superior, Baiju too began as a *qorchi,* a quiver-bearer or guard in the imperial household.[6] His first military campaign was in the late 1220s, when he took part in the attack on Isfahan (Iran).[7] In around 1230, he was placed under the authority of Chormaqan,[8] who had participated in the first western campaigns as a subordinate commander. Chormaqan was later sent westward in pursuit of Muḥammad Khwārazmshāh's son, Jalāl al-Dīn (d. 1231). In charge of *tamma* or garrison troops,[9] stationed in the lush grasslands of Azerbaijan in northwestern Iran and the Caucasus,[10] Chormaqan was ordered to complete the conquest of Iran and bring an end to the troublesome Khwārazmshāh. The Mongols' determination to destroy the Khwārazmshāh thus brought the first significant number of Mongol forces into Western Asia. Baiju was initially assigned a *hazāra,* a company of a thousand, but was promoted to commander of a *tümen,* a unit of ten thousand,[11] and served as Chormaqan's second-in-command. He often acted autonomously, especially toward the end of Chormaqan's life, when his superior commander was debilitated by poor health.

Following the death of Jalāl al-Dīn Khwārazmshāh, in 1231, the Mongol forces under Chormaqan and Baiju continued raiding from their headquarters established in the rich pasturage of the Mughān plain in northeastern Azerbaijan.[12] Chormaqan and Baiju next seized Tabriz (1231), a major city on the trade route, and the nearby town of Maragha. These two urban centers would later serve as the main administrative and cultural centers of the Ilkhanate. They subsequently directed most of their energies against Georgia and Armenia in the Caucasus. Although throughout the 1230s the Mongol armies had seized many Georgian castles, the conquest of the Caucasus occurred piecemeal, and was not completed until 1240.[13]

From 1234 to 1238, there was a lull in Mongol military activity under Chormaqan and Baiju, presumably due to the reformulation of Ögödei's western policy. Ögödei placed Batu Khan at the head of a large force leading a series of campaigns in the west. Known as the European campaign, it was nevertheless aimed at subjugating the nomadic populations north of the Black and Caspian Seas, such as the Qangli and the Qipchaq.[14] Their campaigns extended into the Transcaucasia, eastern Europe, and along the Danube, with some small contingents going as far west as the Dalmatian coast.[15]

After the Mongol imperial forces involved in the European campaign had withdrawn southward to recuperate in 1238, Chormaqan and Baiju's garrison troops resumed their raids in Anatolia, Armenia, and northern Mesopotamia. In the subsequent years, Baiju's raiders continued to terrorize the region's population, Christian and Muslim, rural and urban, from the Caucasus to Baghdad.

These raids now, however, were conducted under the authority of Batu Khan, the senior Chinggisid commander. With Ögödei's death in 1241, Batu outwardly claimed all the imperial possessions in the Caucasus for himself. Chormaqan, it seems, was reluctant to challenge Batu's usurpation of imperial authority. Due to an illness that left Chormaqan paralyzed and deaf, Baiju became the de facto commander-in-chief. Chormaqan likewise left the administrative affairs of his camp in Mughān to his wife.[16] When Chormaqan died sometime in the 1240s, Baiju was officially appointed in his place. Chormaqan's son, Bora, continued campaigning, now under Baiju's authority.[17]

Baiju next (1242–43) turned his energies against the Seljuks of Anatolia. A regional branch of the Great Seljuks, a Turkish dynasty that in the eleventh century took over Iran, Iraq, Syria, Transoxania, and Khwārazm, the Seljuks of Anatolia or Rūm rose as the main Muslim political power in the interior and coasts of formerly Byzantine Asia Minor by the end of the twelfth century. With their administrative center at Konya, the Seljuks controlled the interior plateau of Anatolia as well as the trade emporiums of Sinop on the Black Sea coast and Antalya on the Mediterranean coast; indeed, the Seljuks were at their territorial and economic

FIGURE 2.1. The Kösedağ Plain, with its mountain in the distance.

zenith when the Mongols conquered them. In possession of important trade routes linking the eastern Mediterranean to the Black Sea and Iran, the Seljuks of Anatolia were particularly attractive to the Mongols as a tributary state for the great wealth they commanded.[18]

Although the Seljuk sultan ʿAlāʾ al-Dīn Kayqubād I (r. 1219–37) had first come into contact with Mongol raiders in the early 1230s, it was his son Kaykhusraw II (r. 1237–46) who found himself confronted with an invading army.[19] In the summer of 1242, Baiju, together with other Mongol generals, led a large Mongol force against the largely Armenian city of Erzurum (Karin) on the northeastern frontier of the Seljuk realm.[20] Following the two-month siege and sack of Erzurum,[21] Baiju's armies returned to their winter camp on the Mughān plains. Meanwhile, word of the sack of Erzurum reached the main Seljuk army, which had advanced east from Konya to Erzincan.[22] Aware that the realm was in grave danger, Kaykhusraw II set out to form a regional Muslim-Christian coalition. The Ayyubid princes in northern Mesopotamia as well as the Cilician Armenian ruler, Hetʿum I (r. 1226–70), agreed to join the Seljuk coalition against Baiju's armies. The Seljuk vizier traveled to Syria, where distributing vast sums of gold and silver, he gathered a diverse force of twenty thousand experienced warriors, drawing men from the Turkmen frontier of Anatolia as well as attracting cavalry units from Georgia, the Transcaucasus, and the Qipchaq Steppe. Latin mercenary groups likewise signed up.[23]

Baiju's army reappeared in Anatolia in the summer of 1243, before the reinforcements expected by the Seljuks arrived.[24] Baiju quickly advanced on Anatolia with an immense army of men gathered from Iran and Iraq.[25] Under the influence of hot-headed younger members of his retinue, who were anxious to demonstrate their prowess in battle, the Seljuk sultan headed east to confront Baiju and his army. With a force of allegedly eighty thousand imperial cavalrymen, the sultan marched along the caravan road between Sivas and Erzincan along the mountain known as Kösedağ, stopping at a mountain pass where the Mongol troops would not easily spot them while waiting for reinforcements.[26]

When word came that Mongol army was half the size of that of the Seljuk forces, the sultan's retinue of impetuous young men became emboldened. They left the safety of the mountain hideout to confront their enemy.[27]

THE SELJUK DISASTER AT THE BATTLE OF KÖSEDAĞ AND ITS AFTERMATH

The two armies clashed at the Battle at Kösedağ in a rural location eighty kilometers northwest of Sivas on June 26, 1243.[28] Despite the Seljuk numerical superiority, it was an overwhelming Mongol victory. After razing Sivas to the ground, the Mongols laid siege to Kayseri, where high-ranking Seljuk commanders, officials, and members of the imperial family, including the sultan's mother, had taken refuge. The sultan's mother and her entourage slipped away from the citadel and made their way to Sis in Cilician Armenia just as Baiju ordered his troops to siege the fortress. After some resistance, Kayseri surrendered upon a guarantee of peace terms. Yet, when the city's gates were opened, the Mongol troops slaughtered the entire population and Kayseri was left to burn.[29] Throughout 1244–45, Baiju and his forces ravaged the region, moving south to campaign in Diyarbakır and the Jazira (northern Iraq). They seized the cities of Harran and Ruha (Urfa, Edessa) and took Mardin peacefully after its ruler had fled to Egypt.[30] In 1244, Baiju's Mongol detachments raiding Syria likewise demanded the submission of the crusader principality of Antioch, marking the beginning of papal awareness of the importance of establishing diplomatic relations with the Mongols.[31]

Following the Battle of Kösedağ, the Seljuks realized that further resistance to Baiju was futile. The Seljuk vizier and the judge (*qāḍī*) of Amasya set out for Baiju's mobile camp just outside of Erzurum to negotiate a peace agreement. After approaching Baiju, the Seljuk party

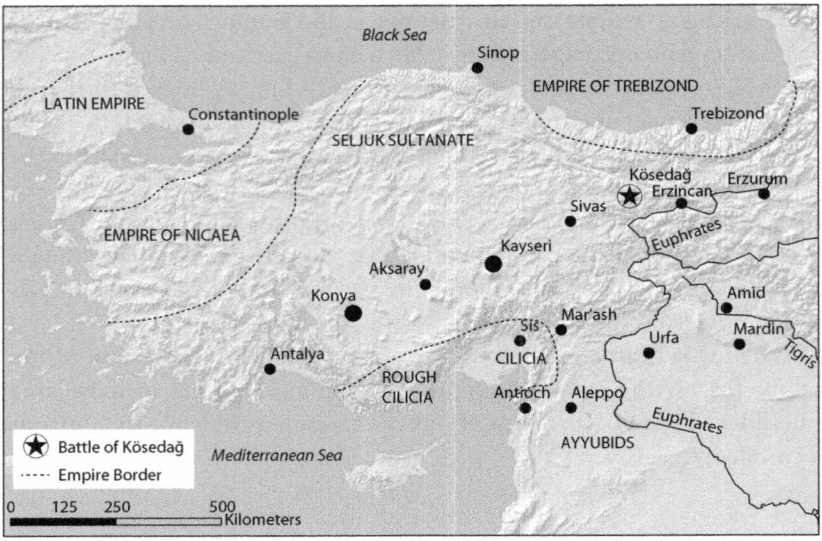

MAP 2.1. The Battle of Kösedağ (1243).

traveled to the plains of Mughān to officiate the peace agreement with Baiju's superior, Chormaqan, and settle on the amount of annual tribute. According to the agreement, the Seljuks were to send the Mongols gold, valuable textiles, and livestock such as horses, camels, cattle, and sheep, as well as slaves as annual tribute.[32] Although peace had been momentarily established, a more solid agreement had yet to be negotiated with the Chinggisids. The Seljuks prepared to send an embassy offering the sultan's obeisance to Batu. Sumptuous gifts for the khan were gathered and the embassy set off, traveling by land and sea, crossing the Caspian before passing onto the Qipchaq Steppe in the north.[33]

Seljuk homage to Batu demonstrated the khan's assumption of imperial authority over the western territories, to the dismay of the imperial regent Töregene Khatun. Baiju, acting on Batu's behalf, likewise found himself in clashes of authority with the Mongol administrators sent by Töregene, such as Arghun Aqa. The latter was appointed in 1242 as the imperial civilian governor of the western territories. Not only was he ordered to circumvent Batu's authority, but also to rein in Baiju and prevent further fiscal abuse by the general who was notorious for his ad hoc extortion of taxes.[34]

After Güyük was nominated qa'an, he sent his general Eljigidei (d. 1251/2) in 1248 to Iran to assert his personal authority in the region, and to wrest control from Baiju, Batu's delegate. Eljigidei was appointed in Baiju's place, and given complete authority over the administration of Anatolia, Georgia, Mosul, Aleppo, and Diyarbakır as well as complete rights to the tribute previously collected, which included the Seljuks' tribute. He in turn accused Baiju of having exacerbated Baghdad's resistance with his aggressive military stance. Yet, with the untimely death of Güyük, as he headed west to battle Batu, Eljigidei never took over Baiju's command.

With Möngke's election as qa'an in 1251, Eljigidei, along with other representatives of Güyük's regime, was implicated in conspiracy against Möngke, and executed.[35] Baiju remained as commander-in-chief of the western territories, despite Möngke's purge of his Ögödeid cousins and their supporters. The succession of Möngke signaled the rise of a new family branch, the offspring of Tolui, Chinggis Khan's youngest son. Möngke sent his two brothers to continue the imperial expansion east and west. His brother Hülegü eventually established his direct control of the western territories, bringing an end to Baiju's de facto autonomy and spurring the second conquest of the already subdued Anatolian Seljuk realm.[36]

THE BATTLE OF AKSARAY (1256): BAIJU'S PLACE IN THE NEW POLITICAL ORDER UNDER HÜLEGÜ

On October 14, 1256, Baiju defeated the Anatolian Seljuks for a second time at the Battle of Aksaray.[37] Baiju's second conquest of the Seljuks, a tributary state since 1243, should be seen in the broader context of the rivalry between the Batuids (or Jochids) and the Toluids. While Batu was among those who orchestrated Möngke's accession, his power threatened the new qa'an and clashed with Hülegü's regional interests. Baiju's 1256 campaign nullified the Batuid claims on the land. The second conquest was also intended to reassert the Mongols' tributary demand and prevent any rebellions, especially in view of Hülegü's planned campaign against the ʿAbbasid caliphate.

Just before the two armies met on the battlefield, in the spring of 1256, the Mongols initiated hostilities by attacking Erzincan. Baiju arrived in Anatolia accompanied by hordes of soldiers, their families and flocks who were evacuated from the plains of Mughān in preparation for the arrival of Hülegü and his vast army.[38] According to an Armenian chronicle, the Mongol commander Qadagha[n] Noyan, a subordinate of Baiju, attacked Erzincan without any provocation.[39] The

Seljuk army at that time had been at Kayseri, preparing for the seasonal campaign against the local Turkmen. Learning of the Mongol attack, they immediately rounded up their armies and headed back to Konya in panic.[40]

The Seljuk and Mongol armies clashed on the plain of Aksaray off the main road between Konya and Kayseri, the two main Seljuk urban centers. That the battle occurred not in the peripheral Seljuk lands of eastern Anatolia, as in the case of Kösedağ, but rather in the center, is significant. The Mongols struck in the heart of Seljuk territory, presaging a more intrusive Mongol presence in Anatolia under Hülegü and the Ilkhans.

After the battle, Baiju remained headquartered for some time near the battle site at the heavily fortified caravanserai located along the Konya-Aksaray road. He monitored the newly submitted Seljuk realm in order to prevent any uprising before he set off in late 1257 to join Hülegü's army for the Baghdad campaign.[41] Baiju also took the precaution of leaving behind a garrison of soldiers and several military governors (*shiḥnas*) in Aksaray.[42]

Following the Seljuk defeat, Konya was spared destruction.[43] A colorful account is offered by the hagiographer of the famous mystical poet Jalāl al-Dīn al-Rūmī (1207–73),[44] who attributes Baiju's sparing of Konya to one of Rūmī's miracles. As Baiju's army was surrounding Konya in order to storm the city, Rūmī fearlessly climbed on top of a hill to pray for the city's safety. His prayers had immediate effect in stopping the assault. The Mongols' arrows changed in midcourse and turned back on their own men. The Mongols were unable to flee, for it was as if their feet had become invisibly bound. Their horses likewise became motionless, stopping in their place, unable to budge. The Mawlānā's spiritual prowess made an impression on Baiju, who although a pagan, understood that he was dealing with someone who had divine protection and whose "anger must be avoided."[45] Konya thus came to terms with Baiju. The city's notables presented valuable gifts to Baiju and the Mongol commander ordered the destruction of the city's battlements, leaving the rest of the city and its residents untouched.[46]

When he learned of the defeat of his forces, the young sultan ʿIzz al-Dīn Kaykāʾūs II (r. 1246–60) fled Konya and headed for his Mediterranean base at Antalya. Rukn al-Dīn Qilich Arslan IV, Kaykāʾūs II's younger brother and rival to the throne, was released from detention at a fortress on the western frontier of the realm. The supporters of the rival prince brought him to Konya and put him on the throne, before setting out to negotiate a peace settlement with Baiju at Aksaray.

Baiju welcomed Rukn al-Dīn on the Seljuk throne, for he, unlike his brother, had not been tarnished by hostilities with the Mongols. Yet, he forbade Rukn al-Dīn and his men from remaining in Konya, where, with its strong fortifications, they could possibly rebel.[47] The new sultan held a feast in Baiju's honor, perhaps in an attempt to ease the general's distrust. This feast, however, ended disastrously with the poisoning death of Baiju's second-in-command, Khwāja Noyan. The Seljuk official responsible for the crime was immediately apprehended and executed in a most gruesome fashion.[48]

When Baiju withdrew from western Anatolia for the east, ʿIzz al-Dīn felt safe enough to return from his temporary exile and made a bid to reclaim the Seljuk throne. In the meanwhile, his brother, Rukn al-Dīn, arrived at Hülegü's camp in Hamadan, Iran, where he was officially recognized as the sole Seljuk ruler.[49] Rukn al-Dīn's officials set about rounding up supplies for the Baghdad campaign upon Hülegü's orders.[50]

THE CONQUEST OF BAGHDAD AND BAIJU'S DEATH

After the caliph al-Mustaʿṣim Bi'llāh refused to submit to Hülegü one last time, Baiju was ordered to prepare for combat. Baiju mobilized an army of allegedly eighty thousand men and headed for the outskirts of Baghdad, where his division would later join Hülegü's main army as part of the right wing. Coming from the direction of Irbil, Baiju crossed the Tigris at Mosul on January 16, 1258, and headed for the suburbs of Baghdad lying to the west of the Tigris. His army camped there while waiting for Hülegü. Hülegü sent ahead one of his most trusted commanders, Suqunchaq, to join Baiju at his encampment.[51] Suqunchaq's vanguard troops met the caliphal army in battle. On the following day, January 17, without any serious engagement between the armies, Suqunchaq and his advance guard retreated. Baiju, having joined the main Mongol army coming from the east, rallied the army to attack. To prevent the ʿAbbasid soldiers from escaping, the Mongols had flooded the hinterland by breaking open a dyke on the Tigris. Few of the caliph's soldiers survived: myriads were killed in battle, and the rest were drowned in the flood. A few days later, on January 22, Baiju's division reached Baghdad's western suburbs. Siege machinery was set up outside the city, and a week later the Mongol army began bombarding the walls, breaching them on February 4. The caliph surrendered. The Mongol armies sacked and burned the city and slaughtered its remaining defenders.[52]

After the Baghdad campaign, Baiju joined the Syrian campaign led by Hülegü in 1260 and died soon afterward.[53] The sources provide conflicting information regarding the circumstances of his death. Some Mamluk sources claim that he was executed by Hülegü because he was suspected of communicating with another ʿAbbasid scion.[54] Another Mamluk historian writes that Baiju died after imbibing a poisoned drink. He explains that Hülegü had concealed his animosity toward Baiju, thus alluding to Hülegü's intention to make use of him in the conquest of Baghdad before doing away with him.[55]

Ilkhanid sources highlight the strained relations between Hülegü and Baiju. Baiju's forced westward migration seems to have inflamed the already tense relationship between the two. Not only did Baiju lose his relative autonomy, but he also lost his prized grazing land to Hülegü's armies. According to Rashīd al-Dīn, Hülegü was particularly annoyed by Baiju's boasting that he "rendered Anatolia submissive."[56] Upon their first meeting, Hülegü treated Baiju harshly, reprimanding him for not having carried out his duties satisfactorily as commander-in-chief of the west: "Since Chormaqan Noyan died, what have you done in his place? . . . What rebel have you brought into submission? Other than frightening the Mongol army with tales of the caliph's might and grandeur, what have you done?"[57] Managing to appease Hülegü, Baiju was then ordered to conquer the rest of the western territories going up to the Mediterranean. Upon this order, Baiju marched to Anatolia, reconquering the Seljuk realm.[58]

BAIJU AMONG CHRISTIANS AND MUSLIMS IN THE WESTERN TERRITORIES

Baiju was one of the earliest Mongols to have come into direct contact with the Franks, or Latin Christians, as a result of his military operations in Syria. In 1244, he sent a raiding party into northern Syria, going as far as the gates of Aleppo.[59] The Syrian attack brought about the submission of Bohemond V, the Frankish ruler of the crusader state of Antioch, and spurred the first papal missions to the Mongols. Thus, in the following year, 1245, Pope Innocent IV (r. 1243–54) sent several missions to the Mongols to establish diplomatic relations, with the particular aim of reaching out to his eastern brethren, the Nestorian or Assyrian Christians. These missions were manned by friars from the mendicant orders of the Dominicans or Franciscans, for not only were they intrepid travelers, but they were also experienced in converting infidels.[60] One of these missions was led by the Dominican friar Ascelin of Cremona. Ascelin, unlike his Franciscan counterpart, John of Plano Carpini (1185–1252), however, never reached Mongolia, but ended his journey, in May 1247, at Baiju's summer camp in the Armenian highlands. Bearing letters from the pope, Ascelin remained there for several months while waiting for an answer from Güyük Qa'an. Subsequently Ascelin returned to Rome on November 1248, accompanied by two Mongol ambassadors relaying the qa'an's demand that Pope Innocent submit. Nothing ever came of this first Mongol-papal diplomatic mission.[61]

After Güyük appointed Eljigidei as commander of the western territories in place of Baiju, Eljigidei sent a diplomatic mission in Güyük's name to Cyprus, where the French king Louis IX was in the midst of preparations for the Seventh Crusade.[62] Coordination with the French on the eve of the Seventh Crusade was crucial to Eljigidei's planned attack on the ʿAbbasid capital of Baghdad in the summer of 1249.[63] Yet, Eljigidei's envoys had the task of repairing relations with the Latin Christians after the earlier diplomatic failure with the pope's envoys. In order to convince the French of their sincerity, Eljigidei's envoys pointed out that Eljigidei was a Christian and that the qa'an was well-disposed toward Christianity, and even on the verge of converting.[64]

BAIJU'S ALLEGED CONVERSION TO ISLAM

Some sources imply that Baiju was hostile to Christians and preferred Muslims over Christians, Yet, typical of Mongols of his generation, Baiju was no less disposed to Christianity than to Islam. He was married to a Nestorian Christian and had Christians in his household. Further Christian military detachments played an important role in Baiju's army, especially the Georgio-Armenian cavalry. Yet, Mamluk historians relate that Baiju submitted to Islam on his deathbed while suffering from the effects of poison. Upon his dying request, his corpse was prepared for burial according to Muslim custom.[65] One must, however, approach such claims with caution.[66] Indeed, this story recalls another alleged early Mongol conversion of the Mongol administrator and governor of Khurasan, Arghun Aqa, Baiju's contemporary and at times, civilian adversary.[67] As in the case of Arghun Aqa, it is difficult to confirm the veracity of Baiju's conversion. Baiju's alleged conversion may be linked to his grandson Sülemish, the Mongol commander-in-chief of Anatolia who rebelled against Ilkhan Ghazan (r. 1295–1304) in 1298–99.[68]

The story's circulation would have been for the benefit of Sülemish's Mamluk allies, who supported him in his failed attempt to gain control of Anatolia, as well as for the anti-Mongol local Muslim population of Anatolia, primarily the Turkmen pastoralists. With Baiju having converted on his deathbed, his grandson Sülemish would have been endowed with the Muslim pedigree that the ruler Ghazan, a recent convert as of 1295, lacked. The claim of Baiju's conversion reflects the Mamluk ideology of seniority in conversion to Islam as a way to nullify Chinggisid dynastic claims of sovereignty—thus granting Sülemish a more legitimate claim to rule over Anatolia than Ghazan, albeit as a Mamluk client.[69] Finally, Baiju's embracing of the Muslim faith during his dying moments may have also been a way of redeeming him, among the Mamluks as well as the Muslims of Anatolia, in light of the destruction that he had waged upon the Muslim world through the conquest of Baghdad.

CONCLUSION: BAIJU'S LEGACY OF CONQUEST IN THE CROSSFIRE OF DYNASTIC STRUGGLE

Often described in the sources as vicious and merciless, and feared by contemporary Christians and Muslims alike, Baiju embodied the violence and destruction associated with the first decades of the Mongol conquests. Baiju was likewise often at odds with civilian Mongol administrators who attempted to bring back the prosperity of lands devastated by conquest and raids. Baiju's military tactics did not stem from the commander's personal predilection for violence and cruelty, but were standard methods employed by the Mongols for rapid and efficient empire building. Referred to as the tsunami strategy,[70] the devastation was meant to be temporary, just like the ad hoc methods of initial taxation and rule by conquering generals such as Baiju. Civilian bureaucrats were tasked with reorganizing the administration of conquered regions. It is not surprising that Baiju was at odds with the methods and goals of the civilian administrators who were sent to contain autonomously acting generals such as himself; indeed, their roles were designed to be conflicting.

Further complicating Baiju's position as commander-in-chief of the western conquests was the fragmentation and overlap of authority among rival members of the Chinggisid family. Baiju's early conquests in the western frontier occurred in the crossfire of dynastic struggle. The 1243 conquest of Anatolia was part of Batu Khan's project of expanding his personal realm, or *ulus,* based in the Western Steppe. The imperial center opposed Batu's claim over these lands, viewing this move as an encroachment on territories which rightfully belonged to the qa'an. Through a series of administrative policies implemented by loyal imperial agents throughout the 1240s, Töregene and Güyük attempted to regain control of the western territories. With Güyük's untimely death in 1248, their efforts failed. Baiju's second conquest of Seljuk Anatolia in 1256 likewise occurred at a turning point in the reconfiguration of power at the Mongol center. This entailed the enthronement of Möngke Qa'an in 1251, and his brother Hülegü's subsequent establishment of the nascent Ilkhanate which encompassed the south-western territories of the empire, including Baiju's conquests.

From the conquest of the Seljuks at the Anatolian frontier to the destruction of the ʿAbbasid caliphate at Baghdad, Baiju significantly shaped the course of history of the medieval Islamic world, just as he opened the papacy's dialogue with the Mongols. Baiju's occupation of Anatolia, beginning in 1256, resulted in a demographic crisis of the Turkmen pastoralists. They were pushed off the vast grazing lands of the Anatolian interior plateau and squeezed into the surrounding mountainous terrain. This in turn spawned a reconfiguration of the political landscape with the rise of the independent Turkish principalities or beyliks in the late thirteenth and early fourteenth centuries in the periphery of Mongol-controlled Anatolia, including the Ottomans.

Baiju's legacy continued through his descendants who remained as commanders in Anatolia. Over three generations, they became Anatolians as much as Mongols, and eventually Muslims. This is best exemplified by Baiju's grandson Sülemish who rebelled in 1298–99 against the Ilkhans with claims to independent rule over Anatolia. Was this a move harkening back to his grandfather's relative autonomy in the region before the arrival of Hülegü? Indeed, Sülemish's rebellion seems to be based on a series of injustices and resentments inflicted on his family by Ilkhanid rulers. His tactics were local as well as transregional: he aligned himself with the most important rising power in the region, the Qaramanid Turkmen, pastoralist tribesmen hostile to the occupying Mongols since Baiju had pushed them off of their grazing lands in the eastern Anatolian plateau, as well as with the Mamluks, the Ilkhanate's implacable foes. Executed by the Ilkhan, Sülemish's fate was the same as that of his grandfather Baiju.[71]

NOTES

1. Rashīd al-Dīn 1994, 2: 1018; Rashīd al-Dīn 1998–99, 2: 499; Gilli-Elewy 2011, 366.

2. Noyan (Mongolian) is a noble or military commander.

3. Jackson 1978, 186; Lane 2003, 62.
4. Peacock and Yıldız 2016, 23; Yıldız forthcoming.
5. Besüd is likewise rendered as Besü'it or Yesü'it.
6. Rashīd al-Dīn 1994, 1: 73, 1: 210; Rashīd al-Dīn 1998–99, 1: 41–42; 1: 109–10; Juwaynī 1958, 1: 147; Atwood 2004, 265; Melville 2006, 146.
7. Al-Nasawī 1965, 167; Jackson 1989, 1.
8. On Chormaqan (Persian Chūrmāghūn): May 1996, 2012.
9. *Tamma* were garrison forces, stationed at the empire's frontiers; they were the main agent for incorporating newly conquered territory. Buell 1980, 45–49; May 2016, 16; Ostrowski 1998a.
10. Rashīd al-Dīn 1994, 1: 73, 1: 210; Rashīd al-Dīn 1998–99, 1: 41–42, 2: 313; Ostrowski 1998a.
11. Rashīd al-Dīn 1994, 1: 73, 1: 210; Rashīd al-Dīn 1998–99, 1: 41–42, 1: 111, 2: 313.
12. Steppe lowlands lying to the west of the Caspian Sea with a mild climate during the winter months. The plains continued to serve as the main winter pasturage for the Mongol army stationed on the western frontier. Juwaynī 1958, 190; Boyle 1968, 303–35; Buell 1977, 29; Qu 2003, 246.
13. *K'art'lis C'xovreba* 1858, 513–17; May 2012, 129–51.
14. See also Shurany's contribution in this volume.
15. Ostrowski 1998b, 465ff.; Jackson 1999, 12–37.
16. Grigor of Akanc' 1949, 317; Kirakos of Ganja 1986, 240–41, 252.
17. Ibn Bībī 1956, 532; Boyle 1968, 337; Kirakos of Ganja 1986, 252; Rashīd al-Dīn 1994, 1: 73; Rashīd al-Dīn 1998–99, 1: 42.
18. Peacock and Yıldız 2013, 1–3.
19. *K'art'lis C'xovreba* 1858, 520; Bar Hebraeus 1932, 398.
20. Ibn Bībī 1956, 515; Aqsarā'ī 1944, 38–39; Grigor of Akanc' 1949, 307.
21. Grigor of Akanc' 1949, 307.
22. Ibn Bībī 1956, 515–17.
23. Ibn Bībī 1956, 518: "*Sarmārī wa Ganjawī wa Gurjī wa Ūjī wa Frang wa Qaymīrī (Qīmīrī) wa Qifchāq*"; also Turan 1971, 432.
24. Ibn Bībī 1956, 520.
25. Ibn Bībī 1956, 521–22.
26. Ibn Bībī 1956, 521.
27. Ibn Bībī 1956, 522–24.
28. Ibn Bībī 1956, 517.
29. Ibn Bībī 1956, 528–30.
30. Rashīd al-Dīn 1994, 2: 816–17; Rashīd al-Dīn 1998–99, 2: 398.
31. Jackson 1980.
32. Ibn Bībī 1956, 531–36; Bar Hebraeus 1939, 408.
33. Ibn Bībī 1956, 541.
34. Juwaynī 1958, 2: 508–9; Rashīd al-Dīn 1994, 2: 807; Jackson 1998, 366–67; Melville 2009, 55.
35. Allsen 1986, 498–500; Jackson 1998, 367.
36. Juwaynī 1958, 2: 508–9; Jackson 1998, 366–67; Melville 2009, 55.
37. Ibn Bībī 1956, 623.

38. These soldiers were the descendants of the original garrison force, which Baiju had inherited from Chormaqan. They consisted of four *tümen* manned primarily by Turkish soldiers, mainly Uighurs, Qarluq, and Kashgarid troops, originating from eastern Turkestan (in Today's Xinjiang, China). Ibn Bībī 1956, 618; Juwaynī 1958, 2: 609; Kirakos of Ganja 1986, 310; Sümer 1969, 1.

39. Galstyan 1962, 68, based on the chronicle of Stepanos the Bishop.

40. Ibn Bībī 1956, 623.

41. Aqsarāʾī 1944, 42.

42. Aqsarāʾī 1944, 43–46; Ibn Bībī 1956, 626.

43. According to another chronicle, Baiju refrained from attacking the city after the city's defenders offered him four camel-loads of valuables, although he did require that they destroy their fortifications. Anonymous 1952, 53–54 [Persian text]; Anonymous 1999, 98. Cahen speculates that the intercession of Baiju's wife may have also been a factor in sparing Konya. Cahen 1988, 247.

44. On Rūmī: Lewis 2000; Chittick 1983.

45. Aflākī 2002, 3: 169, 179–80; 3: 172, 181.

46. Aflākī 2002, 3: 170, 180.

47. Aqsarāʾī 1944, 40; Ibn Bībī 1956, 623–25.

48. Aqsarāʾī 1944, 43; Ibn Bībī 1956, 626; Boyle 1964, 185.

49. Ibn Bībī 1956, 626–87.

50. Aqsarāʾī 1944, 43.

51. A *jarghuchi* (judge), commander of the right wing, and captain of the guard, Suqunchaq (or Suʿunchaq) of the Suldus tribe, had come to Iran with Hülegü. Rashīd al-Dīn 1: 177; Rashīd al-Dīn 1998–99, 1: 95.

52. Boyle 1968, 346–48; Heidemann 1994, 44–47, 49 n. 77; Gilli-Elewy 2011, 363–64.

53. Jackson 1989, 2.

54. Heidemann 1994, 160 n. 5. Following the destruction of Baghdad, the Mamluks established a puppet ʿAbbasid caliphate at the Mamluk court in Cairo.

55. Baybars al-Manṣūrī 1998, 41. He erroneously dates Baiju's death to 1258, immediately after the conquest of Baghdad.

56. Rashīd al-Dīn 1994, 1: 210; Rashīd al-Dīn 1998–99, 1: 111.

57. Rashīd al-Dīn 1994, 2: 993; Rashīd al-Dīn 1998–99, 2: 486–87. Rashīd al-Dīn erroneously dates the meeting between Hülegü and Baiju to March 1257.

58. Rashīd al-Dīn 1994, 2: 993–94; Rashīd al-Dīn 1998–99, 2: 487.

59. Boyle 1963, 211 n. 95.

60. Pelliot 1922–23, 3–30; Voegelin 1940–41, 379; Guzman 1971, 233, 234 n. 14.

61. Voegelin 1940–41, 379; Simon de Saint-Quentin 1965, 93–117; de Rachewiltz 1971; Guzman 1971, 237–39, 244–45; Jackson 1989; Aigle 2014, 46.

62. On the Seventh Crusade: Jackson 2007.

63. Jackson 2007, 66.

64. Jackson 1989, 1; Jackson 1998, 367; Jackson 2007, 66. The Mongol attempt to repair relations with the Latin Christians is indicated by a letter exchanged between the papal legate Odo of Châteauroux and Pope Innocent IV.

The Latin letter is reproduced in d'Achery 1723, 3: 627: "Bacho [Baiju] verò, homo paganus es. & habet Saracenos Consilitarios."

65. Baybars al-Manṣūrī 1998, 41; hence al-Nuwayrī 2004, 259.

66. For Baiju as an early Mongol convert to Islam: cf. Pfeiffer 2006, 373.

67. For Arghun Aqa's conversion: Landa 2018, 77–100.

68. Sümer 1969, 67; Melville 2009, 84; Solak 2014, 64.

69. For the Mamluk argument of seniority in conversion to Islam as legitimizing sovereignty: Broadbridge 2008, 42, 51, 62–64, 83. For the attempt to bring Sülemish into the Mamluk political structure: Broadbridge 2008, 71.

70. May 2012, 146ff.; May 2016, 13–36, esp. 31–32.

71. Rashīd al-Dīn 1994, 2: 1289; Broadbridge 2008, 72.

BIBLIOGRAPHY

Aflākī, Shams al-Dīn Aḥmad. 2002. *Manāqib al-ʿārifīn*. Tr. John O'Kane. *The Feats of the Knowers of God (Manāqeb al-ʿārefīn)*. Leiden: Brill.

Aigle, Denise. 2005. "The Letters of Eljigidei, Hülegü, and Abaqa: Mongol Overtures or Christian Ventriloquism." *Inner Asia* 7: 143–62.

———. 2014. *The Mongol Empire between Myth and Reality. Studies in Anthropological History*. Leiden: Brill.

Allsen, Thomas T. 1986. "Guard and Government in the Reign of the Grand Qan Mongke, 1251–59." *Harvard Journal of Asiatic Studies* 46: 495–521.

———. 1987. *Mongol Imperialism: The Policies of the Grand Qan Möngke in China, Russia, and the Islamic Lands, 1251–1259*. Berkeley: University of California Press.

Anonymous. 1952. [Facsimile of Paris BnF, MS. Suppl. Pers. 1553.] Ed. and tr. Feridun Nâfiz Uzluk. Ankara: Kemal Yayınevi.

———. 1999. *Taʾrīkh-i āl-i Saljūq dar Anāṭūlī* [Anonymous *Saljūqnāma*]. Ed. Nādira Jalālī. Tehran: Daftar-i Nashr-i Mīrāth-i Maktūb, Āyina-yi Mīrāth, sh.1377/1999.

Aqsarāʾī, Karīm al-Dīn Maḥmūd. 1944. *Musāmarat al-akhbār wa musāyarat al-akhyār*. Ed. Osman Turan. Ankara: Türk Tarih Kurumu.

Atwood, Christopher P. 2004. *Encyclopedia of Mongolia and the Mongol Empire*. New York: Facts On File.

Bar Hebraeus. 1932. *Maktbānūt Zabnē*. Tr. Ernest A. Wallis Budge. *The Chronography of Gregory Abu'l Faraj, the Son of Aaron, the Hebrew Physician, Commonly Known as Bar Hebraeus, Being the First Part of His Political History of the World*. Oxford: Oxford University Press.

Baybars al-Manṣūrī al-Dawādār. 1998. *Zubdat al-fikra fī taʾrīkh al-hijra*. Ed. D. S. Richards. Beirut: Das Arabische Buch.

Boyle, John A. 1963. "Kirakos of Ganjak on the Mongols." *Central Asiatic Journal* 8: 199–205, 207–14.

———. 1964. "The Journey of Hetʿum I, King of Little Armenia, to the Court of the Great Khan Möngke." *Central Asiatic Journal* 9: 175–89.

———. 1968. "Dynastic and Political History of the Il-Khans." In *The Cambridge History of Iran*. Vol. 5: *The Saljuq and Mongol Periods*, ed. John A. Boyle, 303–421. Cambridge: Cambridge University Press.

Broadbridge, Ann. 2008. *Kingship and Ideology in the Islamic and Mongol Worlds*. Cambridge: Cambridge University Press.

Buell, Paul David. 1977. "Tribe, *Qan* and *Ulus* in Early Mongol China: Some Prolegomena to Yüan History." PhD diss., University of Washington.

———. 1980. "Kalmyk Tanggaci People: Thoughts on the Mechanics and Impact of Mongol Expansion." *Mongolian Studies* 6: 41–59.

Cahen, Claude. 1988. *La Turquie pré-ottomane*. Istanbul and Paris: L'Institut français d'études anatoliennes d'Istanbul.

Chittick, William C. 1983. *The Sufi Path of Love: The Spiritual Teachings of Rumi*. Albany: State University of New York Press.

d'Achery, Luc. 1723. *Spicilegium sivè Collectio veterum aliquot Scriptorum qui in Galliae bibliothecis, maxime Benedictinorum, latuerunt*. Vol. 3. Paris: Apud Montalant.

de Rachewiltz, Igor. 1971. *Papal Envoys to the Great Khans*. Stanford, CA: Stanford University Press.

Galstyan, A. G. 1962. "Iz 'Letopici' Sebastsi." In *Armyanskie istochniki o mongolakh*, 23–33. Moscow: Izdatel'stvo Vostochnoĭ Literatury.

Gilli-Elewy, Hend. 2011. "*Al-Ḥawādit al-ǧāmiʿa:* A Contemporary Account of the Mongol Conquest of Baghdad, 656/1258." *Arabica* 58: 353–71.

Grigor of Akancʿ [Aknertsʿi]. 1949. "The History of the Nation of the Archers (The Mongols)." Tr. and ed. R. P. Blake and R. N. Frye. "*Harvard Journal of Asiatic Studies* 12: 269–400.

Guzman, Gregory G. 1971. "Simon of Saint-Quentin and the Dominican Mission to the Mongol Baiju: A Reappraisal." *Speculum* 46: 232–49.

Heidemann, Stefan. 1994. *Das Aleppiner Kalifat (A.D. 1261). Vom Ende des Kalifates in Bagdad über Aleppo zu den Restaurationen in Kairo*. Leiden: Brill.

Ibn Bībī. 1956. *Al-Awāmir al-ʿalāʾiyya fī'l-umūr al-ʿalāʾiyya*. Ed. Adnan Sadık Erzi. Ankara: Türk Tarih Kurumu.

Jackson, Peter. 1978. "The Dissolution of the Mongol Empire." *Central Asiatic Journal* 22: 186–244.

———. 1980. "The Crisis in the Holy Land in 1260." *English Historical Review* 95: 481–513.

———. 1989. S.v. "Bāyjū." *Encyclopaedia Iranica* 4.1: 1–2.

———. 1998. S.v. "Eljigidei (Ilčiktāy, Iljīkdāy)." *Encyclopaedia Iranica* 8: 366–7.

———. 1999. "From Ulus to Khanate: The Making of the Mongol States, c. 1220–1290." In *The Mongol Empire and Its Legacy*, ed. Reuven Amitai-Preiss and D. O. Morgan, 12–37. Leiden: Brill.

———. 2005. "The Mongols and the Faith of the Conquered." In *Mongols, Turks, and Others: Eurasian Nomads and the Sedentary World*, ed. Reuven Amitai and Michal Biran, 245–90. Leiden: Brill.

———. 2007. *The Seventh Crusade, 1244–1254. Sources and documents*. Aldershot: Ashgate.

Juwaynī, ʿAlāʾ al-Dīn ʿAtā-Malik. 1958. *History of World Conqueror*. Tr. J. A. Boyle. Manchester: 2 vols. Manchester University Press.

Kʿartʿlis Cʿxovreba [Georgian Chronicles]. 1858. Tr. Marie-Félicité Brosset. *Histoire de la Georgie: depuis l'antiquité jusqu'au XIXe siècle*. Vol. 1. St. Petersburg: De l'imprimerie de l'Academie Impériale de Sciences.

Kirakos of Ganja [Gandzakets'i/Ganakets'i]. 1986. *History of the Armenians.* Tr. Robert Bedrosian. New York: Sources of the Armenian Tradition.

Landa, Ishayahu. 2018. "New Light on Early Mongol Islamization: The Case of Arghun Aqa's Family." *Journal of the Royal Asiatic Society* 28: 77–100.

Lane, George. 2003. *Early Mongol Rule in Thirteenth-Century Iran. A Persian Renaissance.* London: RoutledgeCurzon.

Lewis, Franklin D. 2000. *Rumi, Past and Present, East and West: The Life, Teachings, and Poetry of Jalāl al-Din Rumi.* London: OneWorld.

May, Timothy. 1996. "Chormaqan Noyan: The First Mongol Military Governor in the Middle East." MA thesis, Indiana University.

———. 2012. "The Conquest and Rule of Transcaucasia: The Era of Chormaqan." In *Caucasus during the Mongol Period—Der Kaukasus in der Mongolzeit,* ed. Jürgen Tubach, Sophia G. Vashalomidze, and Manfred Zimmer, 129–52. Wiesbaden, Germany: Ludwig Reichert Verlag.

———. 2016. "Mongol Conquest Strategy in the Middle East." In *The Mongols' Middle East: Continuity and Transformation in Ilkhanid Iran,* ed. Bruno De Nicola and Charles Melville, 13–37. Leiden: Brill.

Melville, Charles. 2006. "The *Keshig* in Iran: The Survival of the Royal Mongol Household." In *Beyond The Legacy of Genghis Khan,* ed. Linda Komaroff, 135–64. Leiden: Brill.

———. 2009. "Anatolia under the Mongols." In *The Cambridge History of Turkey.* Vol. 1. *Byzantium to Turkey, 1071–1453,* ed. Kate Fleet, 51–101. Cambridge: Cambridge University Press.

al-Nasawī. 1965. *Sīrat al-Sulṭān Jalāl al-Dīn Mankubartī* (*sic*). Ed. Mojtabā Minovī. Tehran: BTNK.

al-Nuwayrī, Shihāb al-Dīn Aḥmad. 2004. *Nihāyat al-arab fi funūn al-adab.* Vol. 27. Ed. Najīb Muṣṭafā Fawwāz and Ḥikmat Kishlī Fawwāz. Beirut: Dār al-kutub al-ʿilmiyya.

Ostrowski, Donald. 1998a. "The 'Tamma' and the Dual-Administrative Structure of the Mongol Empire." *Bulletin for the School of Oriental and Asiatic Studies* 61: 262–77.

———. 1998b. "City Names of the Western Steppe at the Time of the Mongol Invasion." *Bulletin for the School of Oriental and Asiatic Studies* 61: 465–75.

Peacock, Andrew C. S., and Sara Nur Yıldız. 2013. Introduction to *The Seljuks of Anatolia. Court and Society in the Medieval Middle East,* ed. A. C. S Peacock and Sara Nur Yıldız, 1–22. London: Taurus.

———. 2016. "Introduction: Literature, Language, and History in Late Medieval Anatolia." In *Islamic Literature and Intellectual Life in Fourteenth- and Fifteenth-Century Anatolia,* ed. Andrew C. S. Peacock and Sara Nur Yıldız, 19–45. Würzburg, Germany: Ergon Verlag.

Pelliot, Paul. 1922–23. "Les Mongols et la Papauté: Documents nouveaux édités, traduits et commentés par M. Paul Pelliot, avec la collaboration de MM. Borghezio, Massé et Tisserant." *Revue de l'Orient chrétien,* 3rd ser., 3: 3–30.

Pfeiffer, Judith. 2006. "Reflections on a 'Double Rapprochement': Conversion to Islam among the Mongol Elite during the Early Ilkhanate." In *Beyond the Legacy of Genghis Khan,* ed. Linda Komaroff, 369–89. Leiden: Brill.

Qu Dafeng. 2003. "A New Study Concerning an Explanation of the Word 'Tamaci' and the Tamaci Army." *Central Asiatic Journal* 47: 242–49.

Rashīd al-Dīn, Faḍlallāh Abū al-Khayr. 1994. *Jāmi' al-tawārīkh*. Ed. Muḥammad Rawshan and Musṭafā Musawī. 4 vols. Tehran: Nashr-i Alburz.

———. 1998–99. *Rashiduddin Fazlullah's Jami'u't-Tawarikh: A History of the Mongols*. Tr. Wheeler M. Thackston. 3 vols. Cambridge, MA: Harvard University, Department of Near Eastern Languages and Civlizations.

Simon de Saint-Quentin. 1965. *Histoire des Tartares*. Ed. Jean Richard. Paris: Librairie orientaliste Paul Geuthner.

Solak, Kürşat. 2014. "Moğol Sülemiş ve Timurtaş İsyanları Karşısında Anadolu'da Türkmenlerin Tutumu." *Cappadocia Journal of History and Social Sciences* 3: 66–74.

Sümer, Faruk. 1969. "Anadolu'da Moğollar." *Selçuklular Araştıramalar Dergisi* 1: 1–147.

Turan, Osman. 1971. *Selçuklular zamanında Türkiye: Siyasi tarih Alp Arslan'dan Osman Gazi'ye (1071–1318)*. 3rd ed. Istanbul: Boğaziçi Yayınları, 1993.

Voegelin, Eric. 1940–41. "The Mongol Orders of Submission to European Powers, 1245–1255." *Byzantion* 15: 378–413.

Yıldız, Sara Nur. Forthcoming. *Mongol Rule in Seljuk Anatolia: Politics of Conquest and History Writing, 1243–1282*. Leiden: Brill.

CHAPTER 3

Qutulun

The Warrior Princess of Mongol Central Asia

MICHAL BIRAN

From the Greek Amazons to China's Hua Mulan and its Disney adaptation, women warriors have caught the imagination of people across time, space and cultures.[1] In the Mongol context, the prowess of the Mongol women, who not only played a pivotal role in the politics and economy of the empire, far greater than that of their sedentary counterparts, but would also ride horses, hunt, and occasionally even fight, greatly impressed their sedentary subjects and neighbors.[2]

The most renowned Mongol female warrior, perhaps the only one who truly deserved the title of Mongol general, is Qutulun (d. ca. 1307). A great-great granddaughter of Chinggis Khan, Qutulun's father Qaidu (r. 1271–1301) was the nemesis of Qubilai Qa'an (r. 1260–94) and founder of the independent Mongol state in Central Asia. Allegedly excelling on the battlefield over all her father's male generals, Qutulun demonstrates both the possibilities and the limitations of women's military careers in the Mongol world. Her exceptional story was famously recorded by Marco Polo as well as by various contemporaneous Persian historians. Qutulun also became the subject of later fascinating adaptations, in Mongolia and beyond. The Mongol princess-general was presented as inspiration for Puccini's famous opera *Princess Turandot* (1924); she has starred in several modern Mongolian novels; and has even become a heroine in the Netflix series *Marco Polo*.

LIFE

Qutulun came from an illustrious Chinggisid branch; yet by the time she was born, the heydays of her lineage had already ended. Her father, Qaidu, was a grandson of Chinggis Khan's son and heir, Ögödei (r. 1229–41). Yet the Ögödeids lost the qa'anate to the descendants of Ögödei's younger brother, Tolui, in the coup of 1251 that enthroned Möngke (r. 1251–59) as the Great Khan. The Ögödeids and their allies were mercilessly purged. Their lands were taken over by other Chinggisids and their *ulus*[3] dissolved. Qutulun's father, however, was among the few Ögödeids who survived the coup. After Möngke's death and during the subsequent power struggle between his two brothers, Qubilai and Arigh Böke (d. 1264), Qaidu strove to restore the Ögödeid cause. Assembling troops through his military skills and charismatic leadership, and taking advantage of the inter-Mongol strife, Qaidu began to carve out a realm for himself in Central Asia, mainly at the expense of his cousins, descendants of Chinggis Khan's second son Chaghadai.[4]

The Chaghadaids supported the Ögödeids in 1251, and also suffered from Möngke's purges, though not as much as the Ögödeids. After Möngke's death, the Chaghadaid Khan Alghu (r. 1260–66) and his successor Baraq (r. 1266–71) also tried to restore their realm. They fought against Qaidu, who, however, eventually forged an alliance with Baraq. In 1271, after Baraq's death, Qaidu declared himself the Ögödeid khan, thereby resurrecting the Ögödeid *ulus*. He then fought for about a decade to assert his authority over the Chaghadaids, finally appointing Baraq's son Du'a as the Chaghadaid Khan (r. 1282–1307). The two cooperated for the next two decades and up to Qaidu's death. Together they ruled over Central Asia from the Oxus River (Uzbekistan's western border) to the Altai region and Xinjiang (in northwest China), a region roughly equivalent to the Chaghadaid and Ögödeid realms that were assigned by Chinggis Khan.[5] Jointly they challenged their Toluid neighbors in China and Iran, and led raids into Afghanistan and India, gradually enlarging their realm and organizing its administration. Throughout his life, Qaidu refused to acknowledge the authority of Qubilai Qa'an, who since overcoming his brother in 1264 presented himself as the Great Khan of the entire empire. Qaidu's refusal to submit to Qubilai had further undermined Qubilai's authority, thereby promoting the empire's dissolution.[6]

Qaidu's preferred way of warfare was border raids, which allowed him to make the best of his nomad army while keeping his main sedentary regions intact. It also enabled him to overcome his numerical inferiority vis-à-vis the armies of Yuan China and Ilkhanid Iran. Throughout his reign, Qaidu led numerous raids, mostly to China and Mongolia, but also elsewhere.[7] Riding alongside her father in his campaigns, Qutulun therefore had many opportunities to practice her skills and gain necessary military experience.

We know very little about Qutulun's life, and most of it seems spiced with legend. Appearing as Qutulun Chaghan (Mongolian: the Lucky Girl of White) in the Persian history of Rashīd al-Dīn (d. 1318),[8] and as Aigiaurac (Turkic: Moonshine) in Marco Polo's (d. 1324) book,[9] the princess grew up alongside her siblings, and, like other nomad girls, was also trained in riding and archery. Both male and female nomads required these skills in their daily management of the herds and the seasonal migrations. Moreover, since unlike swordsmanship, archery demands skill, rather than physical force, women can master it as well as men can. In times of peace, Mongol women herded smaller animals (sheep and goats) and cattle, and when the men were away fighting or hunting, they took care of horses and camels too, handling all the household errands. While managing their camps, women were also responsible for educating their offspring—both male and female—in the art of war, namely riding and archery. Widows (like Chinggis Khan's mother, Hö'elün) were also responsible for protecting their family against their enemies.[10]

Yet, while Mongol women were well versed in archery, and often publicly rode horses, a fact that greatly impressed European, Chinese, and Muslim observers,[11] they did not regularly participate in actual military engagements in imperial campaigns. Although contemporary sources sporadically reference female fighters,[12] these examples are not only rare, but are also mostly unreliable, as many are based on hearsay. Moreover, even when women accompanied their male relatives in the military campaigns or provided them with soldiers from their own camps, they hardly ever took part in the actual fighting.[13]

Qutulun was therefore an exception. Rashīd al-Dīn writes that "she went around like a boy and often went on military campaigns, where she performed valiant deeds."[14] Riding to battle with her father, she frequently entered enemy lines. Demonstrating her skills, she habitually "seized a knight by force as easily as if it were a bird and carried him as prisoner to her people".[15] Excelling not only in bravery and strength but also in intelligence, she soon became her father's favorite. He followed her advice and let her choose her husband herself. This was an unusual privilege. The marriage of a Chinggisid princess was carefully planned by her parents, who used the marriage to cement alliances with either important generals or vassal rulers.[16] Qutulun's sisters were indeed married according to this custom.[17]

Rashīd al-Dīn reports that Qutulun was interested in her distant cousin, the future Ilkhan Ghazan (r. 1295–1304), for a potential spouse. She kept sending him missions and gifts, claiming she would not have any other.[18] Since Ghazan spent his youth as the governor of Khurasan (modern Turkmenistan) near the Ilkhanid border with Qaidu's realm, it is possible that the two knew each other. However, in his very detailed section on Ghazan's reign, Rashīd al-Dīn, who was Ghazan's court historian, mentions neither Qutulun nor any embassies between the two. The marriage, in any case, never took place. The goal of this anecdote was probably to praise Rashīd al-Dīn's patron, Ghazan, allegedly coveted by the most outstanding woman around.

Marco Polo gives further details on Qutulun's marriage plans. According to his often-cited report,[19] after her father agreed to allow her to marry whomever and whenever she pleased, Qutulun declared that she would only take a man who beat her in wrestling: "The bargain was that if the young man were able to vanquish her so that he can put her on the ground by force than she must take him for her husband and that he should have her for wife, and if the king's daughter should vanquish the youth, then he lost a hundred horses or more, according to what he offered, and they were for the damsel."[20] Many candidates responded to the challenge. The wrestling matches took place at court and attracted a considerable audience.

The courtiers watched the beautiful princess, who was "so tall and so big-bodied that it wanted but little that she was a giantess."[21] Dressed like a man,[22] in a narrow and short, albeit richly embroidered, coat, she effortlessly defeated her rivals, allegedly amassing ten thousand horses in her victories.[23] Chinggisid women often had their own herds, soldiers, and camps (*ordos*), but they usually started accumulating their property after they were married and received their bride price, dowry, or assignments from their male relatives.[24] Qutulun, however, literally made her fortune with her own hands.

Around 1280, thus Polo, a real Prince Charming, arrived at Qaidu's court: son of a rich and powerful king, he was young, fair, and strong, and so confident of his victory that he was ready to risk a thousand beautiful horses. Qutulun's parents, enthusiastic about the prospective groom, begged their daughter to give in. Qutulun, however, wanted to lose in a fair fight:

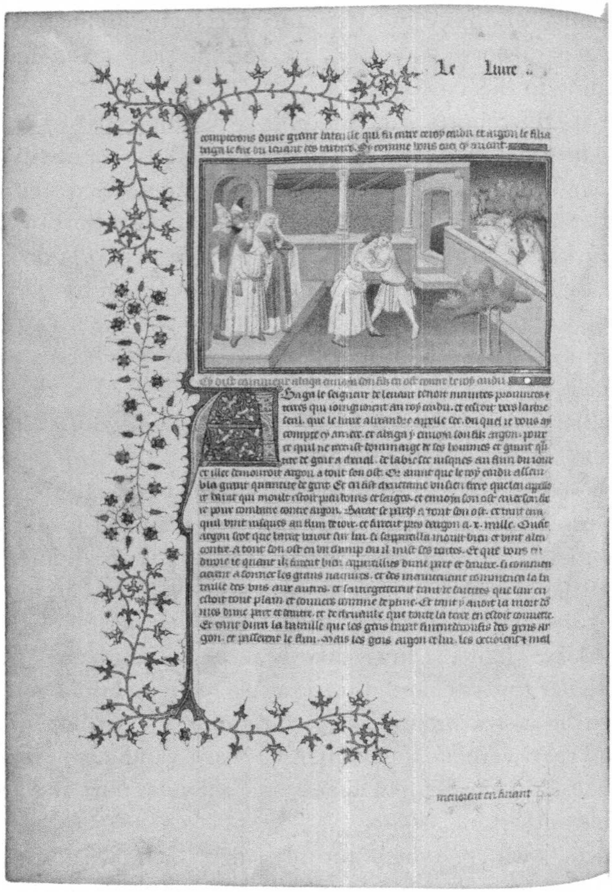

FIGURE 3.1. Qutulun wrestling a suitor. Marco Polo, *Le Livre des merveilles*, MS 2810, fol. 95v (1400–20), BnF.

The two young people had taken hold one of the other with hands and arms and sometimes with feet, the one pulls there and the other here. And they made a very fine beginning, and for a long time one could not overcome the other, but such was the fortune that at last the king's daughter vanquished him and throws [*sic*] him under her on the pavement of the palace most violently. And when he saw himself under her he had very great wrath because of it and very great shame, and did nothing else but, when he was risen, went away as soon as he could with all his company, and went off to his father all ashamed of that which had happened to him, that he had been defeated by a girl. He left the thousand horses.[25]

This story should be taken with a grain of salt. Both tropes, that of a female warrior or wrestler, who excelled over her male peers, and that of the prize-princess who would consider only a suitor who defeated her—in the battlefield or elsewhere—were popular in Muslim and Central Asian epics, as well as in their Chinese and European counterparts.[26] In Qutulun's case, however, the losers had only to pay with their horses, not their heads. Qutulun's story, moreover, did not end with a prince winning over the princess in marriage. Polo's divergence from the common tropes of warrior princesses might lend an aura of credence to his general depiction of Qutulun, even if not to all his details. Certainly, the story attests to the nomadic values apparent in—or ascribed to—Mongol Central Asia, where physical and martial prowess was among the most appreciated talents, and horses were the most prized capital. It also suggests the high reputation of Qutulun's warrior skills.

Eventually, however, Qutulun married a less illustrious husband. She seems to have chosen him herself, either after her father's death or during Qaidu's life, when her extended celibacy gave rise to rumors of incest.[27] We are told that her new spouse was a lively, tall, good-looking man who served as Qaidu's cook.[28] A cook (Mongolian: *ba'urchi*) was a prestigious position in the Mongol world, often a close companion of the ruler, who trusted him to keep his food free of poison, as well as a member of the khan's guard (*keshig*), hence also a warrior.[29] Nothing, however, is known about the military capabilities of Qutulun's husband. In fact, even his name and ethnicity are uncertain;[30] at least outside Central Asia he was not especially notable.

If not for her mentions in the events that followed Qaidu's death in 1301, it would have been easy to dismiss Qutulun's military activity as mere folktale. On his deathbed, Qaidu chose Qutulun's brother, Orus, as his heir, and ordered his sons to follow the commands of his close ally, the Chaghadaid Khan Du'a, due to the latter's experience and wisdom. Du'a, however, had other plans. Qaidu's death gave him an opportunity to get rid of the Ögödeid lordship, and improve his relations with the qa'an in China, Qubilai's successor, Temür Öljeitü (r. 1294–1307). The benefits from ending the conflict for landlocked Central Asia were obvious: it would enable the revival of the overland Silk Roads. The ongoing conflict in Central Asia led to a gradual marginalization of the continental routes, shifting most of the interregional trade to the maritime Silk Roads. The Yuan conquest of south China in

1279 further facilitated the connection between China and Iran through the Indian Ocean, instead of the land routes crossing Central Asia.[31]

By ending the conflict, the Chaghadaids could also focus their military efforts on continuing their expansion into the wealthy lands of the Delhi Sultanate (1206–1526). Securing peace, however, entailed acknowledging Yuan supremacy over the Mongol domains, at the expense of the Ögödeid pretensions.[32] Du'a, therefore, first had to make the Ögödeids succumb to his will. Instead of Orus, he decided to enthrone Qaidu's first-born, Chapar, who suffered from bad health and was notorious for his foolishness. Qutulun "was desirous of leading the military and running affairs";[33] yet loyal to her father's final will, she stood firmly behind her brother Orus. Moreover, she was the first to understand Du'a's plan, and was quick to rebuke the Chaghadaid khan for violating her father's will.[34] Du'a, however, was not impressed by her scolding, stating: "Women's opinions and talk should be about the spindle and spinning wheel, not on the crown and the khanate's throne. What do you have to do with rulership (*pādshāhī*) and government (*ḥukūmat*)?"[35]

The words ascribed to Du'a, however, did not reflect the actual situation of Mongol women. First, while sewing clothes was among their tasks, these clothes were usually made out of animal skin or felt, not of woven material. In this respect, Rashīd al-Dīn's version of the same episode, where Qutulun is sent to the scissors and needles, sounds more plausible.[36] Moreover, Mongol women did have a significant part in politics and government, more than in warfare, although they always came to power through their male relatives—husbands, fathers, or sons. Mongol women did not only impact their spouses and offspring (Chinggis Khan's mother and wife are the best example),[37] but also served as the real power behind their husbands, or as regents after their husbands' death. Thus, for instance, Ögödei's wife, Töregene (r. 1241–46), ruled over the whole united empire from her husband's death to the election of her son Güyük (r. 1246–48) as qa'an, which she had orchestrated.[38] In the Chaghadaid realm, Naishi Khatun, the wife of Yesü Möngke Khan (r. 1246–48), handled the *ulus*'s affairs for her drunken husband.[39] Orghina (r. 1251–59), Chinggis Khan's granddaughter and the widow of the Chaghadaid Khan Qara Hülegü (r. 1244–46, 1259), served as a regent for their minor son Mubārak Shāh, before marrying the new khan, Alghu, whom her son briefly succeeded.[40] Furthermore, the Mongols were willing to appoint women as governors, sometimes on their own right, albeit usually due to their noble husbands—dead or alive.[41]

When she was dismissed by Du'a, however, Qutulun refrained from bringing up these precedents. Instead, she receded to be the guardian of her father's tomb (*qoruq*), on a high mountain between the Ili and the Chu Rivers, probably in one of the southern ranges of the Tian Shan mountains in contemporary Kyrgyzstan. Her camp, near the contemporary Kyrgyz capital, Bishkek, is described as located among various villages, a two-week- to one-month-long journey from Samarqand.[42] The tomb keeper's role also included a military aspect, namely defending the sacred grave against intruders.[43] Yet, assuming this role kept the princess in a relatively secluded place, away from the centers of power, where she could focus on her young family and her camp's prosperity.[44]

Despite her retirement and her reservations about Chapar, when, around 1306, the latter, desperately trying to preserve his realm and authority against Du'a's intrigues, summoned all the Ögödeid troops, Qutlulun came to his help. She arrived with her own *hizāra* (unit of a thousand warriors), just like her brothers and her father's old commanders.[45] Significantly, it was she, not her husband, who led this unit. This matter-of-fact reference to her inclusion among the summoned commanders gives more credibility to her participation in warfare than all the contemporaneous praise of her strength and victories, mentioned above.

The battle, in any case, was decided against the Ögödeids. Du'a summoned Yuan troops from China, and they inflicted a crushing defeat to Chapar's crack troops led by Orus. This, combined with the defection of one of his leading generals, obliged Chapar to surrender to Du'a in late 1306. Du'a sent his loyal commanders to capture the leading Ögödeid princes and generals, including Qutulun.[46] Du'a's nephew was sent to pursue the princess. In early 1307, the Chaghadaid prince reached her camp at night, surprising her family and drowning Qutulun's husband and two sons in the river.[47] Since we hear nothing of Qutulun thereafter, the princess-general was probably killed, either with her family or shortly after.

Moreover, Du'a's victory saw the end of the Ögödeids' political power in the Mongol world: Qutulun's brothers were either killed or found refuge in the neighboring Mongol khanates. The desperate Chapar submitted to the Yuan in 1310, receiving a small appanage in north China, and giving up any aspirations for future restoration of his *ulus*.[48]

"AFTERLIFE"

Qutulun's life ended tragically, but her memory was retained in later historical works,[49] and in folk stories that continued to disseminate among the Steppe nomads, in Mongolia, and elsewhere.[50] Migrating to Europe, some of these stories might have even served as inspiration for the famous opera *Princess Turandot,* by the Italian composer Giacomo Puccini (1858–1924).[51]

In the early eighteenth century, François Petis de la Croix (1653–1713) published a book titled *Mille et un jours: Conte persans* or *The Thousand and One Days: Persian Tales,* an obvious emulation of the Arabic *The Thousand and One Nights.* The author, a son of the first European biographer of Chinggis Khan, also called Petis de la Croix (1622–95), succeeded his father as a secretary and interpreter of Turkish and Arabic for the king of France. He spent his youth in the Middle East, traveling and studying Arabic, Persian, and Turkish, and later became a famous diplomat and one of the renowned orientalists of early modern France.[52] In his introduction to the collection of tales that came out in 1710–12, he declared the book to be a translation of a manuscript given to him in Iran by an Isfahani dervish in 1675. The manuscript, however, was never found and the book seems to have been, at least in part, the fruit of the French author's imagination.[53]

Framed as the stories a nurse tells a beautiful Kashmiri princess who refused to marry, the work includes a long story about Prince Calaf and the Chinese princess.[54] Described as a daughter of Altoun Khan of China, the princess is called Turandot (Persian: *Tūrān-i dukht,* daughter of Turan, the land of the Turks), thereby suggesting that her origin was in Central Asia.[55] Like Qutulun, Turandot agreed to marry only a man who would defeat her, though not in prowess but in wisdom—another very manly feature in the premodern world—by solving her riddles. Unlike Qutulun's case, however, suitors who failed to defeat Turandot lost not only their horses but also their heads. Moreover, contrary to Qutulun's case, the real hero of the story was prince Calaf, a renowned warrior and a learned Muslim scholar, son of the khan of the Nogai Tatars, a Turco-Mongol people settled in the northern Caucasus. After many upheavals, he marries the princess, who eventually falls for him, and overcomes his rivals in the steppe. The scholarly consensus is that this story was the origin of Puccini's *Turandot.*[56]

However, until recently, Turandot's source of inspiration was identified as an unnamed Slavic princess who appears in the famous Persian epic of Niẓāmī (1141–1209), *The Seven Beauties* (*Haft paykār*), compiled in 1197.[57] Like Turandot, and unlike Qutulun, Niẓāmī's princess would marry only a man who would solve her riddles, and those who failed to do so were beheaded. Like Turandot, she is famous for beauty and wit, not military prowess, and eventually she is also defeated by a youth, who, however, was not of royal stock but became a king after marrying her.[58]

In *The Secret History of the Mongol Queens* (2010), the American anthropologist Jack Weatherford suggested that the inspiration for Turandot was Qutulun.[59] Indeed, De La Croix's story has some (late) Mongol features. The prince is a Mongol-Tatar nomad, and the Chinese emperor is also presented as a khan, that is, not ethnically Chinese. Yet Turandot has much more in common with Niẓāmī's princess. Petis de la Croix must have been familiar with Niẓāmī's work, one of the most famous epics in medieval Persian literature, of which he was a connoisseur. He was also well-versed in Mongol history, though did not necessarily know about Qutulun.[60]

Regardless of the story's exact origin, Weatherford's bestseller did further increase Qutulun's popularity in Mongolia and elsewhere. While Qutulun (in modern Mongolian Khotol Tsagaan) had been a part of Mongolia's popular culture before the twenty-first century, she has been mainly remembered in relation to Mongolian traditional wrestling.[61] Weatherford's book, however, linked Qutulun both to the Mongol Empire, making her a much closer relative of Qubilai Qa'an than she ever was, and to an icon of Western culture, Turandot, thereby increasing her attractiveness as a modern Mongolian heroine.

Weatherford's works were extremely influential in Mongolia: *The Secret History of the Mongol Queens* came out after he had already become a mega-celebrity in Mongolia due to the international success of his 2004 bestseller *Genghis Khan and the Making of the Modern World*. The new book was quickly translated into Mongolian, and even read aloud in Mongolia's sacred sites in 2012, the 850th anniversary of Chinggis Khan's birth.[62] Soon enough, his short piece on *The Wresting Princess* also appeared online in Mongolian.[63] The impact of these publications on Qutulun's popularity was quick. Since 2011, she has been featured in Mongolian radio shows, novels, and children's books.[64] She is presented as a proud Chinggisid princess, and at least in one recent popular work, Shüüdertseseg's *Princess Qutulun Chaghan* (*Khotol tsagaan günj*, 2017), her Turandot-connection is noted.[65] The princess has also merited a detailed Wikipedia entry and has appeared as a character in the Netflix series *Marco Polo*.[66] The elaborated folk tales certainly help embellish the princess' life story, much more than the above-discussed few mentions of her in thirteenth- and fourteenth-century sources. We can suspect that Qaidu's strong opposition to Qubilai's

FIGURE 3.2. Qutulun, on the cover of Shüüdertsetseg's *Khotol Tsagaan Günj* (Ulaanbaatar, Mongolia: Admon, 2017), vol. 1. Courtesy of Shüüdertsetseg Baatarsürengiin.

China also contributed to his daughter's popularity in contemporary Mongolia.

CONCLUSION

Qutulun's elaborated "afterlife" notwithstanding, her life story can serve as a starting point for evaluating the role of women in Mongol warfare. Both Polo and the Persian historians portrayed Qutulun's leading position in the army and her active participation in warfare as extraordinary. Indeed, while Mongol women were adept at riding and archery and were certainly involved in military affairs to a far greater extent than their sedentary counterparts, they nevertheless did not have a direct role in Mongol warfare, surely not in comparison to their involvement in politics and economy. Indirectly, however, women did contribute tremendously to the Mongol military machine. First, the women's ability to take full charge of the camps while their husbands were at war enabled most of the Mongol men to join the fighting troops. Second, women attained a prominent role in training the next generation of Mongol warriors. Third, on the elite level, the marriage of Chinggisid princesses often cemented the relations between their fathers (and sometimes brothers) and their generals or vassal rulers, thereby enlarging the troops at their families' disposal. Fourth, women were assigned troops as part of the conquests' booty and sometimes inherited their husbands' contingents, even if they themselves hardly ever led them on campaigns.

Unlike most Mongol women, however, Qutulun was active on the battlefield: she excelled in her military capabilities, and through them achieved freedom, wealth, and prestige. Her freedom, however, was not unlimited. While Qutulun's story demonstrates the potential of female warriors in the Mongol world, it also reflects the limitations imposed on their activities: Qutulun's long celibacy gave rise to ugly rumors that might have forced her to marry. When she tried to take an active part in the succession politics following her father's death, she was humiliated and assigned to the traditional female place. Furthermore, her family's enemies considered her potential leadership a threat leading to her elimination. Despite these limitations and her tragic end, the Chinggisid warrior princess remains very much alive in Mongolia's contemporary popular culture, albeit with a little help from an eighteenth-century French orientalist, an early twentieth-century Italian composer, and a twenty-first-century American author.

NOTES

This study was supported by the Israel Science Foundation (grant 602/12) and made use of the database prepared with the funding of the European Research Council under the European Union's Seventh Framework Programme (FP/2007–13) / ERC Grant Agreement n. 312397.

1. For the Amazons: e.g., Mayor 2014. For Mulan: Frankel 2010, 197–211; Edwards 2016, 17–39.

2. For women under Mongol rule: De Nicola, 2010; Brack 2011; De Nicola 2017; Broadbridge 2018.

3. *Ulus* in Mongolian originally meant the people subject to a certain lord. Later it also became an equivalent of a nation and state, as still apparent in modern Mongolian.

4. On Qaidu: Biran 1997.

5. Chinggis Khan (r. 1206–27) allocated pasturelands to his four sons, hoping (in vain) to avoid future conflicts. Chaghadai received most of Central Asia, from the borders of Uighuria (southeast Xinjiang, China) to the Oxus; Ögödei received a small appanage in Zungaria (north Xinjiang) since as Chinggis Khan's heir he was entitled to inherit *ex officio* the territories that Chinggis Khan left to himself, namely the major sedentary parts under Mongol rule (North China, eastern Iran).

6. Biran 1997, 37–57, 107–12.

7. Biran 1997, 37–68, 87–89.

8. Rashīd al-Dīn 1994, 1: 629–31; Rashīd al-Dīn 1998–99, 2: 309–10; Rashīd al-Dīn, *Shu'ab-i Panjgānah,* fol. 127a. The name Qutulun (*qutu,* with the female suffix *lun*) derives from the Turko-Mongolian term *qutu* (similar to the better-known form *qutlugh*) meaning "lucky" or "fortunate" (Pelliot 1959, 1: 15). The Mongols considered the color white (Mong. *chaghan*) especially sacred, designating charisma and good fortune (Allsen 1997, 59). Qāshānī (1969, 33, 38, 39) has her name as Qutlugh Chaghā (a variant of Rashīd al-Dīn's version), but also as Tīmūr Awhān (*sic*). Unlike Qutulun, which is a distinctly female name, Qāshānī's version(s) are less feminine.

9. Polo 1938, 453.

10. Broadbridge 2018, 9–43.

11. E.g., Giessauf 2007; al-Ṣafadī 1998, 5: 592–93, tr. in Brack 2011, 333–34; Riccoldo da Montecroce 2012, 188, 191; Zhao Gong 2016, 111.

12. E.g., Joinville 1906, 257–59; Ibn al-Athīr 1965–66, 12: 378; al-Dhahabī 1988, 61: 59; Riccoldo da Montecroce 2012, 188; Zhao Gong 2016, 104; Sinor 2007, 264–65; De Nicola 2010, 101–4.

13. Sinor 2007, 265; De Nicola 2010, 101–4, 109–10.

14. Rashīd al-Dīn 1994, 1: 629; Rashīd al-Dīn 1998–99, 2: 309.

15. Polo 1938, 455.

16. Broadbridge 2018, 134–64. On the daughters' husbands, the imperial sons-in-laws: Landa 2016.

17. Mīrkhwānd 1961, 5: 218; Rashīd al-Dīn 1994, 1: 630.

18. Rashīd al-Dīn 1994, 1: 629; Rashīd al-Dīn 1998–99, 2: 309.

19. Polo 1938, 453–56; also Rossabi 1979, 174–75; Rossabi 1988, 104–5; Biran 1997, 2; Lane 2006, 248–50; De Nicola 2010, 102–3; Weatherford 2010a, 116–25; Weatherford 2010b.

20. Polo 1938, 453.

21. Polo 1938, 453–54.

22. When fighting, Mongol women dressed like men. E.g., Ibn al-Athīr 1966, 12: 378; al-Juwaynī 1912–37, 2: 212; al-Juwaynī 1997, 477. However, cross-dressing was also a common topos in women warriors' tales, as seen in the story of Mulan.

23. Polo 1938, 453–54.

24. De Nicola 2010, 109–10; De Nicola 2017, 130–82.

25. Polo 1938, 435–36.

26. Kruck 2014 (Arabic lore); Niẓāmī 2015, 153–79 (Persian); Lewis 1998 (Turkic); Frankel 2010, 187–204, 193 for the *Nibelungenleid*'s Brünnhild; Mayor 2014, 395–410 (Central Asia), 424–25 (China); Colarusso 2002, 364–65 (Caucasus); also Wu Pei-Yi 2002.

27. Rashīd al-Dīn (1911, 12; also *Shuʿab-i Panjgānah,* 127a) claims that her father chose her husband, but in his more detailed and probably later version of Qutulun's story, he writes that she chose her husband herself. Rashīd al-Dīn 1971, 26–27; Rashīd al-Dīn 1994, 1:630; Rashīd al-Dīn 1998–99, 2: 309. Qāshānī (1969, 33), however, claims that she married after her father's death. See also *Muʿizz al-ansāb,* fol. 45a.

28. Rashīd al-Dīn 1994, 1:630; Rashīd al-Dīn 1998–99, 2: 309; Qāshānī 1969, 39.

29. Doerfer 1963, 1: 202–5.

30. He was either a Mongol of the Qorulas tribe (Rashīd al-Dīn 1994, 1: 630; Rashīd al-Dīn 1998–99, 2: 309; *Muʿizz al-ansāb,* fol. 45a) or a northern Chinese (*Khitāʾi*) (Rashīd al-Dīn 1911, 12; Rashīd al-Dīn 1971, 27). His name is rendered as Abtaqūl (Rashīd al-Dīn 1971, 27 n. 74), Ītqūl (Qāshānī 1969, 33) or Ītqūn (Rashīd al-Dīn 1994, 1: 630), all probably variants of the same name.

31. See the articles by Gill, and by Mukai and Fiaschetti in this volume.

32. Biran 1997, 69–72.

33. Rashīd al-Dīn 1994, 1: 631; Rashīd al-Dīn 1998–99, 2: 309.

34. Qāshānī 1969, 32–33.

35. Qāshānī 1969, 33.

36. Rashīd al-Dīn 1994, 1: 631; Rashīd al-Dīn 1998–99, 2: 309–10: "You should mind your scissors and needles. What have you to do with kingship (*mulk*) and chieftainship (*ulus*)?"

37. For the importance of Hö'elün and Börte: Broadbridge 2018, 43–73.

38. E.g., Broadbridge 2018, 164–94.

39. Rashīd al-Dīn 1994, 2: 760; Rashīd al-Dīn 1998–99, 2: 372.

40. De Nicola 2016.

41. For example, Alaqai Khatun, Chinggis Khan's daughter who was married to the chief of the Önggüt tribe, succeeded her husband and even led the tribal army. Broadbridge 2018, 144–58. In the United Empire, the Mongols appointed local women as governors in both Yidu (Shandong) and Akhlat (Anatolia). Wu Pei-Yi 2002; Eastmond 2017, 342–90. See also De Nicola's article in this volume.

42. Rashīd al-Dīn (Rashīd al-Dīn 1994, 1: 630, Rashīd al-Dīn 1998–99, 2: 309) identifies the mountain's name as Shinqūrliq, probably one of the peaks of the Gunchey Alatao range (northern Tianshan mountain, in modern Kyrgyzstan) and said it was two weeks' distance from Samarqand. Qāshānī (1969, 39), describes Qutulun's camp as located near the village Tarsākand, one month's distance from Samarqand. Tarsākand, (literally: the Christians' city, Rashīd al-Dīn's Tarsākīnt), is identified as Qara Jirach, a village in the Alamudun district of the Chui province of Kyrgyzstan, not far from Bishkek, where Christian tombstones were excavated. Klein 2000, 132–36.

43. Rashīd al-Dīn 1994, 1:630; Rashīd al-Dīn 1998–99, 2: 309–10; cf.

Qāshānī 1969, 33, 39. Qāshānī uses the word *kūr* (Persian: tomb). On *qoruq*, the inviolable royal burial grounds: Pelliot 1959, 333 ff.; Barthold and Rogers 1970; Serruys 1974; DeWeese 1994, 181–87.

44. Qāshānī 1969, 39–40.

45. Qāshānī 1969, 39.

46. Qāshānī 1969, 34–40; Waṣṣāf 2009, 281–88. Waṣṣāf, however, never mentions Qutulun; Biran 1997, 74–78.

47. Qāshānī 1969, 39–40. Qāshānī places the events in 1304–5 (704H), but locates them after the demise of the Yuan Qa'an Temür, who died in early 1307. As Du'a died later in 1307, the events must have taken place during this year.

48. Biran 1997, 76–79.

49. E.g., *Mu'izz al-ansāb*, fol. 45a.

50. Mayor 2014, 395–410; Colarusso 2002, 364–65, for the story of Gunda, the heroine of Abkhazia, a region on the Black Sea's eastern shores, which is closer to Qutulun's.

51. On Puccini's *Turandot:* e.g., Fischer 2004, 679–98; Sung 2010.

52. For his biography and works: Sebag 1978, 89–101.

53. Petit de la Croix 1848, 1–3; Sebag 2004.

54. Petis de la Croix 1848, 63–67, 69–117. For an elaborated English version: Petis de la Croix 1892, 177–281.

55. For the blurred borders between China and Turkestan, Turks and Chinese in the medieval Muslim world: e.g., Biran 2005, 97–101. The Altoun Khan here may refer to the Qing emperors of China (1644–1911), who were descendants of the twelfth-century Jin dynasty whom the Mongol called Altan Khan ("the golden khan").

56. E.g., Meier 1941; Bürgel 2008; Sung 2010, esp. 3–24; Weatherford 2010a, 2010b; Shapiro 2018, for the transmission of De La Croix's story—mainly via the versions of Alain-René Lesage (1668–1747), Carlo Gocci (1702–1808), and Friedrich Schiller (1759–1805)—to Puccini. Puccini died before completing the opera, but his colleagues finished it. Turandot was first performed in Milano in 1926, and later staged across the world.

57. Meier 1941; Bürgel 2008; Sung 2010; Shapiro 2018 brings the two options but prefers Niẓāmī's.

58. Niẓāmī, tr. Meisami 2015, 158–73, where the story is elaborated.

59. As far as I can tell, this is the first time this suggestion was raised. Weatherford 2010a, 272–74.

60. He edited his father's biography of Chinggis Khan, adding a very concise appendix listing Chinggisid rulers up to Tamerlane, for whom he composed a biography. Yet the appendix does not mention even Qutulun's father, Qaidu. Petis de la Croix 1710, 221–22.

61. While competing, Mongolian wrestlers wear a *zodog*, an open vest which exposes the chest, and at the end of each match, the winner stretches out his arms to reveal his chest again. These garb and victory dance were traditionally described as connected to Qutulun, as they were allegedly used to ensure that the wrestlers were male, not female. Weatherford 2010b; May 2009, 118–20.

62. See www.macalester.edu/anthropology/facultystaff/jackweatherford/

(accessed on August 23, 2018).

63. See www.budda.mn/news/1790.html (accessed on August 23, 2018).

64. Oyungerel Tsedevdamba 2011 (this children's book originated in a radio show; on the author, a US-educated human (and women's) rights activist, and a former MP and minister: www.oyungerel.org/myprofile.html (accessed August 23, 2018). In 2013, two out of the five winning novels in a state competition for historical novels on Mongol queens were about Qutulun: Purev Sanj's *Khotolon*, and *Khaidu Khaany gaikhamshigt günj Khutulun Chakha* (*Qaidu Khan's wonderful princess Qutulun Chagha*) by Ch. Janchivdorj. Both were first published in a volume titled *Khatan tsadig* (Queens' Stories) in 2014, when Sanzhaagiĭn Batzhargal's novel *Khaĭdu Khaany* (Qaidu Khan) was also first published. I thank Bayasarkhan Dashdangong for sending me the details regarding these works, and Reuven Amitai for providing me with the books.

65. Shüüdertsetseg 2017; Shüüdertsetseg 2018 is an illustrated children book based on the novel. A second volume of the 2017 novel appeared in 2019 but I have not seen it.

66. See https://en.wikipedia.org/wiki/Khutulun (accessed August 24, 2018).

BIBLIOGRAPHY

Allsen, Thomas T. 1997. *Commodity and Exchange in the Mongol Empire: A Cultural History of Islamic Textiles*. Cambridge: Cambridge University Press.

Anonymous. *Muʿizz al-ansāb*. Paris, Bibliotheque Nationale, MS A.F. Pers 67.

Barthold, V.V. and J.M. Rogers. 1970. "The Burial Rites of the Turks and the Mongols." *Central Asiatic Journal* 14: 195–227.

Batzhargal, Sanzhaagiĭn. 2016. *Khaĭdu Khaany: Tuukhen Roman*. Ulaanbaatar: Selenge Press.

Biran, Michal. 1997. *Qaidu and the Rise of the Independent Mongol State in Central Asia*. Richmond, Surrey: Curzon.

———. 2005. *The Qara Khitai Empire in Eurasian History: Between China and the Islamic World*. Cambridge: Cambridge University Press.

Brack, Jonathan. 2011. "A Mongol Princess Making Hajj: The Biography of El Qutlugh, Daughter of Abagha Ilkhan (r. 1265–82)." *Journal of the Royal Asiatic Society* 21: 331–59.

Broadbridge, Anne F. 2018. *Women and the Making of the Mongol Empire*. Cambridge: Cambridge University Press.

Bürgel, Johann Christoph. 2008. "Turandot—von Nizami bis Puccini." *Quaderni di Studi Indo-Mediterranei* 1: 347–64.

Colarusso, John, et al., tr. 2002. *Nart Sagas from the Caucasus: Myths and Legends from the Circassians, Abazas, Abkhaz, and Ubykhs*. Princeton, NJ: Princeton University Press.

De Nicola, Bruno. 2010. "Women's Role and Participation in Warfare in the Mongol Empire." In *Soldatinnen: Gewalt und Geschlecht im Krieg vom Mittelalter bis heute*, ed. Klaus Latzel, Franka Maubach, and Silke Satjukow, 95–112. Paderborn, Germany: Ferdinand Schöningh.

———. 2016. "The Queen of the Chagatayids: Orghīna Khātūn and the Rule of Central Asia." *Journal of the Royal Asiatic Society* 25: 107–20.

———. 2017. *Women in Mongol Iran: The Khatuns, 1206–1335*. Edinburgh: Edinburgh University Press.

DeWeese, Devin. 1994. *Islamization and Native Religion in the Golden Horde*. Philadelphia: University of Pennsylvania Press.

al-Dhahabī, Shams al-Dīn Muḥammad b. Aḥmad, 1988. *Ta'rīkh al-Islām*. Ed. B. 'A. Ma'rūf. Vol. 61. Beirut: Dār al-kitāb al-'arabī.

Doerfer, Gerhard. 1963. *Türkische und mongolische Elemente im Neupersischen, unter besonderer Berücksichtigung älterer neupersischer Geschichtsquellen, vor allem der Mongolen- und Timuridenzeit*. Wiesbaden, Germany: Steiner.

Eastmond, Anthony. 2017. *Tamta's World: The Life and Encounters of a Medieval Noblewoman from the Middle East to Mongolia*. Cambridge: Cambridge University Press.

Edwards, Louise. 2016. *Women Warriors and Wartime Spies of China*. Cambridge: Cambridge University Press.

Fischer, Burton D. 2004. *Puccini Companion: The Glorious Dozen*. Miami: Opera Journeys.

Frankel, Valerie. 2010. *From Girl to Goddess: The Heroine's Journey through Myth and Legend*. Jefferson, NC: McFarland.

Giessauf, Johannes. 2007. "Mulieres Bellatrices oder Apis Argumentosa? Aspekte der Wahrnehmung mongolischer Frauen in abendländischen Quellen des Mittelalters." In *The Role of Women in the Altaic World*, ed. Veronica Veit, 83–92. Wiesbaden, Germany: Harrassowitz.

Ibn al-Athīr, 'Izz al-Dīn 'Alī b. Muḥammad. 1965–67. *Al-Kāmil fī al-ta'rīkh*. Beirut: Dār ṣādir.

Joinville, Jean. 1906. *The Memoirs of the Lord of Joinville: A New English Version*. Tr. Ethel K. Bowen-Wedgwood. New York: E.P. Dutton.

al-Juwaynī [Juvaini], 'Aṭā-Malik. 1912–37. *Ta'rīkh-i Jahāngushā*. Ed. Mīrzā Muḥammad Qazwīnī. London: Luzac.

———. 1997. *Genghis Khan: The History of the World Conqueror*. Tr. John A. Boyle. Manchester: Manchester University Press.

Klein, Wassilios. 2000. *Das nestorianische Christentum an den Handelswegen durch Kyrgyzstan bis zum 14. Jh*. Turnhout: Brespols.

Kruk, Remke. 2014. *Warrior Women of Islam: Female Empowerment in Arabic Popular Literature*. London: I.B. Tauris.

Landa, Ishayahu. 2016. "Imperial Sons-In-Law on the Move: Oyirad and Qonggirat Dispersion in Mongol Eurasia." *Archivum Eurasiae Medii Aevi* 22: 161–97.

Lane, George. 2006. *Daily Life in the Mongol Empire*. Westport, CT: Greenwood Press.

Lewis, Geoffrey, 1998. "Heroines and Others in the Heroic Age of the Turks." In *Women in the Medieval Islamic World: Power, Patronage, and Piety*, ed. Gavin R.G. Hambly, 147–60. New York: St. Martin's Press.

May, Timothy. 2009. *Culture and Customs of Mongolia*. Westport, CT: Greenwood Press.

Mayor, Adrienne. 2014. *The Amazons: Lives and Legends of Warrior Women*

across the Ancient World. Princeton, NJ: Princeton University Press.
Meier, F. 1941. "Turandot in Persien." *Zeitschrift der Deutschen Morgenländischen Gesellschaft* 95: 1–27, 415–21.
Mīrkhwānd, Muḥammad b. Khwāndshāh. 1961. *Taʾrīkh-i rawḍat al-ṣafā*. Vol. 5. Tehran: Markazī-i khayyām pīrūz, 1339sh.
Niẓāmī Ganjavi. 2015. *The Haft Paykar: A Medieval Persian Romance*. Tr. and ann. Julie S. Meisami. Indianapolis, IN: Hackett Publishing.
Oyungerel Tsedevdamba. 2011. *Khotol Tsagaan*. Ulaanbaatar, Mongolia: MonFemNet.
Pelliot, Paul. 1959–73. *Notes on Marco Polo*. 2 vols. Paris: Imprimerie Nationale.
Polo, Marco. 1938. *Marco Polo: The Description of the World*. Ed. and tr. Antoine C. Moule and Paul Pelliot. London: Routledge. Repr. 1976, New York: AMS Press.
Petis de la Croix, Francois (1622–1695). 1710. *Histoire du Grand Genghizcan*. Paris: Claude Barbini.
Petis de la Croix, Francois (1653–1713). 1848. *Les mille et un jours: Contes persans*. Paris: V. Lecou.
———. 1892. *One Thousand and One Days: Persian Tales*. Tr. and ed. Justin H. McCarthy. Vol. 1. London: Chatto & Windus.
Qāshānī, ʿAbd Allāh b. ʿAlī. 1969. *Taʾrīkh-i Ūljaytū*. Ed. Māhīn Hambalī. Tehran: Bangāh-i tarjuma wa nashr-i kitāb.
Rashīd al-Dīn, Faḍl Allah. 1911. *Djami el-tévarikh [sic]:histoire générale du monde*. Ed. Edgar Blochet. Leiden: Brill.
———. 1971. *The Successors of Genghis Khan*. Tr. John A. Boyle. New York: Columbia University Press.
———. 1994. *Jāmiʿ al-tawārikh*. Ed. Muḥammad Rawshan and Muṣṭafā Musawī. 4 vols. Tehran: Nashr-i Alburz.
———. 1998–99. *Rashiduddin Fazlullah's Jamiʿu't-Tawarikh: Compendium of Chronicles: A History of the Mongols*. Tr. Wheeler M. Thackston. Cambridge, MA: Harvard University, Department of Near Eastern Languages and Civilizations.
———. *Shuʿab-i panjgānah*. MS Istanbul, Topkapi Sarayi III, Ahmet, 2937.
Riccoldo da Montecroce. 2012. In *A Christian Pilgrim in Medieval Iraq: Riccoldo da Montecroce's Encounter with Islam*, tr. Rita George-Tvrtković. Turnhout: Brepols.
Rossabi, Morris. 1979. "Khubilai Khan and the Women in his Family." In *Studia Sino-Mongolica: Festschrift für Herbert Franke*, ed. Wolfgang Bauer, 153–80. Wiesbaden, Germany: Steiner.
———. 1988. *Khubilai Khan: His Life and Times*. Berkeley: University of California Press.
al-Ṣafadī, Ṣalāḥ al-Dīn Khalīl b. Aybak. 1998. *Aʿyān al-ʿaṣr wa-aʿwān al-naṣr*. Ed. ʿA. Abu Zayd et al. Beirut: Dār al-fikr al-muʿāṣir/Damascus: Dār al-fikr.
Sebag, Paul. 1978. "Sur deux orientalistes français du XVIIe siècle: F. Pétis de La Croix et le Sieur de La Croix." *Revue de l'Occident Musulman et de la Méditerranée* 25: 89–177.

———. 2004. "Aux origines de l'orient romanesque. Quel est l'auteur des *Mille et Un Jours?*" *IBLA: Revue de l'Institut des Belles Lettres Arabes* 67: 31–60.

Serruys, Henry. 1974. "Mongol 'Qoriγ': Reservation." *Mongolian Studies* 1: 76–91.

Shapiro, Roman. 2018. "The Chinese Princess in the West: From Persian Fairy-tales to Puccini's Opera." Paper read at the fourteenth biennial conference of Asian studies in Israel (ASI18), The Hebrew University of Jerusalem, May 23–24.

Sinor, Denis. 2007. "Some Observations on Women in Early and Medieval Inner Asian History." In *The Role of Women in the Altaic World*, ed. Veronica Veit, 261–68. Wiesbaden, Germany: Harrassowitz.

Sung, Ying-Wei Tiffany. 2010. "Turandot's Homecoming: Seeking the Authentic Princess of China in a New Contest of Riddles." MA thesis, Bowling Green State University. Available at https://etd.ohiolink.edu/!etd.send_file?accession=bgsu1273466517&disposition=inline (accessed August 20, 2018).

Shüüdertsetseg Baatarsürengiin. 2017. *Khotol Tsagaan Günj, Tüükhen Roman.* Ulaanbaatar, Mongolia: Admon.

———. 2018. *Khotolun Günj*. Ulaanbaatar, Mongolia: Shüüder.

Waṣṣāf (Vaṣṣāf) al-Ḥaḍra, ʿAbd Allāh. 2009. *Tajziyat al-amṣār wa tazjīyat al-aʿṣār: Taʾrīkh-i Waṣṣāf*. Ed. Iraj Afshār et al. Tehran: Talāyah.

Weatherford, Jack M. 2010a. *The Secret History of the Mongol Queens: How the Daughters of Genghis Khan Rescued His Empire*. New York: Crown Publishers.

———. 2010b. "The Wrestler Princess." *Lapham Quarterly*. September 27, 2010. Available at www.laphamsquarterly.org/roundtable/wrestler-princess (accessed August 20, 2018).

Wu Pei-Yi. 2002. "Yang Miaozhen: A Woman Warrior in Thirteenth-Century China." *Nan Nü* 4: 137–69.

Zhanchivdorzh, Chimig-Ochiryn, et al. 2017. *Khatan tsadig*. Ulanbaatar, Mongolia: Tört ës, khaadyn san.

Zhao Gong 趙珙. 2016. *Mengda beilu* 蒙韃備錄 [Report of the Mongolian Tatars]. In *Quan Song biji. Di qi bian (er)* 全宋笔记. 第七编(二) [Complete Collection of Brush Notes from the Song Dynasty]. Vol. 7.2. . Zhengzhou, China: Daxiang chubanshe.

CHAPTER 4

Yang Tingbi

Mongol Expansion along the Maritime Silk Roads

MASAKI MUKAI AND FRANCESCA FIASCHETTI

The Mongols' defeat of the Song dynasty (960–1279) in the 1270s enabled them to extend Yuan rule (1260–1368) into South China, and opened a gateway to the "maritime Silk Roads," a series of trade routes and commercial networks that had developed long before the Mongol era. They connected China with major commercial and political centers along the shores of Southeast Asia and the Indian Ocean, leading up to the Persian Gulf, the Red Sea, and the shores of Africa. Access to these routes was crucial for the Yuan: it enabled them to tap into the lucrative and rich trade that could further fuel the empire's expansive aspirations, and also guaranteed an open channel to their allies in western Eurasia, the Ilkhanate (1260–1335), the Mongol state centered in Iran. This channel west was especially significant as long as the continental Silk Roads remained unsecure due to the conflict between the Toluid family in China and Iran and their Ögödeid and Chaghadaid cousins in Central Asia.

From its inception in 1260, the Yuan court combined diplomacy, trade incentives, and military force to gain control over these maritime networks. Yet, Yuan expansion was met with resistance and challenges such as the necessity to adopt new naval technologies and warfare techniques. The different environment and climate required acquiring new navigation knowledge. Further the Mongols dealt with unknown local political and cultural dynamics that they now encountered on the shores of the Indian Ocean and Southeast Asia. For example, trade in the

Southeast Asian archipelago was heavily influenced by the polity of Champa (192–1832, in Central and Southern Vietnam), which remained loyal to the Song dynasty, as well as by the Song refugees who lingered throughout the maritime Southeast.

In the Indian Ocean, the Mongols directed their attention toward the regions of Maʿbar and Kūlam. Maʿbar on the Coromandel Coast, in the southeastern part of present-day Tamil Nadu, was ruled by the Pandya lineage (300 B.C.E.–1650 C.E.).[1] Kūlam lay on the southern end of the Malabar Coast, and was under the hegemony of the Cera king (Ravivarman Kulasekara, ca. 1266/7–1316/17).[2] Both coastal provinces were major nodes in a commercial network that spanned eastern and western Eurasia. The Mongols needed to gain first a footing in their local political scenes to extend their influence to these regions and to the networks they linked. The expertise and mediation skills of non-Mongol personnel, familiar with both the maritime routes and the local conditions, were therefore a crucial asset for facilitating the Mongol expansion. The Han-Chinese general Yang Tingbi (fl. 1270s to 1280s) belonged to this range of individuals who facilitated the Mongol expansion into Southeast Asia and the Indian Ocean. Although he was only a midranking general and not well connected with the empire's elites, his extensive maritime voyages, which covered nearly twenty-eight thousand kilometers, and his military engagements along the empire's maritime frontiers, had a significant impact on developing the Mongol Silk Roads.

Tingbi's career and life are not comprehensively documented in contemporary accounts, but his achievements as a Yuan diplomat left their mark on a variety of documents. Although the *Yuanshi* (History of the Yuan Dynasty)—our main Chinese source for the period—does not devote a chapter to Tingbi's biography, its section on the kingdom of Maʿbar describes in detail the general's activities in the region.[3] Additional fragmentary records and inscriptions further allow us to reconstruct the general's life and career, to a degree. Involved first in the Mongol conflict with the Song, Yang Tingbi fulfilled a leading role in quelling Song resistance in the Fujian region in 1277. A decade later, between the years 1279 and 1283, he reached the height of his career as a Yuan admiral and diplomat when he set on several voyages to Maʿbar and Kūlam.

In the last phase of his career, Tingbi had a pivotal role in guaranteeing the stability of the empire's southeastern frontiers through both diplomacy and military force. The study of his biography thus sheds light on the construction of Yuan diplomatic networks in Southeast Asia and the shaping of Mongol policies toward China's southern frontier regions during the defining stages of the establishment of Yuan imperial rule.

BACKGROUND

The *Yang Tingbi pingkouji* (Record of Yang Tingbi's Subjugation of the Bandits), a stone inscription dated to 1289 (see fig. 4.1),[4] states that the general was born in Enzhou in the Dongping Circuit (in present-day Shandong), a town famous for its legendary heroes.[5] The town gained its fame after the charismatic bandit Song Jiang had settled there in the early twelfth century, together with his band of outlaws.[6] In the mid-1230s, when the Mongols took over the Jurchen Jin dynasty (1115–1234), the Dongping Circuit provided men for one of the five *tümen*s (an army unit of allegedly ten thousand soldiers) in the North China Plain. Subsequently, during the administrative reforms of Ögödei (r. 1229–41), the military unit was placed under the command of the Han Chinese general Shi Tianze (1202–75).[7]

Although we have no records about Yang Tingbi's early career, his first military achievements were most likely linked to the figure of Shi Tianze. Yang Tingbi and his crew might have followed Shi in 1270, when Qubilai (r. 1260–94) appointed him as the supreme general of the Mongol-Yuan forces against the Song. Shi assumed a leading role in the siege of Xiangyang (in present-day Hubei), one of the Yuan's active fronts with the Song army. It was in Xianyang that Shi Tianze assigned Yang Tingbi to the service of the prominent Mongol general Sogatu (d. 1285),[8] who promoted Tingbi's career.[9]

Once Xianyang had fallen to Mongol hands, in 1272, the Yuan troops crossed the Yangtze and fought along the river. Sogatu integrated the surrendered Song soldiers into his army. Their battleships were also seized. The inclusion of enemy soldiers in the Yuan military allowed the Mongols to combine naval and land warfare, significantly advancing their military strategies. The Yuan had already experimented with a combined naval and land approach as early as 1266 in Henan, and in 1270 around Xiangyang. Their mastering of naval warfare eventually led to their final victory over the Song.[10] Under Sogatu's command, Tingbi took part in the maritime clashes against the Song such as the siege on the Song capital of Hangzhou in 1276. His experience during these campaigns laid the foundation for his later overseas missions.

FIGURE 4.1. Thirteenth-century inscription of *Yang Tingbi pingkouji* carved into a cliff in Qixing Yan (Guangdong, China). Photo by Masaki Mukai.

FUJIAN, 1277

After the Mongols had captured Hangzhou, the Song court fled to Fuzhou (in Fujian), turning the city into a refuge for Chinese fugitives and Song loyalists, and the basis from which the Song military remnants were launching their counterattacks.[11] The Mongols were further interested in Fujian's main port city, Quanzhou (Marco Polo's Zaytun), for commercial reasons. A prosperous haven, Quanzhou was the base for an extensive trade network encompassing Southeast Asia and the Indian Ocean. Travelers arriving in the port city reported on finding goods reaching from all corners of maritime Asia (see fig. 4.2). One of them was the Venetian merchant Marco Polo (1254–1324), who reports:

FIGURE 4.2. Luoyang (Wan'an) Bridge, built during the Song period (mid-eleventh century), northeast of Quanzhou (Fujian, China). Luoyang Bridge is one of the most iconic sites in Quanzhou's vicinity since Polo's time. Photo by Masaki Mukai.

"For one shipload of pepper that goes to Alexandria or elsewhere, destined for Christendom, there comes a hundred such, aye and more too, to this haven of Zaytun; for it is one of the two greatest havens in the world for commerce."[12]

Under Sogatu's command, the army advanced to Quanzhou in 1277, upon which they encountered resistance of Song remnants in Chong'an (present-day Wuyi, in northern Fujian). This campaign forms also the background for Tingbi's first explicit reference in historical records (aside from the inscription above), as he played a pivotal role in the Mongol siege on Chong'an.

In typical Mongol fashion, the Yuan attack on Chong'an was organized along three fronts. Tingbi, together with Sogatu's son Baijianu (d. 1311), delivered a pincer attack on the city. Meanwhile, hundreds of Yuan soldiers ambushed the enemy at the bridge leading into the city and at its northern gate. Ambushed from all directions, the Song loyalists were so terrorized that they were entirely set into chaos and disarray. According to some accounts, more than a thousand Song soldiers perished.[13]

Having driven the remaining Song loyalists away from the inland area of Fujian, Sogatu reached Quanzhou. At the time, a famous merchant and the Song superintendent of maritime commerce, Pu Shougeng (d. 1296), resided in the city. Having surrendered to the Yuan and turned against the Song, he slaughtered the Song imperial family residing in Quanzhou, thus helping secure the city for the Mongols.[14]

When the Song loyalists sieged Quanzhou, in response to Pu Shougeng's request, Sogatu rushed to Quanzhou and repulsed the enemy. Rescued by Sogatu, Pu joined forces with the general together with Pu's family naval forces. Subsequently, their private warships were incorporated into Sogatu's forces. Tingbi seems to have followed the combined flotilla of Sogatu and Pu Shougeng in the subsequent campaigns.

1279–80: FIRST VOYAGE TO SOUTH INDIA

The final conquest of the Song and the annexation of Fujian brought the Mongols to directly engage with the Southeast Asian seas. In 1278, Qubilai appointed Sogatu and Pu Shougeng as left vice-ministers (*zuocheng*) of the Mobile Secretariat (*xingsheng;* the provincial government) in Quanzhou. He ordered them to dispatch trade ships carrying ten imperial letters to establish trade relations with various courts in "the southeastern islands" of maritime Asia.[15] Their mission bore immediate fruit and embassies to the Yuan court from both Champa and Maʿbar followed suit.[16]

At the end of 1279, Tingbi was appointed overseer (*darughachi*) of the Commandery-in-Chief (*zhaotaoshi*) in Guangdong,[17] and was entrusted with traveling to Maʿbar and Kūlam in South India.[18] The Yuan considered Maʿbar and Kūlam a high priority, since they provided midroute stations for ships and traders traveling between China and Iran. In early 1280, Tingbi traveled to Kūlam, where King Binadi promised to send tribute to the Yuan court. Tingbi returned that summer to the court with a letter from the king of Kūlam's brother.[19]

His voyage was likely facilitated by the Chinese sailors' prior acquaintance with the Indian Ocean and its shores. Maʿbar had been a major commercial center for Chinese traders well before the Mongol period and some sources attest to the presence of Chinese commercial colonies already under the Song.[20] Similarly, Marco Polo reports that the kingdom of Kūlam was frequented by merchants from South China (*Manzi*), Arabia, and the Levant.[21]

While Yang Tingbi was assigned with establishing relationships with the maritime forces in Maʿbar and Kūlam through diplomacy, Sogatu spearheaded the Yuan military operations in Champa. The routes of the maritime Silk Roads passed through the coast of the Cham kingdom (Champa), a powerful state in Central and Southern Vietnam, with commercial and political influence that extended deep into Southeast Asia. Both Champa and Đại Việt (1054–1400 and 1428–1804), the neighboring kingdom in North Vietnam, enjoyed strong commercial and diplomatic relations with the Song. They sought to maintain their ties with the Chinese dynasty even after the Mongols had demanded their submission.[22]

A strong presence of Song refugees in the Vietnamese territory,[23] as well as the desire of the Cham kingdom to maintain its status in the Southeast Asian commercial network, contributed to the rise of anti-Mongol resistance movements. This negatively affected the Yuan diplomatic missions. In 1282, for example, Yuan envoys were captured and detained by the Cham navy.[24] The Mongols, therefore, saw priority in gaining control over Vietnam, and employed both diplomacy and military pressure to this end.

In November 1281, Sogatu was installed as the head of a Mobile Secretariat (*xingsheng*) in Fujian to oversee Mongol punitive expeditions against Champa.[25] Marco Polo reports that Qubilai dispatched Sogatu with cavalry and infantry to Champa. According to the *Yuanshi,* Qubilai mobilized five thousand men from Jianghuai, Fujian, and Huguang regions. He requisitioned 100 ships and 250 battle ships and put them under Sogatu's command in July 1282.[26] The Cham ruler, Prince Harijit (later known as King Jaya Simhavarman III, r. 1288–1307), escaped from the capital, Vijaya (current Bình Định), and resisted the Mongols through guerilla warfare. The Yuan subsequently sent reinforcements.[27] According to Polo, fearing that the Mongol general would devastate his kingdom, in 1284 the Cham prince sent ambassadors to Qubilai, who ordered his general to retreat. Thereupon, the Cham Kingdom submitted to Mongol rule and agreed to annually present the qa'an with tribute.[28]

Champa's submission was only one of the Mongols' concerns on the maritime Silk Roads. To secure and protect Mongol-sponsored ocean-going travel, the Yuan needed the support of local authorities loyal to them on the other side of the ocean. With this aim, Yang Tingbi was sent on a second mission to South India.

1280–83: SECOND VOYAGE TO SOUTH INDIA

In October or November 1280, Tingbi was appointed commissioner for the Pacification Office (*Julan xuanweisi*) at Kūlam, together with the Uighur general Qasar Qaya (fl. 1280–90). Their mission was to summon the ruler of Kūlam to the qa'an's court. Embarking from Quanzhou in January–February 1281, they arrived at Ceylon (Sri Lanka) after three months of sea voyage. Travelers between Maʿbar and Kūlam usually circumnavigated the southern coast of India, but due to a southwest monsoon, Tingbi's fleet had to change course. With the adverse wind conditions and their food shortage, they were forced to sail to the opposite coast of Maʿbar. From there, they could continue through land routes to Kūlam.[29]

Yang Tingbi and Qasar Qaya arrived at the port of Xincun (lit. "New Village," near present-day Kayal) in Tamil Nadu during April–May 1281.[30] The local magistrate Mayīndira (Ch. *Mayindi*),[31] a member of the royal lineage of the Pandya, and a subordinate of the Pandya ruler Sundara (r. 1216–38), welcomed them. Yang Tingbi's request to use the land route that crossed Maʿbar to reach Kūlam, however, was ignored both by Mayīndira and his minister Bu'ali (Abū ʿAlī).[32] Their refusal might have stemmed from the difficult passage, through a steep mountainous area that separated the southern part of Tamil Nadu and the southern part of Kerala, or from the political fragmentation of the area that made the land route unsafe.[33]

Remaining in Maʿbar, the Yuan envoys found themselves entangled in local political rivalries. A month after their arrival, while they were still waiting for the monsoon season to end, two men (possibly Mayīndira and Abū ʿAlī themselves),[34] hurried to the lodging of Yang Tingbi and Qasar Qaya. They secretly reported that Mayīndira wished to submit to the Yuan and claimed that he had already sent the Iraqi merchant Jamāl al-Dīn al-Ṭibī as envoy to China.[35] However, the Pandya King Sundara and Mayīndira's superior considered al-Ṭibī's embassy an act of rebellion and had planned to execute him. Mayīndira managed to escape and now sought Yuan assistance. The messengers also claimed that King Sundara and his five brothers intended to launch an attack on Kūlam.[36]

The messengers assured them that, if King Sundara was made to surrender through Yuan intervention, Mayīndira would use his influence over the neighboring states along the land route to Kūlam, and convince them to submit to the Yuan. The Mongol envoys could subsequently travel to Kūlam.

In his attempt to establish an alliance with the Mongols, Mayīndira aimed to improve his position vis-à-vis his political and commercial rivals. Yang Tingbi realized that his mission may profit from the situation. He would not only strengthen the relations with the Pandyas, but with the help of Mayīndira, also extend the Yuan commercial and diplomatic network to the polities that were subordinate to them. Qasar Qaya headed back to the Yuan court with this information.

On January 8, 1282, when the northerly winds had subsided and the maritime route was viable, the Yuan court sent another emissary, Andula,[37] to Maʿbar, and ordered Tingbi to proceed to Kūlam, as he promptly did.[38]

FROM MAʿBAR TO KŪLAM

In March–April 1282, Tingbi arrived in the kingdom of Kūlam, where King Binadi and his minister Muḥammad (Ch. *Mahema*) received Qubilai's imperial letter with special reverence. Soon after, the king reciprocated by sending his minister with presents to the Yuan court. In addition, the Chinese sources report that "the head of the *erke'un* [Syriac Christians],[39] and Muḥammad,[40] the leader of the Muslims, and other local [merchant] communities, having heard of the arrival of the imperial envoy, came to meet Tingbi and offered to send annual gifts to the Yuan court and dispatch a representative." Likewise, the kingdom of Somnath (Sumuda, around Gujarat) followed Kūlam's example, sending an envoy to Yang Tingbi requesting submission. Yang Tingbi accepted all their embassies on behalf of the Mongol emperor.

What the Chinese sources frame in terms of "submission," however, refers to a long-established system of tribute-trade relations. The economic outcome of the tribute relations was considered advantageous and attractive for both China and the Southeast Asian courts. The Indian courts saw in their official submission to the Yuan an opportunity to strengthen the lucrative trade with China.[41]

Tingbi began his return journey through Southeast Asia during May–June 1282. Along his route, he successfully secured the submission of the kingdom of Nawang (probably Nagur in Simalungun, North Sumatra) and Samudra (North Sumatra).[42] Thanks to Tingbi's mission, envoys from Kūlam, Nagur, and Somnat, along with the representatives of the Muslim and Christian merchant colonies of Kūlam, arrived on October 7 at the Yuan court carrying tribute (see map 4.1).[43]

On February 20, 1283, a few months after his return, Yang Tingbi was promoted to the rank of pacification commissioner (*xuanweishi*), was honored with imperial gifts of a bow, arrows, a saddle and bridle, and was subsequently sent on a new mission to Kūlam and other states.[44] His mission facilitated the further expansion of Yuan diplomatic and commercial networks in the Indian Ocean.

The success of Tingbi's missions is attested also by a series of Indian sources (mostly in Tamil), which record the increased exchange of embassies and commercial missions between the two countries.[45] Sogatu

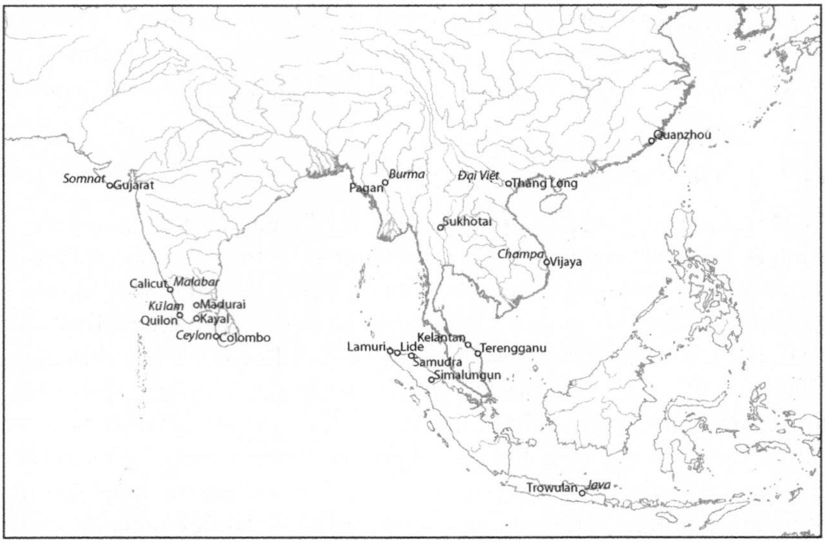

MAP 4.1. Countries along the Routes of Yang Tingbi's Diplomatic Missions.

and Pu Shougeng, too, dispatched their ships to foreign destinations. Owing to the joint efforts of Tingbi, Sogatu, and Pu, the polities situated along the sea route from India, via Sumatra and the Malay Peninsula, to China, had all surrendered by September 20, 1286, when they had sent tribute to the Yuan.[46] Yet, after the transition of power following Qubilai's demise in 1294, Maʿbar remained the only kingdom that continued the tribute-trade relations with the Yuan, at least up to 1314.[47] Neighboring Ceylon and Kūlam ceased sending embassies.

Yang Tingbi's voyages were epoch-making in the history of navigation accomplishments (see table 4.1). Given the distance and the climatic conditions, it is astounding that he managed to travel between China and South India in just one season. He seems to have skipped the Malacca straits, an innovation compared to the route followed by voyagers in earlier periods. The increased maritime traffic triggered by Yuan policies, thus, also seems to have led to improvements in Chinese navigation of the Southeast Asian seas.[48]

1289–91: GUANGDONG AND HAINAN

Returning from his diplomatic missions, Tingbi resumed his military career: he was appointed pacification commissioner at the Western

TABLE 4.1 YANG TINGBI'S VOYAGES IN SOUTH INDIA, 1280–82

Year	Season	Departure	Arrival
1280	Winter	China (Jan.–Feb.)	Kūlam (April)
1280	Summer	Kūlam	China
1281	Winter	Quanzhou (Jan.–Feb.)	Maʿbar (April–May)
1281/1282	Winter	Maʿbar (Dec.–Jan.)	Kūlam (Mar.–April)
1282	Winter	Kūlam	Nakur (May–June)

Circuit of Guangnan (*Guangnan xidao xuanweishi*), and was entrusted with the pacification of the area populated by the Yao and She ethnic groups,[49] in the Guangdong province.[50]

During the early and mid-Yuan period, frequent uprisings mostly headed by local ethnic groups broke out in various parts of South China. The generals in the frontier region had prior knowledge of the local context and showed personal initiative. They took on the role of mediators between the local population and the Yuan Court at Dadu, which, due to its distance, was largely uninformed about the local circumstances. Their role as mediators was crucial for the successful pacification of the uprisings.

Although several officials had undertaken this task prior to Yang Tingbi, they had only partial success. During 1287, the She leader Zhong Mingliang led a series of insurrections in Guangdong, from Guanzhou to the Ningdu district.[51] Subsequently, the Jurchen general Liu Guojie (1234–1305) attempted to suppress the rebellions. His army advanced deep into the mountainous areas of Guangdong and defeated many of the Yao groups. Yet, an epidemic in Hezhou in the summer of 1289 brought Guojie's men to a halt, forcing them to set northward.[52]

The task of pacifying the area now fell to Tingbi. Likely in 1289, he engaged with the rebels in Duanzhou, and in 1290, on the day of the Spring Lantern Festival (January 15), he managed to pacify the rebellion. On May 8, 1290, the relieved residents of Duanzhou carved a record of this event into stone.[53]

Tingbi's last recorded activity was commanding the native Li ethnic group in Hainan Island, which had been incorporated into the Yuan Dynasty in 1278. That same year, some Li people entered the Yuan army as mercenaries and were later enlisted to the Mongols' maritime campaigns.[54]

The subjugation of the Li population was never fully carried out. In 1291, the governor of the Mobile Secretariat at Huguang, Körguz (Ch.

Kuolijisi), mobilized 21,200 soldiers to subdue them. The "inscription recording the pacification of the Li in the *guise* year of the *zhiyuan* period," made in 1293, reports that Yang Tingbi, bearing the title of Guangxi Pacification Commissioner, commanded 14,000 Li mercenaries and joined the battle in Hainan Island.[55] Another stone inscription preserved at Mount Qianfengling (Sharp-Point Peak), in the south of the island (current Ledong Li Autonomous County), tells that the Yuan troops and horses reached the island and camped there on January 11, 1294.[56] After this episode, no further information on Yang Tingbi's destiny or that of his offspring is available.

CONCLUSION

Engaging with the maritime Silk Roads, the Mongols capitalized on technologies and routes that had developed there over centuries. To profit from these pre-established structures, they took advantage of the expertise of capable individuals and their networks. Military commanders, diplomats, and merchants, therefore, found themselves working together in Mongol service to expand the Yuan maritime empire. For the Mongols, war and diplomacy complemented each other, and thus both types of missions may often overlap during the career of one single individual.

Yang Tingbi was such an individual. Starting off as a middle-ranking Han Chinese general, he succeeded to play an important role in the expansion of Yuan authority in Southeast Asia. Tingbi's military performance elevated him to high-ranking administrative posts; it further enabled him to become the leader of one of the most significant diplomatic missions in Yuan history. Furthermore, along with the territorial expansion of the Yuan Dynasty into South China, a growing number of non-Mongol personnel rose to prominence cooperating with senior Mongol military leaders. This, too, applies to Tingbi, whose connection with the general Sogatu was instrumental in his advancement in the Yuan military ranks. Tingbi's success as a diplomat was possibly also related to the extensive information about foreign lands that he could gather through his cooperation with Sogatu and his ally Pu Shougeng.

Through his experience as a diplomat abroad, the ambitious and hard-working Yang Tingbi must have cultivated his skills as a cultural mediator. His overseas experience might have also later facilitated Tingbi's successful engagement with rebellions of the South Chinese ethnic groups like the Yao, the She, and the Li.

This survey of Tingbi's career adds to our understanding of the complex dynamics behind the southward expansion of the Yuan Dynasty. Many players were involved in the landscape of the maritime Silk Roads. The Mongols had to legitimize themselves against the Song, whose political and military elites migrated to Southeast Asian polities, and continued to play a role there, even after the dissolution of the Song dynasty. Local rulers tried to utilize the alliance with the Mongols' military and political power to settle local, regional, and interregional disputes with their neighbors. Furthermore, the southern frontiers, crucial passages between the Yuan realm and the surrounding foreign countries, also represented an ongoing concern for the Mongol administration. The personal initiative, skills, and mobility of individuals like Yang Tingbi enabled the Mongols to acquire the necessary human capital and strategic knowledge to face the challenges of unifying such a vast and ethnically diverse empire.

NOTES

1. Sastri 2005, 192–205.
2. He engaged in raids into the Pandya territory, which were probably the reason for Pandya's planned attack on Kūlam (below). Sastri 2005, 198.
3. Song 1976, 210: 4669–70.
4. The inscription was carved into a cliff in Qixing Yan (Seven Star Crags), north of the city of Zhaoqing (in Guangdong). Tan, Cao, and Xian 2001, 679.
5. *Yang Tingbi pingkouji* (Tan, Cao, and Xian 2001, 679); Mukai 2008, 7; Mukai 2013, 81; Xiang 2014.
6. Song Jiang headed a group of rebels who fought against the Northern Song dynasty (960–1127) in present-day Shandong and Henan. His uprising later served as a background for the fictional heroes and events narrated in the famous Chinese novel *Water Margin*.
7. Su 1996, 6: 92, 7: 115–16. Shi Tianze defeated to the Mongols during their campaign against the Jin dynasty, becoming one of the first Han-Chinese to gain a high position.
8. On the Jalayirid general Sogatu, member of Qubilai's imperial guard (*keshig*): Song 1976, 129: 3150–52; also Mukai 2008, 128–29; Mukai 2013, 82; Xiang 2014, 254–55.
9. Appointed as a chiliarch (commander of a thousand soldiers), Sogatu joined the siege of Xiangyang under the command of Shi Tianze. He recruited his own soldiers out of three thousand young outlaws. In 1271, he was promoted to director-general (*zongguan*), and Shi Tianze assigned him eight hundred soldiers from Dongping (Song 1976, 129: 3151). These troops, which formed the core of Sogatu's army, were probably under the direction of Yang Tingbi. Therefore, Yang Tingbi was probably Sogatu's lieutenant from 1271.
10. Song 1976, 7: 128; Su 1996, 14: 273.

11. In Fuzhou, the eight-year-old Song prince Guang was proclaimed emperor and made nominal commander-in-chief of the army. Lo and Elleman 2012, 278.

12. Yule and Cordier 1920, 2: 235.

13. Song 1976, 129: 3152.

14. Song 1976, 9: 191. On Pu Shougeng: Su 1996, 14: 277; also Rossabi 1988, 92–93; Kuwabara 1989; So 2000, 108, 301–5; Lo and Elleman 2012, 230–31; Chaffee 2017.

15. Song 1976, 10: 204; 210: 4669. The term "southeastern (foreign populations of the) islands" (*daoyi*) is a common Yuan reference to maritime Southeast Asia in general.

16. On September 4, 1280, preceding Yang Tingbi's mission. Song 1976, 11: 225–26; Rockhill 1914, 430–31.

17. This title was mainly granted to Mongol and Central Asian (*semu*) personnel rather than Han Chinese, due to privileges that were associated with it including carrying weapons. Endicott-West 1994, 595–96.

18. The narrative of his voyage appears in *juan* 210 of the *Yuanshi*, which is the main source for the next paragraphs. A translation of the chapter is found in Rockhill 1914, 428–36; cf. Subramaniam 1978; Karashima 1988; Ptak 1993; Fukami 2004; Sen 2006.

19. Song 1976, 210: 4669.

20. Lo and Elleman2012, 186–206.

21. Polo 2004, 463.

22. Vu and Sharrock 2014.

23. Chan 1966.

24. Lo and Elleman 2012, 286–87.

25. Lo and Elleman 2012, 285.

26. Song 1976, 12: 243–44. Chinese junks each carried hundreds of soldiers (Ibn Baṭṭūṭa: a thousand men; Odoric of Pordenone: seven hundred; Wu Zimu: five hundred to six hundred, cited in: Meng et al. 1956, 235). It is therefore possible that Yang's fleet numbered close to a thousand soldiers.

27. Song 1976, 210: 4660–61.

28. Polo 2004, 407.

29. The East Asian monsoon is a seasonal change in the atmospheric circulation in the Indian and Pacific Oceans, caused by the asymmetric heating of land and sea. Only during the "northeastern" monsoon (a drier and calmer season lasting from late October to early March), sailing along the Indian coast was safe. Prange 2018, 27–28.

30. Xincun ("New Village") has been traditionally understood as indicating Pondicherry (Tamil: *Puduchchēri*, in present-day Tamil Nadu), which carries the same meaning (Karashima 1988, 88–89). However, Ptak showed that Xincun in the Yuan sources refers to Punnaikayal (near present-day Kayal), near the center of the Pandya kingdom and Kūlam, which matches Tingbi's intinerary. Ptak 1993.

31. Karashima 1988, 90.

32. Originally from Qalhat (present-day Amman), Abū ʿAlī Sayyid was likely a trader who settled in South India. Later, after Tingbi's visit, Abū ʿAlī

would find asylum at the Yuan court. Liu 1990; also Chen 1980; Ptak 1993; Sen 2006.

33. Between the eleventh and thirteenth centuries, this area was divided between different rulers and lineages, constantly fighting for supremacy and legitimation. Scholars have formulated this territorial segmentation as different "nuclear areas of sub-regional power" (Stein 1984), "fragmentary states" (Stein 1977), or "little kingdoms" (Dirks 1979; Kulke 1993).

34. Liu 1990, 93; Sen 2006, 313 n. 52.

35. Jamāl al-Dīn was the governor of Kish in the Persian Gulf, and his brother Taqī al-Dīn was an influential minister of the Pandya King Sundara. The two traded pearls and horses between Iran, Maʿbar, and China. Kuwabara 1989, 124–25; Elliot 1953, 1: 69; Gill's article in this volume.

36. Maʿbar had a system of joint rulership. Abū ʿAlī's father was the "sixth brother," and Abū ʿAlī was named the "prince of Maʿbar," a designation which appears in the Chinese and Korean sources as well. Allsen suggests, however, that the "prince of Maʿbar" is shorthand for *malik-al tujjār,* the "prince of traders," indicating instead Abū ʿAlī's prominence as a merchant. Allsen, personal communication, cited in Sen 2006, 318. See also Ptak 1993.

37. He carried with him *chao,* Yuan paper money. According to Polo and other accounts, foreign merchants did use Yuan paper money to exchange goods, silver, gold, and pearls, after they reached Yuan territory. It was a common Yuan policy to sponsor all military and official missions with paper money. Vogel 2012, 112–13.

38. Song 1976, 11: 236.

39. Polo, too, mentions Syriac Christians in Maʿbar: Rockhill 1914, 435.

40. It is unclear if the minister Muḥammad and the head of the Muslim community, Muḥammad, are the same individual. According to Ibn Baṭṭūṭa, around the 1340s, a certain Muḥammad, the Muslim leader of Kūlam (Kawlam), took charge of the maritime trade as Shāh Bandar (king of the port). Ibn Baṭṭūṭa 1994, 817.

41. Yang 1968.

42. Sumutula, between Pasai and Acheh in North Sumatra.

43. Song 1976, 12: 245.

44. Song 1976, 12: 250.

45. Sen 2006.

46. These included Maʿbar, Somnath (*Xumenna,* around Gujarat), Ceylon (*Sengjili*), Lamuri (*Nanwuli*), Malandan (*Kelantan*), Nagur (*Nawang*), Terengganu (*Dinghe'er*), Lide (*Laila*), Kelantan (*Jilanyidai*), and Samudra. Song 1976, 210: 4670.

47. The Yuan-Maʿbar relations experienced decline following the dwindling power of the Pandya dynasty in the 1310 to 1320s, after its military conflict with the Delhi Sultanate (1206–1526). After the Delhi Sultans occupied the capital of the Pandya dynasty, Madurai, its viceroy declared his independence from the Delhi court and established the Madurai Sultanate (1335–78). Sen 2006.

48. Fukami 2004, 111–13.

49. The Yao are an ethnic minority spread along the China-Vietnam border. The She mainly resided in Fujian, but also in Guangdong.

50. *Guangnan xidao* was a district in the western part of the Guangnan region, roughly equal to present-day Guangxi region (headquartered at Jingjiang, present-day Guilin) and Hainan Island, a part of Yunnan.

51. The commander Yitmis was first appointed to the task of pacifying the rebellion. He coordinated a successful attack of the three neighboring provinces of Jiangxi, Jianghuai, and Fujian. Yet, further rebellions followed. Song 1976, 15: 319, 322.

52. Toward Daozhou in Huguang (in present-day Hunan). Song 1976, 162: 3809.

53. *Yang Tingbi pingkouji* (Tan, Cao, and Xian 2001, 679); Mukai 2008: 7; Mukai 2013: 81; Xiang 2014: 252. Duanzhou is the old name of Zhaoqing.

54. They were recruited for an attack against Japan in 1283 (that was never carried out), against Champa (nineteen hundred Li soldiers, in 1283), and against Đại Việt (fifteen thousand, in 1287). Wang 2003; Li 2004.

55. Xing 1983, 415. Only a copy of the original stone inscription survives.

56. Tang Zhou 2006, 124.

BIBLIOGRAPHY

Chaffee, John W. 2017. "Pu Shougeng Reconsidered: Pu, His Family, and Their Role in the Maritime Trade of Quanzhou." In *Beyond the Silk Roads: New Discourses on China's Role in East Asian Maritime History*, ed. Angela Schottenhammer and Robert J. Antony, 63–76. Wiesbaden, Germany: Harrassowitz.

Chan, Hok-Lam. 1966. "Chinese Refugees in Annam and Champa at the End of the Sung Dynasty." *Journal of Southeast Asian History* 7: 1–10.

Chen Gaohua 陳高華. 1980. "Yindu Maba'er wangzi Bohali laihua xinkao 印度馬八爾王子孛哈里來華新考 [New Examination of the Arrival in China of the Prince Bohali (from the) India (Polity) of Ma'bar]." *Nankai xuebao* 南开學報 4: 70–73.

Dirks, Nicholas B. 1979. "The Structure and Meaning of Political Relations in a South Indian Little Kingdom." *Contributions to Indian Sociology* 13: 169–206.

Elliot, Henry M. 1953. *The History of India, as Told by Its Own Historians: The Muhammadan Period*. Ed. John Dowson. 2nd ed. Calcutta: Susil Gupta.

Endicott-West, Elizabeth. 1994. "The Yüan Government and Society." In *The Cambridge History of China*. Vol. 6. *Alien Regimes and Border States, 907–1368*, ed. Herbert Franke and Denis C. Twitchett, 587–615. Cambridge: Cambridge University Press.

Fukami Sumio 深見純生. 2004. "Gendai no marakka kaikyō: Tsūro ka kyoten ka 元代のマラッカ海峡: 通路か拠点か [Passage or Emporium? The Malacca Straits during the Yuan Period]." *Southeast Asia: History and Culture* 33: 100–17.

Ibn Baṭṭūṭa. 1994. *The Travels of Ibn Baṭṭūṭa: A.D. 1325–1354*, Vol. 4. Tr. C. F. Beckingham. London: Hakluyt Society.

Karashima Noboru 辛島昇. 1988. "Jūsan seiki matsu ni okeru minami indo to chūgoku no aida no kōryū: Senshū tamiru go kokubun to genshi mābāru den wo megutte 十三世紀末における南インドと中国の間の交流: 泉州タミル語刻文と元史馬八児伝をめぐって [Relations between South India and China at the End of the Thirteenth Century: Concerning the Ch'üan-chou泉州 Tamil Inscription and the Description of Maʿbar in the *Yüan-shih* 元史馬八児伝]." In *Enoki hakushi shōju kinen tōyōshi ronsō* 榎博士頌寿記念東洋史論叢 [Studies in Asian History Dedicated to Prof. Dr. Kazuo Enoki on his Seventieth Birthday], Enoki hakushi shōju kinen tōyōshi ronsō hensan iinkai 榎博士頌寿記念東洋史論叢編纂委員会 [Editorial Committee of 'Studies in Asian History Dedicated to Prof. Dr. Kazuo Enoki on his Seventieth Birthday'], preface by Mori Masao 護雅夫, 77–104. Tokyo: Kyuko Shoin.

Kulke, H. 1993. *Kings and Cults: State Formation and Legitimation in India and Southeast Asia*. Delhi: Manohar Publishers.

Kuwabara Jitsuzō 桑原隲蔵. 1989. *Hojukō no jiseki* 蒲寿庚の事蹟 [On Pu Shougeng 蒲寿庚]. Tokyo: Heibonsha.

Li Bo李勃. 2004. "Yuandai Hainan 'Li bin wanhu fu,' shi zhi niandai kao 元代海南<黎兵 户府>始置年代考 [A Study on the Beginning of Establishment of Li Army Wanhufu]." *Minzu yanjiu* 民族研究 2: 56–62.

Liu Yingsheng 刘迎胜 1990. "Cong 'Bu'ali shendao beiming' kan Nanyindu yu Yuan chao ji Bosiwan de jiaotong 从<不阿里神道碑銘>看南印度与元朝及波斯灣的交通 [Exchanges between South India, the Yuan Dynasty and the Persian Gulf as Seen from the Spirit-Way Stele of Abu Ali]." *Lishi dili* 歷史地理 7: 90–95.

Lo Jung-pang. 2012. *China as a Sea Power, 1127–1368: A Preliminary Survey of the Maritime Expansion and Naval Exploits of the Chinese People during the Southern Song and Yuan Periods*. Ed. and annotated Bruce A. Elleman. Singapore: NUS Press.

Mukai Masaki 向正樹. 2008. "Kubirai chō shoki nankai shōyu no jitsuzō: senshū ni okeru gunji kōeki shūdan to konekushon クビライ朝初期南海招諭の実像: 泉州における軍事・交易集団とコネクション [Another Aspect of the Legation to the Southern Seas during the Early Part of Qubilai's Reign: Military and Trade Groups and Their Connections]." *Tohogaku* 東方学 116: 127–45.

———. 2013. "Mongoru shī pawā no kōzō to hensen: Zensen soshiki kara mita genchō ki no taigai kankei モンゴル・シーパワーの構造と変遷: 前線組織からみた元朝期の対外関係 [The Structure and Transition of Mongol Sea Power: The Foreign Relation of China during the Yuan Period as Seen from the Organization at the Frontier]." In *Gurōbaru hisutorī to teikoku* グローバルヒストリーと帝国 [Global History and Empire], ed. Akita Shigeru 秋田茂 and Momoki Shiro 桃木至朗, 71–106. Osaka: Osaka University Press.

Maspero, Georges. 1928. *Le royaume de Champa*. Paris: Librairie nationale d'art et d'histoire.

Meng Yuanlao 孟元老 et al. 1956. *Dongjing meng hua lu, wai sizhong* 東京夢華錄 (外四種) [Records of a Dream of Past Splendors of the Eastern Capital, and Four Extra Texts]. Shanghai: Shanghai gudian wenxuan chubanshe.

Odoric of Pordenone. 1913. *Cathay and the Way Thither*. Vol. 2. *Odoric of Pordenone*. Tr. Henry Yule and Henri Cordier. Cambridge: Hakluyt Society.

Polo, Marco. 2004. *Le devisement du monde: Le livre des merveilles*. Tr. Louis Hambis. Paris: La Découverte.

Prange, Sebastian R. 2018. *Monsoon Islam: Trade and Faith on the Medieval Malabar Coast*. Cambridge: Cambridge University Press.

Ptak, Roderich. 1993. "Yuan and Early Ming Notices on the Kayal Area in South India." *Bulletin de l'École française d'Extrême-Orient* 80: 137–56.

Rockhill, W.W. 1914. "Notes on the Relation and Trade of China with the Eastern Archipelago and the Coast of the Indian Ocean during the Fourteenth Century Part I." *T'oung Pao* 15: 419–47.

Rossabi, Morris. 1988. *Khubilai Khan: His Life and Times*. Berkeley: University of California Press.

Sastri, K.A. Nilakanta. 2005. *A History of South India: From Prehistoric Times to the Fall of Vijayanagar.* New Delhi: Oxford University Press.

Sen, Tansen. 2006. "The Yuan Khanate and India: Cross-Cultural Diplomacy in the Thirteenth and Fourteenth Centuries." *Asia Major* 19: 299–326.

So, Billy K.L. 2000. *Prosperity, Region, and Institutions in Maritime China: The South Fukien Pattern, 946–1368*. Cambridge, MA: Harvard University Press.

Song Lian 宋濂. 1976. *Yuanshi* 元史 [The Official History of the Yuan]. 15 vols. Beijing: Zhonghua shuju.

Stein, Burton. 1977. "The Segmentary State in South Indian History." In *Realm and Region in Traditional India*, ed. R.G. Fox, 3–51. Durham, NC: Duke University Press.

———. 1984. *All the King's Mana: Papers on Medieval South Indian History.* Madras: New Era Publications.

Su Tianjue 蘇天爵. 1996. *Yuanchao mingchen shilüe* 元朝名臣事略 [Brief Sketches of Famous Yuan Officials]. Beijing: Zhonghua shuju.

Subramaniam, T.N. 1978. "A Tamil Colony in Medieval China." In *South Indian Studies,* ed. R. Nagaswamy, 1: 1–52. Madras: Society for Archaeological, Historical and Epigraphical Research.

Tan Dihua 譚棣華, Cao Tengfei 曹騰騑, Xian Jianmin 冼剣民, eds. 2001. *Guangdong beike ji* 広東碑刻集 [Compilation of Stone Inscriptions in Guangdong]. Guangzhou, China: Guangdong gaodeng jiaoyu chubanshe.

Tang Zhou 唐胄. 2006. *Zhengde Qiongtai zhi* 正徳瓊臺志 [Gazetteer of Qiongtai of the Zhengde period]. Collated by Peng Jingzhong 彭静中, ed. Yuan Dachuan 袁大川. Haikou, China: Hainan chubanshe.

Uematsu Tadashi 植松正. 1984. "Gensho no shazoku no hanran ni tsuite 元初の畲族の反乱について [On Rebellions of *She* people 畲族 in the Early Yuan Period]." In Gendai kōnan seiji shakai shi kenkyū 元代江南政治社会史研究 [Historical Study on Politics and Society in Jiangnan during the Yuan Period], ed. Uematsu Tadashi 植松正, 375–423. Tokyo: Kyuko Shoin.

Vogel, Hans U. 2012. *Marco Polo Was in China: New Evidence from Currencies, Salts, and Revenues*. Leiden: Brill.

Vu Hong Lien, and Peter Sharrock. 2014. *Descending Dragon, Rising Tiger: A History of Vietnam*. London: Reaktion Books.

Wang Xianjun 王献軍. 2003. "Yuan dai 'Li bing wanhu fu' sheli shijian kao 元代<黎兵万户府>設立時間 [A Textual Research into the Time When the

Wanhufu of Li Army Was Established].” *Journal of South-Central University for Nationalities* (Humanities and Social Sciences) 23: 104–6.

Xiang Zhengshu 向正樹 (Mukai Masaki). 2014. “Yang Tingbi pingkouji zai kao: Hubilie chao haishang shili de yi ge shili yanjiu 杨庭璧平寇記再考：忽必烈朝海上势力的一个事例研究 [Yang Tingbi Pin Kou Ji Reexamined: An Individual Research on the Sea Power in Khubilai Khan’s Times].” *Yuanshi Luncong* 元史論叢 14: 251–59.

Xing Menghuang 刑夢璜. 1983. “*Zhiyuan guise ping Li beiji* 至元癸巳平黎碑記.” In *Yashan zhi* 崖山志 [Local Gazetteer of Yashan], ed. Zhang Xi 張巂, Xing Dinglun 刑定綸, Zhao Yiqian 趙以謙, collated by Guo Moruo 郭沫若, 413–15. Guangzhou, China: Guangdong renmin chubanshe.

Yang Lien-sheng. 1968. “Historical Notes on the Chinese World Order.” In *The Chinese World Order: Traditional China’s Foreign Relations*, ed. John King Fairbank, 20–33. Cambridge, MA: Harvard University Press.

Yule, Henry, and Henri Cordier. 1920. *The Travels of Marco Polo: The Complete Yule-Cordier Edition*. 2 vols. New York: Dover Publications.

CHAPTER 5

Sayf al-Dīn Qipchaq al-Manṣūrī

Defection and Ethnicity between Mongols and Mamluks

AMIR MAZOR

A fourteenth-century Arabic author reports the following exchange between two Mamluk officers one night in 1298. As the Mamluk amir (commander) Sayf al-Dīn Qipchaq (d. 1310) was preparing for his fateful defection from his home in Mamluk Syria (1250–1517) to the enemy Mongol state, the Ilkhanate in Iran (1258–1335), another officer, who had been beseeching Qipchaq to change his plans, rebuked him with the following words:

> "Oh *Khawand* [Sir], are you going to defect to the land of the enemy [the Ilkhanate] after you made the *ḥajj* pilgrimage to the Sacred House of God [the Kaʿba in Mecca] and after you spent this [long] period of life in the lands of Islam [the Mamluk Sultanate], and after [you had here your son] amir ʿAlī?"
>
> And Qipchaq replied: "Oh Ḥājj (pilgrim),[1] I thought you were clever. Nothing would change my soul. As for my [belief in] Islam, I am a Muslim wherever I may be, even in [crusader] Cyprus; as for the Ḥajj [the pilgrimage], every year there are several times more pilgrims from the East [the Ilkhanate] than from your lands [Egypt and Syria]; As for [my son] amir ʿAlī, I can make [a son named] amir ʿAlī, amir Ibrāhīm or amir Khalīl . . . from any woman I spit on."
>
> Then, Qipchaq said: "Bring me something to eat." A wooden bowl of ragout (*yakhnī*) was placed in front of him. He took a piece of it, put it on the long-sleeve gown that he wore, and started to sing in Mongolian. Doing this, he [Qipchaq] wanted to show me that he already adopted the appearance of the Mongols and their lifestyle.[2]

This anecdote in the biographical collection of the contemporary Syrian historian al-Ṣafadī (d. 1363) reflects the amir Qipchaq's compromising position, stuck between two worlds. Spending his childhood and youth as a member of the Mongol elite of the Ilkhanate, Qipchaq was taken captive in 1277 and subsequently integrated into the military elite of the Mamluk Sultanate, the Ilkhanate's rivals. There, he would spend the next twenty some years, a formative period of his life.

Even if it is fictional, al-Ṣafadī's dramatic account of Qipchaq's departure serves to stress the officer's divided loyalties. Beseeching Qipchaq to remain in the sultanate, his fellow Mamluk officer argues, first, that his defection would amount to a desertion from, and the corruption of, his Muslim faith, since in the Ilkhanate, the Muslim amir Qipchaq would be surrounded by Mongol infidelity; and second, that Qipchaq would find the separation from his children unbearable. In response, however, Qipchaq reduces the differences between the two realms. One can be a faithful Muslim and start a new family in the Mongol Ilkhanate as well, he argues. Yet, we should wonder whether this religious, ideological and social gap between the two states was as meaningless in Qipchaq's mind as the anecdote's author suggests. By tracing Qipchaq's eventful career, the article explores the roles ethnicity, religious affiliation, and social-cultural solidarity, played across the Mongol-Mamluk frontier, especially in creating divided loyalties among Mongol commanders and defectors, on both sides of the border.

THE MAMLUK MILITARY SLAVERY SYSTEM AND THE MAMLUK SULTANATE

The mamluks were slave soldiers, mainly of Turkic and Central Asian origin, sold and brought from the northeastern boundaries of the Islamic world. The system had deep historical roots. Mamluk military slavery formed the backbone of the Muslim armies already at the start of the ninth century. This system continued largely unchanged until 1250, when a group of mamluk officers in Cairo who had formerly served the Ayyubid sultans (the descendants of Ṣalāḥ al-Dīn, 1171–1250) of Egypt assassinated their new master and overtook the throne. These military slaves became, for the first time in Islamic history, de facto and de jure Muslim rulers and established a thriving Mamluk state that would endure into the sixteenth century.

Through the following decade, and especially after defeating the Mongol forces in the Battle of ʿAyn Jālūt in Palestine (1260), the Mamluks succeeded in expanding their dominium, ruling over Greater Syria (al-Shām) in addition to Egypt. The Mamluk victory in northern Palestine also marked the beginning of more than half a century of incessant Mamluk-Ilkhanid military conflict, which only ended in 1323, when a peace treaty was finally signed.[3]

Despite the ongoing enmity, the military and political elites of the two polities had a lot in common with regard to both their Central Asian Steppe origin and their military techniques. Both armies were primarily based on mounted archers. During the first Mamluk period (1250–1382), most mamluks purchased for the sultanate originated in the Qipchaq Steppe, nowadays part of southern Russia and the Ukraine, and then ruled by the Golden Horde, another Mongol khanate that like the Mamluk Sultanate, was also the Ilkhanate's long-standing rival.

The supply of mamluk slaves to the sultanate's military forces was in fact dependent on the Mongols' military actions. Two earlier Mongol campaigns—the campaign in Central Asia in the 1220s and against the Qipchaqs (and Europe) in the late 1230s—led to the displacement of countless nomads and their migration westward, to the Qipchaq Steppe. Overrun by fresh waves of nomadic migrants and refugees, the Qipchaq Steppe became the main source of supply of military slaves for the Ayyubid sultans of Egypt and their heirs, the Mamluks.[4]

Turkic Qipchaqs were the prevalent group among the slaves sold and purchased in the sultanate. While the Mamluk elite was comprised of diverse ethnicities including Circassians, Georgians, Alans, Kurds, Turkmen, Armenian, Russians, and Mongols, the Qipchaqs were particularly dominant.[5] The young Central Asian slaves were usually brought and enlisted before puberty, and were not Muslims when they entered Mamluk service. After they were brought by the sultan or his amirs, they underwent a prolonged process of military training and acculturation including conversion to Islam. Once they finished their training, the mamluks were manumitted and joined the military ranks. Starting their military career as simple soldiers, the mamluks could advance to higher ranks such as that of an amir, a commander. Most often, however, only a mamluk who was brought and manumitted by the sultan himself would have the opportunity to advance to the highest ranks in the army. Were he to prove himself successful, both on the battlefield and through the political intrigue of the Mamluk elite, the mamluk could potentiality rise in rank to an amir of a hundred mamluks, or even advance to the throne of the sultan.[6]

The training period therefore could determine the future career and fate of the mamluk. During his training, he created his most important relationships developing kinlike relations with his owner and peers. His master (*ustādh*), the officer or sultan who had purchased him, raised, and finally manumitted him—became a father figure to the young mamluk. He would view his fellow mamluks (*khushdāsh*s), all owned by the same master, as his new siblings, and would cultivate with them a relationship of companionship, mutual support, and fraternal-like devotion and loyalty.[7]

FROM THE ILKHANATE TO THE SULTANATE: THE EARLY LIFE OF QIPCHAQ

Qipchaq's career was atypical for the average Mamluk officer. Unlike his peers, he was not brought as a child to the sultanate by slave traders. Instead, he was taken captive by the Mamluk forces in 1277 during the Battle of Abulustayn (Elbistan, in modern South Turkey), one of the major military clashes between the two polities. At this stage, he was a young adult, probably in his early twenties.[8] The recruitment of Mongol captives to the Mamluk military was not uncommon for the sultanate. Apart from Qipchaq, several other Mongol captives were enlisted into the Mamluk ranks and cultivated successful careers as Mamluk officers (see below).

Qipchaq's case was distinct from that of other mamluks in that, he came from an educated Mongol family of high-level scribes, who later served at the court of the Ilkhan Ghazan (r. 1295–1304). Qipchaq himself too fulfilled the role of a scribe (*kātib*) for Ḥasan Taqu, a high-ranking Mongol *noyan* (noble commander) in the Ilkhanate. Mongol scribes were also members of the Ilkhanid guard, the *keshig,* and Qipchaq and his family took part in Mongol military activities. Qipchaq's father was one of the weapon bearers (*silāḥdāriyya*) of Ghazan, and his brother was a senior commander in the Mongol army. As a professional scribe, Qipchaq also had excellent Mongolian writing and speaking skills.[9]

Qipchaq's qualities—his battlefield training and experience, mastery of the Mongolian language and script, and membership in the Mongol elite—considerably raised the prisoner's value from the Mamluk standpoint. These explain his exceptionally fast rise in Mamluk ranks. Immediately after being taken captive, Qipchaq was purchased by the future Mamluk sultan Qalāwūn (r. 1279–90). At the time of captivity (in

1277), Qalāwūn was a senior amir. Yet, two and a half years later, in 1279, when Qalāwūn succeeded the throne, he promoted Qipchaq to the position of commander.[10]

Qipchaq's meteoric rise through Mamluk ranks might have been an exception. Yet, the employment of noble and skilled captives within the military or administration of the sultanate was not uncommon. The Mongols, too, heavily relied on skilled prisoners in both their military and administrative apparatuses. During this period, therefore, captivity could unexpectedly end up on a positive note. Valued for talent and knowledge, captives might have a better chance for social mobility than in their home societies.[11]

Qipchaq's success hinged on his integration into his new environment. The Mongol emir cultivated close ties with other members of the Mamluk military elite, especially with his *khushdāsh*s, i.e. the mamluks of his master, the Sultan Qalāwūn. Qipchaq established a significant bond with his *khushdāsh* and brother-in-arms, the amir Ḥusām al-Dīn Lājīn (Turkish: Lachin). The two concluded a "brotherhood" pact (*ukhūwwa*) already during the reign of their master Qalāwūn.[12] The pact between Qipchaq and Lājīn soon turned out to Qipchaq's advantage. After Sultan Qalāwūn's death, Lājīn was appointed as the viceroy of Sultan Kitbughā (Turkish: Kedbuqa, r. 1294–96), and his appointment also promoted Qipchaq's standing. Qipchaq, moreover, appears to have prized the bond he had formed with Lājīn (based on Mamluk principles) more than any other tie of loyalty. Qipchaq was not on good terms with Sultan Kitbughā, even though the latter was both his *khushdāsh* and a Mongol. The enmity between the two Mongol mamluks was mutual. During Kitbughā's reign, the sultan's confidants plotted against Qipchaq and the Circassian commander Lājīn, while the two "brothers" also collaborated to depose Kitbughā and enthrone Lājīn.[13]

Lājīn's coronation as sultan (r. 1296–99) marked the height of Qipchaq's career as well. At Qipchaq's request, Lājīn appointed him to the powerful position of governor of Damascus, the main district of Greater Syria. He held this post for two years.[14] Despite attempts to break up the pair, Qipchaq and the Sultan Lājīn adhered to their mutual oath of loyalty through most of the period.[15]

Other social relations too helped the Mongol captive put down roots. Qipchaq married his sister and daughter to senior Mamluk amirs.[16] He begot several sons who became emirs. His offspring, moreover, bore Arab-Muslim names, another indication of their assimilation. One of his sons was likely the above-mentioned ʿAlī, who in 1298, had already received the post of an amir. ʿUmar (d. 1336), another son, was appointed amir of forty (mamluks),[17] and Qipchaq's grandson ʿAbd Allāh (d. 1341) was an amir of ten.[18] In general, the Mamluk system was a "one generation nobility." This meant that the sons of the mamluks who, unlike their parents, did not receive the military training associated with being born and raised in the harsh conditions of the steppes, were not supposed to hold military positions. However, it was not uncommon for amirs' sons (*awlād al-nās*) to inherit their fathers' position, usually as low- to middle-rank commanders.[19] That Qipchaq's descendants became amirs is an indication of his powerful position in Mamluk politics. Qipchaq also expanded his network beyond military circles. He appears to have contacts with several distinguished local Muslim religious scholars (*ʿulamāʾ*) who later assisted him in his political affairs.[20] Further, he appears to have been appreciated by the residents of Damascus.[21]

That Qipchaq and other Mongols had succeeded in their careers as Mamluk officers was certainly due to their integration as individuals, either through military captivity or through the slave trade.[22] Mongols also arrived in the sultanate in large groups of defectors from the Ilkhanate due to domestic political struggles. The Mongol defectors, known as *Wāfidiyya* (New Arrivals), did not assimilate into Mamluk society as individual Mongols. Members of the *Wāfidiyya* did not occupy higher political appointments and their influence in the Mamluk political arena was limited.[23] This stands in contrast to the situation in the Mongol khanates, where large-scale defections, usually of commanders with their troops, were a significant channel of military mobility. The promise of successful assimilation and high rank seems to have made such defections to the Mongol side all the more common.[24]

An explanation for the divergent trajectories of the Mongols in the sultanate is found in the unique Mamluk system for cultivating a new generation of Mamluk officers. The Mongols who reached the sultanate in their youth underwent the regular Mamluk system of education, training, and socialization. Yet, Mongol defectors, who upon their defection were often already high-ranking officers in the Ilkhanate and sought refuge in the sultanate along with their families and troops, remained largely alien to Mamluk society and its distinctive social and political regime. Arriving in the sultanate as a young man, Qipchaq belonged to the former category of fully integrated mamluks of Mongol origin.

QIPCHAQ'S DEFECTION TO THE ILKHANATE

Qipchaq's quick rise in Mamluk ranks ended abruptly due to Sultan Lājīn's persecuting policies. A central component of the Mamluk political arena was the removal of the amirs of former sultans from key positions and their replacement with the new sultan's own loyal mamluks. Thus, the incoming sultan would often seek to replace his peers, who were loyal to his former master, with a new generation of mamluks whom he had manumitted himself. When he took the throne, Lājīn indeed imprisoned prominent amirs and removed others from their positions, filling their posts with his own loyal mamluks.

When Qipchaq discovered that, despite his close ties with Lājīn, the latter had been planning on removing him from his lucrative governorship position in Damascus and replacing him with one of Lājīn's personal mamluks, he combined forces with other amirs threatened by Lājīn's plans. The plotters included Qipchaq's brother-in-law Elbegi, the governor of Safed (in modern Israel), and Bektemür al-Silāḥdār, the newly appointed governor of Tripoli (in modern Lebanon). The three were planning, as a last resort, to defect together to the Ilkhanate.[25] Qipchaq first tried to avoid defection, obtaining from Lājīn an *amān* (guaranty of safety) for him and his comrades; however, soon he found himself with no funds and military support. As the army of Aleppo was heading to remove him, he decided to flee to the Ilkhanate.

In January 1299, Qipchaq left Homs and made his way to the Euphrates River, which marked the border between the sultanate and the Ilkhanate. Before crossing over, Qipchaq was informed of the death of Sultan Lājīn and his viceroy. Suspecting, however, that the information was fabricated to lure him to return, he continued nevertheless.[26] Ilkhanid and Mamluk sources are in agreement over Qipchaq's sense of remorse after leaving Syria. Defending Qipchaq's defection, they claim that he was driven by fear for his life.[27]

However, the Syrian author al-Ṣafadī, who was cited at the beginning of this chapter, seems to disagree. They were likely other factors as well facilitating Qipchaq's defection such as the prospects of reuniting with his Mongol family and gaining a lucrative position in the Ilkhanate.[28] Further, the Ilkhanid elite's embrace of Islam following Ghazan's conversion in 1295 might have formed an additional incentive. Although the Mamluk sources tend to doubt the sincerity of the Mongols' conversion to Islam, by the time of Qipchaq's defection, the Ilkhanate was certainly a Muslim-ruled state.[29]

"DOUBLE GAME": QIPCHAQ IN GHAZAN'S SERVICE (1299–1300)

Qipchaq received a warm welcome across the border. After Qipchaq and the amirs were brought before Ghazan in his residence in southern Iraq, celebrations were held for a couple of days. The Ilkhan granted Qipchaq the governorship of Hamadan (in western Iran) and its districts as a *iqṭāʿ* (fiefdom) and bestowed on him generous sums.[30] Furthermore, Ghazan married Qipchaq to his sister-in-law, thereby strengthening Qipchaq's position in the Ilkhanate.[31]

However, already a year after his defection, Qipchaq's loyalty to his new Mongol master was tested. Toward the end of 1299, Mongol forces made another attempt to penetrate Mamluk Syria. The battle between the two armies took place in Wādī al-Khaznadār, north of Homs (see fig. 5.1). This was the first time the Mongols defeated the Mamluks, and for a short while conquered Greater Syria (al-Shām). Qipchaq's role during the battle and the Mongol occupation of Syria reflected his divided loyalty and, moreover, his clear inclination toward the Mamluks.

Already at the battlefield, Qipchaq appeared to be playing a double game. After their initial success against the Mamluks, Ghazan wished to continue fighting to fully eliminate the Mamluk army. Qipchaq, however, claimed that the Mamluks had set a trap, pretending to flee only to ambush the charging forces.[32] Other Mamluk authors depict Qipchaq as enticing Ghazan to continue fighting in the early stages of the battle, when the Mamluks still had the upper hand, in the hope that the Ilkhanid forces would fall to Mamluk hands.[33] The contemporaneous Armenian historian Hayton (Hetʿum) too claims that prior to the battle Qipchaq had secretly corresponded with the Mamluks.[34] Yet, later, noncontemporaneous Mamluk sources blame Qipchaq for persuading Ghazan to attack Syria in the first place, perhaps in order to demonstrate his loyalty to the Ilkhan.[35] In either case, Qipchaq's loyalty during the battle seems to have been a major concern for the Mamluk authors seeking to assess his commitment to the sultanate.

Qipchaq's precarious position and ambivalent attitude toward his Mongol lords became even more acute during the short-lived Mongol occupation of Syria. After the Mamluk defeat, Ghazan appointed Qipchaq to his previous post as governor of Damascus, and his two Mamluk co-defectors as governors of the other main districts of Syria. Bektemür al-Silāḥdār was given Aleppo, and Elbegi was made governor of Safed and Tripoli. Ghazan, however, also appointed at their side

FIGURE 5.1. The Battle of Wādī al-Khaznadār, in Hayton's *Fleur des histoires de la terre d'Orient,* MS Nouvelle acquisition française 886, fol. 31v (1300–1325ad), BnF.

Mongol officials with whom they were to cooperate. The Mongol *noyan* Quṭlugh-Shāh, Ghazan's deputy, functioned as the supreme commander of Syria.[36] These appointments might indicate that the Ilkhan suspected the Mamluk defectors, but they can also be ascribed to the common Mongol policy of dual appointments in the most important posts—a form of "checks and balances."

Governor of Damascus once again, Qipchaq appears torn between demonstrating loyalty to the Mongols and the wish to ameliorate the suffering of the people of Damascus, some of whom still opposed the conquerors. Several accounts claim that he was secretly seeking to assist his former lords, the Mamluks. Qipchaq made efforts to convince the governor of the Damascus citadel, his Manṣūrī *khushdāsh* Sanjar Arjuwāsh, to surrender. Yet, the latter refused to hand over the citadel.[37] Qipchaq also strove to mitigate the suffering of and damages to the local population. For instance, he was quick to collect taxes for Quṭlugh-Shāh from the district's populace and then urged him to leave for Aleppo with his Mongol officers, leaving Qipchaq as sole governor. Indeed, the people of Damascus are said to have been relieved when Ghazan set out, leaving them in the hands of their old governor.[38]

Ilkhanid accounts further support Qipchaq's double game. The pro-Mongol historian Rashīd al-Dīn (d. 1318) claims that Qipchaq and his associates "forgot their commitment" to the Ilkhan. They spread rumors that brought the Mongol supreme general Mūlāy (Mulai), who had remained in Syria after Quṭlugh Shāh's departure, to retreat to the Ilkhanate as well.[39] Similarly, the Ilkhanid court historian Waṣṣāf blames "the opposition and hypocrisy of Qipchaq" for Ghazan's decision to leave Syria and return to the east.[40]

BACK TO THE SULTANATE

Mongol rule in Syria did not last long. Already in June 1300, the entire Mongol army had left the region and Syria returned to Mamluk hands. Qipchaq's own conduct during the short-lived Mongol occupation of Syria might too have contributed to the Mongol retreat, though his contribution to this result should not be overstated.[41] The stubborn resistance of the Manṣūrī amir Sanjar Arjuwāsh to the Mongol forces might have also contributed to the Mongol retreat. Smith and Morgan, however, argue that the environmental conditions in Syria, mainly the lack of sufficient pasture and water for the massive herds of the Mongol army, was the driving force behind the Mongol retreat.[42] Yet, Amitai disagrees arguing that Syria's pastures offered enough fodder for the Mongols' herds. He suggests that the Ilkhanid retreat was triggered by threats to Ilkhanid rule from other frontiers, and possibly faulty intelligence regarding the abilities of the defeated Mamluk army.[43]

After the Mongols' final withdrawal, Qipchaq and his two allies made their way to Cairo. Near Ramla, Palestine, Qipchaq met Baybars al-Jāshnakīr and Salār, the two amirs who had been handling state affairs for the recently enthroned, underage sultan. The two acted as the de facto rulers of the Mamluk Sultanate. Qipchaq begged for their forgiveness, claiming that he and his associates defected from fear of Lājīn and his viceroy. Although in general the Mamluks did not hesitate to severely punish any collaboration with the Mongol enemy, Qipchaq and his allies were forgiven.[44] Continuing to Cairo, Qipchaq and his comrades were officially pardoned and warmly welcomed also by the young sultan al-Nāṣir Muḥammad.[45]

From the Mongol vantage point, Qipchaq's return to the sultanate following his defection to the Ilkhanate was unique. Military defectors most often remained for the rest of their lives in their acquired homes. For instance, the above-mentioned Oirat *Wāfidiyya* remained loyal to the Mamluk Sultanate despite their lack of assimilation.[46]

IN THE FOLD OF THE MAMLUK SULTANATE AGAIN: QIPCHAQ'S LAST DECADE (1300–1310)

In 1300, upon his return to the sultanate, Qipchaq returned to his earlier career as a Mamluk commander. At his request, he was appointed the governor of Shawbak in Transjordan,[47] and in 1301–2, he participated in the expedition against the Bedouin of Upper Egypt.[48] His participation in an area so remote from Shawbak raises the possibility that by this point, he might have already been posted back in Egypt. His contribution to the expedition might have assisted his promotion to the governorship of Hama (west-central modern Syria), which appears to have taken about a year from the expedition.

Qipchaq's loyalty to the Mamluks, however, was tested once again in 1303, when Ghazan's troops returned to Syria. In April that year, Qipchaq participated, now as the governor of Hama, in the decisive battle against the Mongols in Marj al-Ṣuffar, just south of Damascus. During the battle, he commanded the Mamluk right wing, leading the army of Hama.[49] His performance had a crucial role in the Mamluk victory. He successfully drove the fleeing Mongol force away from the water sources, so that the Mongols had to spend the night without water for their men and horses, whereas the Mamluk forces drank their fill.[50] A year later, in 1304, Qipchaq, again heading the army of Hama, took part in the successful expedition against the Armenians of Cilicia (in South Turkey).[51] Qipchaq's military feats safeguarding the Mamluk frontiers left no doubt about where his loyalty lay.

In his final years, Qipchaq was involved in several political intrigues. As the governor of Hama, he collaborated with Qarāsunqur, governor of Aleppo, and Esentemür Kurjī, governor of Tripoli, against the reigning

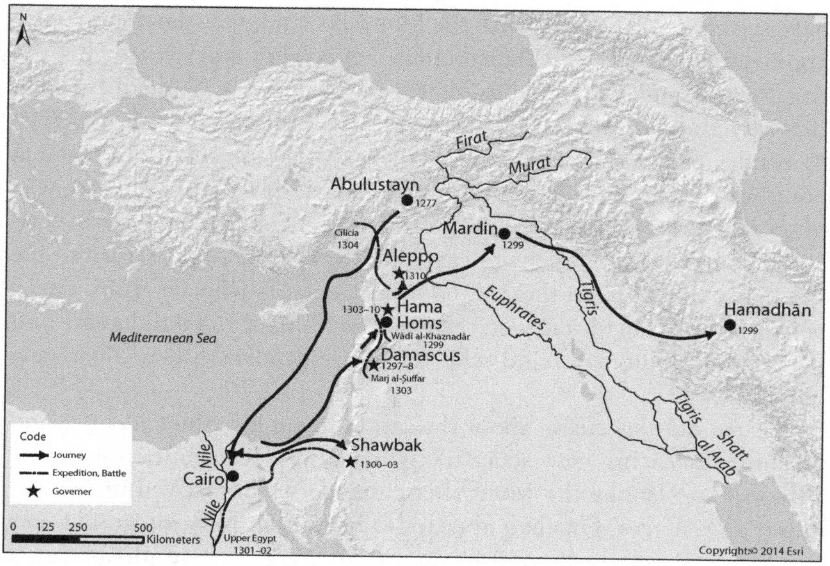

MAP 5.1. Charting the Career of Qipchaq al-Manṣūrī.

sultan Baybars al-Jāshnakīr (r. 1309–10) and in support of the deposed sultan al-Nāṣir Muḥammad b. Qalāwūn (third r. 1310–41). Here too, Qipchaq's political partisanship indicates the little importance that the Mongol officer attributed to his ethnic origins in the Mamluk political scene. The Mongol Qipchaq, the Georgian Esentemür, and the Circassian Qarāsunqur joined forces against the Circassian Sultan Baybars al-Jāshnakīr and his Mongol viceroy Salār.[52] One might see in Qipchaq's support of al-Nāṣir Muḥammad, the son of his former Mamluk master Qalāwūn, a further indication of his loyalty to the Mamluk institution and its legitimate representatives, that is, the house of his patron Qalāwūn. Due to his support of al-Nāṣir Muḥammad, Qipchaq was promoted and appointed governor of Aleppo, a post he held until he died in October 1310 (see map 5.1).[53]

CONCLUSION

Unlike the dialogue the Mamluk author al-Ṣafadī attributed to Qipchaq, with which this article started, Qipchaq appears to have preferred the sultanate over the Ilkhanate. His loyalty was first and foremost to the Mamluks. While in the service of the Ilkhan Ghazan, he seems to have secretly collaborated with the Mamluks, and once the opportunity appeared he returned to the sultanate. Qipchaq's story highlights the two forms of military mobility that were common in Mongol Eurasia: captivity and defection. In the Mongol case, captivity did not necessarily result in "social death"; on the contrary, it could serve as a starting point for the captive's new, glorious career. Military defection, too, was often rewarded in Mongol Eurasia due to the high demand for experienced commanders. Qipchaq's case, specifically due to his return to the sultanate, differs from that of the other generals who defected, either between the Mongol states or between the Mongol-ruled Ilkhanate and the Mamluk Sultanate, and who mostly remained loyal to their new homes.

We can only speculate about the causes, from his ethnic identity and kinship ties to his new social networks, that determined Qipchaq's choices here. Unlike the Mongol commanders who arrived in the sultanate as refugees, Qipchaq appears to have been fully integrated into the Mamluk system despite having been taken captive already as a (young) adult. Although he started his training path at a relatively advanced age, the Mongol mamluk created significant bonds within the Mamluk socio-political elite and more broadly, with other members of Egyptian and Syrian society. While his Mongol identity determined his value for his new Mamluk owners, his Mongol ethnicity seems to have played a minor role, if at all, in his political maneuvering in the sultanate. On the other hand, when he deserted to the Ilkhanate, his Mongol identity and family ties had a significant role in his accommodation. His desertion back to the sultanate suggests that his integration into Mamluk society through socialization and marriage relationships ultimately outweighed his earlier, ethnic and kinship-based ties to the Ilkhanate.

NOTES

1. The title given to an individual who performed the Ḥajj to Mecca.

2. Al-Ṣafadī 1998, 4: 67.

3. On the Mamluk-Ilkhanid struggle and confrontations between 1260–81: Amitai-Preiss 1995. For the later period: Mazor 2015, 113–28.

4. Ayalon 1963; Irwin 1986, 17–18; Allsen 2015, 138–39.

5. Mazor 2015, 36–40.

6. Ayalon 1951a, esp. 5, 9, 25; Ayalon 1953, 467–69; Ayalon 1994, 10–13. An amir of a hundred was a senior military office among the Mamluks (as opposed to a commander of a hundred among the Mongols). He commanded more than a hundred mamluks.

7. Ayalon 1951a, 27–30; Ayalon 1994, 14.
8. Baybars al-Manṣūrī 1998, 155; Ibn Ḥajar 1966, 3:325. Qipchaq died a natural death in 1310. Al-Ṣafadī 1998, 4: 62.
9. Little 1979, 392; Haarmann 1988, 101; Ibn Ḥajar 1966, 3: 326; Amitai 2008, 123–24; al-Ṣafadī 1998, 4: 62; al-Ṣafadī 2009, 24: 178. On Qibjaq's father and brother: Zettersteén 1919, 50.
10. Baybars al-Manṣūrī 1998, 155; al-Maqrīzī 1934–73, 1: 671.
11. Biran 2015, 34–36.
12. Mazor 2015, 175–80, 193–94.
13. Ibn Ḥajar 1966, 3: 326; al-Ṣafadī 1998, 4: 64; al-Ṣafadī 2009, 24: 180.
14. Ibn Taghrī Birdī 1939, 8: 67; al-Ṣafadī 1998, 4: 64; al-Ṣafadī 2009, 24: 180.
15. Al-Ṣafadī 1998, 4:64–65; al-Ṣafadī 2009, 24: 180.
16. Ibn Taghrī Birdī 1939, 8: 204; al-Ṣafadī 1998, 4: 154, 480.
17. Al-Jazarī 1998, 3: 920.
18. Mazor 2015, 286.
19. For *awlād al-nās:* Mazor 2015, 21 n. 16, 187–89.
20. Al-Ṣafadī 1998, 4: 70; 154–55.
21. Ibn Kathīr 1993, 14: 3.
22. There were even sultans and viceroys among these Mongol mamluks, for example, Kitbughā and Salār. Viceroy of the sultanate (1299–1309), Salār was taken captive together with Qipchaq at the battle of Abulustayn (Amitai-2008, 123; Mazor 2015, 249). The Sultan Kitbughā (r. 1294–96) (Amitai 2008, 122–23; Mazor 2015, 241) was taken captive at the Battle of ʿAyn Jālūt in 1260, along with Baydarā, who was appointed viceroy (1290–93) (Mazor 2015, 240), and Bahādur Ḥājj (Mazor 2015, 250–51), who became the chief *ḥājib* (chamberlain). For other Mongols who reached the Sultanate at a young age and became senior amirs: Amitai 2008, 124–26.
23. Ayalon 1951b, esp. 102–3; Amitai 2008, esp. 127–9; Landa 2016. Cf. Nobutaka 2006.
24. Allsen 2015, 127–29, 135.
25. Al-Nuwayrī 1992, 31: 351–52; Ibn Kathīr 1993, 14: 3.
26. Zettersteén 1919, 48–49; al-Maqrīzī 1934–73, 1: 855; al-Nuwayrī 1992, 31: 354–56; al-Yūnīnī 1998, 2: 53–55 (tr. Guo, 1: 110–12); Rashīd al-Dīn 1999, 3: 643.
27. Baybars al-Manṣūrī 1998, 329; Rashīd al-Dīn 1999, 3: 643.
28. On Qipchaq's s joy over meeting his relatives: al-Maqrīzī 1934–73, 1: 871.
29. Boyle 1968, 392, 402; Amitai-Preiss, 1996; Broadbridge 2008, 66–70, 94–95; Morgan 2007, 141–42; Amitai 2013, 75–80.
30. Al-Maqrīzī 1934–73, 1: 871; Ibn Taghrī Birdī 1939, 8: 97–98.
31. Baybars al-Manṣūrī 1998, 318. Qipchaq was married to a sister of Bulughan Khatun, Ghazan's favorite wife.
32. Ibn Ḥajar 1966, 3: 326–27; al-Ṣafadī 1998, 4: 69.
33. Al-Nuwayrī 1998, 31: 385.
34. Amitai 2004, 25.
35. Ibn al-Furāt 1939, 8: 94–95; Little 1970, 93; Amitai 2008, 133.

36. Al-Maqrīzī 1934–73, 1: 894; Baybars al-Manṣūrī 1998, 340–44; Broadbridge 2008, 78–79; Mazor 2015, 114–17.

37. Ibn Kathīr 1993, 14: 9; Baybars al-Manṣūrī 1998, 332–33; Zetterstéen 1919, 64–65; Ibn Taghrī Birdī 1939, 8: 125; al-Yūnīnī 1998, 2: 105–6, 125–26 (tr. Guo, 1: 142–43; 164–65); Amitai 2004, 32–36. According to one report, Qipchaq even tried to deceive the Mongols and defend the Muslims by secretly collaborating with Arjuwāsh: Ibn Ḥajar 1966, 3: 327; Baybars al-Manṣūrī 1987, 158; al-Ṣafadī 1998, 4: 69, 2: 466; al-Ṣafadī 2009, 24: 183.

38. Al-Maqrīzī 1934–73, 1: 895–96, 899; Ibn Ḥajar 1966, 3: 327; Amitai 2004, 37–38.

39. Rashīd al-Dīn 1999, 3: 647.

40. Waṣṣāf 2009, 2.

41. Baybars al-Manṣūrī implies that Qipchaq paid Quṭlugh Shāh a large sum of money for him to retreat. Baybars al-Manṣūrī 1998, 345.

42. Smith 1984, esp. 329–31, 344; Morgan 1985, 233–34.

43. Amitai 2013, 32–35; also: Boyle 1968, 388.

44. "Extenuating circumstances" seem to have played in Qipchaq's favor and his defection was not perceived as betrayal. For instance: al-Yūnīnī 1998, 2: 129; Amitai-Preiss 1995, 45–46.

45. Ibn Taghrī Birdī 1939, 8: 129–30; Ibn Ḥajar 1966, 3: 327; Baybars al-Manṣūrī 1998, 345; al-Ṣafadī 1998, 4: 70; Amitai 2004, 40.

46. See note 23, above.

47. Al-Maqrīzī 1934–73, 1: 902; Ibn Ḥajar 1966, 3: 327.

48. Al-Maqrīzī 1934–73, 1: 920–22; Mazor 2015, 133–34.

49. Baybars al-Manṣūrī 1998, 376; al-Nuwayrī 1998, 32: 29.

50. Ibn Ḥajar 1966, 3: 327; al-Ṣafadī 1998, 4: 70–71.

51. Al-Nuwayrī 1998, 32: 75–76; Stewart 2001, 159–63.

52. On this conflict: Mazor 2015, 134–35, 138–39, 170, 190.

53. Al-Maqrīzī 1934–73, 2: 75; Ibn Ḥajar 1966, 3: 327; al-Ṣafadī 1998, 4: 62, 72; al-Nuwayrī 1998, 32: 157.

BIBLIOGRAPHY

Allsen, Thomas T. 2015. "Population Movements in Mongol Eurasia." In *Nomads as Agents of Cultural Change*, ed. Reuven Amitai and Michal Biran, 119–51. Honolulu: University of Hawai'i Press.

Amitai-Preiss, Reuven. 1995. *Mongols and Mamluks: The Mamluk-Īlkhānid War, 1260–1281. Cambridge:* Cambridge University Press.

———. 1996. "Ghazan, Islam and Mongol Tradition: A View from the Mamlūk Sultanate." *Bulletin of the School of Oriental and African Studies* 59: 1–10.

Amitai, Reuven. 2004. "The Mongol Occupation of Damascus in 1300: A Study of Mamluk Loyalties." In *The Mamluks in Egyptian and Syrian Politics and Society*, ed. Amalia Levanoni and Michael Winter, 21–41. Leiden: Brill.

———. 2008. "Mamluks of Mongol Origin and Their Role in Early Mamluk Political Life." *Mamluk Studies Review* 12: 119–37.

———. 2013. *Holy War and Rapprochement: Studies in the Relations between the Mamluk Sultanate and the Mongol Īlkhānate (1260–1335)*. Turnhout: Brepols.

Ayalon, David. 1951a. *L'esclavage du Mamelouk*. Jerusalem: Israel Oriental Society. Reprint 1979, *The Mamlūk Military Society*. London: Variorum Reprints.

———. 1951b. "The *Wāfidiyya* in the Mamluk Kingdom." *Islamic Culture* 25: 89–104. Reprint 1977, in *Studies on the Mamlūks of Egypt (1250–1517)*. London: Variorum Reprints.

———. 1953. "Studies on the Structure of the Mamluk Army II." *Bulletin of the School of Oriental and African Studies* 15: 448–76. Reprinted 1977, in *Studies on the Mamlūks of Egypt (1250–1517)*. London: Variorum Reprints.

———. 1963. "*The European Asiatic Steppe*. A Major Reservoir of Power for the Islamic World." *Proceedings of the 25th International Congress of Orientalists—Moscow 1960*, 2: 47–52. Reprinted 1979, in *The Mamlūk Military Society*. London: Variorum Reprints.

———. 1994. "Mamluk: Military Slavery in Egypt and Syria." In *Islam and the Abode of War*. 1–19. Aldershot: Variorum, 1994.

Baybars al-Manṣūrī, Rukn al-Dīn. 1987. *Kitāb al-tuḥfa al-mulūkiyya fī al-dawla al-turkiyya*. Ed. ʿAbd al-Ḥamīd Ṣāliḥ Ḥamdān. Cairo: Al-Dār al-miṣriyya al-lubnāniyya.

———. 1998. *Zubdat al-fikra fī taʾrīkh al-hijra*. Ed. D.S. Richards. Beirut: Al-Kitāb al-ʿarabī.

Biran, Michal. 2009. "Central Asia from the Conquest of Chinggis Khan to the Rise of Tamerlane: The Ögödeied and Chaghadaid Realms." In *The Cambridge History of Inner Asia: The Chinggisid Age*, ed. Peter B. Golden, Nicola Di Cosmo, and Allan Frank, 46–66. Cambridge: Cambridge University Press.

———. 2015. "Encounters among Enemies: Preliminary Remarks on Captives in Mongol Eurasia." *Archivun Eurasia Medii Aevi* 21: 27–42.

Boyle, John A. 1968. "Dynastic and Political History of the Īl-Khāns." In *The Cambridge History of Iran*. Vol. 5. *The Saljuq and Mongol Periods*, ed. John A. Boyle, 303–421. Cambridge: Cambridge University Press.

Broadbridge, Anne F. 2008. *Kingship and Ideology in Islamic and Mongol Worlds*. Cambridge: Cambridge University Press.

Haarmann, Ulrich. 1988. "Arabic in Speech, Turkish in Lineage: Mamluks and Their Sons in the Intellectual Life of Fourteenth-Century Egypt and Syria." *Journal of Semitic Studies* 33: 81–114.

Ibn al-Furāt. 1939. *Taʾrīkh al-duwal wa'l-mulūk*. Vol. 8. Ed. Qonstantin Zurayk and N. ʿIzz al-Dīn. Beirut: American Press.

Ibn Ḥajar al-ʿAsqalānī, Aḥmad b. ʿAlī. 1966. *Al-Durar al-kāmina fī aʿyān al-miʾa al-thāmina*. Ed. Muḥammad Sayyid Jād al-Ḥaqq. 5 vols. Cairo: Dār al-kutub al-ḥadītha.

Ibn al-Jazarī, Shams al-Dīn Muḥammad b. Muḥammad. 1998. *Ḥawādith al-zamān wa-anbāʾihi wa-wafayāt al-akābir wa'l-aʿyān min abnāʾihi*. Ed. ʿUmar ʿAbd al-Salām Tadmūrī. 3 vols. Beirut: al-Maktaba al-ʿaṣriyya.

Ibn Kathīr, Ismāʿīl b. ʿUmar. 1993. *Al-Bidāya wa'l-nihāya*. 14 vols. Beirut: Dār iḥyāʾ al-turāth al-ʿarabī.

Ibn Taghrī Birdī, Abū al-Maḥāsin Yūsuf. 1939. *Al-Nujūm al-zāhira fī mulūk Miṣr wa'l-Qāhira*. Vol. 8. Ed. Fahīm Muḥammad Shaltūt et al. Cairo: Dār al-kutub al-miṣriyya.

Irwin, Robert. 1986. *The Middle East in the Middle Ages: The Early Mamluk Sultanate, 1250–1382*. London: Croom Helm/Carbondale: Southern Illinois University Press.

Landa, Ishayahu. 2016. "Oirats in the Ilkhanate and the Mamluk Sultanate in the Thirteenth to the Early Fifteenth Centuries: Two Cases of Assimilation into the Muslim Environment." *Mamluk Studies Review* 19: 149–91.

Little, Donald P. 1970. *An Introduction to Mamluk Historiography: An Analysis of Arabic Annalistic and Biographical Sources for the Reign of an-Malik al-Nāṣir Muḥammad ibn Qalā'ūn*. Wiesbaden, Germany: Franz Steiner.

———. 1979. "Notes on Aitamiš, a Mongol Mamlūk." In *Die Islamische Welt zwischen Mittelalter und Neuzeit: Festschrift für Hans Robert Roemer zum 65. Geburtstag*, ed. Ulrich Haarmann and Peter Bachmann, 387–401. Beirut: Orient-Institut der Deutschen Morganlandischen Gesellschaft/Wiesbaden, Germany: Franz Steiner.

al-Maqrīzī, Taqī al-Dīn Aḥmad b. ʿAlī. 1934–73. *Kitāb al-sulūk li-maʿrifat duwal al-mulūk*. Ed. Muṣṭafā Ziyāda and Saʿīd ʿAbd al-Fattāḥ ʿĀshūr. 4 vols. Cairo: Lajnat al-taʾlīf wa'l-tarjama wa'l-nashr.

Mazor, Amir. 2015. *The Rise and Fall of a Muslim Regiment: the Manṣūriyya in the First Mamluk Sultanate, 678/1279–741/1341*. Mamluk Studies vol. 10. Göttingen: V & R Unipress.

Morgan, David. 1985. "The Mongols in Syria, 1260–1300." In *Crusade and Settlement: Papers Read at the First Conference of the Society for the Study of the Crusades and the Latin East and Presented to R. C. Smail*, ed. Peter W. Edbury, 231–35. Cardiff: University College Cardiff Press.

Nobutaka, Nakamachi. 2006. "*The Rank and Status* of Military Refugees in the Mamluk Army: A Reconsideration of the Wafidiyah." *Mamluk Studies Review* 10: 55–81.

al-Nuwayrī, Aḥmad b. ʿAbd al-Wahhāb Shihāb al-Dīn. 1992, 1998. *Nihāyat al-arab fī funūn al-adab*. Ed. Fahīm Muḥammad ʿAlawī Shaltūt. Vols. 31, 32. Cairo: Al-Muʾassasa al-miṣriyya al-ʿāmma lil-taʾlīf wal-tarjama wa'l-ṭibāʿa wa'l-nashr.

Rashīd al-Dīn Faḍlallāh al-Hamadānī. 1998–99. *Rashīduddin Fazlullah's Jamiʿu't-Tawarikh: a History of the Mongols*. Tr. Wheeler M. Thackston. 3 vols. Cambridge, MA: Harvard University, Department of Near Eastern Languages and Civilizations.

al-Ṣafadī, Khalīl b. Aybak. 1998. *Aʿyān al-ʿaṣr wa-aʿwān al-naṣr*. Ed. ʿAlī Abū Zayd et al. 6 vols. *Beirut: Dār al-fikr* al-muʿāṣir/Damascus: Dār al-fikr.

———. 2009. *Kitāb al-wāfī bil-wafayāt*. Vol. 24. Ed. Muḥammad ʿAdnān al-Bakhīt and Muṣṭafā al-Ḥiyārī. Beirut: Al-Maʿhad al-almānī li'l-abḥāth al-sharqiyya.

Smith, John Masson. 1984. "ʿAyn Jālūt: Mamlūk Success or Mongol Failure?" *Harvard Journal of Asiatic Studies* 44: 307–45.

Stewart, Angus Donal. 2001. *The Armenian Kingdom and the Mamluks: War and Diplomacy during the Reigns of Hetʿum II (1289–1307)*. Leiden: Brill.

Waṣṣāf Shīrāzī, ʿAbd Allāh ibn Faḍl Allāh Sharaf al-Dīn. 2009. *Tajziyāt al-amṣār wa-tajziyat al-aʿṣār (Taʾrīkh-i Waṣṣāf)*. Vol. 4. Ed. Riḍā Hajyān Nijad. Teheran: University of Teheran Press.

al-Yūnīnī, Quṭb al-Dīn Mūsā b. Muḥammad. 1998. *Early Mamluk Syrian Historiography: Al-Yūnīnī's Dhayl Mirʾat al-Zamān*. Ed. and tr. Li Guo. 2 vols. Leiden: Brill.

Zetterstéen, Karl Wilhelm, ed. 1919. *Beiträge zur Geschichte der Mamlukensultane in den Jahren 690–741 der Higra nach arabischen Handschriften*. Leiden: Brill.

CHAPTER 6

Tuqtuqa and His Descendants

Cross-Regional Mobility and Political Intrigue in the Mongol Yuan Army

VERED SHURANY

One of the major markers of, and the most significant changes to, the military system of China under the Mongols (1260–1368) was the rise to dominance of foreign, non-Han Chinese generals, often in a relatively short time span—within one to two generations. The families of military commanders who rose to the highest ranks of the Yuan military and administrative system included Mongols and non-Mongol foreigners. The latter, known in the Chinese Yuan sources as *semu*—non-Chinese and non-Mongol—generals,[1] were in most cases emigrants, often from Central Asia, who had joined and advanced within the Mongol military and administrative ranks. The recruitment of foreign *semu* generals into the Yuan military reflects a broader phenomenon of mobilization and incorporation of military personnel and the armies conquered by the Mongols throughout Eurasia. New guards manned by captives and immigrants were established throughout the Yuan period, to continue Mongol expansion and protect the conquered lands.[2]

From their contribution to the Yuan military campaigns in Central Asia during the second half of the thirteenth century, to their involvement in court intrigue and succession struggles just before the dynasty's collapse (1368), the Qipchaq general Tuqtuqa (1237–97) and his offspring are a case in point for the interregional and social mobility of *semu* generals in Mongol Eurasia. A second, no less significant aspect of the family's story is that its rise to power within the Yuan military system, and the family's growing entanglement within the Yuan political arena, further testify to the changes the Yuan military machine underwent. These entailed the shift in the focus of the Yuan generals from the empire's territorial expansion and the protection of its borders, to internal political power struggles.

The case of Tuqtuqa and his family is interlinked with the broader context of the thirteenth-century "Qipchaq moment" in Mongol Eurasia. From the relatively effective resistance of the Qipchaq mounted archers to the Mongol forces, through the waves of Qipchaq refugees fleeing the Mongol armies or captured and incorporated into the Mongol military, and finally to the flooding of the slave markets along the Steppes with Qipchaq captives and the corresponding rise in demand for Qipchaqs in the Mamluk military slave system—Qipchaqs could be found nearly everywhere in Mongol-dominated Eurasia, within the empire and further afield. Accordingly, references to Qipchaqs are scattered across a multitude of thirteenth- to fourteenth-century historical sources, in diverse languages including Chinese, Persian, Arabic, Latin, Russian, and more. Their dispersal throughout Eurasia was further linked to their flexible formation. Rather than one homogenous ethnic group, the Qipchaq were loosely organized in a supratribal political alliance which incorporated various heterogenous nomadic, mainly Turkic-speaking, tribes.[3]

Prior to the thirteenth century, the Qipchaq confederation was divided regionally, into distinct geographical units, each led by a different tribe. It spread from the Danube all the way across Eurasia to Siberia. Skilled horsemen and archers, the Qipchaqs were recruited and employed as mercenaries by local rulers and communities in Eastern Europe and Central Asia, mainly in Khwārazm (present-day Uzbekistan), Bulgaria, and Hungary, thus gaining considerable experience in the protection of Eurasian frontiers. Beginning with the Mongol conquests, the Qipchaqs became even further geographically dispersed. Surrendering to, or being captured by, the Mongols, they were also incorporated into the Mongol military system. In addition, Qipchaqs were also sold in large numbers to the Mamluk Sultanate of Egypt and Syria (1250–1517), becoming the dominant ethnic group within the Mamluk military system. Fleeing the Mongol armies, some Qipchaqs found refuge in Eastern and Southern Europe, notably in the Balkans, where they were integrated into the military and political elite.[4]

Already during Chinggis Khan's lifetime, the Mongols had gained firsthand experience of the Qipchaq's military might and battlefield expertise on several fronts of the empire's expansion: in Siberia in 1216; in Central Asia in the early 1220s; and during the Mongols' first skirmishes with the Russians in 1223. The Mongols, indeed, deemed the mounted archers of the *Dasht-i Qipchaq* (the Qipchaq Steppe), the region that extended from the Caspian and the Black Seas to the Danube River, a serious obstacle to their expansion. Their subjugation was one of the main reasons for launching the Mongol military campaign in Europe in 1237–41.[5]

Whereas earlier Mongol missions failed, the army that Ögödei Qa'an (r. 1229–41) sent westward in 1235–36, under the command of his nephew Batu (d. 1255),[6] overcame Qipchaq resistance, reaching as far as the gates of Wiener-Neustadt (south of Vienna). Following this Mongol campaign, large numbers of Qipchaqs fled toward Eastern Europe. In Hungary, they would continue to resist the Mongols until their final defeat in 1241, while others, who fled further west, to modern-day Romania and Bulgaria, would settle and establish their own offshoots there. In the Golden Horde, the Mongol state in Eastern Europe, the Qipchaqs became the leading military force. Qipchaq captives were also transferred to China along with other Eastern European troops (e.g., Russians) as the share in the booty of the future qa'an, Möngke (r. 1251–59).[7] Incorporating the skilled men into the Mongols' army facilitated Mongol success and expansion. The Mongols used the conquered population from East Asia to subdue Central and West Asia, and then mobilized troops from Western Asia including Qipchaq captives, to guard their new frontiers in the east.[8]

After fighting alongside Möngke, the Qipchaq forces were later dispatched to join the troops of Möngke's brother and heir, Qubilai Qa'an (r. 1260–94). The Qipchaqs became an essential part of the Yuan army and imperial guards. These elite guards were at the forefront of the Yuan military. They included the qa'an's personal guard (*keshig*) and the imperial palace guards (*suwei*).[9] There appears to have been a significant overlap between these elite military units. The *keshig* and palace guards were both employed as the qa'an's bodyguards and confidants, but when the need arose, were dispatched to the empire's frontiers.[10]

Ethnic groups that were conquered by the Mongols were assimilated into these different guard units. Each guard was named according to its largest ethnic group; for instance, the Qipchaq guard, the Eastern Qipchaqs (Qangli) guard,[11] Asud (Alan) guard,[12] and the Tangut guard.[13] However, the ethnic composition of these guard units was heterogenous. The Qipchaq captives that were initially at Möngke's disposal and later enlisted in Qubilai's army became the basis for the Yuan's Qipchaq guards. However, the Qipchaq units also included Qarluqs,[14] Qangli,

Alans (Asud), Mongols, and Chinese, all under a mostly Qipchaq command.[15]

The ascent of the *semu* generals within the Yuan military ranks was closely interlinked with the challenges Qubilai Qa'an was facing in consolidating his ascent to the throne. In 1260, after proclaiming himself qa'an (emperor of the Mongol Empire), Qubilai found his reign opposed by his brother, who launched attacks from Mongolia against Qubilai's forces. This uprising was further supported by princes of contending Chinggisid branches (the Chaghadaid and Ögödeid lines) who would later challenge themselves Qubilai's rule. To quell their resistance, Qubilai established a personal guard comprised of different ethnic groups, including Kitans, Jurchens, and Chinese.[16] Yet another internal front that Qubilai struggled with during the early 1260s was the rebellions orchestrated by Chinese commanders. Former allies of the Mongols, these commanders either sought to gain their own independence or deserted the Mongols to side with the Han Chinese dynasty of the Southern Song (1127–1279).[17]

Semu generals, and their foreign-based units, were a major asset for Qubilai in these struggles. Since Mongols were reluctant to fight against other Mongols, Qubilai employed the foreign *semu* units that were personally loyal to him against the Mongol resistance. Further the Chinese rebellions increased Qubilai's mistrust of the Han generals, which prompted him to employ his *semu* forces to subdue these rebellions, and moreover to establish additional *semu* guards. The qa'an stationed some of these personally loyal guards in the capital to secure his power. Tuqtuqa's Qipchaq lineage rose to dominance in the context of the consolidation of the new guards.

TUQTUQA'S FAMILY AND ITS RISE THROUGH THE YUAN RANKS

Tuqtuqa's father, Banducha, belonged to an early wave of Qipchaq surrenders, who had joined the Mongols following the western campaigns of the late 1230s. The transition into Mongol service was rapid. Soon after their surrender, possibly as early as in 1239, during the Mongol campaign against Magas,[18] Banducha and his men are found fighting alongside the Mongols. Returning with the Mongol army, Banducha and his troops were next assigned to Qubilai's command. In the early 1250s, Banducha escorted the future qa'an in his first military campaign against the Dali Kingdom (938–1253) accompanied by a small group of

Qipchaq soldiers, which according to the *Yuanshi* (History of the Yuan Dynasty), amounted to a hundred men alone. The subjugation of Dali (nowadays Yunnan, Southwest China) was a major step. From Yunnan, the Mongols were better situated to launch attacks against the Southern Song, and gained access to the continental trade routes of Southeast Asia.[19] Participating in the Dali campaign and later following Qubilai Qa'an during his expedition to the north, Banducha and his son Tuqtuqa showed exceptional skill on the battlefield and subsequently rose in the ladder of command in Qubilai's army.[20]

Banducha and his son were next recruited to Qubilai's imperial palace guards stationed in the capital. Guarding the palace when the border was pacified, they were in close proximity to the emperor. Furthermore, when Qubilai headed military campaigns, the loyal imperial palace guards remained at his side, fighting directly under his command. In the early years of his reign, Qubilai was faced with two active fronts of resistance. Engaged in the ongoing campaign against the Southern Song, Qubilai and his forces were applying war techniques and technologies, mainly navy and siege warfare, that the Mongol armies appropriated from the conquered sedentary subjects.[21]

Yet, on the northern frontier, where Qubilai's rule was challenged by Mongol princes from the steppes of Mongolia and Central Asia, the Yuan army employed nomadic warfare, mainly mounted archery. Trained to fight by shooting arrows from horseback and attack in waves, mounted archers were better equipped for combat in the open spaces of the Steppes, which were not encumbered by fortified cities. The expertise of Banducha and his offspring in nomadic warfare came into use on the northern front. There Banducha and Tuqtuqa accompanied Qubilai in his campaign against his brother, Ariq Böke (d. 1266), and earned the qa'an's esteem. Banducha succeeded to further reinforce his position by brokering marriage alliances with other members of the *semu* elite and with the Yuan imperial lineage itself. He became thereby an imperial son-in-law, a prestigious position in the Yuan elite.[22]

When Qubilai defeated his brother in 1264, he ordered Tuqtuqa, who had by then inherited his father's position in the imperial guard, to garrison the Yuan northern frontier.[23] Qubilai's victory over his brother, however, did not bring an end to his troubles on the northern frontier, where Qubilai was engaged in an extended conflict with Ögödei's rebellious grandson, Qaidu (r. 1271–1301). Further distinguishing himself, Tuqtuqa climbed up the military ranks. His training in nomadic warfare played an important role. It might have been his advice to Qubilai that convinced the qa'an that Qaidu's forces would only be defeated by the same methods of Steppe warfare that Qaidu's forces had employed.[24]

In the second half of the 1270s, Tuqtuqa and his men won several decisive battles there. In 1271, Qubilai sent several Chinggisid princes under the command of his son Nomoghan to fight against Qaidu. However, in 1276, these princes revolted, capturing Nomoghan. Tuqtuqa was dispatched to serve under the general Bayan of the Baarin (1236–95), who returned to the north after heading the conquest of the Song, and successfully led Yuan troops against them.[25] In 1279, along with his Qipchaq warriors, Tuqtuqa took part in the large expedition of the imperial army (*da jun*) against Möngke's son Shiregi (d. ca. 1280). Tuqtuqa and his men were subsequently personally rewarded by Qubilai with lands near the capital in north China and in Jiqing (modern-day Nanjing) in the south. Each Qipchaq household further received a stipend and annual supplies. Tuqtuqa's success in the north further facilitated the expansion of the units under his command. The qa'an ordered all Qipchaq men to register under Tuqtuqa, and the finest Qipchaq soldiers to join the imperial guards. Tuqtuqa, who was promoted to several military and civil posts,[26] was further awarded eight hundred men from the "newly-adhered-army" (*xinfujun*), formerly Southern Song troops.[27]

The stabilization of Qubilai's rule in the 1280s also saw the expansion and diversification of the military base and skills of Tuqtuqa's troops. His men now included further heterogeneous troops, with *semu* soldiers such as the Qangli now fighting alongside the Southern Chinese—known as *nanren*. Each group used different warfare techniques: the *semu* were mostly mounted archers and the Southern Chinese specialized in infantry and siege warfare. Moreover, Tuqtuqa and his household expanded their influence into the Mongolian units as well. In the Yuan army, it was common for commanders and officials to hold several posts simultaneously, as administrators and direct commanders of units and troops. For example, in 1285, Tuqtuqa was appointed assistant director of the Bureau of Military Affairs (*shumiyuan*). This bureau commanded all the military units in the Yuan domain, except for the *keshig*.[28] A year later, in 1286, Tuqtuqa was chosen to lead the newly established Qipchaq guard and manned its administration with Qipchaq men personally loyal to him. In the second half of the 1280s, Tuqtuqa also became the first commander of the new Qarluq Myriarch.[29] Tuqtuqa's meteoric ascent enabled him to reinforce this multiethnic unit with Qipchaq slaves and soldiers who had previously served under other commanders. Its *semu* commanders were of Qipchaq origin and were directly loyal to the emperor, who allegedly trusted them more than his own Mongol troops and commanders.[30]

Qubilai's choice to further rely on and expand his *semu* elite guards paid off during his 1287 campaign against the Mongol rebel prince Nayan,[31] when Qubilai's Mongol troops refused to attack their Mongol adversaries due to ethnic-based solidarity. According to the *Yuanshi,* the qa'an's Mongol forces "stopped their horses and started to speak in their native language, then they put down their weapons and did not fight."[32] According to Marco Polo, when he learned the news, Qubilai summoned his *semu* troops stationed in the capital to subdue Nayan.[33] Faced by the conflicted fealties of his Mongol troops, Qubilai's reliance on his *semu* guards would only increase thereof.[34]

After Tuqtuqa became the commander of the Qipchaq guard, he was ordered twice, in 1286–87 and 1288, to escort Temür Öljeitü, Qubilai's grandson and future heir (Chengzong, r. 1294–1307), to the northern frontier in campaigns against the remnants of Nayan's allies. A year later, in 1289, Tuqtuqa also joined Prince Gammala (1263–1302), another grandson of Qubilai, in a campaign to subjugate Qaidu. Ambushed and surrounded by Qaidu's troops, Gammala and his men were rescued by Tuqtuqa. Later, Tuqtuqa escorted Qubilai himself on an imperial inspection tour to the north. Awarded by Qubilai for his military achievements and the command of his troops, Tuqtuqa was praised, honored, and, just like his father, he was awarded a Chinggisid wife, Talun, Prince Yezhili's younger sister.[35]

In 1294, when Temür Öljeitü ascended the throne, he bestowed on Tuqtuqa gifts and honorary titles such as "Prince of Jurong."[36] This title was also passed to some of Tuqtuqa's descendants. Tuqtuqa returned to the northern frontier, where he died in 1297.[37]

TUQTUQA'S HEIRS

Tuqtuqa's most renowned son was Junqur (1260–1322), who continued his father's outstanding military career and was appointed commander in the Myriarch of the Eastern Wing Mongolian troop (*donglu menggujun wanhufu*). Established toward the end of the 1280s, the Myriarch of the Eastern Wing was another heterogeneous unit that incorporated, in addition to its Mongol members, *semu* groups such as Qipchaqs.[38] The multiethnic composition of these units enabled Qubilai to guarantee the personal loyalty of its men. Further, it helped maintain a balance inside the guard units, avoiding the excessive accumulation of power in the hands of one ethnic group or a single military commander. At the time of Tuqtuqa's death, the northern frontier was still not entirely pacified. Junqur followed in his father's path and led several campaigns with great success. In the early years of Temür Öljeitü's reign, he became general commander of the Left Imperial Army (*zuowei qinjun duzhihuishi*).[39]

Junqur also sought to subdue the rebellious members of the Baarin tribe, former allies of Chinggis Khan, who dwelled between the Yuan and the White Horde (located in present-day Siberia and Western Mongolia). Some of the Baarin cooperated with Qaidu. Breaching the Baarin's defenses, Junqur won several battles against them during the end of the 1290s. Subsequently, Emperor Temür Öljeitü appointed Junqur to commander of the Left Qipchaq guard (*qincha zuo qinjun duzhihuishi*), a post that his descendants would continue to hold after his death. Most of the successful Qipchaq generals, including Tuqtuqa's family, commanded the Left Qipchaq guard—the core of the Qipchaq forces and the main force behind their military success. Junqur also served as a junior assistant director of the Bureau of Military Affairs (*qianshumiyuanshi*), and moved up the ranks in the bureau, becoming part of the central administration. Yet, Junqur did not settle in the capital, choosing instead to continue to fight on the empire's frontiers.[40]

At the turn of the century, Junqur was joined by his son El-Temür (d. 1333) and the two successfully fought together in several campaigns (1299–1301) on the northwestern frontier against rebel princes. These campaigns were led by the eighteen-year-old future emperor, Qaishan (Wuzong, r. 1307–11).[41] Yuan princes were often sent on military campaigns on the empire's frontiers in order to gain valuable military experience and secure the army's loyalty.

Qaishan relied on the Qipchaq commanders' military skills and experience and regularly sought Junqur's advice. Junqur also took part in the Yuan final battle against Qaidu in 1301. While the Yuan army failed, Junqur was victorious in the battles he fought and was rewarded for his performance. Allegedly, it was his success that prompted Qaidu's former allies, Du'a (Chaghadaid Khan, r. 1282–1307) and Malik Temür (d. 1307, the son of Ariq Böke), to seek a peace agreement.[42] The peace was signed in 1304–5, and subsequently the Central Asian princes surrendered to Temür Qa'an.[43]

The conflict between the Yuan and their Ögödeid cousins outlasted the reigns of Qubilai, Temür, and Qaidu. It concluded only in 1310, with the final submission of Qaidu's heir to Qubilai's great-grandson Qaishan.[44] The Yuan retained the Ögödeid forces as border garrisons.

In the 1310s through the 1320s, the Yuan, supported by the Ögödeid remnants, succeeded in defeating the Chaghadaid Mongols of Central Asia, thereby ending the internal strife that had torn apart the Mongol Empire for more than half a century.[45]

The end of the inter-Mongol conflict also marked a major turn in the Qipchaq involvement in Yuan politics. Following the pacification of the frontiers, Junqur turned his attention away from military affairs to the internal Yuan political arena and began meddling in the Yuan succession struggles.[46]

THE ASCENT OF THE *SEMU*

Temür Qa'an's death in 1307, without a male heir, marked the beginning of a bitter succession struggle between the faction of Temür's cousin Ananda (d. 1307) and that of Temür Qa'an's nephews, Qaishan and Ayurbarwada (future Emperor Renzong, r. 1311–20). Junqur and his son El-Temür, along with the Qipchaq guard, supported Qaishan, at whose side they had fought on the northern frontier, together with several high-ranking members of the court.[47]

In April 1307, Ayurbarwada arrived at Dadu and with the support of the grand councilor of the right, Harghasun, took control of the court, arresting and executing prince Ananda and eliminating his supporters. Junqur and his Qipchaq soldiers then accompanied Qaishan to the capital, where he was enthroned. Ayurbarwada conceded to have Qaishan ascend the throne and was appointed as Qaishan's successor, with Qaishan's son guaranteed to be next in line. Junqur played a central role in Qaishan's accession, informing the prince of the political developments in the capital and urging him to return and assume the throne.[48]

After his enthronement, Qaishan generously rewarded his supporters and appointed several of his former fellow soldiers to key positions in the central civil and military administration.[49] Junqur, Qaishan's most trusted commander, was given in marriage a Chinggisid princess, Chaji'er, the daughter of the Toluid prince Yaqudu (d. 1310). Several of Junqur's daughters were also married off to members of the Chinggisid household.[50]

Junqur maintained his post as commander of the Qipchaq guard under both Qaishan and his heir Ayurbarwada. In 1314–15, Junqur led the Yuan army in a campaign against the Chaghadaid Khan Esen Buqa (r. 1310–18), reaching far beyond the Yuan borders, as far as Talas (present-day Shymkent, in Kazakhstan) in the heart of Central Asia, but ultimately failed to end the conflict.[51] During this time, the Qipchaq guard increased in size to the point that, in 1322, it was divided into two separate units: the Left and Right Qipchaq guards.[52]

After Ayurbarwada's death, his son, Shidebala (Yingzong, r. 1321–23), was enthroned through Junqur's active support. Yet, about two years later in 1323, Shidebala's rule was overthrown by the faction of his father's cousin, Yesün Temür (Taiding, r. 1323–28). By then, Junqur was already dead and his son and heir, El-Temür, was confronted by this new political situation.[53]

EL-TEMÜR AND THE FAMILY LEGACY

El-Temür entered the center stage of Yuan history first when he served under Qaishan in the imperial guard and was stationed for ten years on the northern frontier with his father. After Qaishan's enthronement, El-Temür too was appointed to high posts in Qaishan's service such as the associate director of the Palace Provisions Commission.[54] Unlike his forefathers, El-Temür lived at the court for most of his life and was therefore familiar with the dynasty's civil administration.

El-Temür did not play a significant part in the earlier succession struggles at the Yuan court. Yet, he filled a key role in the conflict that escalated into a bloody civil war after Yesün Temür's death in the Yuan summer capital Shangdu,[55] in 1328, leading to the restoration of Qaishan's house on the throne.

Under Yesün Temür, El-Temür and his family lost key positions, as reflected in El-Temür's appointment to a low-ranking post in the Bureau of Military Affairs.[56] Therefore, El-Temür apparently supported, though not immediately, the plan to orchestrate a coup d'état to restore Qaishan's lineage to the throne.[57] He was probably hoping to restore his family's glory and their extensive property.[58]

The 1328 succession struggle known as "the war of the two capitals" was led by *semu* generals, thereby attesting to the *semu*'s growing influence in Yuan politics. El-Temür led the Dadu faction,[59] who supported the candidacy of Qaishan's younger son, Tuq Temür (Wenzong, r. 1328–32), while the opposing Shangdu faction was headed by Dawlat Shāh (d. 1328), a high-ranking Muslim administrator. Together with other high officials and relatives of the royal family loyal to Yesün Temür, he aimed to enthrone the latter's son, Aragibag.[60] El-Temür chose Tuq Temür, Qaishan's younger son, who already had administrative and military experience in both North and South China.[61]

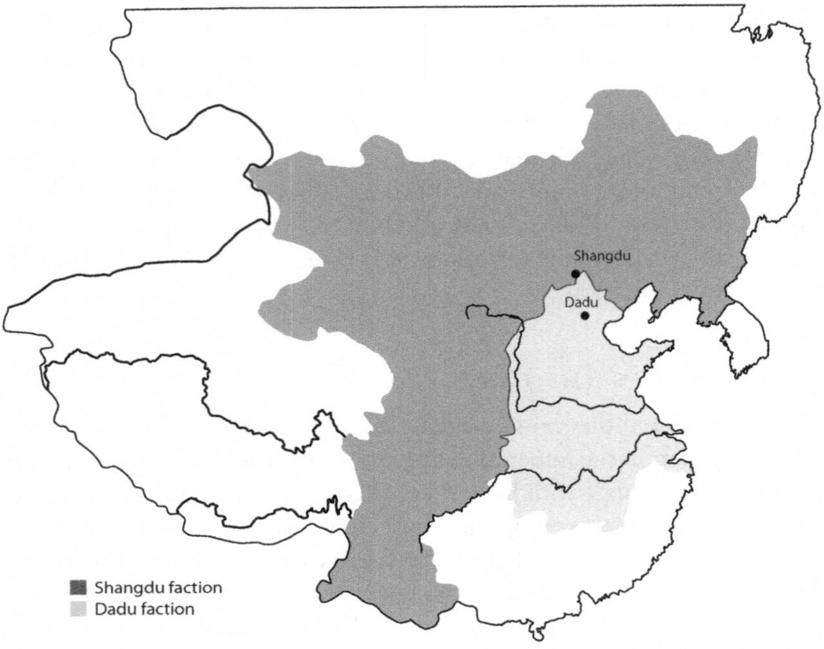

MAP 6.1. The War of the Two Capitals (1328): Territories under Dadu's and Shangdu's Factions (after Tan 1996, 3–4; Dardess 1973, 40; Hsiao, "Mid-Yuan" 1994, 544).

El-Temür's experience in planning military campaigns was instrumental in the coup as well. He had carefully planned his moves even prior to Yesün Temür's death. When the emperor died, away from Dadu, El-Temür managed to take over the capital and to seize control of the main bureaucratic posts and the city's administration, and to place co-conspirators in key positions.[62] El-Temür then ordered his loyal troops to guard strategic areas, while he acquired logistical equipment for the army, and provided food for the soldiers. In October 1328, El-Temür had Tuq Temür enthroned. El-Temür himself, with his brother Sadun (fl. early fourteenth century),[63] then suppressed the Shangdu faction. Dawlat Shāh, the leader of this faction, surrendered to Tuq Temür at the end of 1328, handing over the imperial seal. Dawlat Shāh's surrender ended the war of succession that was, in fact, a power struggle between two leading *semu* commanders, El-Temür and the Muslim Dawlat Shāh (see map 6.1).[64]

El-Temür's faction had the upper hand, not only because of El-Temür's capabilities, but mostly since they had the support of the more populated and richer regions, and therefore more resources and troops at their disposal.[65]

In 1328, El-Temür received the title "Prince of Taiping," which also included a fief in present-day Anhui. Sadun was also rewarded with important posts in the military and administrative system.[66] A year later, the new chief military commissioner post (*dadu dufu*) was established especially for El-Temür. In this post he commanded several elite guard units.[67]

Tuq Temür's reign saw the zenith of El-Temür's power. Not only was he the chief military commander, but he was also appointed the chancellor of the right, namely the equivalent of a prime minister, as well as a member of the Censorate.[68] Practically, El-Temür decided all court affairs, and his Qipchaq guards became the dynasty's most prominent military and political force, disproportionally exceeding all other ethnic groups in the army.[69] Like his forefathers, El-Temür also married into the royal family, and in addition, had his daughter marry the last Yuan emperor, Toghon-Temür (Shundi, r. 1333–70).[70]

El-Temür appears to have continued to meddle in Yuan succession politics. In 1329, Tuq Temür decided to hand his throne to his elder brother Qoshila. Shortly thereafter, however, Qoshila died suddenly, most likely poisoned by El-Temür, who wanted to maintain the key positions he gained under Tuq Temür. The throne was thus restored to Tuq Temür.[71]

At the height of El-Temür's power, Emperor Tuq Temür ordered to build a stone monument in the northern part of Shangdu, honoring El-Temür's support for Tuq Temür's succession. Tuq Temür further ordered a temple built for El-Temür, while the latter was still alive. Relics of El-Temür's temple were unearthed in an archeological excavation carried out at Shangdu in the late twentieth century, in an area near the sacrificial center of the Mongol elite.[72] Dedicated to El-Temür's Qipchaq ancestors, the temple inscribed the history of this foreign family in Yuan service into the city's local landscape (see fig. 6.1).

Toward the end of his life, El-Temür is reported to have conducted an extravagant lifestyle. He spent large sums of money and had many wives.[73] El-Temür died shortly after Tuq Temür's death in 1332, without having the opportunity to influence the succession of the next Yuan emperor.[74] His death also marked the family's downfall. Shortly after, in 1335, El-Temür's descendants were accused of conspiring against the last Yuan emperor, Toghon-Temür, and the family was entirely purged, even Toghon-Temür's wife, El-Temür's daughter, was killed.[75]

FIGURE 6.1. The Yangqun Miao area, the supposed location of El-Temür's ancestral temple, near Shangdu (after Wei 2008, 2: 269). Courtesy of Wei Jian.

CONCLUSION

The ascendancy of Tuqtuqa and his Qipchaq family highlights the composite nature of the Yuan army. Large numbers of its commanders were foreigners, born and bred thousands of miles away from China and Mongolia. Originating from the Western Steppe, transferred eastward during the Mongols' campaigns in eastern Europe, along with the dispersal of other Qipchaq captives and refugees throughout Eurasia, Qipchaq men became the cornerstone of Qubilai's army.

Like other *semu* groups in Yuan China, the Qipchaqs too benefited from Qubilai's mistrust of both the conquered Chinese soldiers and his Mongol troops. Whereas the Qipchaqs were less dominant in the conquest of Southern Song, their expertise in Steppe warfare made them invaluable to the qa'an's continuous attempts to pacify the Yuan northern and western frontiers. From the moment Qubilai Qa'an established the Qipchaq guard as part of the *semu* guards in 1286, the Qipchaqs became one of the emperor's most trusted and loyal units, protecting the palace and the royal family in addition to guarding the Yuan's frontiers. The Qipchaqs were handsomely rewarded for their services, thereby making service in the Qipchaq guard a desirable position. Their numbers in Yuan service kept rising along with the expansion of the *semu* military system. With the increasing enrollment of men in the Qipchaq unit, the unit was divided into two.

Members of Tuqtuqa's family married Chinggisid princesses, in addition to wives from the Mongol elite and of *semu* origin. This combination of marital ties and alliances enabled the family to gain a stronger footing in the Yuan elite. The imperial household also used the marriages to keep an eye on the *semu* family, guaranteeing its loyalty.

The mid to late Yuan succession struggles attest to the changes the dynasty and the agenda of the Qipchaq commanders both underwent. In 1307, Junqur supported the enthronement of Qaishan, a candidate who earned the family's loyalty when he fought alongside the Qipchaqs on the northern and Central Asian frontiers. Moreover, in the bloody succession war of 1328, El-Temür, who had held posts in the capital, chose to support the candidate (Tuq Temür), who was best acquainted with both the Steppe and the Chinese administration.

After he orchestrated Tuq Temür's enthronement, El-Temür held unprecedented power. Yet, after Tuq Temür's demise, the subsequent rise of Merkid Bayan, his rival official (and former ally), under the last Yuan emperor, led to the elimination of El-Temür's family, despite its history of loyalty to the dynasty.

The story of Tuqtuqa and his family demonstrates the growing power of *semu* generals in Yuan China and their transition from military service to civil administration and court politics. Junqur remained stationed at the Steppe and continued to campaign, almost until his death. Yet, when Mongol resistance on the frontier was suppressed and the prominence of frontier commanders was declining, his son El-Temür found the path of civilian service more lucrative. Although he became "kingmaker,"[76] and reached the highest posts in both the civil and military realms, El-Temür was nevertheless fully dependent on the emperor's favor. El-Temür's death sealed the fate of his family, and their fall from fortune was nearly as swift as their rise to power.

El-Temür and his ancestors' temple, built at the height of the family's power, encapsulates the family's journey. It registered the impressive career and meteoric rise of a family that had—just a century earlier—surrendered to the Mongols on the western parts of the Silk Roads, between the Ural and the Volga. It records the process of assimilation into Yuan Chinese society that the foreign Qipchaq family underwent, but also shows that they retained the memory of their distant origin. Thus, it speaks to the complex identities, the opportunities, and the limitations that were created through the establishment of the Yuan military system.

NOTES

This research was supported by the European Research Council under the European Union's Seventh Framework Programme (FP/2007–13)/ERC grant Agreement n. 312397 and the Confucius China studies program. I would like to thank the editors, notably my advisor Professor Michal Biran, and Amit Niv and Eduard Naiman, for their help with the map.

1. The status of the *semuren,* literally meaning "people of various kinds," was between that of the Mongols and the local Chinese: Hucker 1985, 404 (§ 4941); Atwood 2004, 494.

2. Allsen 2015, 137.

3. For more information about the structure of nomadic tribes: Lindner 1982, 689–711; Golden 1990, 280.

4. Baybars al-Manṣūrī 1998, 2–4; Rashīd al-Dīn 1999, 2: 513–14; Golden 1991, 133–34; Golden 2014, 183–84; Amitai-Preiss 1995, 18; Atwood 2004, 340, 455; Jackson 2005, 124; Vásáry 2005, 54–55, 166–67; Allsen 2015, 138–39; Brose 2017, 71–72.

5. Golden 1990, 280; Atwood 2004, 282–83, 455, 479, 521; Allsen 2015, 122; Brose 2017, 69, 71.

6. The mission was also led by the general Sübe'etei Ba'atur (1176–1248), and other princes including two future qa'ans, Güyük (r. 1246–48) and Möngke. Atwood 2004, 455.

7. The booty was for his role in the Western campaigns of 1235–41. For more on the campaigns and the Qipchaqs' fate: Song 1976, 2: 35, 3:43, 121: 2977; Juwaynī 1997, 553–54; Rashīd al-Dīn 1999, 2: 352; Atwood 2004, 455; Jackson 2005, 39–40, 63–67; Vásáry 2005, 62–65, 166–67; Allsen 2015, 138; Brose 2017, 72–73.

8. Allsen 1987, 7; Allsen 2015, 124.

9. Song 1976, 99: 2523–25; Hucker 1985, 330 (§ 3960), 461 (§ 5854).

10. Hsiao 1978, 34.

11. Atwood 2004, 455; Lee 2004, 218.

12. The Alans (known also as Asud or Ossetes) were Iranian nomadic people, originally from the steppe between the Black and Caspian Seas. Under Möngke, they were brought as prisoners to China. In 1272, Qubilai established the Asud Guard. This guard, like others, helped subdue Mongol rebellions, such as Nayan's rebellion in 1287, and fought in the coup d'état of 1323. Atwood 2004, 430.

13. The Tanguts were an Inner Asian people that established the Xi Xia dynasty (982–1227) which controlled today's northwest China, ruling over the Silk Roads to Central Asia. The Xi Xia was the target both of Chinggis Khan's first raids and of his last battle in 1227, where the Great Khan found his death. Following the Xi Xia's fall, Tangut fugitives found their way into the Mongol army and later into the Yuan realm. Dunnell, 1994, 154–214.

14. The Qarluqs were a Turkic people who in the twelfth century ruled southern Kazakhstan and north Xinjiang. In 1211, they submitted to Chinggis Khan and were incorporated into the Mongol army. Atwood 2004, 448–49.

15. Hsiao 1978, 44–47; Lee 2004, 266–67; Liu 2013, 169; Allsen 2015, 139.

16. The Kitans and Jurchens were nomadic tribal peoples living in North China who established the Liao (916–1125) and Jin (1115–1234) dynasties respectively. Lee 2004, 171, 198–200.

17. Most famously the rebellion of Li Tan in 1262: Atwood 2004, 335.

18. The capital of the Asud, currently the capital of the Republic of Ingushetia, Russia. Atwood 2004, 417.

19. See the contribution of Mukai and Fiaschetti in this volume.

20. Song 1976, 128:3131–32.

21. Hill 1973, 104–6; Allsen 1987, 7; Lo 2012, part 3.

22. The sons-in-law (men who married daughters of the Chinggisid lineage, *fuma* or *güregen*) of the Chinggisid line often took part in the military and political sphere, and held positions of power during Mongol rule. Song 1976, 128: 3131–32; Dardess 1973, 42–43; Landa 2016, 163, 168–69; Brose 2017, 72–73.

23. Su 1962, 3: 47; Song 1976, 128: 3132; Yu 2004, 27: 230; Dardess 1973, 42–43; Tu 2012, 102: 641.

24. Rossabi 1988, 77; Biran 1997, 1, 90–91.

25. Song 1976, 117: 2908, 128: 3132; Yu 2004, 27: 230–31; Hsiao 1993, 597–98; Biran 1997, 1, 37–40; Brose 2017, 75.

26. E.g., Marshal of the Second Class. For other appointments: Song 1976, 128: 3132.

27. Song 1976, 128: 3132–33; Yu 2004, 27: 230; Dardess 1973, 43; Hsiao 1978, 15; Brose 2017, 75–77.

28. Song 1976, 128: 3133; Atwood 2004, 606.

29. The Qarluq Myriarch included mainly Qipchaq and Qangli troops.

30. These soldiers were originally part of the troops under the rebellious princes' command who surrendered to Qubilai, as well as the Qipchaqs in the troops of Ananda (Qubilai's grandson). Su 1962, 3: 49; Song 1976, 128: 3133; Atwood 2004, 556; Liu 2013, 171–72, 175; Brose 2017, 75.

31. Nayan was a descendant of Chinggis Khan's brothers, either of the Great Khan's half-brother, Belgütei, or of Chinggis Khan's younger brother Temüge Odchigin. He was stationed in Manchuria and was executed following his rebellion after a campaign personally led by the elderly Qubilai. Atwood 2004, 401.

32. Song 1976, 173: 4048.

33. Polo 1938, 195–97.

34. Lee 2004, 229–32.

35. Yezhili, a grandson of Chinggis Khan's brother, Hachi'un (Qachi'un), was saved by Tuqtuqa from rebels in 1288. Song 1976, 128: 3133–34; Yu 2004, 27: 231; Dardess 1973, 43; Biran 1997, 47; Tu 2012, 102: 642; Brose 2017, 82–83.

36. Jurong is in Jiqing Circuit, near modern Nanjing. Song 1976, 128: 3137–38; Yu 2004, 27: 232, 235; Brose 2017, 77–80.

37. Song 1976, 128: 3135.

38. Liu 2013, 170, 174.

39. Song 1976, 128: 3135.

40. Song 1976, 128: 3135–37; Liu 2013, 172; Atwood 2004, 37.

41. Song 1976, 128: 3136, 138: 3326.

42. Song 1976, 128: 3136–37; Dardess 1973, 10–11; Biran 1997, 52–54; Lee 2004, 211–12.

43. On their surrender and the peace agreement: Qāshānī 1969, 33; Song 1976, 21: 454, 128: 3137; Biran 1997, ch. 3; Dunnell 2014, 185–200; Shurany 2014, 28–45.

44. This was Qaidu's son Chapar (r. c. 1303–10). Biran 2016.

45. For the last phase of the conflict: Liu 2005, 339–58.

46. Liu 2013, 169–70; Allsen 2015, 137.

47. These members included the Toluid prince Yaqudu (Junqur's future father-in-law) and Harghasun (d. 1308/9). Song 1976, 114:2873–74, 117: 2909; Dardess 1973, 13; Hsiao 1994, 505–6; Atwood 2004, 215; Zhao 2008, 243; Humble 2015, 324; Brose 2017, 80–81.

48. Song 1976, 128: 3137; Hsiao 1994, 506–7; Liu 2013, 169.

49. Dardess 1973, 16–17; Brose 2017, 81.

50. Chaji'er's father Prince Yaqudu was a great-grandson of Tolui, Chinggis Khan's youngest son and Qubilai's father. Song 1976, 128: 3136; Dardess 1973, 17; Brose 2017, 83–84.

51. Atwood 2004, 86, 556; Liu 2005, 348–50.

52. Song 1976, 99: 2529–30, 138: 3331; Ye 1983, 109–11; Farquhar 1990, 272–73 (§ 50.1, 50.2); Allsen 2015, 122.

53. The rebellion was led by Temür's grandson Tegshi (d. 1323), the commander of the Asud Guard, a key force in the coup d'état. The Qipchaqs where not dominant in this revolt, perhaps because Junqur had died in 1322. Song 1976, 128: 3137–38, 207: 4599–600; Dardess 1973, 18; Hsiao 1994, 532–33; Liu 2013, 169–70.

54. Song 1976, 138: 3326.

55. Shangdu, in today's Inner Mongolia, was established by Qubilai already in the 1250s, and later served as the Yuan summer capital. The Yuan emperors moved between Dadu and Shangdu, spending the hot season in cooler Shangdu.

56. Song 1976, 138: 3326.

57. El-Temür was approached by several princes and officials who were former supporters of Shidebala and probably wanted to avenge his murder. Cleaves 1950, 53 n. 173; Dardess 1973, 42; Hsiao 1994, 542–43.

58. Song 1976, 184: 4235–36; Cleaves 1950, 53 n. 173; Dardess 1973, 42–43; Hsiao 1994, 542–43.

59. This faction included, in addition to El-Temür, Bayan of the Merkid (d. 1340, not to be confused with Bayan of the Baarin, conqueror of the Song), a powerful Mongol official during the reign of the two last Yuan emperors. The Dadu faction also included imperial family members such as Junqur's widow Chaji'er. Song 1976, 138: 3326–27; Hsiao 1994, 542–43.

60. Hsiao 1994, 541.

61. Song 1976, 138: 3326–7; Hsiao 1994, 542–43.

62. El-Temür also plotted with co-conspirators in Shangdu, but they were prematurely caught.

63. Sadun led the vanguard and was El-Temür's right-hand man.

64. Song 1976, 138: 3326–31; Cleaves 1950, 53 n. 173; Dardess 1973, 38–42; Hsiao 1994, 543–44; Tu 2012, 126: 757.

65. The Dadu faction controlled Beijing, and most of the areas of the Central Plains (i.e., China proper, both north and south) such as the area of Zhongshu (which was the seat of the central secretariat—the province of the capitals), Henan, Huguang, Jiangxi, and Jiangzhe. The Shangdu faction strongholds included Manchuria, Mongolia, Shaanxi, Gansu, Sichuan, and Yunnan, namely more peripheral areas (see map 6.1). Dardess 1973, 40; Hsiao 1994, 544.

66. Song 1976, 138: 3328, 3330–34; Dardess 1973, 48; Hsiao 1994, 547; Tu 2012, 126: 757–58.

67. The guards El-Temür commanded in this position included among others the Left and Right Qipchaq, the general commander of the Longyi Attendant Guard, Imperial Army, and the Qarluq Myriarchy. Farquhar 1990, 271–75 (§§ 50–50.7). Also: Song 1976, 99: 2529–30, 138: 3331–32; Dardess 1973, 47–48; Hsiao 1978, 228 n. 176; Ye 1983, 109–10; Robinson 2009, 39–40; Tu 2012, 126: 757–59; Allsen 2015, 121.

68. El-Temür therefore oversaw the government's "Three Branches of Power"—civil (Central Secretariat), military (Bureau of Military Affairs), and the Censorate. Song 1976, 138: 3331; Ye 1983, 109–11; Lee 2004, 258–59.

69. The Qipchaq guards were about twice the size of the Asud guards and much larger than the Tangut guards. Lee 2004, 249; Liu 2013, 170.

70. El-Temür married Örüg, who seems to have been the daughter of Qoshila. Song 1976, 114: 2878–79; Dardess 1973, 49, 192 n. 74; Brose 2017, 83–84.

71. Song 1976, 31: 701; Dardess 1973, 26–27; Liu 2013, 170.

72. At Quishu Gou of Yangqun Miao area. Song 1976, 35: 796, 138: 3332; Wei 2008, 1: 70, 85–87, 692–707.

73. These could be *topoi* of El-Temür as a bad minister.

74. Song 1976, 138: 3333; Hsiao 1994, 557.

75. Bayan of the Merkid, El-Temür's former ally might have been behind the plot against El-Temür's descendants. Song 1976, 138: 3334; Dardess 1973, 56–57; Hsiao 1994, 567–68; Robinson 2009, 119.

76. Hsiao 1994, 549, 559.

BIBLIOGRAPHY

Allsen, Thomas T. 1987. *Mongol Imperialism: The Policies of the Grand Qan Möngke in China, Russia, and the Islamic Lands, 1251–1259*. Berkeley: University of California Press.

———. 2015. "Population Movements in Mongol Eurasia." In *Nomads as Agents of Cultural Change: The Mongols and Their Eurasian Predecessors*, ed. Reuven Amitai and Michal Biran, 119–51. Honolulu: University of Hawai'i Press.

Amitai-Preiss, Reuven. 1995. *Mongols and Mamluks: The Mamluk-Ilkhanid War, 1260–1281*. Cambridge: Cambridge University Press.

Atwood, Christopher P. 2004. *Encyclopedia of Mongolia and the Mongol Empire*. New York: Facts on File.

Baybars al-Manṣūrī. 1998. *Zubdat al-fikra fī ta'rīkh al-Hijra*. Berlin: Verlag Das Arabische Buch.

Biran, Michal. 1997. *Qaidu and the Rise of the Independent Mongol State in Central Asia*. Richmond, Surrey: Curzon Press.

———. 2016. S.v. "Chapar b. Qaidu." In *Encyclopaedia of Islam*, 3rd edition. Online version.

Brose, Michael C. 2017. "Qipchak Networks of Power in Mongol China." In *How Mongolia Matters: War, Law, and Society*, ed. Morris Rossabi, 69–86. Leiden: Brill.

Cleaves, Francis W. 1950. "The Sino-Mongolian Inscription of 1335 in Memory of Chang Ying-Jui." *Harvard Journal of Asiatic Studies* 13: 1–131.

Dardess, John W. 1973. *Conquerors and Confucians: Aspects of Political Change in Late Yüan China*. New York: Columbia University Press.

Dunnell, Ruth W. 1994. "The Hsi Hsia." In *The Cambridge History of China*. Vol. 6. *Alien Regimes and Border States, 907–1368*, ed. Herbert Franke and Denis Twitchett, 154–214. New York: Cambridge University Press.

———. 2014. "The Anxi Principality: [Un]Making a Muslim Mongol Prince in Northwest China during the Yuan Dynasty." *Central Asiatic Journal* 57: 185–200.

Farquhar, David M. 1990. *The Government of China under Mongolian Rule: A Reference Guide*. Stuttgart: Franz Steiner.

Golden, Peter B. 1990. "The Peoples of the South Russian Steppes." In *The Cambridge History of Early Inner Asia*, ed. Denis Sinor, 256–84. Cambridge: Cambridge University Press.

———. 1991. "The Qipčaqs of Medieval Eurasia: An Example of Stateless Adaptation in the Steppes." In *Rulers from the Steppe: State Formation on the Eurasian Periphery*, ed. Gary Seaman and Daniel Marks, 2: 132–57. Los Angeles: Ethnographics Press.

———. 2014. "Qipčaq." In *Turcology and Linguistics: Éva Ágnes Csató Festschrift*, ed. Nurettin Demir, Birsel Karakoç, and Astrid Menz, 183–202. Ankara: Hacettepe University.

Hill, Donald R. 1973. "Trebuchets." *Viator* 4: 99–114.

Hsiao, Ch'i-Ch'ing. 1978. *The Military Establishment of the Yuan Dynasty*. Cambridge, MA: Harvard University Press.

———. 1993. "Bayan." In *In the Service of the Khan: Eminent Personalities of the Early Mongol-Yüan Period (1200–1300)*, ed. Igor de Rachewiltz, et al., 584–607. Wiesbaden, Germany: Harrassowitz.

———. 1994. "Mid-Yüan Politics." In *The Cambridge History of China*. Vol. 6. *Alien Regimes and Border States, 907–1368*, ed. Herbert Franke, and Denis Twitchett, 490–560. New York: Cambridge University Press.

Hucker, Charles O. 1985. *A Dictionary of Official Titles in Imperial China*. Stanford, CA: Stanford University Press.

Humble, Geoffrey. 2015. "Princely Qualities and Unexpected Coherence: Rhetoric and Representation in '*Juan*' 117 of the '*Yuanshi*.'" *Journal of Song-Yuan Studies* 45: 307–37.

Jackson, Peter. 2005. *The Mongols and the West, 1221–1410*. Harlow, Essex: Pearson Longman.

Juvaini [Juwaynī], ‘Ala-ad-Din ‘Ata-Malik. 1997. *Genghis Khan: The History of World Conqueror.* Tr. John A. Boyle. Manchester: Manchester University Press.

Landa, Ishayahu. 2016. “Imperial Sons-In-Law on the Move: Oyirad and Qonggirad Dispersion in Mongol Eurasia.” *Archivum Eurasiae Medii Aevi* 22: 161–98.

Lee, Yonggyu. 2004. “Seeking Loyalty: The Inner Asian Tradition of Personal Guards and its Influence in Persia and China.“ PhD diss., Harvard University.

Lindner, Rudi P. 1982. “What Was a Nomadic Tribe?” *Comparative Studies in Society and History* 24: 689–711.

Liu, Yingsheng. 2005. “War and Peace between the Yuan Dynasty and the Chaghadaid Khanate (1312–1323).” In *Mongols, Turks, and Others: Eurasian Nomads and the Sedentary World,* ed. Reuven Amitai and Michal Biran, 339–58. Leiden: Brill.

———. 2013. “From the Qipčaq Steppe to the Court in Daidu: A Study of the History of Toqtoq’s Family in Yuan China.” In *Eurasian Influences on Yuan China,* ed. Morris Rossabi, 168–177. Singapore: Institute of Southeast Asian Studies.

Lo, Jung-pang. 2012. *China as a Sea Power, 1127–1368: A Preliminary Survey of the Maritime Expansion and Naval Exploits of the Chinese People during the Southern Song and Yuan Periods.* Ed. Bruce A. Elleman. Singapore: NUS Press/Hong Kong: Hong Kong University Press.

Polo, Marco. 1938. *The Description of the World.* Tr. and ann. Arthur C. Moule and Paul Pelliot. London: Routledge.

Qāshānī, ‘Abd al-Qāsim ‘Abdallah b. ‘Alī. 1969. *Ta’rīkh-i Ūljaytū.* Ed. Mahīn Hamblī. Tehran: BTNK.

Rashīd al-Dīn, Faḍlallāh. 1999. *Rashiduddin Fazlullah’s Jami‘u’t-tawarikh: Compendium of Chronicles: A History of the Mongols.* Vol. 2. Tr. Wheeler M. Thackston. Cambridge, MA: Harvard University, Department of Near Eastern Languages and Civilizations.

Robinson, David M. 2009. *Empire’s Twilight: Northeast Asia under the Mongols.* Cambridge, MA: Harvard University Press.

Rossabi, Morris. 1988. *Khubilai Khan: His Life and Times.* Berkeley: University of California Press.

Shurany, Vered. 2014. “Islam in Northwest China under the Mongols: The Life and Times of Prince Ananda (d. 1307).” MA thesis, Hebrew University of Jerusalem.

Song, Lian 宋濂. 1976. *Yuanshi* 元史 [The Official History of the Yuan]. Reprint. Beijing: Zhonghua shuju 北京: 中華書局.

Su, Tianjue 蘇天爵. 1962. *Yuanchao mingchen shilüe* 元朝名臣事略 [A Review of the Illustrious Ministers of the Yuan Dynasty]. Beijing: Zhonghua shuju.

Tan, Qixiang 譚其驤, ed. 1996. *Zhongguo lishi ditu ji, di qi ce* 中國歷史地圖集, 第七册 [The Historical Atlas of China: The Yuan Dynasty Period and the Ming Dynasty Period, vol. 7]. Beijing: Zhongguo ditu chubanshe.

Tu, Ji 屠寄. 2012. *Mengwu’er shiji* 蒙兀兒史記 [Historical Records of the Mongols]. Published in *Yuanzhi erzhong* 元史二種. Shanghai: Shanghai guji chubanshe.

Vásáry, István. 2005. *Cumans and Tatars: Oriental Military in the Pre-Ottoman Balkans, 1185–1365*. Cambridge: Cambridge University Press.

Wei, Jian 魏堅. 2008. *Yuan Shangdu* 元上都 (上, 下) [Shangdu Site of the Yuan Dynasty, I, II]. Beijing: Zhongguo dabaike quanshu chubanshe.

Ye, Xinmin 葉新民. 1983. "Yuandai de Qincha, Kangli, Asu, Tangwu wei jun 元代的欽察, 康裡, 阿速, 唐兀 衛軍 [Qipchaq, Qangli, Asud, and Tangut Guards in the Yuan Dynasty]." *Neimenggu shehui kexue* 内蒙古社會科學 6: 109–15.

Yu, Ji 虞集. 2004. "Jurong jun wang shiji bei 句容郡王世績碑 [Stele Inscription Dedicated to the Accomplishment of the Ancestors of the Prince of Jurong]." In *Quan Yuan wen* 全元文 [Complete Literary Works of the Yuan Dynasty], ed. Li Xiusheng, 27: 229–37. Nanjing: Fenghuang chubanshe.

Zhao, George Qingzhi. 2008. *Marriage as Political Strategy and Cultural Expression: Mongolian Royal Marriages from World Empire to Yuan Dynasty*. New York: Peter Lang.

PART TWO

Merchants

CHAPTER 7

Jaʿfar Khwāja

Sayyid, Merchant, Spy, and Military Commander of Chinggis Khan

YIHAO QIU

From the inception of the Mongol empire, even prior to Chinggis Khan's subjugation of the eastern Islamic world (1219–25), Muslims were found in Mongol service. Joining the Mongols primarily from Central Asia and Iran, they served in various capacities, most notably as administrators of the Mongols' newly conquered sedentary territories. Jaʿfar Khwāja (fl. 1201–21?), an early follower of Chinggis Khan, is one of the first examples of a Muslim taking part in the nascent imperial enterprise. Based on Jaʿfar Khwāja's biography in the official *Yuanshi,* or *History of the Yuan Dynasty,*[1] along with other contemporaneous Chinese, Persian, and Arabic accounts, this chapter explores Jaʿfar Khwāja's career within the broader context of the early stages of the expanding empire. The diverse functions that Jaʿfar Khwāja fulfilled in Mongol service demonstrate the significant role of Muslims in the emerging empire and the great opportunities of social mobility that Mongol service provided in return.

BACKGROUND: THE CONTINENTAL SILK ROADS PRIOR TO CHINGGIS KHAN

Jaʿfar Khwāja's initial interactions with Chinggis Khan's world were related to his trade activities. Behind these was a long history of east-west commercial relations along the Silk Roads, largely facilitated by Central Asian Muslim traders. Commercial ties between the Islamic world and

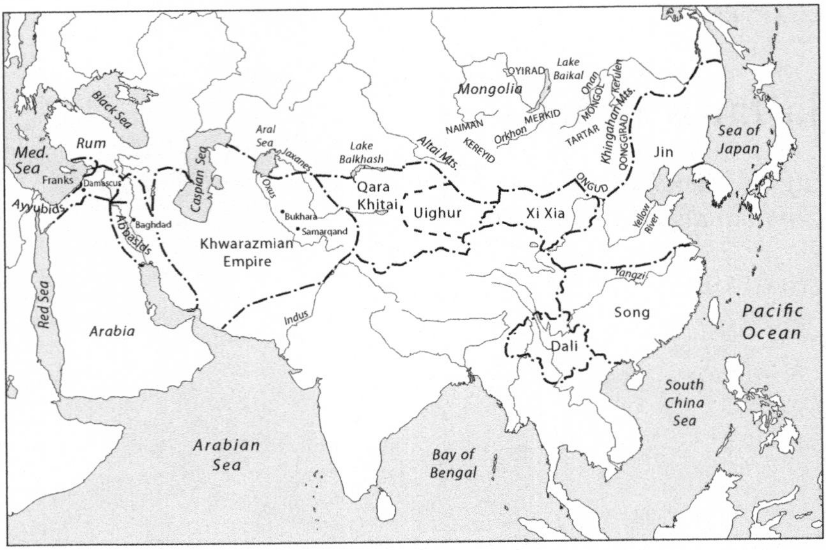

MAP 7.1. Regional Polities Along the Silk Roads before Chinggis Khan's Rise (after Biran 2007, 24).

China flourished during the Umayyad era (661–750) and the earlier part of ʿAbbasid rule (eighth to ninth centuries). After the tenth century, several new regional polities arose in East and Central Asia, including the Buddhist Kitan Liao (907–1125), the Tangut Xixia (1038–1227), the Gaochang (Qocho) Uighur kingdom (843–1209). Later the Qara Khitai (1124–1218), and the Muslim Qarakhanids (ca. 955–1213) and Khwārazmshāhs (1077–1231) appeared as well. These polities divided the continental Silk Roads into regional commercial networks. Although the political dissolution and occasional conflicts did not necessarily result in the disruption of trade, they certainly complicated the inter-Eurasian exchange between China and Islamic World (see map. 7.1).[2]

Since, unlike their Khitan predecessors, the Jurchen Jin emperors (1115–1234) could not bring Mongolia under their control, the Jurchens sought to pacify the tribal groups in the steppes by establishing a series of trading border markets along the boundary with the Mongolian Plateau (today's Inner Mongolia).[3] These trade stations were mainly situated along strategic routes leading to the Steppe and along the Silk Roads. Some of these stations can even be traced back to settlements that Sogdian immigrants to China established between the fourth and tenth centuries.[4]

Under the Jin dynasty, the trade further east was largely handled by Uighur, mostly Buddhist, merchants from Gaochang.[5] During the twelfth century, the majority of caravans traveling eastward from the Islamic world reached only as far as the Xi Xia (Northwestern China), rarely going further eastward, to China proper.[6] Yet, certain Muslim merchants from Central Asia, especially from Kashgar (in western Xinjiang, China, the Eastern Qarakhanid capital) and Balāsāghūn (in Kyrgyzstan, the Qara Khitai capital), maintained the Jin's western trade. The Jurchens identified them as "Muslim Uighurs," ordering resident Muslim merchants to settle in the Uighur immigrants' villages.[7] Further, Zhongdu (also known as Yanjing, present-day Beijing), the Jin capital, had a major settlement of Central Asian immigrants—Buddhist Uighurs and Muslims.[8]

However, Central Asian merchants also maintained direct trade relations with the tribes of Mongolia. The Jin rulers restricted the kind of commodities exchanged in the Jin-controlled border markets. They banned the exportation of ironware and weapons to the Steppe people. Central Asian merchants filled this gap, providing the Mongolian nomads with the desired commodities, including daily necessities such as clothes. The flow of trade commodities from Central Asia had special importance for the nomads' daily life. Even a temporary interruption in the trade could lead to serious shortages in the Steppe.[9]

Central Asian traders engaged in long-distance trade were useful for the Mongols in other capacities as well: they were well known for their multilingual competence.[10] Furthermore, since the Mongols were usually denied entry into China, according to Jin law,[11] they employed itinerant merchants as informants, and even as spies, to collect intelligence on their sedentary neighbors.

JA'FAR KHWĀJA'S EARLY LIFE

According to Chinese sources, Ja'far Khwāja was a descendant of the prophet Muḥammad (*Saiyi,* i.e., Sayyid);[12] his homeland was "the Great West" (*daxi*), a term that denoted Central Asia or regions further west including the Middle East. He might have kept a certain connection to the Islamic communities in Central Asia and eastern Iran since the contemporaneous (or near contemporaneous) Muslim authors Jūzjānī (1193–ca. 1260) and al-Baṭīṭī (fl. 1260) both report his name and achievements during the Jin conquest.[13] They identified Ja'far Khwāja as an Arabic-speaking Shi'ite of Middle Eastern origin.[14]

Ja'far Khwāja had his initial audience with Temüjin, the future Chinggis Khan, at the turn of the thirteenth century, when Temüjin had won a series of battles against his rivals, the Tatars and Taychi'uts.

Encouraged by these victories, Jaʿfar Khwāja entered Temüjin's service, like other Muslim merchants such as Ḥasan (Asan),[15] probably hoping to receive in exchange for his loyalty favorable trade agreements and protection for his caravans.[16]

Jaʿfar Khwāja is described, not only as an astute businessman, but as a skilled rider and archer. According to Jaʿfar's (Chinese) biography, the Mongols understood "Sayyid" as a western title equivalent to a tribal chief (*zuzhang*), which might have contributed to the warm reception Jaʿfar met from Temüjin.[17] Moreover, his Chinese biography also emphasizes his impressive appearance: He was "full of heroic spirit" and had "eagle-eyes and a broad forehead."[18]

By 1203, Temüjin's alliance with his patron, Ong-khan, chief of the Kereyit tribe, began to crumble. After his victory over the Tatars, Temüjin sought a marriage alliance with Ong-khan's family. Ong-khan's son, Senggum, however, rejected his marriage proposal out of jealousy or due to personal enmity, convincing Ong-khan to reject Temüjin's proposal. Pretending to agree to the marriage, they made plans to capture Temüjin during the betrothal banquet. However, two horse herders who served Senggum secretly warned the future Chinggis Khan. When Senggum and Ong-khan realized that their plot was uncovered, they pursued Chinggis Khan and defeated him on the frontier of Manchuria.[19]

Accompanied by a few warriors, Temüjin escaped toward the nearby Khalkha River.[20] When he and his men took refuge in the area of Baljuna (Mong. "the muddy water"), the future Chinggis Khan made his famous covenant with his loyal followers. Raising his hands to heaven, Temüjin swore: "If I can achieve my great enterprise successfully, I will share my fate with all of you, and if I violate my oath, I [will be a failure and disappear] just like the river's water."[21] Jaʿfar Khwāja appears among the allegedly nineteen individuals who witnessed Temüjin's oath, which indicates that he might have been among Temüjin's most trusted companions (*nökör*, pl. *nököd*). Like other participants in the Baljuna covenant, Jaʿfar Khwāja might have been a leading member of Chinggis Khan's guard (*keshig*).[22] Yet, even if he was not close to Temüjin before the covenant, he certainly became so thereafter.

JAʿFAR KHWĀJA'S ACTIONS DURING THE CONQUEST OF THE JIN

After the Baljuna incident, Temüjin defeated the Kereyit (1203) and the Naiman (1204), and united the various Mongol tribes. He was enthroned as emperor and received the title Chinggis Khan in a grand assembly (*quriltai*) in 1206. Shortly thereafter, Chinggis Khan turned to conquer North China. In the years preparing for this campaign, he gathered intelligence about the Jin from defectors, refugees, merchants, and diplomatic envoys.[23]

With his diplomatic skills and knowledge of the Jin, Jaʿfar Khwāja easily stood out among Chinggis Khan's informants. He made a name for himself as an "envoy" (Ch. *yilizhi,* Per. *īlchī,* Mong. *elchi*), a title which became his epithet in the Muslim accounts as well.[24]

Jaʿfar Khwāja's first mission to the Jin took place shortly after 1209.[25] With the mounting tension between Chinggis Khan's nascent polity and the Jin, Jaʿfar's journey to Jin territory was fraught with dangers. Jaʿfar was sent to the Jin court with Chinggis Khan's letter to the emperor. The letter urged the Jurchen ruler to submit to the Mongols and pay them tribute. The demanded tribute included not only commodities, but human talent as well. The Jin emperor was asked to hand over several individuals, notably multilingual translators.[26] Enraged by their demands, the Jin emperor threatened that "if Chinggis Khan does come to this country, he will discover what our ever-victorious forces can wield."[27] Then he ordered Jaʿfar Khwāja imprisoned.

The detention of Chinggis Khan's envoy was probably meant to prevent Jaʿfar Khwāja from providing the Khan information about the Jin's plan to carry out an assault against the Mongol threat. Jaʿfar, however, fled. Safely returning to Mongolia through a secret path that he had discovered by chance, he proceeded to report the Jin's plans to Chinggis Khan.[28] The detainment of his envoy provided Chinggis Khan with a *casus belli* to declare war against the Jin.

According to one contemporaneous Muslim account, after hearing about the Jin emperor's conduct, Chinggis Khan climbed to the top of a mountain, placed his belt around his neck, and for three days straight remained there praying for heaven's help. On the fourth day he returned, proclaiming that heaven granted him victory and incited his men against the Jin to wreak his personal vengeance against the former Jin emperor.[29] Announcing in 1211 the new title of his regime, "the Great Mongolian Nation" (Mong. *Yeke Mongghol Ulus*), Chinggis Khan then led his troops marching southward.[30] With the assistance of his allies, the Önggüt tribal chief, Chinggis Khan made inroads into Jin domains, annihilating the main force of the Jurchen army.[31] The Mongol troops launched a month-long siege of Zhongdu (present-day Beijing), the Jin capital, but eventually had to withdraw due to lack of appropriate siege weapons. In the following year, several contingents continued to weaken the Jin defense lines, later conquering a series of cities in Hebei province.[32]

In 1213, Chinggis Khan rejected the Jin emperor's second peace offer. The Mongol armies gathered and marched to the Juyong Pass, a strategic fortress that protected the thoroughfare southward to the Jin capital.[33] It was envisioned as a natural boundary separating the nomad and the sedentary worlds.[34]

Foreseeing the Mongol attack on the Juyong Pass, the Jin prepared the garrison for defense against the Mongols. Iron was melted to seal the fortress's gates, and iron-caltrops were scattered over a radius of hundreds of kilometers. Seeing that the Juyong Pass was well defended, Chinggis Khan summoned Jaʿfar Khwāja, who suggested a secret passing through the so-called Black Forest,[35] which would enable the Mongol troops to arrive at the Juyong Pass within one night and surprise the Jin garrisons.[36] As a traveling merchant, Jaʿfar Khwāja was aware of the secret paths that were used for centuries by cross-border businessmen to evade border guards and traverse to the interior regions of the Jin Empire, to trade or smuggle commodities.[37]

Chinggis Khan therefore ordered Jaʿfar Khwāja to guide General Jebe (d. 1223) and his squadron past the forest via the secret path; while Chinggis Khan himself outflanked the Juyong Pass from the southwest with his elite force.[38] At dawn, the garrisons of the Jin encountered devastating blows from two directions and remained defenseless. The soldiers were massacred and the fortress was seized by the Mongols.[39]

In addition to guiding the Mongol troops through the Juyong Pass, Jaʿfar Khwāja also participated in the subsequent military actions.[40] He did not merely serve the chief commander, Jebe, as his assistant, but also took charge of persuading the local governors to surrender. The "Provincial Governor *Bazha*" (*xingsheng Bazha*), who accepted the submission of the local garrisons stationed in Zhuozhou (in today's Hebei province), can be identified with Jaʿfar Khwāja, though he was only granted the official title of provincial governor (*xingsheng*) several years later.[41] With Chinggis Khan's permission, Jaʿfar Khwāja issued appointment letters to the local governors urging them to abandon resistance to their new Mongol overlords.[42]

The fall of the Juyong Pass signaled the collapse of Jin defenses on the northwest frontier. North China was now defenseless against the Mongol incursions. The Song envoys themselves admitted that it was this battle that "exhausted the manpower and military resources which were accumulated by the Jin government in the last hundred years, and thus led to the state's fatal decline."[43]

The sources are split as to Jaʿfar Khwāja's role in the Mongol victory. Whereas the *Secret History* and Rashīd al-Dīn relate only the meritorious services of the Mongol commanders—Jebe, Qatai, and Bocha[44]—other historians, both Chinese and Muslim, speak to Jaʿfar Khwāja's distinguished service during the Jin conquest.[45]

During the spring of 1214, Chinggis Khan besieged Zhongdu once again, and established his headquarters in its northern suburb. After plundering north of the Yellow River, the Right Wing of the Mongol army under the command of Chinggis Khan's sons and the Left Wing led by his brothers gathered outside the city. By this point, however, the Mongol army's provisions were depleted and epidemics broke out among the men due to the food shortage. Continuing the siege on Zhongdu would have put Chinggis Khan's troops in jeopardy.[46] In what appears to be a graphic historical topos, the papal ambassador to the Mongols, John of Plano Carpini (d. 1252), claims that the starved "Tatar" army resorted to cannibalism, eating one in every ten men.[47] Under duress at the siege, Chinggis Khan declined his generals' advice; he dispatched Jaʿfar Khwāja as his ambassador for peace negotiations with the Jin.[48]

The Jin emperor Weishao wang (Wanyan Yongji, r. 1208–13) was murdered in a palace coup just prior to the siege, and was succeeded by his nephew Xuanzong (Wanyan Xun, r. 1213–24). In February 1214, the new emperor accepted Jaʿfar Khwāja at his court. Jaʿfar conveyed Chinggis Khan's message: "Your districts and the counties in Shandong and Hebei are now in my possession, leaving you with only Yanjing. Heaven has weakened you so much that if I were to attack you now, in your distress, what would Heaven think of me? I therefore intend to turn back with my army. We would appreciate if you provided me with supplies for the troops, thus lessening my generals' resentment."[49] Jaʿfar next presented Chinggis Khan's conditions for peace, which included tributes of gold, rare commodities, brocade, and horses. In addition, Chinggis Khan demanded that a Jurchen princess be granted to him in marriage, along with five hundred slaves, male and female. At Chinggis Khan's orders, the Jin Left prime minister (*zuo chengxiang*), Wanyan Fuxing, was to personally accompany the princess and the gifts to his encampment.

At Jaʿfar Khwāja's insistence, the Jin emperor was also made to bow down toward the north at the court, in order to make public his submission to Chinggis Khan.[50] Fearing a Mongol attack, the Jin emperor fully accepted Chinggis Khan's conditions. He assigned the former emperor Weishao wang's favorite daughter, the "Little Princess" (*xiao jiejie*), considered the prettiest and brightest, as Chinggis Khan's intended wife. Both the Chinese and Persian sources write that the princess, designated as "Gongzhu Empress" (Ch. *gongzhu huanghou;* or Per. *gūnjū khātūn*), was treated well by the Mongols. She became one of Chinggis' four chief wives, and was allotted the fourth *ordo* (the royal camp).[51]

JAʿFAR KHWĀJA AS THE ADMINISTRATOR OF ZHONGDU

In May 1214, after realizing that the fate of the Jin Empire was sealed, the Jurchen emperor decided to move the imperial court to the southern capital (in today's Kaifeng). His decision was regarded a sign of weakness and had disastrous consequences for his state. A month later, the Jin crack troops stationed in the capital's suburbs rebelled and joined the Mongols.[52] Supported by the rebels, the Mongol troops next marched southward and laid siege to Zhongdu. The Jin capital however resisted Chinggis Khan's forces for a year.[53]

After the city was reduced to cannibalism, the chief Jurchen commander Fuxing committed suicide and the survivors of the city submitted. The extended siege and military conflicts had devastating results. The Khwārazmshāh's envoy, who arrived in Yanjing shortly after the city's fall, reported that corpses were piled up like a snow hill and the city's streets were greased with human fat.[54]

According to Jaʿfar's *Yuanshi* biography, Chinggis Khan credited Jaʿfar with the successful siege. Observing the view from the city wall, he told Jaʿfar: "Shoot with your bow, [and I will] grant [you] all the land within the range of your fallen arrows as your fief."[55] Jaʿfar's fiefdom included the palace of the "Fourth Prince" (the Jin emperor's fourth son), which became Jaʿfar's residence.[56] Chinggis Khan also appointed Jaʿfar Khwāja the "chief *darughachi* [Mong. governor] under heaven, in charge of the civil affairs over the regions from the north side of the Yellow River to the south side of the Iron Gate."[57]

Jaʿfar Khwāja's official title, *darughachi,* reflects his status: he was the imperial agent dispatched to oversee the administration of submitted urban centers. The *darughachi,* a central institution in Mongol administration, derives from the government system of the Qara Khitai that had ruled Central Asia during the twelfth century, until their defeat by the Mongols in 1218.[58] Jaʿfar appears to have been the first *darugh-*

achi assigned to China, and his appointment was a significant stage in the formation of the nascent imperial Mongol bureaucracy in China.

Aside from the administrative official Jaʿfar Khwāja, Samghar (*Samuha*), a Mongol *jarghuchi* (judge, Ch. *duanshiguan*), was assigned as Chinggis Khan's representative, and Bujir (*Buzhi'er*) as the commander of the Mongol troops stationed in Zhongdu.[59] The three were to take charge of the local affairs supervising the recruited local elites. This arrangement represents the initial pattern that would inform the empire's dominant dual-administrative system. It required that Mongol appointees and local elites collaborate in governing the local affairs.[60] Jaʿfar Khwāja was a polyglot. He is recorded conversing freely with Chinese intellectuals, and likely had earlier knowledge of Chinese, which was spoken in Central Asia under the Qara Khitais.[61] Proficiency in Chinese would have been advantageous in his administrative tasks.

Spending his later years in Yanjing, Jaʿfar Khwāja gradually lost his power in the Mongol government to junior officials. A Southern Song envoy who visited the city in 1221 records that Jaʿfar (*zhaba*) had aged. He refers to Jaʿfar as the last of Chinggis Khan's meritorious ministers (*gongchen*).[62]

The final section in Jaʿfar Khwāja's *Yuanshi* biography is dedicated to his contacts with the patriarch of the popular Daoist Quanzhen sect, Qiu Chuji (known also as Changchun, "Everlasting Spring," 1148–1227). In the second decade of the thirteenth century, Qiu Chuji earned a growing reputation for providing spiritual and physical shelter for the masses in North China, who had greatly suffered during the turbulent era of the Mongol invasion.[63] The Mongols too were attracted to the Daoist scholar, who was famous for his alleged longevity. Chinggis Khan summoned him to his camp near the Hindukush and honored him there in 1222 with a golden tablet and the title "Spirit Immortal" (*shenxian*).[64]

Jaʿfar played the role of intermediary between Qiu Chuji and Chinggis Khan: in 1219 he was sent to Laizhou (in present-day Shandong province) to invite the patriarch to an audience with the khan, probably due to Jaʿfar's earlier acquaintance with the Daoist master.[65] In 1223, when Qiu returned from Central Asia, Jaʿfar, in his capacity as the provincial governor, sent the master a letter inviting him in accordance with Chinggis Khan's orders, to move into the Taiji Palace (*Taiji gong*, present-day Baiyun guan, in Beijing).[66] The next year, Qiu Chuji was granted Qionghua Island (today's Jade Island in Beihai Park, Beijing), located within the domains of the former Jin palace, to build a new Daoist temple. The land was granted through "the donation of His

Excellency, the provincial governor and *xuancha* [*darughachi*, judge] Ja'far."[67]

Aside from their official contacts, Ja'far and Qiu seem to have been on friendly terms. Ja'far's biography reports on a private conversation between the two. Qiu had asked Ja'far whether he preferred to become a highly dignified individual, or that his family would grow and prosper. Ja'far's answer was that "dignified status is meaningless since people are all destined to die. I wish my family to be safe and my descendants to continue the family line." Qiu approved of his answer.[68] This cordial talk between the Muslim governor on behalf of the Mongols and their Daoist protégé represents the commonplace interreligious encounters and interconfessional alliances under the Mongols' pluralistic rule.

According to his biography, Ja'far's "wish" came true. He enjoyed longevity, dying at the age of 118. He had at least two sons, Alaqan (*Alihan*) and Minglikcha, and seven grandsons, most of whom continued to serve as high-ranking officials in the central and local administration.[69] Persian chronicles report that in September 1304, one of his descendants, a Muslim named Muṣṭafā, reached the court of Ilkhan Öljeitü (r. 1305–16) in Iran as the ambassador of Yuan Emperor Temür (r. 1294–1307) to proclaim the general peace agreement among all four Chinggisid *ulus*es.[70]

CONCLUSION

Ja'far Khwāja's story demonstrates the versatility as well as the geographical and social mobility of Muslim merchants in Mongol China. He was one of Chinggis Khan's early supporters, and his skills—a combination of financial, linguistic, and military capabilities, along with his noble origins and impressive appearance—enabled him to fulfill key positions during the Mongol conquest of North China and in the nascent Mongol administration.

The Mongols appreciated the financial and trade-related skills of their subject Muslim merchants, which enabled them to play a vital role in the empire's trade, both inside the empire and further afar. Through their political, administrative and economic privileges, the families of the Muslim merchants accumulated significant assets. They often migrated and dispersed within the domains of the Mongol Empire, especially in Yuan China.

Ja'far Khwāja's story is also more broadly indicative of the instrumental role Muslims had in the process of the establishment of the

Mongol Empire. Muslims participated in the Mongols' imperial enterprise, not only serving as trade partners, but also taking part in military and political campaigns and later as governors and administrators in non-Muslim lands as well, especially China. They contributed their military and intellectual skills to the successful and swift conquests of North China and Central Asia. In return for their aid, the Mongol rulers promoted their Muslim allies to leading positions, often superior to the local Han Chinese population. After he was appointed governor of North China, Ja'far Khwāja and his family settled there and continued to serve the Mongols for several generations. Maintaining their Muslim identity, the migrant family also came to terms with Chinese traditions and customs. Thus, the career and life of Ja'far Khwāja and his descendants demonstrates not only the Mongol preference to employing foreign, mainly Muslim, administrators in China, but also speaks to the integration of these individuals and their families into the Chinese environment and society.

NOTES

1. Song 1976, 120: 2960–61.
2. Biran 2013, 250; Hansen 2013; Biran 2015.
3. The first series of border markets was established under Jin Taizong (r. 1123–35). Tuotuo 1975, 81: 1826.
4. The Sogdians were an ancient Iranian people who originated in the Zerafshan valley, in today's Uzbekistan and Tajikistan. They were famous as traders in Central Asia and China. Rong 2001, 37–110.
5. Biran 2015, 582.
6. Zhao 1983, 13: 14a–b.
7. Such an instance of resettling appears in the *Official History of the Jin Dynasty* (*Jinshi*). Tuotuo 1978, 121: 2637.
8. Hong Hao 2000, 1: 95.
9. Ibn al-Athīr, for example, reports that the 1218 shortage of clothes in Mongolia was caused by the Khwārazmshāh's conquest of Transoxania from the Qara-Khitai. Biran 2005, 138.
10. Peng 2014, 85.
11. Zhao 1983, 13: 13b.
12. Song 1976, 120: 2960; *Yuan dianzhang* 2011, 1: 246.
13. Al-Baṭīṭī is the author of a recently published Arabic work on the Mongols, allegedly composed in 1260 (658H) in the Middle East. A few anachronisms (e.g., using post-1260 names for places) suggest that it was a later compilation. While it is difficult to assess the authenticity of the work, the fact that it refers to Ja'far is significant. Baṭīṭī 2015, 70.
14. *Min al-shī'a al-sadīda 'arabī al-nasab wa-l-lisān*. Al-Baṭīṭī 2015, 70; Jūzjānī 1964, 2: 100, 103; Jūzjānī 1881, 2: 954, 965.

15. Ḥasan (Asan), who met the future Chinggis Khan in Baljuna and joined his ranks, is probably Ḥasan Ḥajjī, who appears in the Persian sources. He was Chinggis Khan's companion and trader, who accompanied Jochi, Chinggis Khan's eldest son, in the campaign against Khwārazm and was slain by the inhabitants of Suqnaq near Uṭrār (West Kazakhstan) around 1219. *The Secret History*, de Rachewiltz 2006, 1: 104, 2: 657–58.

16. Ratchnevsky 1993, 72.

17. Song 1976, 120: 2960.

18. Song 1976, 120: 2960. A pair of bright piercing eyes was one of the most admired features for the contemporary Mongols. It was also used to judge someone's personal qualities. *The Secret History*, de Rachewiltz 2006, 1: 14.

19. Ratchnevsky 1993, 69; *The Secret History*, de Rachewiltz 2006, 1: 88.

20. The *Secret History* (de Rachewiltz 2006, 1: 95) reports the number of Chinggis Khan's followers as 2,600. However, Rashīd al-Dīn (1998, 1: 186) supplies another number: 4,600.

21. Song 1976, 120: 2960.

22. Cleaves argues that Chinggis Khan's men numbered nineteen. Yet, a recently published fourteenth-century source, the *Akhbār-i mughūlān* (Mongol News), notes that seventy faithful followers accompanied Temüjin there. Cleaves 1955, 391–92; Shīrāzī 2010, 19; Lane 2012, 545; *The Secret History*, de Rachewiltz 2006, 1: 114, 2: 658.

23. Li Xinchuan 2000, 2: 842; Yelü Ahai's biography: Song 1976, 150: 3549.

24. Jūzjānī 1964, 2: 100; Jūzjānī 1881, 2: 954; Baṭīṭī 2015, 70; Ibn al-Dawādārī 1972, 7: 235.

25. Yuan 2004, 571. Yuan only mentions that this event occurred in the beginning of the *Da'an* period (1209–11), hence around 1209.

26. The list included experts in economic and diplomatic affairs, such as Ma Qingxiang, a Nestorian Uighur fluent in six languages, who was a skilled translator in the Department of State Affairs (*shangshusheng yishi*).

27. Khondamīr 1994, 1: 12–13.

28. Jūzjānī 1881, 2: 954; Song 1976, 120: 2961.

29. Jūzjānī 1964, 2: 100; Jūzjānī 1881, 2: 954. This vengeance likely refers to the fate of Chinggis's great-grandfather's brother, and the ruler of the short-lived twelfth-century Mongol state, Hambaqai (Ambaqai) Khan. Hambaqai was captured by the Tatar people, and delivered to the Jin emperor. He was nailed to a wooden donkey and left to die a slow and painful death. Rashīd al-Dīn 1998, 1: 130.

30. Chen Xiaowei 2016, 233–46.

31. Tuotuo 1975, 93: 2066; Song 1976, 1: 15. Chinggis Khan's troops defeated the Jin army first at Yehu Ridge (*Yehu ling*, in today's Wanquan county, Hebei province) and then at the Juyong Pass (*Juyong guan*, in today's Changping district, Beijing).

32. Cheng Zhuo 2013, 3: 1253.

33. The Joyong Pass lies on a ravine that cuts through the mountains, located around sixty kilometers north of Zhongdu. *The Secret History*, de Rachewiltz 2006, 2: 891.

34. Xiong 2001, 251.

35. The Black Forest (*hei shulin*) can be identified as the pine forest located to the east of the Juyong Pass. Gu 2005, 1: 432–33.

36. Song 1976, 120: 2961; Jūzjānī 1964, 2: 100; Jūzjānī 1881, 2: 953–54; Tuotuo 1975, 103: 2267.

37. Al-Baṭīṭī 2015, 70.

38. The Zijing Entrance also appears as the "Zijing Pass" (*Zijing guan*). Tuotuo 1975, 86: 1326, 101: 2228.

39. Song 1976, 120: 2961; Jūzjānī 1964, 2: 100–101; Jūzjānī 1881, 2: 954; *The Secret History*, de Rachewiltz 2006, 1: 247.

40. A contingent of Qarluqs, a Turkic tribe whose members were mostly Muslim, also fought with the Mongols in the battle. Ja'far Khwāja might have commanded them because of their shared faith. Huang 2008, 1: 426.

41. Song 1976, 152: 3606. Tu Ji points out that Bazha is a variant of Ja'far. Tu 1989, 50: 444; also Pelliot 1933–35, 925–26.

42. Ma 1991, 239.

43. Zhao 1983, 13: 14b.

44. *The Secret History*, de Rachewiltz 2006, 1: 175–76; Rashīd al-Dīn 1998, 1: 218.

45. For example, the Mamluk historian Ibn al-Dawādārī (fl. 1309/10–1335/6), mentioned Ja'far Khwāja—with his designation of *īljī* (envoy)—as Chinggis Khan's spy to the Jin. Ibn al-Dawādārī 1972, 7: 235; Haarmann 1974, 29–30. Baṭīṭī (2015, 70) even attributes to Ja'far Khwāja the capture of the emperor himself and states that due to this feat, Chinggis Khan gave him the Jin emperor's throne and wife. This exaggerated account might have originated in Ja'far's later appointment as the Jin capital's governor.

46. Rashīd al-Dīn reports that due to the unusual heat, "the Mongol troops were all afflicted [with an epidemic or in distress] (*ranjūr shuda ast*)." Rashīd al-Dīn 1994, 1: 449. Cf. Rashīd al-Dīn 1998, 1: 220; *The Secret History*, de Rachewiltz 2006, 1: 177.

47. Plano Carpini 1996, 52. This account might have been based either on the rumors of Jin cannibalism during a later Mongol siege or on European perceptions about Mongol barbarism. It might also reflect the Mongols' desperate situation during this siege, though the Mongols would more likely choose to resort to feeding off their livestock. Guzman 1991, 31–68.

48. Tuotuo 1975, 14: 302–4, 306; Yang 2003, 363–69.

49. Song 1976, 1: 17; Li Xinchuan 2007, 2: 850. Translated in Ratchnevsky 1993, 113.

50. Li Xinchuan 2000, 2: 850–51.

51. She bore him five children. *The Secret History*, de Rachewiltz 2006, 1: 177; Tuotuo 1975, 14: 303–4; *Shengwu qinzhenglu jiaozhu* 1983, 13: 67a–b; Rashīd al-Dīn, *Shu'ab-i panjgāna*. MS Topkapi Sarai, III Ahmet, 2937, fol.105b; Ḥamdallāh al-Mustawfī 2011, 7: 205.

52. In the contemporary Chinese sources, these crack troops were called the *Jiu* army. It constituted of a multiethnic group of men, many of whom (e.g., the Khitans and Tatars) were nomads, and was mainly stationed along the Jin's northwestern border. Cai 2012, 215–47.

53. Yüwen 1986, 1: 344.

54. Jūzjānī 1964, 2: 103; Jūzjānī 1881, 2: 965.

55. Song 1976, 120: 2961. Measuring the fief by a bowshot was a traditional Mongolian practice. Chinggis Khan implemented this practice when he enfeoffed his meritorious attendants with the estates of the Jin capital. Chan 1991, 75–76.

56. Liu 1983, 4. Subsequently, part of this palace was used as the offices of Yanjing's Branch Secteriat (*Yanjing xingshangshu sheng*), the main institution of Mongol administration in the region.

57. *Huanghe yibei, tiemen yinan tianxia dudaluhuachi:* Song 1976, 120: 2961. The "Iron Gate" refers to the Juyong Pass; the Jin people had melted iron to seal the gate.

58. Buell 1979, 131–32; Biran 2005, 119–22.

59. *Yuan dianzhang* 2011, 1: 246. On this text: Hong Jinfu 2012, 48. On Samghar's military merits: Song 1976, 1: 17, 150: 3556, 155: 3611; on Bujir's biography: Song 1976, 124: 3059; de Rachewiltz 1993, 131–34.

60. Aigle 2006–7, 65–72.

61. Li Zhichang 1983, 13: 2a–2b; Biran 2005, 127–28.

62. Zhao 1983, 13: 10b.

63. de Rachewiltz and Russell 1984, 1–27; Yao 1986, 201–19.

64. Li Zhichang 1983, 13: 9b. The journey was recorded by Chanchun's student Li Zhichang and is an important source on Central Asia under Chinggisid rule.

65. Song 1976, 120: 2961, 202: 4524.

66. Li Zhichang 1983, 13: 14a; Chen Yuan 1988, 539.

67. Li Zhichang 1983, 13: 15a; Chen 1988, 457.

68. Song 1976, 120: 2961.

69. Song 1976, 120: 2961.

70. Qāshānī 1969, 32.

BIBLIOGRAPHY

Aigle, Denise. 2006–7. "Iran under Mongol Domination: The Effectiveness and Failing of a Dual-Administrative System." *Bulletin d'études orientales* 57: 65–78.

Al-Baṭīṭī, Ḥusayn b. ʿAlī. 2015. *Aḥwāl mulūk al-tatār al-mughūl.* Ed. Rasūl Jaʿfariyān. Qom, Iran: n.p.

Biran, Michal. 2005. *The Empire of the Qara Khitai in Eurasian History: Between China and the Islamic World.* Cambridge: Cambridge University Press.

———. 2007. *Chinggis Khan: Makers of the Muslim World.* Oxford: One-World.

———. 2013. "Unearthing the Liao Dynasty's Relations with the Muslim World: Migrations, Diplomacy, Commerce, and Mutual Perceptions." *Journal of Song-Yuan Studies* 43: 221–51.

———. 2015. "The Qarakhanids' Eastern Exchange: Preliminary Notes on the Silk Roads in the Eleventh and Twelfth Centuries." In *Complexity of Interaction along the Eurasian Steppe Zone in the first Millennium* C.E., ED. JAN

Bemmann and Michael Schmauder, 575–95. Bonn: Rheinische Friedrich-Wilhelms Universität Bonn.

Buell, Paul D. 1979. "Sino Khitan Administration in Mongol Bukhara." *Journal of Asian History* 13: 121–51.

Cai Meibiao 蔡美彪. 2012. "*Jiu yu Jiujun zhi yanbian* 乣與乣軍之演變 [Studies on the *Jiu* People and Evolution of the *Jiu* Army]." In *Liao, Jin, Yuan shi kaosuo* 遼金元史考索 [Studies of the History of Liao, Jin, and Yuan Dynasties], ed. Cai Meibiao, 215–47. Beijing: Zhonghua shuju.

Chan, Hok-lam. 1991. "Siting by Bowshot: A Mongolian Custom and Its Sociopolitical and Cultural Implications." *Asia Major* 4: 53–78.

Chen Xiaowei 陳曉偉. 2016. "Zai lun 'Da Menggu guo' guohao de chuangjian niandai wenti 再論"大蒙古國"國號的創建年代問題 [Resurveying the Date of the Establishment of the Reign Title 'the Great Mongol State']." *Zhonghua wenshi luncong* 中華文史論叢 [Journal of Chinese Literature and History] 1: 233–46.

Chen Yuan 陳垣. 1988. *Daojia jinshi lue* 道家金石略 [Collection of the Inscriptions and Epigraphs of the Daoist School]. Beijing: Wenwu chubanshe.

Cheng Zhuo 程卓. 2013. "Shi Jin lu 使金錄 [Reports of a Mission to the Jin State]." In *Songdai riji congbian* 宋代日記叢編 [Anthology of the Diaries Written in the Song Dynasty], 3 vols., ed. Gu Hongyi 顧宏義 and Li Wen 李文, 3: 1244–57. Shanghai: Shanghai shudian.

Cleaves, Francis W. 1955. "The Historicity of the Baljuna Covenant." *Harvard Journal of Asiatic Studies* 18: 357–421.

de Rachewiltz, Igor, ed. 1993. *In the Service of the Khan: Eminent Personalities of the Early Mongol-Yüan Period,* Wiesbaden, Germany: Harrasowitz.

———. 2006. *The Secret History of the Mongols: A Mongolian Epic Chronicle of the Thirteenth Century*. 2 vols. Leiden: Brill.

de Rachewiltz, Igor, and Terence Russell. 1984. "Ch'iu Ch'u-chi (1148–1227)." *Papers on Far Eastern History* 29: 1–27.

Gu Zuyu 顧祖禹. 2005. *Du shi fangyu ji yao* 讀史方輿紀要 [Important Notes on Reading the Geography Treatises in the Histories]. 12 vols. Ed. He Cijun 賀次君 and Shi Hejin 施和金. Beijing: Zhonghua shuju.

Guzman, Gregory G. 1991. "Reports of Mongol Cannibalism in the Thirteenth-Century Latin Sources: Oriental Fact or Western Fiction?" In *Discovering New Worlds: Essays on Medieval Exploration and Imagination,* ed. Scott D. Westrem, 31–68. New York: Garland Publishing.

Haarmann, Ulrich. 1974. "Altun Hān und Čingiz Hān bei den ägyptischen Mamluken." *Der Islam* 51: 1–36.

Ḥamdallāh al-Mustawfī. 2011. *Ẓafarnāma*. Vol. 7. Tehran: Pazhuhishgāh-i 'ulūm-i insābī wa muṭāli'āt-i farhangī, 1390sh.

Hansen, Valerie. 2013. "International Gifting and the Kitan World, 907–1125." *Journal of Song-Yuan Studies* 43: 273–302.

Hong Hao 洪皓. 2000. *Songmo jiwen* 松漠紀聞 [Records of the Pine Forests in the Plain]. In *Yuzhang congshu shibu* 豫章叢書·史部 [*Yuzhang congshu:* Volumes of Historical Works]. Vol. 1. Ed. Tao Fulü 陶福履 and Hu Sijing 胡思敬. Nanchang, China: Jiangxi jiaoyu chubanshe.

Hong Jinfu 洪金富. 2012. "Yuan dianzhang dianxiao shili xu《元典章》點校釋例續 [Case-studies of the *Yuan dianzhang*]." *Yuanshi ji minzu bianjiang yanjiu jikan* 元史及民族與邊疆研究集刊 [Studies on the Mongol-Yuan and China's Border Areas] 24: 46–54.

Huang Jin 黃溍. 2008. *Huang Jin quan ji* 黃溍全集 [Huang Jin's Literary Collection]. Ed. Wang Ting 王頲. Tianjin, China: Tianjin guji chubanshe.

Ibn al-Dawādārī, Abū Bakr b. ʿAbdallāh b. Aybak. 1972. *Kanz al-durar wa-jāmiʾ al-ghurar.* Vol. 7. Ed. Ulrich Haarmann as *Der Bericht über die frühen Mamluken.* Cairo: Deutsches Archäologisches Insitut Kairo.

Jūzjānī, Minhāj al-Sirāj. 1964. *Ṭabaqāt-i Naṣirī.* Ed. ʿAbd al-Ḥayy Ḥabībī. 2 vols. Kabul: Pūhanī Maṭb.

———. 1881. *Tabakat-i-Nasirī: A General History of the Muhammadan Dynasties of Asia: including Hindustan, from* A.H. *194 (810* A.D.*) to* A.H. *658 (1260* A.D.*) and the Irruption of the Infidel Mughals into Islam.* Tr. H.G. Raverty. London: Gilbert & Rivington.

Khondamīr [Khwāndamīr], Ghiyāth al-Dīn b. Humām al-Dīn al-Ḥusayn. 1994. *Habibu's-siyar: The Reign of the Mongol and the Turk; Genghis Khan-Amir Temür.* Vol. 3, pt. 1. Ed. and tr. Wheeler M. Thackston. Cambridge, MA: Harvard University Press.

Lane, George. 2012. "Mongol News: The *Akhbār-i Moghulān dar Anbāneh Qutb,* by Quṭb al-Dīn Maḥmud ibn Masʿūd Shīrāzī." *Journal of the Royal Asiatic Society* 22: 541–59.

Li Xinchuan 李心傳. 2000. *Jianyan yi lai chao ye za ji* 建炎以來朝野雜記 [Miscellaneous Notes on Inner and Outer Politics since the Jianyan Reign (1127–30)]. Ed. Xu Gui 徐規. Beijing: Zhonghua shuju.

Li Zhichang 李志常. 1983. "Changchun zhenren xi you ji jiaozhu 長春真人西遊記校注[Commentary of the Report of a Travel of the Spirit Immortal Changchun (i.e., Qiu Chuji)]." In *Wang Guowei yishu* 王國維遺書 [Posthumous Writings of Wang Guowei], vol. 13. Ed. Zhao Wanli 趙萬里, Wang Guohua王國華, Shanghai: Shanghai shudian chubanshe.

Liu Qi 劉祁. 1983. *Gui qian zhi* 歸潛志 [Memories in Retirement]. Beijing: Zhonghua shuju.

Ma Zuchang 馬祖常. 1991. *Shi Tian xiansheng wenji* 石田先生文集 [Ma Zuchang's Literary Collection]. Ed. Li Shuyi 李叔毅. Zhengzhou: Zhongzhou guji chubanshe.

Pelliot, Paul. 1933–35. "Sur un passage du *Cheng-wou ts'ing-tcheng lou.*" In *Qing zhu Cai Yuan pei sheng liushiwu sui lunwen ji* 慶祝蔡元培先生六十五歲論文集 [Festschrift in Honor of Cai Yuanpei on His Ninetieth Birthday], ed. Institute of History and Philology, Academia Sinica 中央研究院歷史語言研究所, 2: 907–38. Beijing: Academia Sinica.

Peng Daya 彭大雅. 2014. *Hei Da shilüe jiaozhu* 黑韃事略校注 [Annotated Short Notes on the Black Tartars]. Ed. Xu Quansheng 許全勝. Lanzhou, China: Lanzhou daxue chubanshe.

Plano-Carpini, John of. 1996. *Historia Mongalorum: The Story of the Mongols Whom We Call the Tartars.* Tr. Erik Hildinger. Boston: Branden Publishing.

Qāshānī, Abū al-Qāsim ʿAbdallāh b. Muḥammad. 1969. *Tārīkh-i Ūljāytū.* Ed. M. Hambly. Tehran: Shirkat-i intishārāt-i ʿulūmī wa farhangī, 1348sh/1969.

Ratchnevsky, Paul. 1993. *Genghis Khan: His Life and Legacy*. Ed. and tr. Thomas Nivison Haining. Oxford: Blackwell.

Rashīd al-Dīn, Faḍl Allāh. *Shu'ab-i panjgāna*. MS Topkapi Sarai, III Ahmet, 2937.

———. 1994. *Jāmi' al-tawārīkh*. Ed. Muḥammad Rawshan. Tehran: Nashr-i Alburz, 1373sh/1994.

———. 1998. *Rashiduddin Fazlullah's Jami'u't-Tawarikh: Compendium of Chronicles; A History of the Mongols*. Tr. and ed. Wheeler M. Thackston. 3 vols. Cambridge, MA: Harvard University, Department of Near Eastern Languages and Civilizations.

Rong Xinjiang 榮新江. 2001. *Zhonggu Zhongguo yu wailai wenming* 中古中國與外來文明 [Medieval China and Foreign Civilizations]. Beijing: Sanlian shudian.

Shengwu qinzheng lu jiaozhu 聖武親征錄校注 [Commentary of Emperor Shengwu's Conquest Wars]. 1983. In *Wang Guowei yishu* 王國維遺書 [Posthumous Writings of Wang Guowei], vol. 13, Ed. Zhao Wanli 趙萬里, Wang Guohua 王國華. Shanghai: Shanghai shudian chubanshe.

Shīrāzī, Maḥmūd b. Mas'ūd Quṭb al-Dīn. 2010. *Akhbār-i mughūlān*. Ed. Irāj Afshār. Qom, Iran: Kitābkhāna-i Ayatallāh Marashī Najafī, 1389sh/2010.

Song Lian 宋濂. 1976. *Yuanshi* 元史 [Official History of the Yuan Dynasty]. Beijing: Zhonghua shuju.

Tu Ji 屠寄. 1989. *Mengwu'er shiji* 蒙兀兒史記 [Historical Records of the Mongols]. Shanghai: Shanghai guji chubanshe.

Tuotuo 脫脫. 1975. *Jinshi* 金史 [The Official History of the Jin Dynasty]. Beijing: Zhonghua shuju.

Xiong Mengxiang 熊夢祥. 2001. *Xijin zhi jiyi* 析津志輯佚 [Re-compilation of the Gazetteer of Xijin]. Beijing: Beijing guji chubanshe.

Yang Zhijiu 楊志玖. 2003. *Yuandai huizu shigao* 元代回族史稿 [Studies on the Hui Muslims in the Yuan Dynasty]. Tianjin: Nankai daxue chubanshe.

Yao Tao-Chung [Daozhong]. 1986. "Ch'iu Ch'u-chi and Chinggis Khan." *Harvard Journal of Asiatic Studies* 46: 201–19.

Yuan dianzhang 元典章 [Statutes of the Yuan Dynasty]. 2011. Eds. Chen Gaohua陳高華 et al. 4 vols. Tianjin: Tianjin guji chubanshe.

Yuan Haowen 元好問. 2004. *Yuan Haowen quanji* 元好問全集 [Yuan Haowen's Literary Collection]. Ed. Yao Dianzhong 姚奠中. Shanxi, China: Shanxi guji chubanshe.

Yüwen Maozhou 宇文懋昭. 1986. *Da Jin guo zhi jiaozheng* 大金國志校正 [Recension of the Unofficial History of the Jin State]. Ed. Cui Wenyin 崔文印. 2 vols. Beijing: Zhonghua shuju.

Zhao Gong 趙珙. 1983. *Mengda beilu jianzheng* 蒙韃備錄箋證 [Annotated Edition of a Refined (Report) of the Mongol-Tartars]. In *Wang Guowei yishu* 王國維遺書 [Posthumous Writings of Wang Guowei], vol. 13. Ed. Zhao Wanli 趙萬里, Wang Guohua 王國華. Shanghai: Shanghai shudian chubanshe.

CHAPTER 8

Diplomacy, Black Sea Trade, and the Mission of Baldwin of Hainaut

JOHN GIEBFRIED

Today the Polos are commonly remembered as the first lay European travelers to the court of the Great Khans. Yet, a quarter-century before Marco Polo left home and a decade before Niccolò and Maffeo Polo traveled east in search of wealth, Baldwin of Hainaut, an ambassador of the crusader emperor of Constantinople, left on an embassy to the court of the Great Khan Möngke (r. 1251–59). Unlike Marco Polo, Baldwin had no Rustichello to record his tales into a great epic, but he did meet and pass on advice to the Franciscan friar William of Rubruck, an envoy bound for Mongol lands on a mission for King Louis IX of France (r. 1226–70). Rubruck's report to the king is our only source for Baldwin's own voyage, and provides clues that allow historians to reconstruct his mission. Baldwin's journey would blaze a trail from Constantinople, across the Black Sea to Crimea and the Eurasian Steppe.

CRUSADERS IN CONSTANTINOPLE

The roots of Baldwin of Hainaut's mission can be seen in the capture of Constantinople by the army of the Fourth Crusade in 1204. That crusade ended with Count Baldwin IX of Flanders being elected as Baldwin I (1204–5), the first ruler of the Latin Empire of Constantinople (1204–61). However, resistance to crusader rule from both Greeks and Bulgarians left them unable to consolidate their conquest. Instead, a sixty-year struggle for control of the old Byzantine world ensued between the

Latin Empire and their Venetian allies, the kingdom of Bulgaria, and three Greek successor-states based respectively in Epirus, Nicaea, and Trebizond.[1]

The ambassador Baldwin of Hainaut (not to be confused with Emperor Baldwin) was not one of the crusaders who conquered Constantinople. However, he was a close relative of the new imperial family. The Belgian historian Charles Verlinden has claimed that Baldwin of Hainaut was the son of Countess Margaret of Flanders, and the grandson of Emperor Baldwin I.[2] However, an unpublished Flemish charter demonstrates that Baldwin was instead Margaret's cousin and thus also a cousin to several rulers of crusader Constantinople, including its longest-reigning monarch, Emperor Baldwin II (r. 1237–61), himself the nephew of Baldwin I.[3] At some point before 1219, Baldwin of Hainaut traveled East to Constantinople and was given a place within the aristocracy of the Latin Empire. Documentation for his life in Constantinople is scarce. He is mentioned as a witness to a charter issued in 1219.[4] After this, he vanishes from the historical record for exactly twenty years.

In 1236, the Mongols began their great invasion of eastern Europe. Among their primary targets were the nomadic Cumans, a Turkic people known also as Qipchaqs, who had violently refused to accept Mongol rule. Instead, large numbers of fleeing Cumans flooded into the Balkans.[5] The largest group went to Hungary, where they were welcomed by King Bela IV (r. 1235–70).[6] But many more made their way further south, where they concluded alliances with Bulgaria and the Latin Empire.

The alliance between the Cumans and the Latin Empire was sealed by pagan rituals in which the parties drank from a cup of each other's blood, diluted with water and wine, to become "blood brothers," and enacted a ritual whereby a dog ran a gauntlet of soldiers from both parties, who then chopped it to bits, symbolizing the fate of anyone who broke the pact.[7] The crusaders, for their part, sealed the alliance in a more traditionally Christian way: marriages between three leading Latin nobles and three daughters of the Cuman chiefs.[8] Thus, to seal the alliance, Baldwin of Hainaut married the daughter of the Cuman king Saronius.[9] This marriage might explain why, a dozen years later, Emperor Baldwin II chose Baldwin of Hainaut to lead an embassy to the Mongol court. Through his wife, Baldwin likely became familiar with the languages and traditions of the Steppe. Perhaps she even accompanied him. Doing so would have been an advantage, as the fourteenth-century Florentine merchant Francesco Pegolotti reports that a merchant traveling the Steppe will be more comfortable if he brings a woman fluent in the Cuman language.[10]

This Cuman alliance won the Latin Empire short-term gains against the Greeks, but it also earned them the wrath of the Mongols, who devastated Hungary and then turned south toward the Latin Empire, Bulgaria, and their Cuman allies.[11] Emperor Baldwin II emerged victorious in the first encounter with the Mongols, only to be defeated in a subsequent battle, both around 1242.[12] Nevertheless, the lack of siege equipment meant the Mongols could not capture crusader strongholds and thus their forces simply withdrew eastward.[13] The result of this attack, combined with the defeat of the Turks and their allies at the Battle of Kösedağ soon afterward (1243),[14] meant that all the major powers in the Aegean save one, the Greek empire of Nicaea, were severely weakened by Mongol aggression. Filling that vacuum, Nicaea emerged as the dominant player in the region.[15]

MEETING THE MONGOLS

The Mongol invasion of Eastern Europe caught the West almost entirely by surprise. Little was known about the Mongols or their intentions, and so in 1246, Pope Innocent IV (r. 1243–54) called the Council of Lyons to discuss, among other things, how Europe should respond to the Mongols. There the religious and secular leaders of Europe, including Baldwin II, agreed to send out five teams of Franciscan and Dominican friars to find the Mongols and uncover their intentions.[16] One group, led by the Franciscan John of Plano Carpini, traveled across eastern Europe, Russia, and the Steppe just in time to witness the enthronement of the Great Khan Güyük (r. 1246–48).[17] The other ambassadors would be less lucky. They had all been dispatched to the Middle East, to follow the traditional way to the East along the Silk Roads. Instead, the missions of Andrew of Longjumeau, Ascelin of Cremona,[18] Dominic of Aragon, and Laurence of Portugal, all failed to make any significant contacts with the Mongols, although the latter two appeared to have refocused more successfully on diplomacy with Eastern Christians.[19]

A second wave of embassies soon followed, instigated by further contact between the Mongols and Europeans. While on crusade in the East, King Louis IX dispatched two such missions, one led by Andrew of Longjumeau and another by William of Rubruck. In the time between these missions, Emperor Baldwin II, Louis's cousin and ally in the East, sent an embassy of his own to the Mongols, led by Baldwin of Hainaut.

The exact circumstances leading to Baldwin of Hainaut's journey are unclear. Nevertheless, one existing theory can be discarded. This is the suggestion that after his battle with the Mongols, Baldwin II was captured and made to submit himself and his empire to the Mongols.[20] According to this theory, the purpose of Baldwin of Hainaut's trip a decade later was for crusader Constantinople to pledge their allegiance to the new Great Khan Möngke and receive a confirmation of their titles, or *yarligh,* a royal decree, from him.[21]

This is a problematic hypothesis because there is no evidence for Baldwin making submission. Moreover, Baldwin II likely would have been excommunicated for submitting to the Mongols, as was the crusader-prince of Antioch when he had done so.[22] Instead, Baldwin sat at the right hand of Pope Innocent at the Council of Lyons.[23] Surely an avowed vassal of a pagan horde would not get such treatment. Moreover, when William of Rubruck lists the vassals of the Mongols in the Aegean Basin, he does not include the Latin Empire.[24]

A more credible reason for this embassy was expressed in two recent articles by Aleksandar Uzelac, who argues that Baldwin II wanted to gain Mongol aid in his wars against his Greek rivals. Uzelac terms this Baldwin's "nomadic diplomacy," a willingness to find allies among Steppe tribes, as he had with the Cumans, because western European rulers, distracted by pressing needs at home and in the Holy Land, were not interested in coming to his aid.[25]

In any case, the immediate cause of Baldwin of Hainaut's mission is difficult to establish. Uzelac points to two possibilities: the visit of a Mongol envoy to the papal court following the legation of Ascelin of Cremona, and the second mission of Andrew of Longjumeau, made in response to the promise of an alliance made by a Mongol viceroy to Louis IX on Cyprus in 1249.[26] However, if Baldwin of Hainaut had been dispatched at either of these moments, he would have arrived too early to meet with the Great Khan Möngke (r. 1251–59).

A better possibility is the embassy of a Syrian Christian charlatan named Theodolus. He was originally part of Andrew of Longjumeau's second mission, but abandoned the group, later going on alone to meet Möngke.[27] There he spun a fanciful story about bringing a letter from Heaven sealed with gold ink that predicted the Mongols would rule the world, which he had accidentally lost.[28] Nevertheless, Möngke deputized Theodolus to lead an embassy to Louis IX and the pope to get their submission. His journey took him across the Steppe, through the Black Sea, to Nicaea, where he was detained by the Greek emperor.[29]

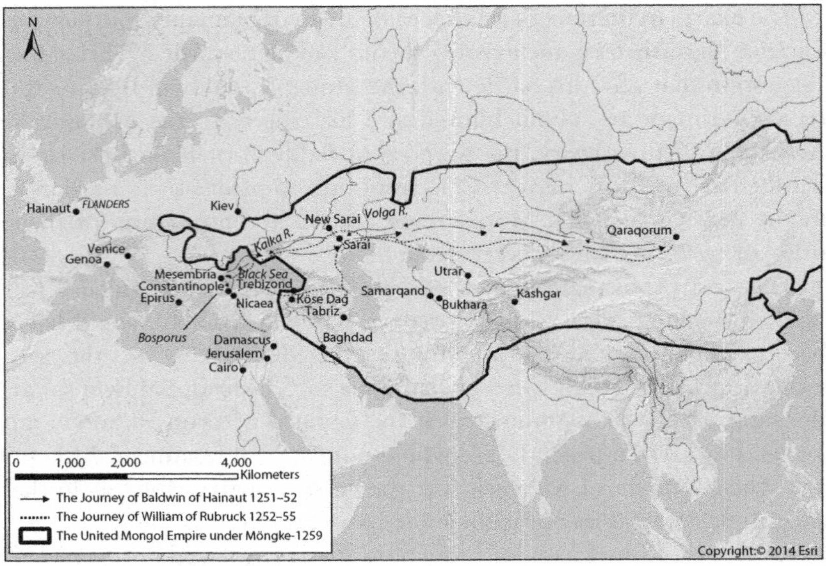

MAP 8.1. The World of Baldwin of Hainaut, ca. the 1250s.

Unable to produce a letter showing his credentials, the hoaxer was locked up and all the gifts and tribute he collected along the way were confiscated.[30] It seems highly illogical that this embassy, which we know was collecting tribute from cities it passed through, would sail directly past Constantinople, the first major city of the Latin West on his route, only to stop shortly thereafter at the less than friendly city of Nicaea. Therefore, Theodolus almost certainly stopped in Constantinople, and his visit might have convinced Emperor Baldwin II to send Baldwin of Hainaut off to Möngke. While not conclusive, this theory best fits the evidence and allows Baldwin to set off in time to meet the Great Khan.

Thus, Baldwin of Hainaut left Constantinople in late 1251 or early 1252, crossing the Black Sea and going overland to the camp of Sartaq, the pro-Christian son and heir to Batu Khan (r. 1227–55), the first ruler of the Golden Horde. There he was interrogated by Sartaq's principal secretary about who among the rulers of Europe was the most powerful.[31] From there he continued to Qaraqorum, probably via Batu's court at Sarai.[32] Then he returned home to Constantinople, where he met with William of Rubruck, a Franciscan friar sent by Louis IX to Sartaq's court to open relations with the prince and who unknowingly was about to make the identical trip to Möngke's court (see map 8.1).

If Mongol military aid against the Greeks was on the agenda for Baldwin of Hainaut, none was forthcoming. However, the mission did serve to either open or intensify preexisting diplomatic relations between the Golden Horde and Constantinople.[33] Moreover, Baldwin's mission coincides with the start of a decade of increased political, military, and economic involvement around the Black Sea by the Latin Empire and its Venetian allies. Emperor Baldwin II provided William of Rubruck with signed diplomatic credentials for the Mongols, and Venetian merchants in Crimea advised William on the best means of travel to the Mongol camp.[34] These both suggest a familiarity with the Mongol court by Baldwin and the Venetians. At the same time, Baldwin II also tried to strike a marriage alliance with the Greek empire of Trebizond, a Mongol vassal and Black Sea trade hub.[35] Venice also voted to reinforce Constantinople by paying for a garrison of a thousand men-at-arms.[36] Moreover, in 1258, a Venetian fleet captured the city of Mesembria on the Black Sea's western coastline.[37] Three years later, the Venetians and the crusaders launched an attack on the island of Daupnousia. This small island is the first port after the opening of the Bosporus going east and thus when cross-winds block ships from entering the Bosporus, Daupnousia provides safe harbor.[38] The reason for this spate of activity in the 1250s possibly lies in a major shift in global trade: the creation of a new Silk Road.

SHIFTING SILK ROADS

For decades, historians have understood that although the idea of a Silk Road is a useful shorthand for the patterns of premodern Eurasian trade, the image of one simple discrete path for all long-distance trade across Asia is an oversimplification of the facts on the ground.[39] For the purposes of this chapter, however, it is fair to say that in the centuries leading up to the rise of the Mongols, there was a westward flow of silk, spices, and other luxuries from East Asia on a series of interconnected land routes, which we can call "Silk Roads," through Central Asia, Persia, and Mesopotamia to the Eastern Mediterranean, where Italian traders could take these goods to the European market.[40]

The arrival of the Mongols brought many changes to these Silk Roads, primarily because for the first time, most of Eurasia was controlled by only one power. One key development that happened during their rule, as this chapter will show, was the development of another more northerly Silk Road that traveled across the Eurasian Steppe and terminated at the Black Sea. In the 1250s, the Silk Roads saw dramatic upheaval due to a Mongol invasion and intra-Christian struggle in the Holy Land.[41] Möngke's brother, Hülegü (1218–65), led a Mongol invasion westward across the Middle East, devastating and conquering cities on the old Silk Roads, most famously Baghdad, which was taken in 1258.[42] Meanwhile, long-simmering rivalries among Christians in the Holy Land erupted over a dispute regarding the monastery of St. Sabas in Acre.[43] The War of St. Sabas quickly evolved into a full civil war in the Kingdom of Jerusalem with Genoa, the Hospitallers, and a faction of the kingdom's barons fighting against Venice, the Templars, and other Jerusalemite barons. Acre was devastated by full-scale urban warfare, with siege engines on both sides firing day and night until the Genoese quarter fell after a year-long siege.[44]

The fighting soon spread to the Aegean, which became an important theater in a trans-Mediterranean war between Venice and Genoa.[45] In 1261, Genoa allied itself with Venice's enemy, the Greek empire of Nicaea, pledging naval support in exchange for Venice's possessions and trade rights in the Aegean and Black Seas.[46] Later that year, Greek forces retook Constantinople. In that same year, Hülegü (r. 1260–65), now established as the first ruler of the Ilkhanate, the Mongol state based in Iran and Mesopotamia (1260–1335), attacked his fellow Mongol, Berke, Khan of the Golden Horde (r. 1257–66), seizing all of Berke's lands south of the Caucasus Mountains, most importantly the city of Tabriz.[47]

Previous historians have seen this moment as the catalyst for a great transformation. Berke was left isolated on the Steppe, unable to tap into the riches of the Silk Roads.[48] In response, he allied himself with the Mamluk Sultanate in Egypt to combat their shared Mongol rivals: the Ilkhanate. He also developed a new branch of the Silk Road by courting Western merchants—primarily the Genoese—who had just set up shop in the Black Sea after their Greek allies displaced the Venetians.[49] From their bases in Crimea they could both gain access to silk, spices, and other luxuries and transport military aid from the Golden Horde to their Egyptian allies.

However, the final section of this chapter will demonstrate that this new Silk Road predates the falls of Constantinople and Tabriz in 1261. Moreover, it will examine how diplomatic contacts by men like Baldwin of Hainaut were crucial in the development of this new trade network. Yet, before the development of the trade links in the Mongol period can be analyzed, the nature of Black Sea trade before the arrival of the Mongols must be first discussed.

THE EVOLUTION OF BLACK SEA TRADE

For most of the Middle Ages, the Black Sea served as a conduit for goods coming from Russia, Scandinavia, and the Steppe to Constantinople. Russia was set up by Vikings as a trading entrepot between Scandinavia and Byzantium, sending everything from honey to furs to the famed Varangian Guards, the personal bodyguard of the Byzantine emperors, southward to Constantinople.[50] Winding its way down the Dnieper River, this trade made Kiev the center of medieval Russia. Before 1204, the Byzantine Empire strictly limited access to Black Sea trade to Italian merchants.[51] After the Fourth Crusade captured Constantinople in 1204, these restrictions ceased to exist.

The extent to which Venice traded in the Black Sea in the years between the Fourth Crusade and the Mongol conquest of Russia in the late 1230s is debatable. Only three Venetian commercial documents mentioning trade in the Black Sea survive from this period, and they reveal little more than the names of the merchants involved.[52] However, John of Plano Carpini does meet Venetian merchants in Kiev, and both Christian and Muslim authors document the continuing trade in furs, including black fox, squirrel, miniver, and beaver, before and after the Mongol conquest.[53]

Trade also flourished in another commodity during this period: slaves.[54] The slave trade was a staple of Black Sea commerce going back centuries, but the increased supply of slaves following the Mongol invasions led to a boom in this market. It is notable that the first recorded transaction involving slaves, in this case a Russian woman sent from Constantinople to Venice, dates to 1223, the same year as the great Mongol victory at the Kalka River.[55] Soon the market would be so saturated that even William of Rubruck would pick up a slave boy named Nicholas to help him on his travels.[56] The Venetians found an active market for these slaves in the Middle East, where rulers were seeking to reinforce their armies with slave soldiers, or mamluks.[57] In fact, this trade became so extensive, even before 1261, that Pope Innocent IV had to step in and chastise Venetian and other Italian merchants for selling so many Christian slaves to Muslims.[58] After 1261, the Genoese took this trade to yet another level, shipping huge numbers of slave soldiers to Egypt to reinforce the Mamluk army.[59]

Yet, while these trades were lucrative for Venice and Genoa, it was the presence of two other goods in Crimean markets, silk and spices, first reported by William of Rubruck during his visit there in the early 1250s, that made this market especially valuable.[60] Perhaps that is why Venice and the Latin Empire expended so much effort to secure the region in the 1250s. With trade in the Eastern Mediterranean under threat, both from conflict between Muslims and Mongols and from the War of St. Sabas, Venice was doubling down on the Black Sea. Genoa, too, at that point losing the war in the Levant, decided that rather than winning back the Holy Land, it was best to seize the Black Sea from their arch-rival with Greek aid. This is a clear indication of how highly both sides valued the revenues that could be gained from Black Sea trade. Now the trade there in Eastern luxuries in this early period was not as high in volume, but the potential for more trade did exist, fed by the prospect of diplomacy.

It appears therefore that trade in the goods which would characterize this Silk Road under Berke all predate his reign. Instead, I suggest that this route had its origins in the diplomatic policies of his elder brother, Batu. In the 1250s, the central axis of Mongol power ran westward from Möngke's base in Qaraqorum to Batu's lands on the Steppe.[61] His semi-independent status, due to his role as Möngke's kingmaker and his frontline location, meant that envoys from Europe and the Middle East who sought to parley with the Mongols would travel to his court, bringing him gifts. He would then dispatch them on to Qaraqorum as an act of fealty to his cousin.[62]

Along the way to his court, however, there was another port of call, that of Batu's senior vassals, his son Sartaq and younger brother Berke. Rubruck reports how Sartaq's camp was positioned along the route that Russians, Vlachs, Bulgarians, Circassians, Alans, and those coming from Crimea, would take to Batu's court.[63] Sartaq, who had the reputation of being a Christian, received generous gifts from these Christian visitors. Likewise, Berke, whose camp was located in Georgia, along the routes taken by envoys from Anatolia and the Middle East, embraced Islam, receiving generous gifts from the envoys from the Islamic world.[64]

In the Mongol world, tribute and trade went hand in hand. For instance, it is not clear whether Niccolò and Maffeo Polo, bringing jewels to Berke's court, sold them to the khan at a profit, or simply gave them to him and in turn were richly rewarded.[65] This generosity was a tried and true method to win merchants to Mongol courts. Ögödei would pay extravagant amounts to merchants, even if their goods were not of the best quality, and his son Güyük was famously generous.[66] Either way, the courts of these Mongol rulers became magnets for trade long before 1261. Rubruck observed that Batu's camp was followed wherever it went by a bazaar.[67] Before the reforms of Möngke, traders followed diplomats in the use of the Mongol postal relay system free of charge.[68] That being said, there were probably far more merchants doing business regionally, rather than those making the journey from Crimea to China, but such was surely the case along the traditional Silk Roads.[69]

Batu's northern diplomatic "superhighway" to Qaraqorum and the trade network that would grow up around it had two main selling points: speed and safety. Less than a century later, the Florentine merchant Pegolotti would call the Crimea to China route the safest and quickest way to the East.[70] Yet, this was true even in the time of the earliest Christian diplomatic missions to the Mongols. All three envoys who attempted the northern journey, Carpini, Rubruck, and Baldwin of Hainaut, made it successfully to the Mongol heartland and home again with little difficulty. Meanwhile, of those who went south on the traditional Silk Road routes, only Andrew of Longjumeau on his second journey made it to the Mongol court. But even with the full protection and support of the Mongol viceroy, Andrew was still tossed in prison in Aleppo on his return journey.[71]

However, while Carpini was able to travel in relative safety from Lyons to Mongolia in the mid-1240s, it took him fifteen months to reach Güyük's court, substantially longer than the eight months it took for Rubruck to travel from Constantinople to Möngke's court.[72] The reason for this is the long overland travel through Eastern Europe. What made a trade route from the Golden Horde to Italy possible was the ability for merchants to sail across the Mediterranean, past Constantinople, through the Black Sea and right up to the Mongolian doorstep of Crimea. This Black Sea shortcut is the great legacy of Baldwin of Hainaut's mission to the Mongols. As the first known European to take this route, he blazed a trail that diplomats like Rubruck and traders like the Polos would soon follow.[73] Within a century, it would be the primary link between Europe and East Asia.

Thus, it is not surprising that even in the infancy of this trade corridor across the Black Sea, Venice and their allies in the Latin Empire made controlling this trade their top priority, especially considering the volatility of the southern route. Unfortunately, this desire to control the Black Sea was their undoing. On a June night in the summer of 1261, while the Venetian fleet was away trying to take Dauphnousia, a Greek army, originally off to harass Bulgarians, found Constantinople virtually unguarded, and surprised and overwhelmed an underdefended gate, capturing the city.[74] This attack restored the Byzantine Empire and gave their Genoese allies a dominant position in the Black Sea trade for nearly half a century, bringing unparalleled wealth to that city. As for the protagonists of our story, the emperor Baldwin II would spend the last decade and a half of his life going around Europe selling all he owned, fruitlessly looking for aid to restore him to the throne.[75] His cousin Baldwin of Hainaut also returned an exile, but in 1262 he received lands from his other cousin Countess Margaret of Flanders and settled down to the quiet life of a minor local lord in modern-day Belgium.[76] Here he faded to a footnote in the history of the greatest land empire ever assembled.

NOTES

This research was supported by the European Research Council under the European Union's Seventh Framework Programme (FP/2007–13)/ERC grant Agreement n. 312397.

1. Wolff 1962, 200–201.
2. Verlinden 1952, 125–28.
3. *Charter of Countess Margaret of Flanders to Baldwin of Hainaut, 1262.*
4. Tafel and Thomas 1856–57, 2: 214–15.
5. Vásáry 2005, 63–64; also Shurany's chapter in this volume.
6. Jackson, 2005, 61.
7. Joinville 1995, 244; Joinville 2009, 475.
8. Trois-Fountaines 1874, 950.
9. Vásáry 2005, 66.
10. Pegolotti 1936, 21–22; tr. Yule and Cordier 1914, 3:153.
11. Giebfried 2013, 132–33.
12. Giebfried 2013, 133.
13. Giebfried 2013, 133.
14. On the battle of Kösedağ: Yıldız's contribution in this volume.
15. Giebfried 2013, 133–35.
16. Jackson 2005, 87; Roncaglia 1953, 36; Baldwin 1985, 472.
17. For an overview of Carpini's mission: Dawson 1980, xv–xvii.
18. On Ascelin's failed mission: Yıldız's chapter in the volume.
19. Baldwin 1985, 472–75; Dawson 1980, xviii–xix. On Lawrence of Portugal: Roncaglia 1953, 33–44; on Ascelin of Cremona: Guzman 1971, 234–49; and on Dominic of Aragon: Tisserant 1924, 340–55.
20. Richard 1992, 118; Hamilton 2014, 50.
21. Richard 1992, 118.
22. Richard 1999, 410–11.
23. Abulafia 1988, 361.
24. Jackson 2005, 117.
25. Uzelac 2012, 64–65.
26. Uzelac 2015, 67.
27. Rubruck, ed. van den Wyngaert 1929, 253–54; tr. Jackson 2009, 184.
28. Rubruck, ed. van den Wyngaert 1929, 254; tr. Jackson 2009, 184.
29. Rubruck, ed. van den Wyngaert 1929, 254–5; tr. Jackson 2009, 185–86.

30. Rubruck, ed. van den Wyngaert 1929, 255; tr. Jackson 2009, 186.
31. Rubruck, ed. van den Wyngaert 1929, 151; tr. Jackson 2009, 115.
32. Rubruck, ed. van den Wyngaert 1929, 201; tr. Jackson 2009, 200.
33. Uzelac 2015, 70–71.
34. Uzelac 2015, 69–71.
35. Joinville 1995, 294; Joinville 2009, 293.
36. Norden 1903, 759–60.
37. Riant 2004, 1: 157.
38. Geanakoplos 1959, 99.
39. Christian 2000, 2–6; Hansen 2017, 5–8; Jackson 2017, 210–11.
40. Lambton 1988, 333–34; Jackson 2005, 295–301; Jackson 2017, 214–17.
41. Karpov 2011, 419–20.
42. Jackson 2017, 128–31, 164–68; also Hoduos's and Yıldız's articles in this volume.
43. Marshall 1992, 39–40.
44. Marshall 1992, 225–28.
45. Longnon 1962, 220–21.
46. Geanakoplos 1959, 84–85, 87–89.
47. Ciocîltan 2012, 148.
48. Saunders 1977, 67–76; Ciocîltan 2012, 148–57.
49. Ciocîltan 2012, 150–52.
50. Frankopan 2017, 122–23.
51. Jacoby 2007, 698.
52. Della Rocca and Lombardo 1971, 18–20, 83–84, 200–201.
53. Carpini, ed. van den Wyngaert 1929, 129; tr. Dawson 1980, 71; Ciocîltan 2012, 142, 146–47.
54. Frankopan 2017, 114–32.
55. Jacoby 2007, 690–91.
56. Rubruck, ed. van den Wyngaert 1929, 170; tr. Jackson 2009, 69.
57. On the mamluk slave markets: Mazor's article in the volume.
58. Jacoby 2007, 690–91.
59. Saunders 1977, 73.
60. Rubruck, ed. van den Wyngaert 1929, 166; tr. Jackson 2009, 64.
61. Ciocîltan 2012, 51–53.
62. Ciocîltan 2012, 53.
63. Rubruck, ed. van den Wyngaert 1929, 209; tr. Jackson 2009, 126.
64. Rubruck, ed. van den Wyngaert 1929, 209; tr. Jackson 2009, 127.
65. Polo 1986, 105; Polo 2016, 3.
66. May 2016, 104.
67. Jackson 2017, 215.
68. May 2016, 106.
69. Jackson 2017, 211.
70. Pegolotti 1936, 22–23; tr. Yule and Cordier 1914, 3: 152.
71. Jackson 2009, 35.
72. Carpini, ed. Van Den Wyngaert 1929, lx, 116; tr. Dawson 1980, xv, 61; Rubruck, ed. Van Den Wyngaert 1929, 164; tr. Jackson 2009, 61, 176.

73. Uzelac 2015, 70–71.
74. Wolff 1962, 231.
75. Wolff 1962, 232.
76. *Charter of Countess Margaret of Flanders to Baldwin of Hainaut, 1262.*

BIBLIOGRAPHY

Abulafia, David. 1988. *Frederick II: A Medieval Emperor.* Oxford: Oxford University Press.

Allsen, Thomas. 1997. *Commodity and Exchange in the Mongol Empire: A Cultural History of Islamic Textiles.* Cambridge: Cambridge University Press.

Baldwin, Marshall W. 1985. "Missions to the East in the Thirteenth and Fourteenth Centuries." In *History of the Crusades.* Vol. 5. *The Impact of the Crusades on the Near East.* ed. N.P. Zacour and H.W. Hazard, 452–518. Madison: University of Wisconsin Press.

Charter of Countess Margaret of Flanders to Baldwin of Hainaut, 1262. Archives Départementales du Nord, CC série B 1357, n. 1293.

Ciocîltan, Virgil. 2012. *The Mongols and the Black Sea Trade in the Thirteenth and Fourteenth Centuries.* Tr. Samuel P. Willcocks. Leiden: Brill.

Christian, David. 2000. "Silk Roads or Steppe Roads? The Silk Roads in World History." *Journal of World History* 11.1: 1–26.

Dawson, Christopher. 1980. *The Mission to Asia.* Toronto: University of Toronto Press.

della Rocca, Roberto Morozzo, and Agostino Lombardo. 1971. *Documenti del commercio veneziano nei secoli XI/XIII.* Turin: Bottega d'Erasmo.

Frankopan, Peter. 2017. *The Silk Roads: A New History of the World.* New York: Vintage Books.

Geanakoplos, Deno John. 1959. *Emperor Michael Palaeologus and the West, 1258–1282.* Cambridge: Cambridge University Press.

Giebfried, John. 2013. "The Mongol Invasions and the Aegean World (1241–61)." *Mediterranean Historical Review* 28: 129–39.

Guzman, Gregory G. 1971. "Simon of Saint-Quentin and the Dominican Mission to the Mongol Baiju: A Reappraisal." *Speculum* 46: 232–49.

Hansen, Valerie. 2017. *The Silk Road: A New History with Documents.* Oxford: Oxford University Press.

Hamilton, Bernard. 2014. "The Latin Empire and Western Contacts with Asia." In *Contact and Conflict in Frankish Greece and the Aegean, 1204–1453*, ed. Nikolaos G. Chrissis and Mike Carr, 43–63, Farnham, England: Routledge.

Jackson, Peter. 2005. *The Mongols and the West, 1221–1410.* New York: Pearson.

———, tr. 2009. *The Mission of Friar William of Rubruck: His Journey to the Court of the Great Khan Möngke, 1253–1255.* Indianapolis: Hackett.

———. 2017. *The Mongols and the Islamic World.* New Haven, CT: Yale University Press.

Jacoby, David. 2007. "Byzantium, the Italian Maritime Powers, and the Black Sea before 1204." *Byzantinische Zeitschrift* 100: 677–99.

Joinville, John of. 1995. *La vie de Saint Louis.* Ed. Jacques Monfrin. Paris: Dunod.

———. 2009. *Chronicles of the Crusades.* Tr. Caroline Smith. New York: Penguin Books.

Karpov, Sergei. 2011. "Main Changes in the Black Sea Trade and Navigation, 12th-15th Centuries." In *Proceedings of the 22nd International Congress of Byzantine Studies,* ed. Iliiā̆Iliev et al., 417–30. Sofia: Bulgarian Historical Heritage Foundation.

Lambton, Ann K.S. 1988. *Continuity and Change in Medieval Persia: Aspects of Administrative, Economic, and Social History, 11th-14th Century.* Albany: State University of New York Press.

Longnon, Jean. 1962. "The Frankish States in Greece, 1204–1500." In *A History of the Crusades. The Later Crusades, 1189–1311,* vol. 2, ed. Robert Lee Wolff, Kenneth M. Setton, and Harry W. Hazard, 234–75. Madison: University of Wisconsin Press.

Marshall, Christopher. 1992. *Warfare in the Latin East, 1192–1291.* New York: Cambridge University Press.

May, Timothy. 2016. "Commercial Queens: Mongolian Khatuns and the Silk Road." *Journal of the Royal Asiatic Society* 26: 89–106.

Norden, Walter. 1903. *Das Papsttum und Byzanz.* Berlin: Behr.

Pegolotti, Francesco Balducci. 1936. *La pratica della mercatura.* Ed. Allan Evans. Cambridge, MA: Medieval Academy of America Press.

Phillips, Jonathan. 2005. *The Fourth Crusade and the Sack of Constantinople.* New York: Penguin.

Polo, Marco. 1986. *Il milione.* Ed. Ruggiero M. Ruggieri. Florence: Olschki.

———. 2016. *The Description of the World.* Tr. Sharon Kinoshita. Indianapolis: Hackett.

Queller, Donald, and Thomas Madden. 1999. *The Fourth Crusade: The Conquest of Constantinople.* Philadelphia: University of Pennsylvania Press.

Riant, Paul-Édouard-Didier. 2004. *Exuviae sacrae Constantinopolitanae.* 2 vols. Paris: Éditions du le Comité des Travaux Historiques et Scientifiques.

Richard, Jean. 1992. "À propos de la mission de Baudouin de Hainaut: L'empire Latin de Constantinople et les Mongols." *Journal des savants* 1: 115–21.

———. 1999. *The Crusades, c.1071-c.1291.* Tr. Jean Birrell. Cambridge: Cambridge University Press.

Roncaglia, Martiniano. 1953. "Frere Laurent de Portugal OFM et sa légation en Orient (1245–1248)." *Bollettino della badia greca di Grottaferrata* 7: 33–44.

Saunders, John Joseph. 1977. "The Mongol Defeat at Ain Jalut and the Restoration of the Greek Empire." In *Muslims and Mongols: Essays on Medieval Asia,* ed. G.W. Rice, 67–76. Christchurch, Australia: University of Canterbury Press.

Tafel, Gottlieb Lukas Friedrich, and Georg Martin Thomas. 1856–57. *Urkunden zur älteren Handels-und Staatsgeschichte der Republik Venedig, mit besonderer Beziehung auf Byzanz und die Levante: Vom neunten bis zum Ausgang des fünfzehnten Jahrhunderts.* 3 vols. Vienna: Hofund Staatsdruckerei.

Tisserant, Eugene. 1924. "La légation en Orient du franciscain Dominique d' Aragon, 1245–47." *Revue de l'oriente chrétien* 24: 336–55.

Trois-Fontaines, Alberic of. 1874. *Chronica Alberici Monachi Trium Fontium, a monacho NoviMonasterii Hoiensis interpolata*. Ed. Paul Scheffer-Boichorst. In *Monumenta germaniae historica*. Series scriptores 23. Stuttgart: Hiersemann.

Uzelac, Aleksandar. 2012. Balduin od Enoa i 'Nomadska Diplomatija' Latinskog Carstva" [Baldwin of Hainaut and 'the Nomadic Diplomacy' of the Latin Empire]." *Istorijski časopis* 61: 45–65.

———. 2015. "The Latin Empire of Constantinople, the Jochids and Crimea in the Mid-Thirteenth Century." *Golden Horde Review* 3: 62–76.

Van den Wyngaert, Anastasius, ed. 1929. *Itinera et relationes Fratrum Minorum saeculi XIII et XIV.* Florence: Quaracchi.

Vásáry, István. 2005. *Cumans and Tatars: Oriental Military in the Pre-Ottoman Balkans, 1185–1365*. Cambridge: Cambridge University Press.

Verlinden, Charles. 1952. "Boudewijn van Henegouwen: een onbekende reiziger door Azie" [Baldwin of Hainaut: An Unknown Traveler of Asia]." *Tijdschrift voor Geschiedenis* 65: 122–29.

Wolff, Robert Lee. 1962. "The Latin Empire of Constantinople." In *A History of the Crusades. The Later Crusades, 1189–1311*, ed. Robert Lee Wolff, Kenneth M. Setton, and Harry W. Hazard, 187–233. Madison: University of Wisconsin Press.

Yule, Henry, and Henri Cordier, tr. 1914. *Cathay and the Way Thither.* 3 vols. London: Hakluyt Society.

CHAPTER 9

Jamāl al-Dīn al-Ṭībī

The Iraqi Trader Who Traversed Asia

MATANYA GILL

In the 1250s, two brothers from a Baghdadi family of potters set sail on a dangerous journey, across the Indian Ocean, carrying a precious cargo of pearls. Their maritime journey took them from the Island of Kish in the Persian Gulf to the Swahili coast in Africa. From there, they headed to the Pandyan kingdom of Maʿbar in South India (nowadays Tamil Nadu), and then, to south China continuing to their destination in northern China. This chapter unravels the story of one of these brothers, the local Baghdadi merchant and entrepreneur Jamāl al-Dīn Ibrāhīm al-Ṭībī (1232–1306). Jamāl al-Dīn's successful career is a case in point for how local merchants took advantage of the new commercial opportunities that Mongol rule offered. Under the Mongol aegis, the Ṭībī family developed their personal and the imperial trade networks beyond the local arenas, transforming them into a trade enterprise that extended throughout the Mongol-dominated continental and maritime routes across Asia and further beyond.

To promote the flow of trade to and supply their courts, as well as increase their wealth, the Mongol rulers introduced new institutions and laid the foundations and infrastructure for promoting trans-Eurasian trade. The *ortaq* was one of these special institutions.[1] The khans, their wives, princes, members of the Mongol elite, and even government officials would enter a commercial, contractual partnership with a merchant. The Mongol partners provided the merchant with investment capital for his commercial venture, and granted him the privileges associated with the lucrative *ortaq* status. In return, the merchant provided his Mongol partner the lion's share in the profits. Although, as the empire expanded and underwent centralization, *ortaq* privileges changed, they generally included subsidized transportation, the protection of the *ortaq*'s property and person, and in some instances, even tax exemptions. Through the *ortaq* system, the Mongols had an active role, as consumers, investors, and entrepreneurs, in the thriving of long distance, trans-Asian trade. While Muslims and Uighurs were particularly prevalent in the *ortaq* and non-*ortaq* merchant ranks of the empire, Syriac Christians, Armenians, and other communities took part in the trade as well.[2]

Studying *ortaq* commercial partnerships under the Mongols presents some difficulties. The term itself rarely appears in the sources and the details of such Mongol investment in trade are not clearly stated. Merchants mixed their own private financial interests and commercial engagements with their official *ortaq* business, and the Mongols themselves often blurred the lines between private capital and imperial lands, properties and privileges. Furthermore, the *ortaq* system was not the sole mechanism that merchants employed to expand their local enterprises into interregional trade networks. Other means included kinship and patronage ties, gifting, and official state appointments, especially as diplomats, envoys, governors, or tax collectors.

This article explores the role of Ilkhanid-based merchants in the expansion of trade through the story of one of the most prominent merchants. Based in Ilkhanid-ruled Baghdad and the Island of Kish in the Persian Gulf, Jamāl al-Dīn al-Ṭībī and his family established and maintained a trade network that interlinked markets in western, southern, and eastern Asia. Its reach extended from Iraq, Iran, Syria, Anatolia, and Europe, to Africa, Yemen, India, and China. Jamāl al-Dīn and his sons further used their trade activities and ties to the Mongol court to gain beneficial positions in the Ilkhanid administration and government. Although scholars have examined the role of the Ṭībīs in the expansion of Ilkhanid trade,[3] the Arabic sources have not yet been exhausted. Juxtaposing these with other, contemporaneous sources in Persian and Chinese, enables us to better reconstruct their commercial activities and expansion.

Jamāl al-Dīn's success is further interlinked with the changes that the land routes, which complemented the Indian Ocean maritime trade routes, went through under Mongol hegemony. Jamāl al-Dīn al-Ṭībī's maritime voyage to China signaled a new stage in the Mongol expansion into the maritime networks. During the latter half of the thirteenth century, especially following the Mongols' defeat of the Song dynasty in 1279 and the Mongol annexation of their thriving ports, the main channel for trade relations between the two allied Mongol states, the Ilkhanate of greater Iran (1260–1335) and the Yuan in China (1260–1368), shifted from the continental Silk Roads to the maritime routes that extended from the Persian Gulf to South India and China. The Mongols' efforts to secure maritime trade further facilitated connections between maritime and continental paths creating a trans-Asian trade networks that crisscrossed most of the Old World.[4] *Ortaq* and private merchants played a significant role in facilitating this expansion of maritime-continental trade networks, on both the Yuan and Ilkhanid ends.

Previous scholarship had suggested that the gradual decline of the ʿAbbasid Caliphate from the eleventh century, and especially, the Mongol conquest of Baghdad in 1258, led to the shift in the mainline routes of the western Indian Ocean trade, from the Baghdad-centered, Iraq-Persian Gulf route, to the Red Sea route that interlinked Cairo and Yemen with South India.[5] The Ṭībīs' impressive commercial network, however, shows that Baghdad maintained its central place as an intercontinental trade hub in the Indian Ocean–linked commerce under the Ilkhans.

The Baghdad-based Ṭībīs and their expanding trade relations facilitated the city's recovery of its role as the leading center for the manufacturing and trading of pearls. Baghdad-manufactured pearls found their way to the markets of China, India, Yemen, and Europe. The city remained the Tībīs' center of operation and funding while they expanded their enterprise through the Indian Ocean trade. The family's story further highlights the significance of Ilkhanid and Iraqi commercial relations with the Rasūlid dynasty in Yemen (1228–1454).

JAMĀL AL-DĪN'S RISE AND EARLY CAREER

Jamāl al-Dīn was born in Baghdad in 1232 to a Muslim family that originated in the town of al-Ṭīb, near the city of Wāsiṭ in southeast Iraq. His father, Muḥammad b. Saʿdī al-Ṭībī, emigrated from Wāsiṭ to Baghdad during the reign of the ʿAbbasid caliph al-Nāṣir (r. 1180–1225). The Ṭībis were a family of potters, making and selling *sawāmil*—clay drinking vessels that were used by the locals in the rural areas of Wāsiṭ. Leaving the family business in his youth, Jamāl al-Dīn learned how to pierce pearls (*thaqb al-luʾluʾ*) in Baghdad, and after mastering the profession, he began to work as a pearl merchant.[6]

Baghdad was famous for its pearl industry. Reporting what he learned about the city's flourishing pearl industry and its trade relations with the Indian Ocean before the Mongol conquest (in 1258), the famous Venetian traveler and merchant Marco Polo (1254–1324) writes that:

> Baudac [Baghdad] is a great city . . . where the chief prelate who was called calif of all the Saracens of the world is, just as at Rome for the most part is the see of the Pope of all the Christians of the world . . . from which one can go to the Sea of India. Up and down it, merchants come and go with their wares. You must know that the length of the river from Baudac to the Sea of India is eighteen days' journey. The merchants who wish to go to India descend the river as far as a city called Kisi [Kish] and there enter the Sea of India. I will add, too, that on this river, between Baudac and Kisi, there is a great city called Bastra [Basra]. . . . And almost all the pearls that are brought from India [Indian Ocean] to Christian countries [Europe], are pierced in Baudac.[7]

Yet, according to Polo's account, after the Mongol conquest of Baghdad, Tabriz took over Baghdad's place as the new commercial hub, where European merchants now purchased pearls, silk, and other luxuries. Tabriz became the new destination for merchandise that was transported across the Indian Ocean, and through the Persian Gulf, Baghdad, and Mosul.[8] Jamāl al-Dīn's story, however, shows that, in contrast to Polo's account, Baghdad kept its central position in pearl trade, alongside the thriving markets of Tabriz.

This transcontinental trade in pearls was driven not only by their European demand, but also by patterns of Mongol elite consumption. Pearls, especially the big white pearls, pierced (*luʾluʾ*) or unpierced (*durr*), were luxury items in high demand among members of the Mongol elite. The Mongols associated the color white with good fortune and charisma. Precious rarities, pearls were used in jewelry and clothes, for medicine, and as barter for other commodities or services.[9]

In the 1250s, the young pearl merchant Jamāl al-Dīn traveled to Baghdad and the Island of Kish, a major emporium in the Persian Gulf, where pearl hunting was the main industry. There he purchased a big cargo of white pearls to pierce and sell in Baghdad.[10] Saving up a sum of two thousand dirhams from his ventures, Jamāl al-Dīn set out on the long voyage to China to further purchase and trade pearls in an effort to expand his commercial business (see map 9.1).[11]

Jamāl al-Dīn was accompanied in his voyage by his younger brother, Taqī al-Dīn ʿAbd al-Raḥman (d. 1303). Their route passed between

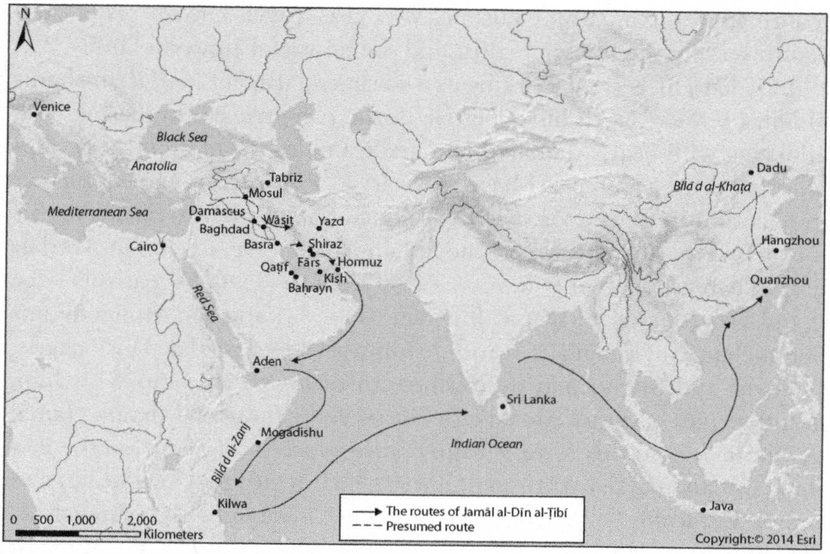

MAP 9.1. The Travels of Jamāl al-Dīn al-Ṭībī.

Baghdad and Kish through Wāsiṭ. From Kish, the two brothers sailed to China, first passing through several stations along the Indian Ocean Basin that also served as pearl fishing centers. Like the Persian Gulf and the South China shores, the Indian Ocean Basin too had an abundance of pearl-production sites.[12] The brothers first headed to the Swahili coast of southeast Africa, then to the kingdom of Maʿbar in South India, and from there to South China, probably heading from there to north China.[13] After making their fortune in China, the two brothers set out on their homeward voyage to the Ilkhanate. In the late 1260s, they sailed from China to Maʿbar, where Jamāl al-Dīn's brother settled after entering the service of its Pandyan ruler. While his brother remained in Maʿbar, Jamāl al-Dīn continued to the Persian Gulf, heading next to the city of Shiraz in southern Iran.[14] From the moment of his return, Jamāl al-Dīn gradually climbed his way up to Mongol service and to the court, where opportunities for gaining investment capital and profit were more abundant.

Upon his arrival in Shiraz, Jamāl al-Dīn established ties with Shams al-Dīn Muḥammad b. Malik Tāzīku al-Yazdī (d. 1300), who was employed at the time in the administration of Fārs (a province on the shores of the Persian Gulf) and took part in the local governance of Shiraz since 1265. Shams al-Dīn, whose commercial businesses extended from China to India and Europe, was also a well-known *ortaq* merchant, serving the Ilkhanid court and the powerful Juwaynī family.[15]

Jamāl al-Dīn started working as a commercial agent (*wakīl*) in Shams al-Dīn's service. With his expertise in the piercing, embroidering, and adorning with pearls, Jamāl al-Dīn made a name for himself as the supplier of pearls and pearl-based jewelry.[16] His career gained further momentum in the 1270s, when he joined Shams al-Dīn Tāzīku on his journey to the court (*ordo*) of the Ilkhan Abaqa (r. 1265–81) in Azerbaijan. There, Jamāl al-Dīn was introduced to Tāzīku's patrons—the grand vizier Shams al-Dīn al-Juwaynī (d. 1284) and the Mongol Amīr Suqunchaq (Sughūnjāq, d. 1290).[17] Impressed by Jamāl al-Dīn's pearls, Juwaynī and Suqunchaq established an *ortaq* partnership with him, granting him together an investment of sixty thousand dinars. Jamāl al-Dīn then used this fortune to purchase pearls in Hormuz on the Persian Gulf and make extravagant jewelry inlaid with precious stones and pearls. Returning to the court, he presented Juwaynī with his merchandise and provided him with a lavish gift. The jewelry was valued at 360,000 dinars. We should note that gifts played a significant role in such commercial engagements, and were often used to return the partner's investment or loan, or to grant him his share in the profit, as well as for providing the merchant with new capital to invest.[18]

Juwaynī and Suqunchaq awarded Jamāl al-Dīn drafts (*ḥawālat*) against the annual incomes of Shiraz, and Jamāl al-Dīn then headed to Shiraz, where he collected the due revenue.[19] This was a common practice at the Mongol courts: short in cash, the court, the commander, or the ruler might grant a merchant, as payment or investment, drafts on the expense of future tax revenue that in most cases, the merchant was to collect himself.[20]

Jamāl al-Dīn successfully took advantage of his new access to the court, further expanding his commercial network. Annually returning to the court, he would sell his lavish jewelry to the wives of the ruler and other ladies. Abaqa's retinue paid him with merchandise, whereas Juwaynī and Suqunchaq provided him with extensive drafts, which allegedly included the annual incomes of Baghdad and Tabriz, making Jamāl al-Dīn very wealthy.[21] While the exchange of drafts or tax farming rights for investment capital or payment often became a heavy burden on the peasantry and the taxpayer subjects, who had to directly deal with the greedy merchants seeking to exhaust the revenue potential of the areas assigned to them, the Arabic biographers favorably mention Jamāl al-Dīn's compassionate and just treatment of the subjects.[22]

In the 1280s and 1290s, Jamāl al-Dīn continued to benefit from his commercial relations. The death in 1277–78 of the ruler of Hormuz, Maḥmūd Qalhatī, who was his rival and competitor in the Persian Gulf, further facilitated his expansion into the Indian Ocean. Beginning in 1281, he was the leading merchant in the Persian Gulf, and under the Ilkhan Arghun (r. 1284–91), was contracted to collect taxes in the district of Fārs.[23]

At this point, we see Jamāl al-Dīn using his fortune and commercial relations with the court to advance to official capacities in Ilkhanid administration. In 1293, the Ilkhan Geikhatu's (r. 1291–95) vizier, Ṣadr al- Dīn Khālidī Zanjānī (d. 1298), assigned Jamāl al-Dīn to the governorship of Fārs for four years, during which he was free to collect the province's taxes for himself. For this position, Jamāl al-Dīn paid the court, was suffering from a depleted treasury, the handsome sum of a thousand *tumans* (equivalent to ten million Ilkhanid silver dinars). Jamāl al-Dīn's payment to the court provides one possible explanation why the vizier Ṣadr al- Dīn's later attempts to accuse him of embezzlement were thwarted.[24]

Furthermore, the court authorized Jamāl al-Dīn to supervise the maritime trade out of the Persian Gulf. His brother Taqī al-Dīn, who remained in India, was appointed that very same year (1293) vizier for the kingdom of Maʿbar and thus gained control over the Pandyan dynasty's ports along the Southeast Indian Coromandel Coast.[25] The presence of Muslim merchants in South Indian maritime trade centers is attested as early as the ninth century. Through their access to commercial and kinship networks as well their administrative and linguistic skills, Muslim merchants quickly became central figures in the political and bureaucratic elites of the South Indian polities. Taking on official capacities, the Muslim merchants maintained their commercial enterprises, which often worked to the advantage of both parties. The merchants advanced their own financial interests, while the ruling elites received access to transregional trade and information networks, and guaranteed the flow of luxury items to their courts.[26]

The simultaneous rise of Jamāl al-Dīn and Taqī al-Dīn across the Indian Ocean enabled the Ṭībī brothers to gain what amounted to a monopoly over Ilkhanid maritime trade routes. They amassed such wealth that Jamāl al-Dīn now had his own private fleet of about a hundred boats in the Persian Gulf. Taqī al-Dīn made sure that no merchant could purchase in Maʿbar any goods from China, before Jamāl al-Dīn's agents inspected the merchandise and claimed the most valuable items for the Ṭībīs.[27]

The Ṭībī brothers, who started off as pearl merchants, now extended their monopoly into the horse exportation as well, shipping horses bred in Iran and Iraq to South India and China, where horses for military usage were in high demand. The Mongol Yuan and the Pandyan dynasties both had difficulty in importing horses via land routes due to their enmity with their neighbors, the Chaghadaids in Central Asia and the Delhi Sultanate (1206–1526) in North India, respectively.[28] So, the maritime routes became the main supply channel for high-quality Arabian horses.

The Ṭībīs shipped horses from Kish and the Persian Gulf to Maʿbar, and from there to China. Each year, Jamāl al-Dīn would send about ten thousand horses to Maʿbar. The price was fixed at 220 dinars per horse, to be paid even if the horses died in transit.[29] The enforcement of such an agreement, which severely disadvantaged their customers in India and China, indicates that high demand for horses and profitability made the risky transactions still worthwhile for importers.

The growing reputation of the Ṭībī brothers as leading Indian Ocean merchants, and their monopoly on Ilkhanid trade to India and China, also drew the attention of dynasties and individuals outside the Ilkhanate who subsequently sought to cooperate with them. The Rasūlid rulers (1228–1454) in Yemen, who had also been exporting large numbers of horses to India, established commercial cooperation and cultivated close ties with the family.[30]

While Jamāl al-Dīn's business thrived, his relations with his former patron, Shams al-Dīn Tāzīku, went sour and the two became bitter rivals. When, in 1294, Shams al-Dīn Tāzīku was impoverished, Jamāl al-Dīn agreed to provide him with only two hundred dinars, less than the price of one horse,[31] perhaps because Jamāl al-Dīn was driven by ambition to eliminate his mercantile competition.

Tāzīku's impoverishment was connected to power struggles over Hormuz. Jamāl al-Dīn, however, found a way both to calm the situation at Hormuz and advance his hold on the maritime trade. He entered an alliance with Bahāʾ al-Dīn Ayāz, a Turkish general who had first served the ruler of Hormuz, Maḥmūd Qalhatī, but after his patron's death (1277–78), rebelled against the Qalhatīs. Jamāl al-Dīn granted Bahāʾ al-Dīn asylum in Kish and assisted him in taking possession of Hormuz from the Qalhatī family. In return, Bahāʾ al-Dīn acknowledged the Ṭībīs' supremacy in the Persian Gulf.[32]

When Jamāl al-Dīn had become famous for his generous donations to charity as well, he fostered close ties with the Sufi Shaykh ʿIzz al-Dīn al-Fārūthī (d. 1296), telling him about his travels and providing him with handsome annual support. His donations to the shaykh continued when the latter migrated to Damascus in the early 1290s, and Jamāl al-Dīn also settled al-Fāruthī's debts after his death.[33] His ongoing support for the Sufi master after the latter moved to Syria, is a possible indication that Jamāl al-Dīn had at least indirect connections also with the Mamluk Sultanate (1250–1517), which ruled in Egypt and Syria, and this despite the ongoing Mamluk-Ilkhanid enmity. The ongoing commercial and scholarly connections between Ilkhanid-ruled Iraq and Syria even during their rivalry (1260–1323),[34] and the ample information on Jamāl al-Dīn in the Mamluk sources, seem to support this conclusion.

JAMĀL AL-DĪN'S FALL FROM GRACE

The reign of the Ilkhan Ghazan (1295–1304) saw the height of Jamāl al-Dīn's power in the Ilkhanid government, as well as his steep fall. In 1296, the Ilkhan put him in charge of Iraq's taxation and financial management, and leased him lands near Baghdad and Shiraz.[35] However, Jamāl al-Dīn had difficulties paying his annual lease for these lands, and therefore, in 1298 he was summoned to the court at Tabriz. To win the Ilkhan's favor, Jamāl al-Dīn brought with him his eldest son, Fakhr al-Dīn (d. 1304), in the hope that his son's previous acquaintance with the Ilkhan might mitigate the case against him. Upon his arrival at the *ordo* (the court), Jamāl al-Dīn submitted the income and accounting books, and was detained there for the next two years.[36] He was unable to extend his earlier leases, but he received a new lease for Kish for four years beginning in 1298, in return for the sum of seven hundred thousand dinars per annum.[37]

During Jamāl al-Dīn's court detainment, his son Fakhr al-Dīn became Ghazan's envoy and *ortaq* merchant to Yuan China. In addition to conducting trade on the Ilkhan's behalf and maintaining the Ilkhanid alliance with the Yuan, Fakhr al-Dīn was also tasked with the delivery of silk stuffs from Ghazan's appanages in China, which had not been collected since the 1250s.[38] For this diplomatic-commercial mission, Fakhr al-Dīn received from the Ilkhan a sum of a hundred thousand dinars as capital for trade, as well as military support consisting of experienced sailors and archers, both Persians and Turks. Jamāl al-Dīn, however, was the one who supplied the junk ships for this voyage. Jamāl al-Dīn, moreover, also filled his son's assigned ships with his own merchandise and the merchandise of his partners in Baghdad and Baṣra, including pearls and jewels valued at eighty thousand dinars.[39]

Fakhr al-Dīn's voyage to China did not set out immediately from Tabriz, but from Baghdad, and only in 1301, almost three years after first corresponding with the Rasūlid sultan al-Mu'ayyad Hizabr al-Dīn Dāwud b. Yūsuf (r. 1296–1321) regarding the promotion of the commercial activities between the Ṭībī family and Aden port.[40] Fakhr al-Dīn seems to have been unable at that time to sail along the coasts of North India due to the tensions between the Delhi Sultanate and horse traders who dealt with the Pandyan dynasty, the Delhi Sultanate's rivals, and therefore used the Aden port to reach Ma'bar in southwest India. There, Fakhr al-Dīn sailed to China in a ship led by Yang Shu (1282–1331), a young Chinese *ortaq* merchant who was captain of a Yuan governmental ship that set out from south China for trade in India. Fakhr al-Dīn's journey to China probably took about a year.[41]

If Jamāl al-Dīn was hoping that the profits of his son's trade would enable him to keep up with the payments for the annual lease for the governorship of Kish, he was wrong. In 1302, while his son was still on his way to China, Jamāl al-Dīn lost his position as ruler of Kish. He had declared to the Ilkhans that during the period he governed the coastal districts, the annual revenue of Kish had amounted to four hundred thousand dinars. However, an Iraqi merchant and competitor of Jamāl al-Dīn in the Indian Ocean trade, Nūr al-Dīn Aḥmad b. al-Ṣayyād (d. after 1303), argued at the court that the annual revenue should amount to 1,300,000 dinars, a much higher sum than the one Jamāl al-Dīn had guaranteed.[42] Based on this testimony, the vizier Rashīd al-Dīn (d. 1318) ordered Jamāl al-Dīn's dismissal, appointing Nūr al-Dīn in his place.

Rashīd al-Dīn, nevertheless, permitted Jamāl al-Dīn and his commercial agents to continue their activities through the Persian Gulf without interference. The only condition was that Jamāl al-Dīn pay the government taxes on the goods his ships carried through Kish. These taxes were to be paid in full, even if his ships did not arrive at Kish and disembarked at other Ilkhanid ports.[43]

The Ṭībīs' trade empire took a further hit when Jamāl al-Dīn's brother Taqī al-Dīn died in 1303. Jamāl al-Dīn attempted to reestablish his brother's commercial connections in the kingdom of Ma'bar, sending there another son, Sirāj al-Dīn 'Umar (d. 1315), with two hundred thousand dinars to guarantee Taqī al-Dīn's position and secure the huge property that his brother had left behind.[44] In 1305, Jamāl al-Dīn was informed that his oldest son, Fakhr al-Dīn, had died on his return voyage from China, where he had stayed for four years. Fakhr al-Dīn was buried in Ma'bar alongside his uncle, and his father, Jamāl al-Dīn, lost all hope of regaining his fortune through his son's eastern commercial adventure.[45] Yet, that same year the newly enthroned Ilkhan Öljeitü (r. 1304–16) summoned Jamāl al-Dīn from Kish to Shiraz to take charge of the city's fiscal affairs after a sharp decline in the city's revenue. Jamāl al-Dīn accepted the office even though he was ill, and held this post until his death in 1306, at the age of 76. After his death, the inhabitants of Shiraz raised a handsome tomb over his remains, and a public prayer for him was held in Baghdad.[46]

Jamāl al-Dīn's sons and relatives succeeded him as local governors and merchants until the mid-fourteenth century, continuing to trade with Yemen, India, China, and even Venice, from Kish, Baghdad, and Tabriz.[47]

CONCLUSION

The story of Jamāl al-Dīn and his brother Taqī al-Dīn, who established a trade empire across the Indian Ocean in the second half of the thirteenth century, is closely entwined with the expansion of the Mongol polities, the Ilkhanate in Iran and the Yuan dynasty in China, into the Indian Ocean maritime trade, especially after the Song defeat in 1279, when the Yuan gained access to the Song ports in South China.

The Mongol conquests and rule in the Middle East and Iran brought a change to the regional and transregional trade routes. As Polo reports, under Ilkhanid rule, Tabriz became the new trading center of the eastern Islamic world. Yet, the Ṭībīs, who had their humble beginnings in Baghdad, kept the city as their center of operation for their transregional pearl, and later horse, trade enterprises. Baghdad remained an important hub in the extensive networks that connected the land routes leading from Basra, Tabriz, al-Hijaz, Khurasan, Central Asia, and Europe to the Indian Ocean, as well as the trade between Yemen and the Mamluk Sultanate.[48]

In their rise to fortune and moreover, in the expansion of their trade operation in precious items, from pearls to horses, the Ṭībīs successfully exploited several mechanisms. Merchants often relied on their kinship ties, and Taqī al-Dīn's settlement in Maʿbar, and his subsequent appointment as vizier for the Pandyans were clearly important steps in facilitating the Ṭībīs' expansion, especially in their horse-trading venture. Together, the brothers appear to have gained a monopoly on the Indian Ocean trade for a short while in the 1290s.

Equally significant was the Mongol *ortaq* system of commercial partnership. Jamāl al-Dīn had to build his patronage relationship with the

Ilkhanid elite from the bottom up. Beginning as an agent for another *ortaq* merchant and governor (Shams al-Dīn Tāzīkū), he then entered a commercial partnership with a Mongol governor (Suqunchaq) and a powerful vizier (Juwaynī), finally climbing to the service of the Mongol rulers in a beneficial and lucrative *ortaq* position and selling his merchandise directly at the court. The flow of precious gifts and profits guaranteed that the Mongols would continue to provide him with capital or leases on the income of Ilkhanid-ruled lands and cities, either to pay for his merchandise or to invest in his enterprise. In other cases, in return for drafts and leases, Jamāl al-Dīn paid the court large sums, offers that were often accompanied by appointments to governorships or similar posts that also enabled Jamāl al-Dīn to advance his financial and trade-related business. This system of exchanging leases and official posts allowed Ilkhanid patrons to transfer future tax revenues as capital for trade or payment, and was especially beneficial when the patrons lacked cash to invest, or when the state treasury was temporarily deflated.[49]

Jamāl al-Dīn's advancement to working directly with the Mongol elite gave him a significant advantage over other traders without direct ties to the court. The Mongols' appetite for profit and extravagant commodities created the conditions for fierce competition between merchants, as well as opportunities for great social and economic mobility. It also set the stage for the swift downfall of the same merchants.

The Ṭībīs were, indeed, in need of allies in their Eurasian trade network, and cultivated close relations with the Yemen Rasūlids. While Yemen and the Persian Gulf offered two competing separate paths, cooperation between the ports existed as well. The Ṭībīs' enterprise exemplifies the rise of a trans-Asian commercial system under Mongol auspices, and the opportunities Mongol rule offered to local and regional entrepreneurs.

NOTES

This research was supported by the European Research Council under the European Union's Seventh Framework Programme (FP/2007–13)/ERC grant Agreement n. 312397.

1. A term of Turkic origin, *ortaq* came to mean in Mongolian "partner," "friend," and later, "comrade." Allsen 1989.

2. On the *ortaq* system: Allsen 1989; Endicott-West 1989.

3. E.g., Aubin 1953, 89–100; Lambton 1987, 107–8; Lambton 1988, 335–41; Allsen 1997b, 22; Fiorani Piacentini 2004; Aigle 2005, 124, 142–53; Kauz 2006; Yokkaichi 2008a, 2008b; Chaffee 2013; Qiu 2014, 2, n. 4–5.

4. Allsen 1997b; Yokkaichi 2008a, 74; Kuroda 2009; Manz 2010,157–58; Biran 2015, 550–51.

5. Ashtor 1976, 250, 262–64;Wing 2013, 304–5.

6. Al-ʿAsqalānī 1993, 1:60; al-Dhahabī 1987–2004, 61:71; al-Birzālī 2006, 3:325–26; al-Yūnīnī 2013, 22:346.

7. Polo 1938, 1:101.

8. Polo 1938, 1:104.

9. Serjeant 1942, 82–84; Balazs 1960, 327; Allsen 1997a, 18–19, 28–29; Donkin 1998, 105–12; Atwood 2004, 429, 265.

10. Al-Ṣuqāʿī 1973, 32; al-Yūnīnī 2013, 22: 346. For the Island of Kish and its connection to Baghdad: Polo 1938, 1: 101; Ibn Baṭṭūṭa 1853, 2: 244–46; Ibn Baṭṭūṭa 1956–2000, 2: 407–9; Qiu 2014: 3.

11. Ibn al-ʿImād 1986–93, 8: 26; al-ʿAynī 2009–10, 4: 438; al-ʿAsqalānī 1993, 1: 60;al-Birzālī 2006, 3: 325–26; al-Dhahabī 1987–2004, 61: 71.

12. Ptak 1993, 147.

13. The Arabic term used for the Swahili coast is "Bilād al-Zanj,"i.e.,"the land of the blacks.""*Al-Ṣīn*" might refer to China in general, but here probably means South China, since Jamāl al-Dīn continued from *al-Ṣīn* to *Bilād al-Khaṭā*, North China. Bosworth 1978; Becker and Dunlop 1986. On the pearl industries in these regions: Donkin 1998, 196–204.

14. Al-Dhahabī 1987–2004, 61: 71; Ibn al-ʿImād 1986–93, 8: 26; al-ʿAynī 2009–10, 4: 438; al-ʿAsqalānī 1993, 1: 60.We have no further information about this voyage. Jamāl al-Dīn likely returned to Shiraz after 1268, when his brother Taqī al-Dīn entered the service of the Pandyan king of Maʿbar, Jatavarman Sundara Pandyan II (r. 1268–93). The Pandyans were an ancient Tamil dynasty that ruled parts of South India, from around 400 B.C.E. to the first half of the seventeenth century C.E. Rockhill 1914, 433; Subrabmanya Aiyer 1917, 172–75.

15. Tāzīku made his initial fortune in 1262–63 by providing food for the troops of Ilkhan Hülegü (r. 1260–65) during the war with Berke Khan (ruler of the Golden Horde, 1257–67). His career flourished in the 1260s and 1270s, as he established close ties with the Juwaynīs. Al-Ṣuqāʿī 1973, 32–33; Lambton 1988, 335; Jaʿfarī 2005, 243; al-Yūnīnī 2013, 22: 347–48; Rashid al-Dīn 1994, 2: 1061; Anonymous 1976, 283. On the Juwaynīs: Lane 2003, 177–212.

16. Al-Ṣuqāʿī 1973, 32–33; al-Yūnīnī 2013, 22: 346; al-Dhahabī 1987–2004, 61: 71.

17. Suqunchaq was a Mongol general from the Suldus tribe who served as the governor of Shiraz and Fārs in the 1270s to 1280s. Rashid al-Dīn 1994, 2: 1178; Lane 2003, 135–44; Limbert 2004, 21–22. Dhahabī states that this meeting took place during the early days of Abaqa's reign—probably after 1272, when Suqunchaq became governor and was tasked with securing Ilkhanid trade in the Persian Gulf. Al-Dhahabī 1990, 387; Waṣṣāf 1853, 1: 194–95; Āyatī 2004, 114; Aubin 1953, 84–87; Aigle 2005, 122–23; Qāshānī 1969, 157; Zarkūb Shīrāzī 1931, 65–66; Kauz 2006, 57.

18. Allsen 1989, 119–20.

19. Al-Ṣuqāʿī 1973, 32; al-Yūnīnī 2013, 22: 346–47; al-ʿAynī 2009–10, 4: 439.

20. İnalcık 1986;Lambton 1988, 334.
21. Al-Ṣuqāʿī 1973, 32; al-Yūnīnī 2013, 22: 347.
22. For abuse: Allsen 1989, 102, 105.
23. Yule 1870, 348; Aubin 1953, 85; Waṣṣāf 1853, 2: 221–22; Āyatī 2004, 126;Qāshānī 1969, 151–60; Martinez 1975, 192; Kauz 2006, 58; Qiu 2014, 5–6.
24. Waṣṣāf 1853, 3: 268–69, 332–35; Āyatī 2004, 187–88; Rashīd al-Dīn 1994, 2: 1273; Anonymous (Pseudo-Ibn al-Fuwaṭī) 2005, 535;Lambton 1988, 335–41; Aigle 2005, 149–50.
25. Elliot and Dowson 1871, 3: 32–35; Zarkūb Shīrāzī 1931, 73; Āyatī 2004, 15;Rashīd al-Dīn 2005, 41–42;Aubin 1953, 89–99; Lambton 1988, 335–41; Limbert 2004, 24; Aigle 2005, 142–43; Kauz 2006, 58, 66; Chaffee 2013, 46–47.
26. Haridas 2016.
27. Rashīd al-Dīn 2005, 40–42.
28. Vallet 2006, 291–92; Yokkaichi 2008b, 87–97.
29. Elliot and Dowson 1871, 3: 32–35; Rashīd al-Dīn 2005, 41; Kauz 2006, 66.
30. Jamāl al-Dīn's brotherTaqī al-Dīn's name appears as a horse trader in a list of the Indian rulers to whom the Rasūlid dynasty granted precious gifts in 1293–94. Jāzim 2003–5, 1: 515, 519. On the relations between Yemen and Taqī al-Dīn: al-ʿAsqalānī 1993, 3: 412; al-Ṣafadī 1998, 4: 372–73. On the Rasūlid dynasty (1228–1454): Smith 1995; Vallet 2010.
31. Waṣṣāf 1853, 3: 296–300; al-Ṣuqāʿī 1973, 33; Qāshānī 1969, 151–61; al-Yūnīnī 2013, 22: 348; Aigle 2005, 147–53; Kauz 2006, 58–60.
32. Waṣṣāf 1853, 3: 296–300; Qāshānī 1969, 151–61; al-Ṣuqāʿī 1973, 33; al-Yūnīnī 2013, 22: 348; Aubin 1953, 89–100; Aigle 2005, 147–53; Kauz 2006, 58–60.
33. Al-Dhahabī 1987–2004, 61: 71; al-ʿAynī 2009–10, 4: 438–39;al-Yūnīnī 2013, 22: 347.On al-Farūthī, a shaykh of the Rifāʿiyya order: Ohlander 2012.
34. On these relations: Amitai-Preiss 1995, 208–11; Gill 2015, 43–49, 66–70.
35. ʿAzzāwī 1935, 1: 378; Ibn al-ʿImād 1986–93, 8: 26;Rashīd al-Dīn, ed. Rawshan 1994, 2: 1157; Anonymous (Pseudo-Ibn al-Fuwaṭī) 2005, 534, 539.
36. Ibn al-Fuwaṭī 1995, 1: 224–25, 2: 525; Āyatī 2004, 193–94; Qiu 2014, 6–7.
37. Lambton 1987, 115; Āyatī 2004, 223–24; Kauz 2006, 60.
38. Appanage lands were assigned to Mongol princes after large campaigns, especially during the United Empire period. After the empire's dissolution, a number of appanages remained under the rule of a different family branch (e.g., the Hülegüid appanages in China), that would be then responsible for securing their revenues for their owners. Rulers sometimes used these future revenues to invest or pay their agents, including *ortaq* merchants. See: Allsen 1989, 111; Allsen 2001, 33–34, 43–47.
39. Elliot and Dowson 1871, 3: 45–47; al-Dhahabī 1987–2004, 61: 71; al-Ṣafadī 1998, 1: 118; Allsen 2001, 49.
40. Waṣṣāf 1853, 3: 303–9.
41. On Yang Shu: Park 2012, 112–13; Chaffee 2013, 50–51.On Fakhr al-Dīn voyage: Qiu 2014.

42. Nūr al-Dīn Aḥmad b. al-Ṣayyād served under the Mongols as the local governor of Wāsiṭ and Iraq during the 1280s. Ibn al-Fuwaṭī 1995, 2: 22–23; Anonymous (Pseudo-Ibn al-Fuwaṭī) 2005, 479, 484–85, 496, 529; Ja'farī 2005, 243.

43. Waṣṣāf 1853, 4: 405; Āyatī 2004, 224;Aubin 1953, 98; Lambton 1987, 115–16.

44. Elliot and Dowson 1871, 3: 45;Āyatī 2004, 261; Yokkaichi 2008b, 87–97. Sirāj al-Dīn was killed in 1315 by Malik Kafur (d. 1316), a prominent slave-general of the Delhi Sultanate who served under the Sultan 'Alā' al-Dīn Khiljī (r. 1296–1316) and invaded Ma'bar. Waṣṣāf 1853, 5: 646–47; Shīrazī 1949, 546–47.

45. Waṣṣāf 1853, 3: 303–9, 4: 505–6; Elliot and Dowson 1871, 3: 35, 45–47; Ibn al-Fuwaṭī 1995, 2: 525; al-Ṣafadī 1998, 1: 18; Allsen 2001, 34, 49–53; Yokkaichi 2005, 125–36; Kauz 2006, 64–65; Qiu 2014, 14–15.

46. Elliot and Dowson 1871, 3: 47; Ibn al-'Imād 1986–93, 8: 26; al-Birzālī 2006, 3: 326; al-Yūnīnī 2013, 22: 346; Lambton 1987, 118.

47. Qāshānī 1969, 161–63; Ibn al-Fuwaṭī 1995, 1: 224–25; Lambton 1988, 341–42; Fiorani Piacentini 2004, 251–60; Limbert 2004, 25; Aigle 2005, 160–61; Kauz 2006, 60–61; Martinez 2008–9, 220–21.

48. Amitai-Preiss 1995, 208–11; Gill 2015, 43–49, 66–70.

49. Lambton 1987, 108; Lambton 1988, 334;Atwood 2004, 429–30; de la Vaissière 2014, 107–8.

BIBLIOGRAPHY

Aigle, Denise. 2005. *Le Fārs sous la domination mongole: Politique et fiscalité(XIIIe–XIVe s.)*. Paris: Association pour l'avancement des études iraniennes.

Allsen, Thomas T. 1989. "Mongolian Princes and Their Merchant Partners, 1200–1260."*Asia Major* 2: 83–126.

———. 1997a. *Commodity and Exchange in the Mongol Empire: A Cultural History of Islamic Textiles*. Cambridge: Cambridge University Press.

———. 1997b. "Ever Closer Encounters: The Appropriation of Culture and the Apportionment of Peoples in the Mongol Empire." *Journal of Early Modern History* 1: 2–23.

———. 2001. *Culture and Conquest in Mongol Eurasia*. Cambridge: Cambridge University Press.

Amitai-Preiss, Reuven. 1995. *Mongols and Mamluks: The Mamluk-Īkhānid War, 1260–1281*. Cambridge: Cambridge University Press.

Anonymous. 1976. *Ta'rīkh-i shāhī Qarākhitā'iyān*. Ed. Muḥammad Ibrāhīm Bāstānī Pārīzī. Tehran: Bunyād-i farhang-i Īrān.

Anonymous (Pseudo-Ibn al-Fuwaṭī). 2005. *Kitāb al-ḥawādith li-mu'allif min al-qarn al-thāmin al-hijrī wa-huwa al-kitāb al-musammā wahman bi'l-ḥawādith al-jāmi'a wal-tajārib al-nāfi'a*. Ed. Bashshār Ma'rūf. Qum, Iran: Intishārāt-i Rashīd.

al-'Asqalānī, Aḥmad b. 'Alī b. Ḥajr. 1993. *Al-Durar al-kāmina fī a'yān al-mi'a al-thāmina*. 3 vols. Beirut: Dār al-jīl.

Ashtor, Eliyahu. 1976. *A Social and Economic History of the Near East in the Middle Ages*. London: Collins.

Atwood, Christopher P. 2004. *Encyclopedia of Mongolia and the Mongol Empire*. New York: Facts on File.

Aubin, J. 1953. "Les princes d'Ormuz du XIIIe au XVesiècle."*Journal asiatique* 241: 138–77.

Āyatī, ʿAbd al-Muḥammad. 2004. *Taḥrīr-i taʾrīkh-i Waṣṣāf*. Tehran: Pizhūhishgāh-i ʿulūm-i insānī wa muṭālaʿāt-i farhangī.

al-ʿAynī, Badr al-Dīn Maḥmūd b. Aḥmad. 2009–10. *ʿIqd al-jumān fī tārīkh ahl al-zamān: ʿAṣr salāṭīn al-mamālīk*. Ed. Muḥammad Amīn. 4 vols. Cairo: Dār al-kutub wal-wathāʾiq al-qawmiyya.

ʿAzzāwī, ʿA. 1935. *Tārīkh al-ʿIrāq bayna iḥtilālayn: Ḥukūmat al-Mughūl*. Baghdad: Maṭbaʿat Baghdād.

Balazs, Étienne. 1960. Review of *Economic Structure of the Yüan Dynasty*, translation of chapters 93 and 94 of the *Yüan shih*, tr. Herbert Franz Schurmann. *Journal of Asian Studies* 19: 325–27.

Becker, C.H. and Dunlop, D.M. 1986. S.v. "Baḥr al-Zandj." *Encyclopaedia of Islam*. 2nd ed. Online version accessed January 15, 2018, http://referenceworks.brillonline.com/entries/encyclopaedia-of-islam-2/bah-r-al-zand-j-SIM_1066.

Biran, Michal. 2015. "The Mongol Empire and the Inter-Civilizational Exchange." In *The Cambridge History of the World*, vol. 5, ed. Benjamin Z. Kedar and Merry Wiesner-Hanks, 534–58. Cambridge: Cambridge University Press.

al-Birzālī, al-Qāsim b. Muḥammad. 2006. *Al-Muqtafī ʿalā kitāb al-rawḍatayn al-maʿarūf bi-taʾrīkh al-Birzālī*.Ed. 'Umar 'Abd al-Salām Tadmurī. Beirut: al-Maktaba al-ʿaṣriyya.

Bosworth, C.E. 1978. S.v. "Ḳarā Ḵh̲iṭāy." *Encyclopaedia of Islam*. 2nd ed. Online version accessed January 14, 2018, http://referenceworks.brillonline.com/entries/encyclopaedia-of-islam-2/kara-khitay-SIM_3890?s.num=2&s.q=%E1%B8%B2ara+K%CC%B2h%CC%B2it%C4%81i.

Chaffee, John. 2013. "Cultural Transmission by Sea: Maritime Trade Routes in Yuan China." In *Eurasian Influences on Yuan China: Cross-Cultural Transmissions in the 13th and 14th Centuries*, ed. M. Rossabi, 41–59. Singapore: University of Singapore Press.

de la Vaissière, Étienne. 2014. "Trans-Asian Trade, or the Silk Road Deconstructed (Antiquity, Middle Ages)." In *The Cambridge History of Capitalism*, ed. Larry Neal and Jeffrey. G. Williamson, 1: 101–24. Cambridge: Cambridge University Press.

al-Dhahabī, Muḥammad b. Aḥmad. 1990. *Muʿjam shuyūkh al-Dhahabī*. Ed. Rawḥīyah ʿAbd al-Raḥmān al-Suyūfī. Beirut: Dār al-kutub al-ʿilmiyya.

———. 1987–2004. *Tārīkh al-islām wa-wafayāt al-mashāhīr wa'l-aʿlām*. Ed. ʿAbd al-Salām Tadmurī. Beirut: Dār al-kitāb al-ʿarabī.

Donkin, R.A. 1998. *Beyond Price: Pearls and Pearl-Fishing; Origins to the Age of Discoveries*. Philadelphia: American Philosophical Society.

Elliot, H.M., and J. Dowson, J. 1871. *The History of India: As Told by Its Own Historians; The Muhammadan Period (Vol. III)*. London: Trübner.

Endicott-West, Elizabeth. 1989. "Merchant Associations in Yuan China: The *Ortogh*." *Asia Major* 2: 127–54.

Fiorani Piacentini, Valeria. 2004. "The Mercantile Empire of the Ṭībīs: Economic Predominance, Political Power, Military Subordination." *Proceedings of the Seminar for Arabian Studies* 34: 251–60.

Gill, Matanya. 2015. "Commerce in the Ilkhanid State (1260–1335) as Reflected by Ibn al-Fuwaṭī's (d.1323) Biographical Dictionary." MA thesis (in Hebrew), Hebrew University of Jerusalem.

Haridas, V.V. 2016. *Zamorins and the Political Culture of Medieval Kerala.* Delhi: Orient Black Swan.

Ibn Baṭṭūṭa, Abū ʿAbdallāh Muḥammad. 1853. *Voyages d'Ibn Battûta.* Ed. and tr. C. François Defrémery and B. R. Sanguinetti. 5 vols. Paris: Édition Anthropos.

———. 1956–2000. *The Travels of Ibn Baṭṭūṭa,* A.D. *1325–1354.* Tr. H.A.R. Gibb. 5 vols. Cambridge: Cambridge University Press.

Ibn al-Fuwaṭī, Kamāl al-Dīn ʿAbd al-Razzāq b. Aḥmad. 1995. *Majmaʿ al-ādāb fī muʿjam al-alqāb.* Ed. Muḥammad al-Kāẓim. 6 vols. Tehran: Muʿassasat al-ṭibāʿa wa'l-nashr.

Ibn al-ʿImād, Shihāb al-Dīn ʿAbd al-Ḥayy. 1986–93. *Shadharāt al-dhahab fī akhbār man dhahab.* Ed. ʿAbd al-Qādir al-Arnāʾūṭ. Beirut: Dār Ibn Kathīr.

İnalcık, H. 1986. S.v."Ḥawāla." *Encyclopaedia of Islam.* 2nd ed. Online version accessed January 15, 2018, http://referenceworks.brillonline.com /entries/encyclopaedia-of-islam-2/h-awa-la-SIM_2807.

Jaʿfarī, Jaʿfar b. Muḥammad. 2005. *Tārīkh-i Yazd.* Ed. Īraj Afshār. Tehran: Shirkat-i intishārāt-i ʿilmī wa-farhangī.

Jāzim, Muḥammad, ed. 2003–5. *Nur al-ma'arif, Lumière de la Connaissance: Règles, lois et coutumes du Yemen sous le règne du sultan rassoulide al-Muzaffar.* Sanaa, Yemen: Centre français d'archéologie et de sciences sociales de Sanaa.

Kauz, Ralph. 2006. "The Maritime Trade of Kish during the Mongol Period." In *Beyond the Legacy of Genghis Khan,* ed. Linda Komaroff, 51–68. Leiden: Brill.

Kuroda, Akinobu. 2009. "The Eurasian Silver Century,1276–1359: Commensurability and Multiplicity." *Journal of Global History* 4: 245–69.

Lambton, Ann K.S. 1987. "Mongol Fiscal Administration in Persia (Part II)." *Studiaislamica* 65: 97–123.

———. 1988. *Continuity and Change in Medieval Persia: Aspects of Administrative, Economic and Social History, 11th-14th Century.* London: I.B. Tauris.

Lane, George. 2003. *Early Mongol Rule in Thirteenth-Century Iran. A Persian Renaissance.* London: Routledge Curzon.

Limbert, John W. 2004. *Shiraz in the Age of Hafez: The Glory of a Medieval Persian City.* Seattle: University of Washington Press.

Manz, Beatrice F. 2010. "The Rule of the Infidels: The Mongols and the Islamic World." In *The New Cambridge History of Islam* 3, ed. David O. Morgan and Anthony Reid, 128–68. Cambridge: Cambridge University Press.

Martinez, Arsenio Peter.1975."International *Trade Cycles:* Bullion Transfers and Economic Policy in *Mongol* Western Asia." PhD diss., Columbia University.

———. 2008–9. "The Eurasian Overland and Pontic Trades in the Thirteenth and Fourteenth centuries."*Archivum EurasiaeMedii Aevi* 16: 127–223.

Ohlander, Erik S. 2012.S.v. "Al-Fārūthī, ʿIzz al-Dīn." *Encyclopaedia of Islam*. 2nd ed. Online version accessed January 8, 2018, http://referenceworks.brillonline.com/entries/encyclopaedia-of-islam-3/al-faruthi-izz-al-din-COM_27006.

Park, Hyunhee. 2012. *Mapping the Chinese and Islamic Worlds: Cross-Cultural Exchange in Pre-modern Asia*. Cambridge: Cambridge University Press.

Polo, Marco. 1938. *The Description of the World*. Tr. A.C. Moule and P. Pelliot. London: George Routledge & Sons.

Ptak, Roderich. 1993. "Yuan and Early Ming Notices on the Kayal Area in South India."*Bulletin de l'École française d'Extrême-Orient* 80: 137–56.

Qāshānī, ʿAbū al-Qāsim ʿAbd Allāh. 1969. *Tārīkh-i Ūljāytū*. Ed. M. Hambly. Tehran: Shirkat-i intishārāt-i ʿilmī wa farhangī.

Qiu Yihao. 2014. "Background and Aftermath of Fakhr al-Dīn Ṭībī's Voyage: A Resurvey on the Interaction between the Ilkhanate and the Yuan at the Early 14th Century." Paper read at the international conference New Approaches on the Il-Khans, Ulanbataar, Mongolia, May 21–23.

Rashīd al-Dīn. 1994. *Jāmiʿ al-tawārīkh*. Ed. Muḥammad Rawshan and Muṣṭafā Mūsawī. 4 vols. Tehran: Nashr-i Alburz.

———. 2005. *Jāmiʿ al-tawārīkh: Tārīkh-i Hind wa Sind wa Kashmīr*. Ed. Muḥammad Rawshan. Tehran: Markaz-i nashr-i mīrāth maktūb.

Rockhill, W.W. 1914. "Notes on the Relations and Trade of China with the Eastern Archipelago and the Coast of the Indian Ocean during the Fourteenth Century."*T'oung Pao* 15: 419–47.

al-Ṣafadī, Khalīl b. Aybak. 1998. *Aʿyān al-ʿaṣr wa-aʿwān al-naṣr*. 6 vols. Beirut: Dār al-fikr al-muʿāṣir.

Serjeant, R.B. 1942. "Material for a History of Islamic Textiles Up to the Mongol Conquest."*Ars islamica* 9: 54–92.

Shīrazī, Muʿīn al-Dīn Abū al-Qāsim Junayd. 1949. *Shadd al-izār fī ḥaṭṭ al-awzār ʿan zawwār al-mazār*. Ed. Muḥammad Qazwīnī and ʿAbbās Iqbāl. Tehran: Chāpkhānah-yi majlis.

Smith, G.R. 1995. S.v. "Rasūlids."*Encyclopaedia of Islam*. 2nd ed. Online version accessed December 14, 2017, http://referenceworks.brillonline.com/entries/encyclopaedia-of-islam-2/rasu-lids-COM_0912.

Subrabmanya Aiyer, K.V. 1917. *Historical Sketches of Ancient Dekhan*. Ed. K.S. Vaidyanathan. Madras: Modern Printing Works.

al-Ṣuqāʿī, Faḍl Allāh b. Abī al-Fakhr. 1973. *Tālī kitāb wafayāt al-aʿyān*. Ed. Jacqueline Sublet. Damascus: Institut française d'études orientales.

Vallet, Eric. 2006. "Yemeni Oceanic Policy at the End of the Thirteenth Century."*Proceedings of the Seminar for Arabian Studies* 36: 289–96.

———. 2010. *L'Arabie marchande: État et commerce sous les sultansRasūlides du Yémen (626–858, 1229–1454)*. Paris: Publications de la Sorbonne.

Waṣṣāf, Sharaf al- Dīn ʿAbd Allāh ibn Faḍl Allāh. 1853. *Tajziyat al-amṣār wa-tazjiyat al-aʿṣār*. Bombay. Reprint, Tehran 1338/1959–60.

Wing, Patrick. 2013. " 'Rich in Goods and Abounding in Wealth:' The Ilkhanid and Post-Ilkhanid Ruling Elite and the Politics of Commercial Life at Tabrīz,

1250–1400." In *Politics, Patronage, and the Transmission of Knowledge in 13th–15th Century Tabrīz*, ed. Judith Pfeiffer, 301–21. Leiden: Brill.

Yokkaichi, Yasuhiru. 2005. "Az Sīraf bah Kīsh: Tijārat-i Uqiyānūs-i Hind wa Kīsh dar ʿaṣr-i Mughūl [From Sīraf to Kīsh: Maritime Trade in the Indian Ocean under Mongol Rule]." *Proceedings of the International Congress of Siraf Port, 14–16 November,* 125–36. Bushehr, Iran: Bonyād-i Irānshināsi.

———. 2008a. "Chinese and Muslim Diasporas and the Indian Ocean Trade Network under Mongol Hegemony." In *The East Asian Mediterranean: Maritime Crossroads of Culture, Commerce, and Human Migration,* ed. Angela Schottenhammer, 73–103. Wiesbaden, Germany: Harrassowitz.

———. 2008b. "Horses in the East-West Trade between China and Iran under Mongol Rule." In *Pferde in Asien: Geschichte, Handel und Kultur / Horses in Asia: History, Trade, and Culture,* ed. Bert Fragner et al., 87–97. Wiesbaden, Germany: Harrassowitz.

Yule, Henry. 1870. "An Endeavour to Elucidate Rashiduddin's Geographical Notices of India." *Journal of the Royal Asiatic Society* 4: 340–56.

al-Yūnīnī, Quṭb al-Dīn Mūsā b. Aḥmad. 2013. *Dhayl mirʾāt al-zamān fī tārīkh al-aʿyān li-Sibṭ Ibn al-Jawzī.* Vol. 22. Ed. ʿAbbās Hānī al-Jarrākh. Beirut: Dār al-kutub al-ʿilmiyya.

Zarkūb Shīrāzī, Abū al-ʿAbbās Aḥmad Abī al-Khayr. 1931. *Shīrāznāma.* Ed. Bahman Karīmī. Tehran: Maṭbaʿa-yi rūshanāʾī.

CHAPTER 10

Taydula

A Golden Horde Queen and Patron of Christian Merchants

SZILVIA KOVÁCS

The Mongol Empire is celebrated for the relative independence and political involvement of its elite female members. The wives and princesses of the Mongol imperial household took part in the empire's decision-making process, if not also more directly in its government and administration. Owning their own properties, which were administered by their personal mobile courts (*ordo*), female elite members were also in many cases economically independent. Thus, they were relatively free to participate in the political sphere, in governing, and even in the empire's diplomatic efforts, and they had the required capital to promote trade and commercial enterprises at the transregional and intercontinental levels.[1]

Taydula (d. 1361),[2] the most renowned queen (*khatun*) in the history of the Golden Horde, is a prominent example of the involvement of women in the empire's political and commercial arenas. Ruling alongside her husband Özbek Khan (r. 1313–41), Taydula used her patronage and support for the Christian communities to promote her interests in trade and the Horde's diplomatic relations. Narrative sources and charters issued by Taydula herself confirm her image as deeply involved in the politics and commerce of the Horde.

The Golden Horde ruled a vast territory that extended at its height from the upper Volga and the Kama River, in the north, to the upper Irtysh in the east, the lower Danube in the west, and the Crimean Peninsula, the Caucasus, the Ustyurt Plateau, the lower Amu Darya and the midstream of the Syr Darya, in the south (today's Ukraine, parts of Russia, Kazakhstan, and northern Uzbekistan). Although the empire's territory also encompassed sedentary communities with agricultural and urban-based economies,[3] it was, nevertheless, largely a nomadic empire with a Steppe-based economy. Unlike their rival kin in Ilkhanid Iran or their distant kin in Yuan China, the Golden Horde's vast territories had never beforehand been united under one single imperial apparatus. Rulers of the Horde therefore had less to rely on when it came to their sedentary subjects' administrative and cultural traditions.

The Horde's population was mostly comprised of different Turkic-speaking groups such as the Cuman-Qipchaqs and the Volga Bulghars, and a minority of Mongol conquerors, who gradually assimilated into the Turkic-speaking population. In addition to the Turkic and Mongol nomads, Iranian-speaking peoples lived in the North Caucasus and Khwārazm, and a smaller Jewish community resided in the Crimea. The empire had a considerable Christian population as well, due to the conquered principalities of the Rus' and the Greek, Armenian, and Italian colonies in the Crimea. The Christians in the Crimea lived mostly in cities, and their settlements functioned as transit markets in the Levant trade. The ethnic and religious diversity of the empire was reflected in its religious policies. Mongol rule evinced a pluralistic attitude toward the religions of its subjects. Their religious pluralism persisted even after Özbek Khan, Taydula's husband, converted to Islam in 1312/3, which made the gradual process of the Horde's Islamization irreversible.

Contemporaneous sources say nothing about Taydula's ethnicity. Later accounts report she was Qipchaq. The Turkic Qipchaq were the biggest nomadic group in the Horde. However, researchers now suggest that she belonged to the Qongrat, a Mongol tribe that traditionally enjoyed close marriage ties with the Chinggisids.[4] Taydula was not originally Özbek's principal wife. She occupied the position only after the death of his first principal wife.[5] This, in any case, may explain why her ethnic identity was never recorded.

In 1332, when the famous traveler Ibn Baṭṭūṭa (1304–77) reached Özbek's court to the north of the Caucasus, Taydula had been already the khan's principal wife. Ibn Baṭṭūṭa writes that Özbek had three children from Taydula, two of whom, Tinibek (r. 1341–42) and Janïbek (r. 1342–57), would later become khans, and another, an unidentified daughter, married Hārūn Bek, son of the Horde's governor of Khwārazm.[6] According to another Arabic author, after Özbek's death, Taydula took part in the conspiracy against her husband's eldest son, Tinibek, and helped her favorite son, Janïbek, assume power in his place.[7]

Taydula's position in Özbek's court drew the Moroccan traveler's attention. He reports the seating arrangement in Özbek's golden pavilion after the Friday prayer: Taydula was to the right of the khan, and Kabak Khatun next to her. The khan's two other wives, Bayalūn and Urdujā, were seated to his left.[8] Ibn Baṭṭūṭa was astounded by the magnificence of the khatuns' retinues. They had numerous slave girls, pages, and slave boys. The traveler's observations suggest that the khatuns' *ordo*s were administered by female ministers (viziers) and female chamberlains. When he visited Taydula, she was surrounded by her female attendants, who were cleaning cherries. The khatun received him in her tent and provided him with *kumiss,* a typical Mongolian alcoholic beverage made of fermented mare's milk. Ibn Baṭṭūṭa notes that she possessed about three hundred wagons with her chests, robes, furnishings, and food, but claims that she was nevertheless "close-fisted."[9] Furthermore, in an anecdote which likely consists more of fantasy about the harem than reality, Ibn Baṭṭūṭa reported that Taydula attained her position as Özbek's favorite wife due to her sexual prowess or unique female anatomy. He writes that the khan adored her "because he finds her every night just like a virgin," and moreover, that "the vagina of this khātūn has a conformation like a ring."[10] However, a more likely explanation for Taydula's high regard was her strong and commanding character.

It was Taydula's political ambition and her relentless involvement in the succession struggles after Özbek's death that left the greatest mark on the history of the Horde. The Horde reached its zenith during the reign of Taydula's husband. Signs of decline began appearing during the reign of their son Janïbek. The murder of Berdibek (r. 1357–59), Janïbek's son, was then followed by twenty years of decay and chaos, from which the Horde never fully recovered. The empire disintegrated, and new polities were formed in the 1430s. The major successor states, the khanates of Qazan and Astrakhan, would be furthermore conquered by the Russians in 1552 and 1556.

The ambitious Taydula, who enjoyed a senior position during the reign of her husband, son, and grandson, tried to retain her power even during the last year of her life.[11] When the Batuid line (descendants of Chinggis Khan's grandson and Jochi's son, Batu) died out following the murder of her grandson, Berdibek (1359), Taydula was reported to have invited the Shibanids, another Jochid family line, to assume the throne of the Horde. She might even have strived to consolidate her new alliance with the Shibanids through marriage. According to a sixteenth-century historian, Ötemish Ḥājjī, the aging khatun found the Shibanid Prince Khiḍr (r. 1360–61) so attractive that she dyed her hair black in the hope that the khan would marry her. Khiḍr was, indeed, inclined to marry the influential woman, but was advised against it.[12] The khatun met a gruesome death in the first years of the anarchy that afflicted the Golden Horde for about twenty years (1359–80). Captured during a battle near Sarai, the Horde capital on the Volga River, she was allegedly bound to a sledge drawn by an unbroken horse. The horse was driven into a valley with a water-worn ravine, where it dashed the sledge bearing the Mongol queen into pieces.[13]

TAYDULA AND THE BLACK SEA TRADE

Laying at the intersection of several international trade routes, the Golden Horde was crossed from north to south by merchants marketing the products of the northern forests—fur, felt, leather, wax, and slaves; it was traversed from east to west by travelers and traders from Europe heading to Central Asia, and even China. The Mongol elite were greatly interested in the cultivation of this interregional commerce, and female elite members were also involved in the promotion of the Horde's trade, providing even their own capital to this end. The Black Sea trade was of supreme importance for the empire.[14] The most important centers of trade were Italian colonies: Venetian Tana (today Azov) on the mouth of Don River, and the Genovese city of Caffa (today Feodosia) in the Crimea. From these ports, a multitude of goods was shipped to different parts of the Mediterranean: slaves, hides, fleece, wheat, barley, millet, wax, salt, cheese, and fish from the Steppe and the Taiga forest, as well as products from the East, mainly silk and spices (see map 10.1).

Taydula's support for the Christians, Catholic and Orthodox alike, living in the empire was interlinked with her broader interest in European trade activities in the Black Sea region. In the spring of 1344, the senate of Venice sent delegates to Janïbek Khan's court to resolve the conflict that erupted a year earlier in Tana between the Italian merchants and the local population and that quickly spiraled into a full-fledged war between the Horde and the Italian trade colonies in the Black Sea region. The Venetians tried to end the conflict through diplomatic means. According to the Venetian delegates' report of April 28, 1344, alongside Janïbek and other members of the court, the delegation also met a khatun whose name is not documented.[15] Tana, the Venetian

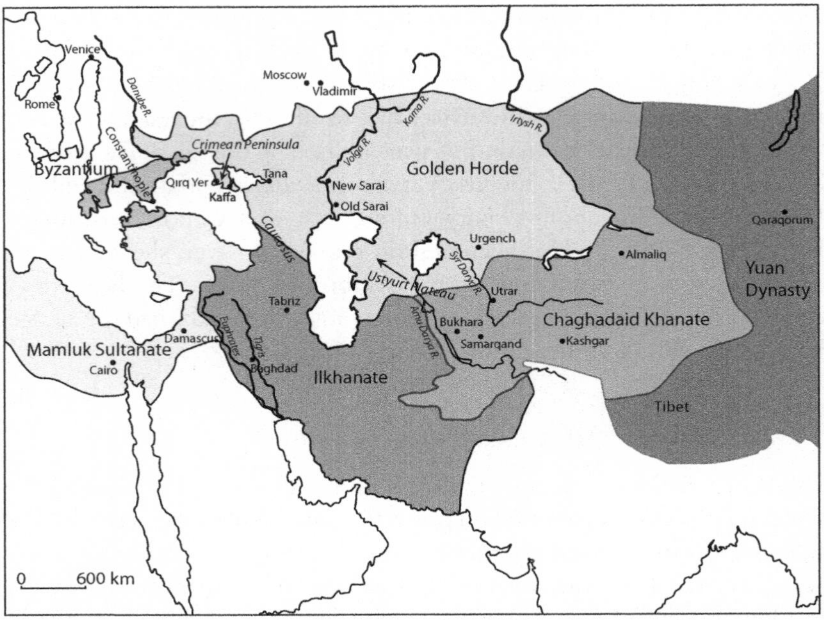

MAP 10.1. The Golden Horde and Its Trading Partners

trade emporium in the Black Sea region, was the European post linking to the main east-west continental route. During the fourteenth century, the route passed through Sarai (the Golden Horde capital), Urgench (in Khwārazm), Almaliq (the Chaghadaid capital in contemporary North Xinjiang), and China, transferring a significant volume of luxury products to Europe. Taydula had direct economic interest in this trade since a portion of the import duties paid by the Christian ships docking at Tana was assigned to her treasury. We learn this from a decree issued in 1358 by her grandson Berdibek Khan, ordering the khatun to transfer a fixed amount of her income from these levies to the khan's toll collectors.[16] The Venetians seem to have not only seen in Taydula a patron of the Christian communities, but also to have considerable sway with the khan and further a personal interest in the flourishing of the Black Sea trade through Venetian cooperation.

Taydula remained interested in the prosperous trade of Tana. In 1353–54, the Venetians caused damages to Golden Horde traders, who then turned to Berdibek Khan to redress their grievances. In September 1358, the khan ordered that the consul and Tana's merchants immediately pay recompense.[17] However, the khatun considered the compensation (2,830 *sommo,* i.e. 529.776 kg of silver) too heavy for the Venetian trade colony, so she decided to relieve the Venetians' financial burden. The letter she sent to the Doge of Venice in 1359 was translated into Latin. It testifies that she paid off 550 *sommo* (102.96 kg of silver), which amounted to one-fifth of the total Venetian debt.[18] But why would the Mongol queen carry out this act of benevolence? First, it could have reinforced her reputation as the "patron of Christians."[19] Second, her contribution to alleviating the tense relations between Venice and the Horde would have enhanced her political position. Yet, she might have also expected to be compensated. In the letter she sent to the Doge of Venice, she enclosed a detailed payment note containing the list of individuals who received her money.[20] The list also included some names that were not among the damaged traders (e.g., her treasurer or translator), and that was probably the reason why the Doge's delegate, Giovanni Dolphin (r. 1356–61), protested Taydula's supposed magnanimity.[21] Despite their objections, the khatun sent the money to the listed individuals in the presence of the Venetian delegates.[22]

TAYDULA AS PATRON TO THE CHRISTIANS

Taydula facilitated and promoted favorable relations between the ruling Mongol elite and their Christian subjects. The Chinggisid conquerors were known for assuring their subjects' religious freedom. The subdued peoples freely practiced their cults, as long as they did not question the conquerors' authority or their practices contravened Mongol indigenous beliefs. The Mongol rulers exempted from taxation the representatives of the religions, who, in return, were expected to pray for the ruler and his family. The religious specialists were further expected to facilitate the pacification and integration of the newly conquered territories into the empire. The priesthood of the Rus' Church, indeed, was also exempted from paying tax in the Horde, in exchange for their representatives' prayers for the rulers and their families.[23]

The wives of the khans also took part in maintaining the relations between the Mongol rulers and the religious institutions of the subdued peoples.[24] Mongol support for, and patronage of, religious communities need not necessarily be solely politically motivated, but was also reinforced, in some cases, by the religious affiliation and the commitment of male and female members of the royal household. For example, Yāylāq, the principal wife of the Mongol commander Noghai (d. 1299), the khan maker of the Golden Horde, was both a patron of the Franciscan community and was baptized by the Franciscans. She not only provided the Franciscans with a building in the city of Qırq Yer (today Çufut Qale) in the Crimea, but also guaranteed their safety.[25] However, the khatuns' support of religious communities and institutions was not conditioned on their affiliation with that religion. The religious affiliation of Sorqaqtani Beki (d. 1252), the wife of Chinggis Khan's youngest son, Tolui, with the Church of the East did not prevent her from donating money for building and maintaining a *madrasa,* a Muslim college, in Bukhara.[26]

Taydula's personal religious affiliation remains an open question. Because of her role as a patron of Christian communities in the Golden Horde, some historians suggest that she was a clandestine Christian in her husband's Muslim-dominated court.[27] However, our best source on Taydula, Ibn Baṭṭūṭa, does not mention her Christian affiliation. To the contrary, he describes one of his companions performing a Quran recitation at her court.[28] And her son Janïbek and grandson Berdibek were certainly Muslims.

Taydula appears as the patron of the Christians mostly after Özbek's death in 1341. Nevertheless, some sources suggest that she had already intervened on behalf of the Christian communities beforehand. As mentioned above, Özbek's conversion to Islam did not result in the persecution of Christianity. Shortly after he took the throne, on March 20, 1314, the khan himself issued an edict, *yarligh* (Mong. *jarlig*), to the Franciscans granting them privileges, exempting them from different taxes, and confirming the royal protection on their churches and convents.[29] Ibn Baṭṭūṭa's account further raises the possibility that each of Özbek's wives was assigned with providing patronage to a different religious community. It seems that Taydula was assigned the Christian denomination and another of his wives, Urdujā, was given the Muslim community.[30] Perhaps it was due to her benevolence toward the Christians that Taydula was asked by the prince of Tver, Aleksandr Mikhaïlovich (r. 1337–39), to intervene for his sake at the court once he learned in 1339 that the khan decided to execute him.[31]

In the letter Pope Benedict XII (r. 1334–42) addressed at "Taydola, Empress of Tartary in the Northern Parts" in 1340, the pope thanked Taydula for her support of the Catholic Christians living in the Golden Horde, writing that Özbek's emissaries informed him of her pious and benevolent attitude. He asked her to continue her good deeds and urged her to convert to the "Catholic faith."[32] The pope too seems to have misconstrued her patronage of the Christians as a sign of her personal inclination toward the Christian faith.[33]

TAYDULA'S RELATIONSHIP WITH THE RUS' CHURCH IN THREE EDICTS

After the establishment of the Golden Horde in the second half of the 13th century, the Mongol conquerors normalized their relations with the Orthodox Church. In several *yarlighs*, the rulers of the Horde assured the Rus' church tax exemption, as well as guaranteeing the protection of their property and cultic buildings. In return, representatives of the Rus' Church were instructed to pray for the khan and his kin. Six Golden Horde regal edicts (*khanskie i͡arlyki*) to the Rus' Church are known from the thirteenth to the fourteenth centuries.[34] These documents have come to us only through church collections and in their Russian translations, not in their original Mongol or Turkic versions.[35] Out of the six decrees, four documents (1267, 1351, 1357, and 1379) granted fiscal immunity and other privileges to the Church, and two decrees (1347 and 1354) were free-passage documents (*proezzhai͡a gramota*), which guaranteed free and safe travel for a certain bishop from Sarai, and the Metropolitan Aleksiĭ, the head of the Rus' Church. Three out of these six decrees were issued by queen Taydula, two (1347 and 1354) granting free travel and one charter (in 1351) granting the tax exemptions.

The fourteenth-century Egyptian encyclopedist al-ʿUmarī notes that the khatuns in the Golden Horde were not only active participants in the political life, but could also issue decrees of their own volition.[36] Taydula's decrees evince the unique authority and privilege attributed to the women of the royal household in the Golden Horde and more broadly, in the Mongol Empire. They are further indicative of the clear hierarchical structure at the court and the existence of a well-developed chancellery practice in the Horde. Thus, the documents issued by Taydula are referenced as charters, *gramota,* whereas the edicts issued by the Golden Horde rulers, for example, Berdibek in 1357, were titled *al tamgha yarlighs* (edicts with red seal).[37] Taydula probably did not have the right to use on her edicts the imperial red seal, which was reserved for the khan alone.[38]

The first charter (1347) issued by Taydula is also unusual due to its addressees. Other *yarlighs* issued by the khans and the two other charters issued by Taydula address the officers of the Golden Horde who were appointed to the Rus' territory or Golden Horde subjects. However, in Taydula's 1347 free passage charter, the addressees appear to be Simeon Ivanovich, the Grand Duke of Moscow (r. 1340–53), and his subordinate princes, that is, members of the Rus' principality. The identity of the metropolitan who received the charter raises some problems. We do not know of any metropolitan named Ioan at this time. He might have been a lower-ranking church official, perhaps a bishop, in Sarai. An orthodox bishopric existed in the Horde's capital since 1261. The bishopric was established for political, rather than religious purposes, and the bishops were tasked with solidifying the relationship between the metropolitans and the Golden Horde's khans. The bishops assigned to the Horde sought to gain influence at court so they could intervene on behalf of the Rus', and possibly also the Byzantine Empire. Ioan, bishop of Sarai, required Taydula's protection to travel through the northeastern territory of the Rus'. The main text of the charter implies that such trips were regularly carried out.[39] In the next part of the charter, Taydula cautions from preventing the free passage, harassing, or confiscating the horses of the prelate and his men.[40]

The second charter issued by Taydula in 1351 was bestowed on the head of the Rus' Church, the Metropolitan Feognost (r. 1328–53), and the addresses were the officials of the Horde. It shows once more Taydula's role as an intermediary between the Mongol court and the Church.[41] Charters granting fiscal immunity and other privileges to the Rus' Church were mainly issued when new khans assumed the throne or new metropolitans were appointed. According to a Russian chronicle, the Metropolitan Feognost arrived at the court of the recently enthroned Janïbek to ask for the *yarligh,* but contrary to former practice, the khan demanded taxes from Feognost.[42] Yet, Feognost was able to acquire the document from Janïbek after the Metropolitan bribed the khan, the khatun, and the leading officers. Janïbek's 1342 *yarligh* did not survive, but Taydula's charter of 1351 was likely based on the khan's edict.[43] It is also possible that the khan's *yarligh* had to be reissued by Taydula because it was not observed.[44] Taydula's charter says that the khan gave a donation to the metropolitan, and handed him a *yarligh* with the imperial red seal (*s aloi͡u tamgoi͡u i͡arlyk*). The charter states that ever since Feognost was installed in the office of the Metropolitan in Vladimir, he had been praying for Janïbek, Taydula and their children. The charter next enumerates the kinds of taxes that were not to be levied on the metropolitan, and forbids anyone from confiscating his lands, water sources, gardens, vineyards, and mills.[45]

Taydula's final charter is another free passage guarantee, from 1354 (see appendix, below).[46] It clearly indicates the name of the intended individual (Aleksiĭ), his position (metropolitan), and the destination of his travels (Tsar'grad/Constantinople). In the spring of 1353, metropolitan Feognost died of the plague.[47] Aleksiĭ, his designated successor, traveled to the Golden Horde asking for the pass. From there, he set out to Constantinople with the pass issued to him on February 11 so that he could be consecrated as metropolitan by the patriarch in Constantinople. The free passage document forbids stopping, harassing, or confiscating the horses of Aleksiĭ and his men for they were praying for Janībek, his children, and his mother, Taydula.

Beyond this remarkable documentary evidence, the significance of Taydula's support for the Rus' Church can be gauged from the later Russian legendary adaptations. There, she was not only assigned a preference to Christianity, but was also made to play a role in establishing the Rus' Church's claim to have acquired Mongol patronage for the Christians through the performance of miracles. Thus, the sixteenth-century Nikon Chronicle writes that Taydula was afflicted by eye disease and sent for the Metropolitan Aleksiĭ. The metropolitan blessed Taydula with holy water and she recovered her sight at once. In return, Taydula bestowed generous gifts, including a holy vestment, on Aleksiĭ and his attendants.[48]

CONCLUSION

Although medieval Mongol society was patriarchal and patrilineal, women of the elite played crucial roles at the highest levels of society. They participated in politics, economy, and religious patronage. Like many other Mongol khatuns, Taydula too had a politically active and influential role, especially when it came to succession struggles. She supported her son Janībek's succession, and later, Khiḍr's assumption of the Golden Horde throne.

The ambitious khatun also used her influence to facilitate trade throughout the empire. She was involved and had directly invested in the Black Sea trade. She supported the Venetian traders, helping them to resolve their conflicts with the court and obtain privileges and financial gains. Her close contacts with the Latin Christian traders' communities in Tana were driven by mutual economic interests.

Taydula's patronage of the Christian subjects seems to have been mainly linked to her trade interests. Unlike other khatuns, Taydula did not donate for the building of Christian churches, cloisters, or schools, as the above-mentioned Yāylāq had done, nor did Taydula supply them with holy books, as did Ögödei's wife Töregene (r. 1242–46).[49] Rather, in line with Mongol male rulers, Taydula supported the representatives of the Rus' Church with exemptions from taxpaying and safe-conduct passes. Although Taydula issued these charters by the orders of khans and under their authority, she nevertheless granted the edicts in her own name. Hence, she joins the short list of female members of the Mongol elite whose names appear on edicts and chancellery documents.[50]

While Taydula's support for the Christians was motivated by the prospects of political and economic gain rather than spiritual convictions, and she resorted to a pragmatic approach common to the Mongols' broader religious policies, she nevertheless significantly contributed to strengthening the interactions between Orthodox Rus' Christianity and the Turkic-Mongol culture of the Golden Horde. The tale of her miraculous recovery from illness at the hands of the Metropolitan Aleksiĭ might have been designed to commemorate and extol the role played by the Church in safeguarding the protection of the Christians under the Muslim Mongols, but it is further indicative of the significant influence that the Church rightfully attributed to the Mongol queen.

APPENDIX

Taydula's 1354 yarligh to Metropolitan Aleksiĭ

By Janïbek's *yarligh* [royal edict], [this is my] Taydula's word [i.e. order].[51]

To the commanders[52] of ten thousands and thousands, and to the commanders of hundreds and tens,[53] to the administrative chiefs of districts and towns,[54] to the commanders [of the districts and towns], to the passing envoys, to the many people, and to all.

To all, if Metropolitan Aleksiĭ goes to Tsar'grad [Constantinople], and wherever he is, [we order that] none hinder his passage and that [none] use force against him.[55] Moreover, wherever he stays, [none] should capture either him or his men, nor obstruct his passage. His horses and anything else [of his] should not be taken from him. They are to leave them alone in peace, because he prays for Janïbek, his children and us [for Taydula]. We order so.

Now, whosoever hereupon commits violence [against Aleksiĭ and his men], he will be charged according to the Great Custom.[56]

So saying, we have issued a sealed charter[57] in the year of the Horse,[58] in the month of Aram,[59] on the second [day] of the old,[60] [when] the *ordo* camped in Gulistan.[61] It was written by . . . .[62] The petition was presented [to Taydula] by Temir Khoja.[63]

NOTES

1. May 2016, 89–106; De Nicola 2017, 130–81: for the khatuns' involvement in trade, 145–49.

2. Her name meant either "having a foil tail" (Pelliot 1949, 102–4; Zimonyi 2005, 307) or "born in the house of a maternal uncle" (Grigor'ev and Grigor'ev 2002, 196).

3. Found in the Rus', Khwārazm, Volga Bulgharia, and the Crimea.

4. Ivanics 2011, 213; Ivanics, 2017, 156, 251. For the Chinggisids' relations with the Qongrats: Landa 2016, 165–73, 193–95.

5. The Khan's principal wife was the first wife he married and/or the wife who gave birth to his potential male successors. If she did not give birth to a son (or died), she might be replaced by another. Özbek's first principal wife was Bayālūn (d. 1323) (PSRL 18: 89). She is not to be confused with Bayalūn, Özbek's third wife and daughter of the Byzantine emperor. Ibn Baṭṭūṭa (1962, 2: 483, 486) mentions that Taydula replaced the mother of Özbek's daughter, Īt Kujujuk. However, Taydula was probably already one of Özbek's wives before she became principal wife since Tinibek, Taydula's and Özbek's son, had been already married seven years after Taydula was promoted to principal wife. Tizengauzen 1941, 101.

6. Ibn Baṭṭūṭa 1962, 2: 486; Ibn Baṭṭūṭa 1971, 3: 544. The translator, Gibb, states Khurasan, but this is a mistake. I thank Prof. Peter Jackson for drawing my attention to this.

7. According to Shams al-Dīn al-Shujā'ī, they had a third brother, Ḥiḍrbek, who was also killed by Janïbek (Tizengauzen 1884, 254–55, 263–64). The seventeenth-century *Defter-i Chinggis-name* states that Taydula was married to Janïbek. Ivanics and Usmanov 2002, 82–83; Ivanics 2017, 251. This is unlikely since the Mongol custom of levirate enabled the son to marry his father's widow as long as she was not his own mother. This confusion perhaps stems from the important role of Taydula, Janïbek's mother, at his court.

8. Ibn Baṭṭūṭa 1962, 2: 483.

9. Ibn Baṭṭūṭa 1962, 2: 485–86.

10. Ibn Baṭṭūṭa 1962, 2: 485–87. Either Ibn Baṭṭūṭa or his informant associated Solomon's ring, a symbol of wisdom, with Taydula's ring-shaped vagina, which gave her control over Özbek. Zimonyi 2005, 308–9.

11. After her grandson, Berdibek, had his father Janïbek killed, Taydula tried to convince Berdibek to show mercy toward his eight-month-old brother, but Berdibek is reported to have killed the baby with his own hands. Tizengauzen 1941, 129.

12. Utemish-khadzhi 1992, 109, 112.

13. Utemish-khadzhi 1992, 113.

14. See Ciocîltan 2012; and Giebfried's chapter in this volume.

15. Thomas 1880, 321.

16. Predelli 1899, 50; Grigor'ev and Grigor'ev 2002, 147, 153.

17. Predelli 1899, 52, Grigor'ev and Grigor'ev 2002, 185–91.

18. Predelli 1899, 53–54; Grigor'ev and Grigor'ev 2002, 204–17.

19. Grigor'ev and Grigor'ev 2002, 202.

20. The letter and the payment list are recorded separately (Predelli 1899, 53–54). Yet, it is clear from their content that they are connected (Grigor'ev and Grigor'ev 2002, 196–217). However, the currency units in the two sources differ: *sommo* in the letter, while the list contains *bess*, namely bezant (i.e., Byzantine gold solidus). The amount of 550 *sommo* mentioned in the letter roughly corresponds to the 10,998 bezants that appear in the list (Grigor'ev and Grigor'ev 2002, 207). The Armenians are the seventh on the list. They received the largest amount of money from Taydula (5,000 bezants). *Bazimano* (to whom Taydula gave 540 bezants) is probably the same individual named *Bassimat* (Bachman?) in Berdibek Khan's letter. This merchant lodged a complaint to Berdibek Khan after he was plundered by the Venetians. Predelli 1899, 52; Grigor'ev and Grigor'ev 2002, 187, 201.

21. Cf. Ibn Baṭṭūṭa 1962, 2: 486. The dating of the charter is in compliance with the practice of the chancellery of the Horde: Year of the Pig, second month, fifth [day] of Gibbous Moon (March 4, 1359). Grigor'ev and Grigor'ev 2002, 199, 202.

22. Predelli 1899, 53; Grigor'ev and Grigor'ev 2002, 204–17. Gulistan, where Taydula received the Venetians, may have been the winter residence of the khans of the Golden Horde; it was somewhere in the Volga region. Fedorov-Davydov 1994, 22–23.

23. Atwood 2004, 237–56; Jackson 2005, 245–90.

24. De Nicola 2017, 182–222.

25. Golubovich 1913, 444–45.

26. Juwaynī 1997, 552–53.

27. Grigor'ev and Grigor'ev 2002, 127; Howorth 1880, 172, 178.

28. Ibn Baṭṭūṭa 1962, 2: 487.

29. Hautala 2014.

30. Grigor'ev 1990, 37–38.

31. The prince sent one of his servants to the *t͡sarit͡sa* (empress), possibly Taydula, but he and his son were executed nonetheless. PSRL 15 2000, 49–50.

32. Golubovich 1923, 4:228.

33. Ryan 1998.

34. Legal and diplomatic documents had the same form throughout the Mongol Empire. For the structure of *yarligh*s: Herrmann 2004, 9–32. For chancellery practice in the Horde: Vásáry 1987; for the Chaghadaid realm: Biran 2008. For Mongolian documents: Ligeti 1972; Cerensodnom and Taube 1993. Cf. Atwood 2004, 239–41, who compares Golden Horde and Yuan edicts.

35. Cherepnin 1955, 463–65.

36. Al-ʿUmarī 1968, 136.

37. Taydula's 1351 charter also mentions the order issued by Janïbek (presumably in 1342) as *s alot͡u tamgot͡u t͡arlyk*. A similar distinction between the designation of empress' edicts (*yizhi*) and the emperor's edicts (*shengzhi*) is found in Yuan China (Zhao and Guisso 2005, 18). For Berdibek's 1357 edict: Cherepnin 1955, 469–70; cf. Schurmann 1956, 346–48.

38. Grigor'ev 1990, 41. All of Taydula's charters were composed while the court was residing in her winter quarters, which is where she seems to have engaged with her Christian subjects. There are additional structural and formal

differences between Taydula's charters and the regal *yarlighs*. Whereas the khans' edicts all start with the invocation of divine powers, the khatun's three charters with a reference to the khan's and her orders instead. For example, the first charter issued by Taydula (1347), probably begun with "By Janïbek's order, my Taydula's word" (Priselkov 1916, 79–81; Grigor'ev 1990, 38, 39, 42; Cherepnin 1955, 468, 470–71; Predelli 1899, 53). This was a common opening for decrees issued by the khan's non-Chinggisid subordinates—commanders or governors (for example, Matsui 2007, 61; Matsui 2008, 158; cf. Herrmann 2004, 73, 79, etc).

39. The Rus' Church's mission in Sarai traveled home to acquire church tools and liturgical books, and to purchase clothes and food.

40. The charter appears to have been sealed (*nishenem gramotu*). Cherepnin 1955, 467. Following Mongolian chancellery protocol, the edict ends with the date and place of signing: the eighth month of the Year of the Pig, the fifth day of the waning moon (September 25, 1347), when the *ordo* was at the Yellow Reed (*Zheltoi Trosti*), probably the Basin of Sarykamish (Grigor'ev 1990, 40–42).

41. Grigor'ev 1991, 85–86.

42. PSRL 10 1885, 215.

43. According to Taydula's charter, the Rus' Church was exempted from paying the *poshlina* (direct tax) and *podvoda* (cart tax), and from providing *korm* (food), *zapros* (extra demands), *dar* (gift, tax to the landlord) and *pochestie* (contribution-in-kind). Cherepnin 1955, 468. For taxes in the Golden Horde: Vernadsky 1953, 219–23; Schurmann 1956, 343–59. The *podvoda* and the *korm* were taxes related to the postal relay system (Turk. *yam*, Mong. *jam*).

44. Cf. Spuler 1965, 228.

45. It was issued with a *nishān* (seal), and written in Sarai, during the year of the Rabbit, in the month of Aram (the first month of the Uighur calendar), on the eighth day of the new moon, i.e., March 7, 1351 (on its dating: Pliguzov 1987, 579).

46. Cherepnin 1955, 470; Grigor'ev 1993, 149–54. For a similar edict: Matsui 2008, 160.

47. The Black Death reached the Horde in the 1340s and the Crimea in 1346. A report on eighty-five thousand dead in the Crimea suggests a considerable depopulation across its territories. The plague led to the political instability that ensued in 1360. Schamiloglu 2017, 325–43.

48. PSRL 11 1897 32–33; Kriptsov 2005, 50–51.

49. De Rachewiltz 1981, 45.

50. E.g. Töregene's decree (Zhao and Guisso 2005, 19); salary/tax assessment from the wife of Ilkhan Abū Saʿīd (r. 1316–35), Dilshād Khatun. Herrmann 2004, 102–6.

51. Cherepnin 1955, 470; Grigor'ev 1993, 149–54. I thank Professor István Ferincz for his help in checking the translation. Traditional Mongol documents use the formula *üge manu* "our word" (Turk. *sözümüz*, alternatively rendered in the singular as "my word," Turk. *sözüm*). The documents drew their authority from strictly maintaining the longstanding imperial protocol and invoking Chinggisid precedents. The structure of the edicts included an introductory

section (*protocollum*) that usually contains: 1. an invocation (*invocatio*), which is missing in Taydula's charters; 2. the name of the issuer (*intitulatio*); 3. the addressees (*inscriptio*), usually the Mongol officers. The second section (*contextus*), the main body of the document, includes a legitimizing explanation for the exemption, and the detailed content of the decree, which usually would provide fiscal immunity or safe passage to the Church and its members. In return, representatives of the Church are required to pray for the khan and his family (*narratio* and *dispositio*). Then, there is a general warning (*sanctio*) addressed at anyone who disobeys the *yarligh*. The final section (*eschatocollum*) starts with a reaffirmation of the decree (*corroboratio*, e.g., "The charter was sealed") and concludes where and when the document was issued (*datatio*), and in some cases, details also the witnessing parties and officials, and the name of the scribe (*subscriptio*). The charters of the Golden Horde sometimes end with a chancellery note pertaining to the office routine of the chancellery (e.g. the name of the official who presented the petition). Although Taydula's charters were preserved only in their Latin and Old Church Slavonic translations, it is clear that the dating of the original documents, too, was carried out according to Mongol chancellery practice, using the traditional Mongolian animal cycles to identify the year, as well as providing the month and the day according to the lunar cycle.

52. Here, the title *kn͡iaz'*, literally prince, signifies a commander (for *amir* or *beg* probably).

53. This reflects the traditional Inner Asian decimal military system which became the basic units of taxation in the Horde. In the Horde's administration, a *temnik* was a commander of ten thousand men, a *tys͡iachnik* commander of a thousand men, a *sotnik* commander of a hundred men, and a *des͡iatnik* commander of ten. Vernadsky 1953, 207, 254, 223–24, 321.

54. The Russian *volosteli* stands for Mongol *darughachi* (or *darugha* > Rus. *doroga*); he was a chief official, a supervisor of a territorial and/or administrative unit and had multiple functions: inspecting state revenue, conducting census, collecting taxes, supervising the postal system, and maintaining order. A threefold division of the *darugha*s (district, town and village) can be observed in the Horde. *Volosteli* were *darugha*s of districts (*volosti*), and the *gorodnye dorogi* were *darugha*s of towns (*goroda*). Vásáry 1976, 188–90. In the Russian chronicles, they are often referred to as *baskak*s (Turk. *basqaq*). Vernadsky 1953, 211–12, 220; Vásáry 1976, 187–97.

55. Metropolitans were elected by the Rus' Church and appointed by the patriarch in Constantinople. Therefore, when Aleksiĭ asked for the pass, he was not yet officially a metropolitan. Taydula used his title (metropolitan) in advance.

56. Schurmann 1956, 349. The phrase . . . *na velikoĭ poshline* (literally "the great custom") refers to the Mongol *Yeke Jasaq* (i.e., Great Yasa), the legal code ascribed to Chinggis Khan.

57. In this case the Persian *nishān*, "sign, signal, marker character, seal, stamp," means seal.

58. *Eita* (< Turk. *At*).

59. Turk. *Aram*, the first month (January–February) of the Uighur calendar.

60. *V vtoryi vetkha.* Rus. *vetkha* is the genitive of *vetkho*, from *vetkhiĭ* (old) referring to the last third of the month (Schurmann 1956, 346). In some Middle Mongolian documents, "the first ten days and the last nine or ten days are expressed by cardinal numbers from one to ten plus *sine* 'new' or *qagucin* 'old' respectively. The days of the middle of the month are formed by cardinal numbers from eleven to twenty." Rybatzki 2003, 270–71. The date corresponds to February 11, 1354. Cherepnin 1955, 480.

61. Gulistan was probably the winter residence of the Horde rulers, in the Volga region. See note 22.

62. Usually, the name of the scribe appears here. For example, in Berdibek's 1357 *yarligh, seunch' Temur' mi͡ur' bakshii*, i.e., Sevünch Temür mīr-bakshi, appears as the name of the scribe. Cherepnin 1955, 470; Vásáry 1987, 37.

63. In the chancellery practice of the Horde there were mediators who presented petitions in the name of supplicants. Vásáry 1987, 38–44. Temir Khoja is unidentified.

BIBLIOGRAPHY

Atwood, Christopher P. 2004. "Validation by Holiness or Sovereignty: Religious Toleration as Political Theology in the Mongol World Empire of the Thirteenth Century." *International History Review* 26: 237–56.

Biran, Michal. 2008. "Diplomacy and Chancellery Practices in the Chagataid Khanate: Some Preliminary Remarks." *Oriente Moderno* 88: 369–93.

Cerensodnom, Dalantai, and Manfred Taube. 1993. *Die Mongolica der Berliner Turfansammlung*. Berliner Turfantexte XVI. Berlin: Akademie-Verlag.

Cherepnin, L[ev] V[ladimirovich]. 1955. *Pami͡atniki russkogo prava*. Ed. L.V. Cherepnin. Moscow: Gosudarstvennoe izdatel'stvo i͡uridicheskoĭ literatury.

Ciocîltan, Virgil. 2012. *The Mongols and the Black Sea Trade in the Thirteenth and Fourteenth Centuries*. Boston, Leiden: Brill.

De Nicola, Bruno. 2017. *Women in Mongol Iran: The Khātūns, 1206–1335*. Edinburgh: Edinburgh University Press.

de Rachewiltz, Igor. 1981. "Some Remarks on Töregene's Edict of 1240." *Papers on Far Eastern History* 23: 39–63.

Fedorov-Davydov, G[erman] A[lekseevich]. 1994. *Zolotoordynskie goroda Povolzh'i͡a*. Moscow: Izdatel'stvo Moskovskogo universiteta.

Golubovich, Girolamo. 1913. *Biblioteca bio-bibliografica della Terra Santa e dell'Oriente Francescano*. Vol. 2. Florence: Collegio di S. Bonaventura.

———. 1923. *Biblioteca bio-bibliografica della Terra Santa e dell'Oriente Francescano*. Vol. 4. Dal 1333 al 1345. Florence: Collegio di S. Bonaventura.

Grigor'ev, A[rkadiĭ] P[avlovich]. 1990. "Proezzhai͡a gramota Taĭduly ot 1347 g.. Rekonstrukt͡sii͡a soderzhanii͡a." *Vestnik Leningradskogo universiteta; Istorii͡a, i͡azykoznanie, literaturovedenie*, ser. 2, 3: 37–44.

———. 1991. "Zhalovannai͡a gramota Taĭduly ot 1351 g.. Rekonstrukt͡sii͡a soderzhanii͡a." *Vestnik Leningradskogo universiteta: Istorii͡a, i͡azykoznanie, literaturovedenie*, ser. 2, 1: 85–93.

———. 1993. "Proezzhaî͡a gramota Taĭduly ot 1354 g.. Rekonstrukt͡sii͡a soderzhanii͡a." *Vostokovedenie: Filologicheskie issledovanii͡a* 18: 149–54.

Grigor'ev, A[rkadiĭ] P[avlovich], and V[adim] P[avlovich] Grigor'ev. 2002. *Kollekt͡sii͡a zolotoordynskikh dokumentov XIV veka iz Venet͡sii: istochnikovedcheskoe issledovanie.* St. Petersburg: Izdatel'stvo Sankt-Peterburgskogo universiteta.

Hautala, Roman. 2014. "I͡Arlyk khana Uzbeka frant͡siskant͡sam Zolotoĭ Ordy 1314 goda: latinskiĭ tekst, russkiĭ perevod i kommentarii." *Golden Horde Review* 3.5: 31–48.

Herrmann, Gottfried, 2004. *Persische Urkunden der Mongolenzeit: Text- und Bildteil.* Documenta Iranica et Islamica 2. Wiesbaden, Germany: Harrasowitz.

Howorth, Henry H. 1880. *History of the Mongols from the 9th to the 19th Century.* Part 2. *The So-called Tartars of Russia and Central Asia.* London: Longmans, Green.

Ibn Baṭṭūṭa. 1962–71. *The Travels of Ibn Baṭṭūṭa,* A.D. *1325–1354.* Tr. H. A. R. Gibb. Vols. 2 and 3. Cambridge: Cambridge University Press.

Ivanics, Mária. 2011. "Die Frauen der Khane in der Goldenen Horde und in ihren Nachfolgestaaten." *Chronica: Annual of the Institute of History University of Szeged* 11: 211–20.

———. 2017. *Hatalomgyakorlás a steppén.* A Dzsingisz-námé *nomád világa* [Practicing Power in the Steppe. The Nomadic World of the Chinggis-name]. Budapest: MTA Bölcsészettudományi Kutatóközpont Történettudományi Intézet.

Ivanics, Mária, and A. Mirkasym Usmanov. 2002. *Das Buch der Dschingis-Legende: Däftär-i Čingiz-nāmä.* I. Studia Uralo-Altaica 44. Szeged, Hungary: Department of Altaic Studies, University of Szeged.

Jackson, Peter. 2005. "The Mongols and the Faith of the Conquered." In *Mongols, Turks, and Others: Eurasian Nomads and the Sedentary World,* ed. Reuven Amitai and Michal Biran, 245–90. Leiden, Boston: Brill.

Juwaynī, 'Alā' al-Dīn 'Aṭā Malik. 1997. *Genghis Khan: The History of the World Conqueror.* Tr. J. A. Boyle with a new introduction and bibliography by David O. Morgan. Manchester: Manchester University Press.

Kript͡sov, D[mitriĭ] I͡U[r'evich]. 2005. "Dar Khanshi Taĭduly mitropolitu Aleksei͡u: Real'nost' ili legenda?" *Drevnii͡ai͡a Rus': Voprosy medievistiki* 3: 50–51.

Landa, Ishayahu. 2016. "Imperial Sons-in-Law on the Move: Oyirad and Qonggirad Dispersion in Mongol Eurasia." *Archivum Eurasiae Medii Aevi* 22: 161–97.

Ligeti, Louis. 1972. *Monuments préclassiques 1. XIIIe et XIVe siècles.* Monumenta Linguae Mongolicae Collecta II. Budapest: Akadémiai Kiadó.

Matsui, Dai. 2007. "An Uigur Decree of Tax Exemption in the Name of Duwa-Khan." *Shinzhlėkh Ukhaany Akademiĭn mėdėė* 4: 60–68.

———. 2008. "A Mongolian Decree from the Chaghataid Khanate Discovered at Dunhuang." In *Aspects of Research into Central Asian Buddhism: In Memoriam Kōgi Kudara,* ed. Peter Zieme, 159–78. Turnhout: Brepols.

May, Timothy. 2016. "Commercial Queens: Mongolian Khatuns and the Silk Road." *Journal of the Royal Asiatic Society* 26: 89–106.

Pelliot, Paul. 1949. *Notes sur l'histoire de la Horde d'Or: Suivies de quelques noms turcs d'hommes et de peuples finissant en "ar."* Oeuvres posthumes de Paul Pelliot 2. Paris: Libr. d'Amérique et d'Orient.

Pliguzov, A[ndreĭ] I[vanovich]. 1987. "Drevneĭshiĭ spisok kratkogo sobranii͡a i͡arlykov, dannykh ordynskimi khanami russkim mitropolitam." In *Russkiĭ feodal'nyĭ arkhiv XIV—pervoĭ treti XVI veka*, ed. V.I. Buganov, 571–94. Moscow: Akademii͡a nauk SSSR, Institut Istorii.

Predelli, Riccardo. 1899. *Diplomatarium Veneto-Levantinum, sive acta et diplomata res Venetas, Graecas atque Levantis illustrantia. a. 1351–1454.* Vol. 2. Venice: Sumptibus Societatis.

Priselkov, M[ikhail] D[mitrievich]. 1916. *Khanskie i͡arlyki russkim mitropolitam.* Petrograd: Tipografii͡a "Nauchnoe di͡elo."

PSRL 10. 1885. *Letopisnyĭ sbornik imenuemyĭ Patriarshei͡u ili Nikonovskoi͡u letopis'i͡u: Polnoe sobranie russkikh letopiseĭ.* Vol. 10. St. Petersburg: Tipografii͡a ministerstva vnutrennikh del.

——— 11. 1897. *Letopisnyĭ sbornik imenuemyĭ Patriarshei͡u ili Nikonovskoi͡u letopis'i͡u: Polnoe sobranie russkikh letopiseĭ.* Vol. 11. Saint Petersburg: Tipografii͡a I.H. Skorokhodova.

——— 15. 2000. *Rogozhskiĭ letopiset͡s: Tverskoĭ sbornik; Polnoe sobranie russkikh letopiseĭ.* Ed. with a foreword to the edition of 2000 by B[oris] M[ihaĭlovich] Kloss. Vol. 15. Moscow: I͡Azyki russkoĭ kul'tury.

——— 18. 2007. *Simeonovskai͡a letopis': Polnoe sobranie russkikh letopiseĭ.* Ed. with a foreword to the edition of 2007 by B[oris] M[ihaĭlovich] Kloss. Vol. 18. Moscow: Znak.

Ryan, James D. 1998. "Christian Wives of Mongol Khans: Tartar Queens and Missionary Expectations in Asia." *Journal of the Royal Asiatic Society* 8: 411–21.

Rybatzki, Volker. 2003. "Names of the Months in Middle Mongol." In *Altaica Budapestinensia MMII: Proceedings of the 45th Permanent International Altaistic Conference (PIAC) Budapest, Hungary, June 23–28, 2002*, ed. Alice Sárközi and Attila Rákos, 256–90. Budapest: Budapest Research Group for Altaic Studies, Hungarian Academy of Sciences.

Schamiloglu, Uli. 2017. "The Impact of the Black Death on the Golden Horde: Politics, Economy, Society, Civilization." *Golden Horde Review* 5: 325–43.

Schurmann, H[erbert] F[ranz]. 1956. "Mongolian Tributary Practices of the Thirteenth Century." *Harvard Journal of Asiatic Studies* 19: 304–89.

Spuler, Bertold. 1965. *Die Goldene Horde: Die Mongolen in Rußland 1223–1502.* 2nd ed. Wiesbaden, Germany: Harrassowitz.

Tizengauzen, V[ladimir] [Gustavovich]. 1884. *Sbornik materialov, otnosi͡ashchikhsi͡a k istorii Zolotoĭ Ordy: Izvlechenii͡a iz sochineniĭ arabskikh.* Vol. 1. St. Petersburg: S.G. Stroganov.

———. 1941. *Sbornik materialov, otnosi͡ashchikhsi͡a k istorii Zolotoĭ Ordy: Izvlechenii͡a iz persidskikh sochineniĭ.* Vol. 2. Moscow: Izdatel'stvo Akademii nauk SSSR.

Thomas, Georgius Martinus. 1880. *Diplomatarium Veneto-Levantinum, sive acta et diplomata res Venetas, Graecas atque Levantis illustrantia. a. 1300–1350.* Vol. 1. Venice: Sumptibus Societatis.

al-ʿUmarī, Aḥmad Ibn-Yaḥyā Ibn Faḍlallāh. 1968. *Das mongolische Weltreich: Al-'Umarī's Darstellung der mongolischen Reiche in seinem Werk Masālik al-abṣār fī mamālik al-amṣār.* Ed. with paraphrase and commentary by Klaus Lech. Asiatische Forschungen Bd. 22 Wiesbaden, Germany: Harrassowitz.
Utemish-khadzhi. 1992. *Chingiz-name.* Ed. with facsimile, translation, transcription, textological commentary by V. P. I͡Udin. Prepared for edition by I͡U. G. Baranov. Commentary and index by M. Kh. Abuseitova. Alma-Ata, Kazakhstan: Gylym.
Vásáry, István. 1976. "The Golden Horde Term *Daruġa* and Its Survival in Russia." *Acta Orientalia Academiae Scientiarum Hungaricae* 30: 187–97.
———. 1987. *Az Arany Horda kancelláriája* [The Chancellery of the Golden Horde]. Keleti értekezések 3. Budapest: Kőrösi Csoma Társaság.
Vernadsky, George. 1953. *A History of Russia.* Vol. 3: *The Mongols and Russia.* New Haven, CT: Yale University Press.
Zhao, George Q., and Richard W. L. Guisso. 2005. "Female Anxiety and Female Power: The Political Involvement of Mongol Empresses during the 13th and 14th Centuries." In *History and Society in Central and Inner Asia: Papers Presented at the Central and Inner Asia Seminar, University of Toronto, 16–17 April 2004*, ed. Gillian Long, Uradyn Erden Bulag, Michael Gervers, 17–46. Toronto: Asian Institute, University of Toronto.
Zimonyi, István. 2005. "Ibn Baṭṭūṭa on the First Wife of Özbek Khan." *Central Asiatic Journal* 49: 303–9.

PART THREE

Intellectuals

CHAPTER 11

Rashīd al-Dīn

Buddhism in Iran and the Mongol Silk Roads

JONATHAN BRACK

Buddhism was not entirely a newcomer to Iran when it first arrived at the doorsteps of the Iranian world under the Mongol auspices in the mid-thirteenth century. Eastern Iran was a center of Buddhist activity and learning, mainly in the second and third centuries C.E. In the centuries following the seventh-century expansion of Islam into the Persian-speaking world, Muslims continued to encounter Buddhism, mainly through the abundant Buddhist artifacts and ruins that dotted the eastern parts of Iran and Khurasan, or through the contributions of Buddhist scholars to the Arabic translation of Sanskrit medical treatises in the cosmopolitan intellectual scene of ninth-century Baghdad.[1] Yet by the eleventh century, Muslim contacts with real-life Buddhists became so infrequent that, the Central Asian scholar al-Bīrūnī (d. 1048) was unable to find a Buddhist informant with whom to consult about the Buddhist creed.[2]

This reality drastically changed after the Mongol conquest of the eastern Islamic world. Hülegü (r. 1260–65), founder of the Ilkhanate, the Mongol state centered in Iran, Iraq, and Azerbaijan (1260–1335), was an avid supporter of Buddhists, especially of the Tantric Tibetan schools. With Hülegü's and his descendants' financial and political support, Buddhism succeeded in establishing its reach far into the Islamic domains, erecting "a corridor of Buddhist temples between the Black Sea and the area south of the Caspian Sea, along the routes that linked Anatolia to the Indus River Valley."[3] Clusters of Buddhist shrines were especially

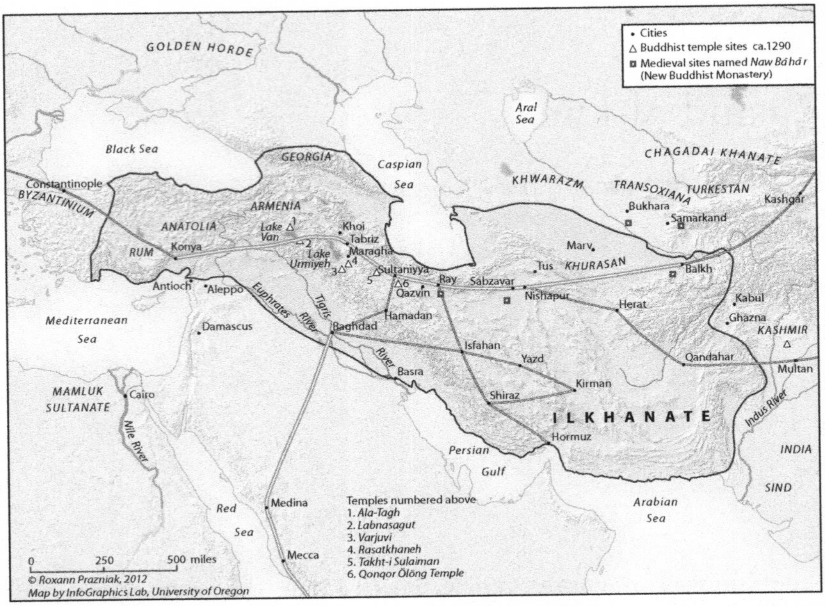

MAP 11.1. Map of Buddhist Sites in Ilkhanid Iran. Courtesy of Roxann Prazniak (originally published in Prazniak 2014, 653).

prevalent near sites frequented by the Ilkhans' mobile royal camps (see map 11.1). The generous patronage that Hülegü and his offspring, the Ilkhans, provided the Buddhist schools in the Hülegüid appanages in western Tibet created a strong incentive for Tibetan, Kashmiri, and Indian Buddhist monks to visit the Ilkhanid court.[4] The revival of Buddhism in Iran lasted roughly four decades. It abruptly ended with the conversion of Hülegü's great-grandson, Ghazan (r. 1295–1304), to Islam and his subsequent succession to the Ilkhanid throne. Ghazan implemented a series of Islamization policies and presented a hostile attitude toward the Buddhists. He ordered the ransacking and destruction of their monasteries and shrines, including those established by his own father, Ilkhan Arghun (r. 1284–91).[5]

Our knowledge of this "era of Buddhist revival" in Mongol-ruled Iran remains vague. Our main evidence is derived from the Ilkhanid Muslim authors, who appear to have had little interest in the reentrance of Buddhism to Iran, or purposefully chose to remain silent on the topic.[6] Things become slightly clearer during the reign of Hülegü's grandson, the Ilkhan Arghun, who showed interest in the Buddhist monks,[7] especially for their medical expertise.[8] His generous patronage attracted Buddhist priests from India and Kashmir to the court, where the Muslims encountered them.[9]

One important source on these Muslim-Buddhist interactions and daily encounters at Arghun's camp are the animated autobiographical accounts of the Sufi Shaykh ʿAlāʾ al-Dawla Simnānī (d. 1336). During the summer of 1288, Simnānī was detained in the Ilkhan's summer camp at Qonqur Öläng (in northwestern Iran, near where the city of Sulṭāniyya would be later built), where he was made to partake in disputations with Buddhist priests, who by his own account, had especially gathered from across Asia—India, Tibet, Kashmir, and Uighur territory—to dispute with him. As Devin DeWeese shows, Simnānī's accounts attest to the centrality of the interfaith, Buddhist-Muslim, debates in the intellectual life at Arghun's court.[10]

From martial spectacles and sportive tournaments to "intellectual duels," public contests were at the front and center of a sedentary economy of luxury entertainment the Mongols became accustomed to as their empire expanded. Court-sponsored debates fulfilled numerous functions, from educating the ruler and his milieu or providing intelligence, to the enhancement of the khan's prestige through the display of the diverse human talent accumulated at his court. From the standpoint of its participants, interfaith debates formed an opportunity to display rhetorical skill, convince the khan or his representatives of the superiority of their faith, and gain the court's support and patronage—perhaps even lay the foundation for a future conversion of the ruler and his household (or fend off the advances of other religious contenders).[11] In the Mongol Empire and Ilkhanid Iran, the forum of the court debate was also an opportunity for exchange of ideas and production of knowledge on the religious other.

This chapter explores the works of the Ilkhanid vizier, historian and theologian Rashīd al-Dīn (ca. 1247–1318) as a vital source for the Buddhist participation at the Ilkhanid interfaith debates, and more broadly, for the Buddhist influence at the court. We focus here on new evidence on Rashīd al-Dīn's attitude toward the Buddhists, especially considering the vizier's prominent role in facilitating the transfer and integration of new knowledge on Buddhism in the Islamic world.

RASHĪD AL-DĪN: BIOGRAPHICAL SKETCH

Rashīd al-Dīn Faḍlallāh al-Hamadānī was born to a Jewish family of physicians, who originated from the city of Hamadan in western Iran.[12]

Hamadan was home to a thriving Jewish community at the time. Despite Rashīd al-Dīn being a prolific author, he himself tells us very little about his family history, and next to nothing about his early life. He lists his grandfather, the "great physician" Muwaffaq al-Dawla,[13] and his descendants, among those "released" in 1256 by the Mongol forces from the Ismāʿīlī stronghold of Maymūndiz in northern Iran, together with the Shīʿī polymath Naṣīr al-Dīn Ṭūsī (d. 1274).[14] There, Rashīd al-Dīn claims, his grandfather and family were held against their will by the mad Ismāʿīlī Imam. After their safe delivery, Muwaffaq al-Dawla and his children gladly joined the service of Hülegü.[15] Rashīd al-Dīn's narrative of his family's release, however, raises some difficulty. It is plausible that Rashīd al-Dīn's grandfather had initially sought refuge with the Ismāʿīlīs due to the turmoil ensued by the Mongol invasions, and that they were later captured with the surrender of the stronghold.[16] However, the narrative also suspiciously echoes Ṭūsī's earlier account.[17] It might reflect therefore the vizier's attempt to provide his family with a more glamorous account of their start at the Mongol service, some fifty years after the events in question.

Rashīd al-Dīn, in any case, was probably nine years old when his family surrendered.[18] The family settled in Maragha in western Iran, where Ṭūsī established his famous observatory.[19] Under Ṭūsī's management, the observatory and city would become the central intellectual hub in the first few decades of the Ilkhanate. Rashīd al-Dīn's grandfather, and his father, ʿImād al-Dawla, became physicians (or pharmacists) at the Mongol court.[20] We know next to nothing about Rashīd al-Dīn's youth, though he likely followed the footsteps of his father and grandfather as a medical practitioner.[21] Jewish physicians frequented the court attending on the Ilkhan and his family, and some used this proximity to gain political influence and high-ranking administrative posts. The Jewish physician Saʿd al-Dawla (d. 1291), for example, was the Ilkhan Arghun's vizier, from 1289 until his execution in 1291.[22] Rashīd al-Dīn too appears to have gradually risen in prominence, progressing from the practice of medicine at the courts of the Ilkhans Abaqa (r. 1265–82) and Arghun, to consulting with chief commanders (*amīrs*) on the affairs of the state, and finally, to more formal assignments to administrative tasks.[23]

We are also ignorant about the time and circumstances of Rashīd al-Dīn's conversion to Islam.[24] Although he was accused of being a Jewish sympathizer and worse, a heretic and pseudo convert[25]—accusations that he fended off in his extensive theological collections (below)—he remained vague about his own conversion. While his father, ʿImād al-Dawla, remained Jewish,[26] Rashīd al-Dīn implies in one instance that his father's fraternization with eminent Muslims, especially the pious individuals and educated scholars, and his own upbringing in their company, convinced Rashīd al-Dīn to embrace Islam.[27] It seems, in any case, that by the end of the Ilkhan Abaqa's reign, and around the age of thirty (c. 1277), Rashīd al-Dīn had already converted.[28] That his Jewish past continued to haunt him is evident in a contemporaneous Christian account which states that a Jewish individual named Rashīd al-Dawla served as a cook for the Ilkhan Geikhatu (r. 1291–95).[29] No other account corroborates the claim that Rashīd al-Dīn had an official role at Geikhatu's court, and thus that this Jewish cook is Rashīd al-Dīn. However, the identification of Rashīd al-Dīn as cook, if not during Geikhatu's reign, then possibly under his successors, is not without grounds.

The cook, *ba'urchi,* was a highly coveted and greatly esteemed position in the Mongol imperial guard (the *keshig*), indicating an individual on intimate terms with the Mongol ruler. "The kitchen was the starting point of many an illustrious career in the empire," as Thomas Allsen notes.[30] Further the profession of cook was intertwined with medical expertise; and the fear of poisoning the ruler clearly demanded that a trustworthy individual be assigned. Rashīd al-Dīn is reported to have served as Ghazan's "glorious cook." Some even state that the Ilkhan would not eat from anyone else's hands, except for Rashīd al-Dīn's and his son's.[31]

Rashīd al-Dīn's and his family's long years of faithful court service paid off when he was appointed governor of Yazd in central Iran, a city to which he already had established ties. Rashīd al-Dīn had traveled to Yazd to study medicine, and subsequently cultivated financial interests in the city, as well as personal relationships forged by marriage ties to notable Yazdi *sayyid* (descendants of the Prophet) families.[32] However, already in 1298, he was promoted to a leading administrative position (or senior advisor) at the court, sharing the running of the state with the vizier Saʿd al-Dīn Sāvajī (d. 1312). While the division of labor between the two, and even the exact description of Rashīd al-Dīn's official post, remain unclear, Rashīd al-Dīn is portrayed as carrying the main load of state administration.[33] The two, Sāvajī and Rashīd al-Dīn, would have a tense relationship leading up to Sāvajī's execution in 1312.[34] While Rashīd al-Dīn maintained his influential position for nearly two decades, a near-record time for an Ilkhanid vizier, his tenure was far from uneventful. His two decades in office, which marked the height of his court career and influence, were tumultuous, filled with court intrigue and conspiracies, in which he played both as target and conspirer. The fall of one of his rivals would often mark the rise of a new opponent or the formation of a new faction in his opposition.[35]

Rashīd al-Dīn's success at court is assigned to his talent as statesman and political player,[36] but also to his profound understanding of Mongol cultural norms and his cultivation of an intimate relationship with the Mongol rulers, especially the Ilkhan Öljeitü (r. 1304–16).[37] Nevertheless, he shared the same fate as other Ilkhanid ministers. In 1318, shortly after Öljeitü's death, Rashīd al-Dīn was accused of poisoning the Ilkhan with a laxative and was executed together with one of his sons.[38]

Yet, the most remarkable aspect about the vizier's career is not his political shrewdness, nor his role as the alleged architect of Ghazan's reforms in the Ilkhanid government;[39] rather, it is his impressive scholarly productivity, especially considering his demanding government tasks. As an author, Rashīd al-Dīn is primarily famed for his world history, the *Compendium of Chronicles* (*Jāmiʿ al-tawārīkh*), singled out as one of the earliest examples of world history, as well as "the most important single historical source for the Mongol Empire."[40] According to Rashīd al-Dīn's introduction, the first volume titled the *Blessed History of Ghazan* (*Tārīkh-i mubārak-i Ghazanī*), which included the history of the Mongols and the Turks, from their origins to Chinggis Khan and his successors in China, Iran, the Qipchaq Steppe, and Central Asia was commissioned by Ghazan, but completed only after the ruler's death. The second volume, commissioned already by Ghazan's successor Öljeitü, is a world history (*ta'rīkh-i ʿālam*) consisting of the histories of the pre-Islamic rulers, the Muslims from the Prophet to the end of the ʿAbbāsid caliphate, and the "rest of the world": the Oghuz Turks and the Seljuks, the Chinese, the Jews, the Franks, and India. This chapter on India further included a section on the Buddha's life and teachings (below).[41] Handsomely rewarded by the Ilkhan for his work, Rashīd al-Dīn used the award to establish his famous pious foundation in eastern Tabriz, the *Rabʿ-i Rashīdī* (Rashīd al-Dīn's quarter, which included the vizier's tomb complex, a hospice, hospital, library, mosques, and a classroom).[42]

The two volumes demonstrate the vizier's remarkable openness to various cultures beyond the scope of Islam. Yet, his main achievement is the integration of the Mongols' history, genealogies, and present into Islamic history.[43] Aside from his historical-genealogical magnum opus, Rashīd al-Dīn was also a prolific author in other fields, especially theology and philosophy, and this vision of integration and inclusiveness is prevalent there as well.

On the theological, philosophical, and scientific fronts, starting with Öljeitü's enthronement in 1305, Rashīd al-Dīn produced an impressive number of treatises, mainly on topics related to *kalām* (Islamic theology) and *tafsīr* (Quranic commentaries), which he then collected into several compilations.[44] Like his other works, his theological writings are closely interlinked with the broader social-historical context of the Ilkhanid court. They reflect the competitive atmosphere of the court, where intra- and interfaith debates and intellectual disputations were frequently orchestrated. Rashīd al-Dīn presents his treatises as answers to questions posed to him during such court sessions or in more informal exchanges, by Muslims—both Sunnīs and Shīʿīs, Christians, and Buddhists, and most significantly, by Öljeitü himself.[45]

Equally significant as a historical source is Rashīd al-Dīn's medical and agricultural studies. There we find evidence for the vizier's strong interest in recording new information on East Asia, particularly Chinese medicine, agronomy, language, and script. The contacts Rashīd al-Dīn cultivated at the court, and especially his productive collaboration with the Mongol chancellor (*chingsang*) Bolad (d. 1313), Qubilai's (r. 1260–94) envoy and chief consultant to the Ilkhanid rulers, became a conduit for the transfer of information on China and the Mongols.[46] Noteworthy in this regard is the Persian translation project—headed by the vizier—of Chinese medical treatises, the first of its kind ever in the Muslim world.[47] Buddhism constituted another area of expertise where Rashīd al-Dīn's court contacts played a significant role in expanding Muslim horizons.

RASHĪD AL-DĪN'S *LIFE AND TEACHINGS OF THE BUDDHA*

Rashīd al-Dīn's account of Buddhism has long captivated scholars of Islam and Buddhism alike.[48] With remarkable illustrations of scenes from the Buddha's life and eastern scenery scattered throughout,[49] this section in the vizier's broader chapter on the *History of India* in the second volume of his world history, the *Compendium of Chronicles*,[50] has been regarded a prime example of interecumenical exchange in Mongol Eurasia. Aside from a few exceptions such as a peculiar account on the Buddha's achievement of nirvana in a dome-shaped structure made of pure crystal,[51] the three main foci of Rashīd al-Dīn's account—

FIGURE 11.1. *Shakyamuni offering fruit to the devil* (1314). *Jāmiʿ al-tawārīkh*, MSS 727, fol. 34a. Courtesy of the Nasser D. Khalili Collection.

the Buddha's biography, the Wheel of Life, and the worship of the Buddha Maitreya—offer a rather faithful and straightforward account of the Buddha's life and doctrine (see fig. 11.1).[52]

Scholars suggest that what made the vizier's account the best-informed description of Buddhism in the medieval Muslim world was his access to "real-life" Buddhist informants at the court.[53] Rashīd al-Dīn names one of his collaborators for the *History of India,* a Buddhist monk (*bakhshī*) named Kamālashrī, his main source for the chapter.[54] Rashīd al-Dīn states only that Kamālashrī "was born and bred in Kashmir and is knowledgeable in the *nom* (*nūm*), which is the book (*kitāb*) of Shākimūnī [Shakyamuni]."[55] To the best of our knowledge, however, Kamālashrī does not appear outside of the chapter on the *History of India,* not in the *Compendium* nor in any other Ilkhanid account. The recent revelation that Rashīd al-Dīn based his second volume of the *Compendium* including his chapter on the *History of India,* on the work of the Shīʿī Ilkhanid court historian ʿAbdallāh al-Qāshānī (d. after 1317) and therefore, that it was al-Qāshānī who relied first on Kamālashrī's words or on some work produced by the monk, raises doubts about Rashīd al-Dīn's personal collaboration with the Kahsmiri Buddhist.[56]

In any case, the identity of Kamālashrī has long puzzled historians, who raised several intriguing, yet far from definitive, speculations, from a Kashmiri monk based in China to a Tibetan translator.[57] The question of the textual basis for Rashīd al-Dīn's version of Buddhism is equally, if not more confounding. There is strong evidence to indicate the influence of Tibetan Tantric Buddhist traditions (Varjayāna). Rashīd al-Dīn praises Tantric Buddhism as a superior teaching.[58] Yet, the chapter's Tibetan "orientation" is largely overshadowed by its reproduction of translations of early Indian Sanskrit works, and the distinct allusions to Chinese Buddhism that can be traced to specific Chinese textual traditions.[59] Furthermore, evidence for the presence of the Chinese Chan Buddhist monks and/or manuscripts in the Ilkhanate is found in another short account on the Buddha's life from the vizier's chapter on China (*History of China*) in his *Compendium*. This version, which also includes the impregnation of the Buddha's mother by a mysterious ray of light, strikingly differs from the story of the Buddha in Rashīd al-Dīn's *History of India*. Scholars have demonstrated that this account of the Buddha and more broadly the vizier's *History of China* likely draw on a Chinese Buddhist chronicle composed under Mongol Yuan rule in China. The vizier's acquaintance with Chinese history and culture was mediated through Chinese Buddhism, and accordingly colored by its worldview.[60] That certain aspects of Rashīd al-Dīn's description of Buddhism seem to reflect Buddhist elements that became especially prevalent in Yuan China,[61] indeed raises the possibility that the *History of India* includes a Persian translation of a description of the Buddhist doctrine that was *not* the product of Ilkhanid Buddhism, but rather commissioned and composed at the other end of Eurasia, in the Buddhist centers in Mongol-ruled China.

Tracing the different influences prevalent in the Buddhist section is further complicated by the fact that, as Yoeli-Tlalim explains, even if we were able to single out one specific text or tradition, be it Tibetan, Tangut, Sanskrit Indian, Chinese, or Central Asian Uighur, that was embedded into the *History of India*, we cannot determine with certainty the origination of the work from this tradition since the same works were transmitted between different languages, and circulated orally as well as textually.[62] Put differently, the *History of India* should be considered a product of Mongol Eurasia, which "brought together not only the Buddhist and Muslim worlds; it also brought together for the first time, Buddhists of many different cultural backgrounds and religious affiliations".[63]

Rashīd al-Dīn's description of the Buddha has also been noted for its relatively positive view of Buddhism. The Muslim vizier generously utilizes Muslim terms to explain Buddhist ideas, thus, fostering certain commonalties between Buddhism and Islam. For example, the Buddhist demon Mara is addressed as the Muslim devil, Iblīs, and the Buddha's spiritual advancement is cast in Sufi terminology: nirvana is envisioned as the Muslim mystic's self-annihilation in the divine.[64] Elverskog concludes that Rashīd al-Dīn was attempting "to make the Dharma comprehensible and possibly even palatable to a Muslim audience."[65] On the face of it, indeed, Rashīd al-Dīn's view of Buddhism in the *History of India* seemingly differs from the generally Muslim negative attitude toward the Buddhists.

REFUTING BUDDHISM AT THE ILKHANID COURT

Rashīd al-Dīn, however, harbored a more ambivalent attitude toward the Buddhists. Thus, he ended his seemingly amicable detailed description of Buddhism in the *Compendium* on a soberer tone, appending the first of his three treatises refuting the Buddhist theory of reincarnation. He explains that he was driven by his wish to ascertain that the Buddhists' misguided belief in the reincarnation of the soul (*tanāsukh*) would not taint the faith of his Muslim readers.[66]

In his three refutations of reincarnation,[67] Rashīd al-Dīn disproves theories of metempsychosis (the transmigration of the souls) and presents Muslim views on the thereafter. He explores a range of topics, from preexistence versus the temporal origination of the soul, reward and punishment in the afterlife, and the exclusive compatibility of each body and soul, to the torments of the grave and the eternal heaven or hell. The three treatises amount therefore to something more than refutations; they are guide books, accounting for all that the Muslim believer, specifically the vizier's Mongol patron and Muslim convert, the Ilkhan Öljeitü, should expect to experience after his corporal demise.[68]

Rashīd al-Dīn's refutations of the Buddhist reincarnation are generally structured as a hypothetical disputation with a theoretical contender;[69] yet on several instances, the vizier relates some of his actual experiences with the Buddhists. In one example, Rashīd al-Dīn shares his methodical insights on how to dispute with the "idol worshipers"—the Buddhists—on matters such as the resurrection of the dead. There he advocates for the use of rational argumentation (*ma ʿqūl baḥth*):

> Since I was occupied with writing the *Compendium of Chronicles*, I requested to learn their [the idol worshipers, i.e., the Buddhists] history, and by these means, also gain knowledge about their states, stories and the principles of

> their creed, and during this, I rationally discussed with them each matter. Since they [the Buddhist monks] have a wise and tender (*laṭīf*) nature and they listen to reason and speak with reason, it became known from their words that their school/dogma (*madhhab*) too does not say that the world is fully ancient and they too believe it is impossible that the world is completely eternal and uncreated; but they say that it will exist for a great, endless number of years, and although they do not believe in the deluge of Noah, they do agree with the general deluge (*ṭūfān-i kullī*) and the End of Time.[70]

The vizier's praise for the monks' fine character, erudition, and reason immediately draws one's attention. Buddhism had a long tradition of rational argumentation, scholastic disputation, and public debate, prevalent first in the Buddhist schools of Tibet and India, and later in Chinese Buddhism.[71] Similar traditions of rational disputation were also found in the Islamic world. Further the gradual assimilation of Greek philosophical methods of reasoning and rational demonstration into Islamic theology (*kalām*) reached its zenith during the Ilkhanid period.[72]

The culmination of this process is discernable in the vizier's own theological expositions. The latter conceives himself as following the footsteps of earlier Muslim theologians by demonstrating the congruency of Muslim scripture and divine revelation with reason.[73] This paragraph suggests not only that the Muslims were aware of the Buddhist methods of rational argumentation and noticed the affinities between the two scholastic traditions, but also that the parallels could work as a bridge for cross-cultural, Buddhist-Muslim, commensurability.

The vizier's statement about having conducted his intellectual exchanges with the Buddhists under the pretext of working on the chapter on India in his *Compendium* is interesting as well. Since Rashīd al-Dīn claims he began work on the second volume, which includes the *History of India,* after presenting the Ilkhan Öljeitü with the first volume commissioned by his predecessor, Ghazan (above), this would place these conversations at the start of Öljeitü's reign in 1305. However, by then, Ilkhanid Buddhism had already undergone a decade-long decline, as Islam was gaining a stronger hold among the Mongol elite.[74]

Indeed, unlike the court of his father Arghun, there are no references to the presence of eminent Buddhists at the court during Öljeitü's reign. It is true that Muslim authors tended to ignore the significant Buddhist presence in Arghun's court as well. Yet, it is still reasonable to expect that if Buddhist monks were present at Öljeitü's court, they would be mentioned in the context of the numerous court debates and intellectual engagements under Öljeitü. However, Rashīd al-Dīn, who extensively documents the discussions at the court and records his "debates" with the religious "others"—a Byzantine Christian physician for example, refrains from mentioning any disputation with Buddhist interlocutors. Further, despite Rashīd al-Dīn's extensive efforts in refuting the Buddhist reincarnation, the only concrete and explicit reference in his theological oeuvre (or elsewhere in his writings) to a specific debate with a Buddhist is when a monk in Arghun's retinue challenges Rashīd al-Dīn with the classic Buddhist "chicken and egg" enigma:[75]

> One day, one of the Buddhist monks (*bakhshī*)[76] in the retinue of the great king, the deceased great khan,[77] Arghun Khan (r. 1284–91), tested me in the presence of the king asking me what came first, the bird or the egg. The monk thought that I would fail to answer. Although I had never heard this question, nor had I ever investigated or reflected on its meaning, I remained confounded [only] for a brief moment. For after a single moment passed, God All Mighty from his grace and honor divulged [the answer] to this poor one [Rashīd al-Dīn]. Although he who tested me himself did not grasp [its meaning] and was repeating something like a famous [Buddhist] fable, in so much that it was futile for him [to ponder on it] . . . from repeating and studying it many new insights were revealed [to Rashīd al-Dīn].[78]

ÖLJEITÜ AND THE BUDDHIST SACRED RELICS

Other references to the Buddhist "experience" in the vizier's refutations of reincarnation similarly point to the Ilkhan Arghun's court as the height of Buddhist influence and Buddhist-Muslim exchanges. A conversation between Rashīd al-Dīn and Öljeitü suggests that Öljeitü's acquaintance with Buddhism was mainly based on his experiences growing up at his father's camp. Öljeitü asks Rashīd al-Dīn about the *Śarīra* (*shārīn*)—small, jewel-like, indestructible relics found after the cremation of Buddhist sages.[79] His father, Öljeitü reports, was an avid collector of these karma-generating relics, and Öljeitü personally tested them confirming their indestructibility. He wonders why the Muslim dead do not produce similar remarkable treasures. Öljeitü's question here alerts us to the Mongol attraction to sacred relics, and their perceivable, tangible power, their empirically tested indestructibility.

Rashīd al-Dīn's answer to the Ilkhan, indeed, cuts to the heart of these devotional objects' power of persuasion. First, he states that we the Muslims do not cremate our dead but had we done so, one would likely find in the ashes something better and greater than the *Śarīra;* second, the *Śarīra* does not constitute a sacred relic but a warning from God that our bodies belong to us for eternity, and therefore, are not to be mutilated; finally, the Buddhist saints might leave behind pea-size relics, but the bodies of the Muslim saints, he explains, are entirely fireproof. Sufi shaykhs consume and walk on fire without inflicting harm on themselves and Abraham was not harmed in the fire-pit into which he was thrown.[80]

There is a lot to discuss about this rich anecdote. What is significant for us here is that Öljeitü reports on his memories from his father's camp, rather than on his current interactions with Buddhists. Was Ilkhanid Buddhism by the time of Öljeitü's reign, in the first decade of the fourteenth century, already a relic of the past, or does Rashīd al-Dīn simply wish to convince us of Islam's victory by relegating this experience to the period prior to Ghazan's conversion? It is difficult to tell. Yet the vizier's writings suggest that, as far as Rashīd al-Dīn, himself a Sunnī Muslim, was concerned, it was the growing influence of Shīʿīsm, another Muslim sect, over the Mongol ruler that posed the greatest threat, far more alarming than a Buddhist "relapse."[81] Öljeitü indeed would eventually convert to Shīʿī Islam, not return to Buddhism.[82]

The *History of India* with its detailed and well-informed description of Buddhism might have therefore resulted from an earlier moment of interecumenical intellectual exchanges, in the late 1280s at Arghun's court. Rashīd al-Dīn's exposure to the monks at Arghun's court, and the mélange of Eurasian Buddhist traditions they introduced to the Ilkhanate, had a significant impact on the vizier's intellectual trajectory over the centuries to come. In his account about the monk's "chicken and egg" enigma, Rashīd al-Dīn states indeed that the Buddhist challenge helped him arrive at new insights on several important issues such as the creation of Adam and the divine source of human knowledge.[83]

CONCLUSION

As DeWeese notes, the Sufi Simnānī's accounts of his time at Arghun's court, especially his reports on his debates with the Buddhist monks, attest to the fluid and eclectic religious environment of the Mongol ruler's camp, but also testify to the competitive and tense atmosphere between the different religious practitioners.[84] The same combination, a competitive atmosphere with a religiously eclectic environment, is also reflected in the few autobiographical anecdotes that place Rashīd al-Dīn at the Ilkhanid Buddhist court "scene."

The vizier's firsthand impressions from the monks he met express his ambivalent stance toward Buddhism: he describes the monks as "wise and tender" in one instance, and in another, as ignorant of the potential of their own traditions, stressing his superior stance in the interfaith debates;[85] his history provides the most comprehensive account on the Buddha's life and teachings in the Islamic world, but he chooses to supplement it with his refutation of the Buddhist reincarnation. His ambivalence toward Buddhism indicates a conscious attempt to situate Buddhism in a familiar, albeit borderline place. For the vizier, its presence in Iran is not entirely acceptable, but tolerable, so long as it does not threaten Muslim domination.[86]

Rashīd al-Dīn's answer to Öljeitü's question on the Buddhist relics demonstrates the vizier's proficiency as a contender at the Ilkhan's competitive court debates. It is further indicative of his skills as a cultural mediator in Mongol service. He addresses the intellectual challenge that the indestructability of the Buddhist relics posed for refuting the Buddhist karmic theory (the Mongol ruler's own empirical observation after all could not be questioned), on the one hand, while on the other, he transforms his predicament into a demonstration of the superior efficacy of Muslim saintly power. The cremated Buddhist sages leave behind them small, indestructible relics, whereas the bodies of Muslim prophets and saints are fully fireproof. Rashīd al-Dīn's answer, thus, boils down to a Buddhist-Muslim "fire ordeal," a theme that would have strongly appealed to, and resonated with, the Mongols' Inner Asian mythic traditions of fire contests.[87] This anecdote demonstrates, once more, that Rashīd al-Dīn's most prized asset was his remarkable acquaintance with the cultural norms and the traditions of his Mongol patrons, and especially, his ability to translate between the Mongols and Islam. It enabled a member of a Jewish family of physicians in Mongol service to gradually advance to the most influential position in the Ilkhanid government, and moreover, hold on to his powerful post for a near record-long period of two decades. It further speaks to his role as a convertor and an agent of Islam among the Mongol elite.

Thomas Allsen had good reason, therefore, to consider Rashīd al-Dīn the most influential cultural broker in Ilkhanid Iran. Yet as recent research has shown, cultural brokerage required more than mediating across cultural boundaries or blurring difference; on the contrary, cultural brokers were also those responsible for emphasizing and sustaining cultural differences. As one scholar has put it: "difference is their [cultural brokers'] stock in trade; but integration is what they offer."[88] Elverskog wonders whether Rashīd al-Dīn's focus on the Buddhist heaven and hell in the *History of India* was an attempt to establish a common link between Islam and Buddhism.[89] However, Rashīd al-Dīn's extensive treatment of these topics might also be seen as an attempt to explain, reiterate, and emphasize the differences between the two religions (and the superiority of the one—Islam—over the other—Buddhism) for the "outsider" Mongols. In Mongol eyes, the two transcendental religions, with their elaborate salvific schema, might not have been seen all that different after all.

Buddhism had a considerable impact on the vizier. Unlike the other individuals in this volume who traveled along the Silk Roads and beyond, Rashīd al-Dīn himself did not physically traverse Mongol Eurasia or even step beyond the domains of Islam proper; yet, his work testifies to his great knowledge of Eurasia as it was being remolded by the Mongol conquests and rule. One might suggest that it is a true testimony to the unparalleled rise in the mobility of objects, people, ideas, and religions across Mongol-ruled Eurasia, that one could learn and even experience so much of this cosmopolitan world without ever subjecting himself or herself to the pain and risks of distant travel.

NOTES

The article was written with the support of the Martin Buber Society of Fellows at the Hebrew University of Jerusalem.

1. Prazniak 2014, 655–57.
2. Sachau 1910, 249; Elverskog 2010, 82–90.
3. Prazniak 2014, 661–66, on 661; also: Sperling 1990; Grupper 2004, 5–77; Azad 2011, 209–30.
4. Elverskog 2010, 149; Prazniak 2014, 655; Samten and Martin 2014, 297–331.
5. According to Rashīd al-Dīn, most of the monks chose to convert to Islam; yet since their conversion was insincere, Ghazan sent them to their homelands. Rashīd al-Dīn 1994, 2:1357; Rashīd al-Dīn 1998–99, 3: 676. On Ghazan's early training with the Buddhists and support for Buddhism prior to his conversion: Rashīd al-Dīn 1998–99, 3:591; Jackson 1988, 535–36.
6. Prazniak 2014, 652.
7. The reign of his brother and successor, Geikhatu (1291–95), too was favorable to the Buddhists: Grupper 2004, 50–63.
8. On Arghun's interest in Buddhist life-prolonging medicine and his possible poisoning due to a concoction offered to him by an Indian monk: Yoeli-Tlalim 2013, 200. Also: Buell 2011, 189–208.
9. Prazniak 2014, 663.
10. DeWeese 2014, 35–76.
11. Lane 2016.
12. On Rashīd al-Dīn's Jewish background: Netzer 1994.

13. His full name was Abū al-Faraj ʿĀlī/Eli, son of Abī Shujāʿ. Kamola 2013, 104.

14. The Nizārī Ismāʿīlīs, known as the Assassins (for their clandestine political assassinations of their enemies), were a branch of the revolutionary Shīʿī Ismāʿīlī sect. Resisting the Seljuk pro-Sunnī policies, the Nizārīs established their own polity centered on a network of isolated mountain strongholds extended throughout the Iranian domains. Virani 2007; on Ṭūsī: Isahaya's chapter in this volume.

15. Rashīd al-Dīn 1957, 3: 35–37; Rashīd al-Dīn 1998–99, 3: 483, 485; Netzer 1994, 122. Ṭūsī might have been the one who introduced the family to Hülegü. Krawulsky 2011, 119–20.

16. The family's flight could have been encouraged by the residence of Jewish communities among the Ismāʿīlī strongholds. Benjamin of Tudela 1907, 120–21.

17. Ṭūsī 1964, 24–25.

18. Krawulsky 2011, 120.

19. Ibn al-Fuwaṭī 1995, 2: 62, 5: 613.

20. Ibn al-Fuwaṭī 1995, 2: 62.

21. On his medical training, Kamola 2013, 111–12; Pfeiffer 2016, 80–81; Hoffmann 2013, 9.

22. Fischel 1969, 90–117; Amitai 2013, 39–41; Brack 2019.

23. According to the vizier's protégée Munshī Kirmānī, Geikhatu offered Rashīd al-Dīn the vizierate, but he declined, remaining as court physician and unofficial advisor. Munshī Kirmānī 1959, 112; Kamola 2013, 113.

24. Shabānkāraʾī (d. 1337), a near-contemporary Ilkhanid author, even suggested that the Jewish (*mūsawī*) doctor had converted as late as Öljeitü's reign. Shabānkāraʾī 1984, 270.

25. Qāshānī 2005, 54–55, 131–32, 240–41; Krawulsky 2011, 132–33. The Mamluk sources are united in emphasizing Rashīd al-Dīn's previous Jewish identity, and further accuse him of falsifying and corrupting the Quran. Amitai-Preiss 1996, 32–33; Chipman 2013, 115–26; also Brack *2019*.

26. The title (*laqab*) ʿImād al-Dawla (state pillar), instead of ʿImād al-Dīn (al-Dawla was commonly used for non-Muslim—Jewish and Christian—state officials), indicates that he remained Jewish.

27. Rashīd al-Dīn's "Answer to the Adversaries." Krawulsky 2011, 123, 132–33; Rashīd al-Dīn 2013 (facsimile copy of MS. 2235 Gulistan Palace Library), 79r–79v.

28. Amitai-Preiss 1996, 26.

29. Bar Hebraeus 1932, 496; Amitai-Preiss 1996, 26.

30. Allsen 2001, 127–29.

31. Amitai-Preiss 1996, 25–26. In his *waqfiyya* (endowment deed) for the *Rabʿ-i Rashīdī,* the vizier depicts himself as a "humble cook" employed in a charity kitchen in comparison to the magnanimity of the Ilkhan. Hoffman 2013, 12.

32. Mancini-Lander 2019, 1–24.

33. Kamola 2013, 124–25.

34. Qāshānī 2005, 122–28.

35. Morgan 1994, 443–44.
36. Morgan 1997, 179–88.
37. Shabānkāra'ī 1984, 270. Rashīd al-Dīn repeatedly reasserts his close relationship with the Ilkhans Ghazan and Öljeitü in his theological writing.
38. Kamola 2013, 1.
39. For the reforms: Petrushevsky 1968, 494–95; Lambton 1988, 135–37, 140–48, 176–80; Morgan 1994; Kamola 2013, 182–83.
40. Morgan 1994, 443–44; Melville 2008, 462–68.
41. The second volume was also meant to include the history of Öljeitü's reign, but this section has either been omitted or was never completed. Öljeitü also commissioned a third volume on geography, which is also absent. Melville 2008, 462–68.
42. Blair 2016; Hoffmann 2014.
43. Pfeiffer 2013, 57–70.
44. Van Ess 1981, 12–21; Krawulsky 2011, 77–86.
45. For example, the questions of a Byzantine physician, possibly the Constantinople-born bishop George Chioniades (c. 1240–c. 1320): Rashīd al-Dīn 1993, 2: 52–53; Togan 1966, 9–15.
46. Allsen 2001, 72–80; Lambton 1998, 126–54.
47. On the *Tānksūqnāma:* Allsen 2001, 144–60; Lo and Wang 2013; Berlekamp 2010; and Isahaya's chapter in this volume.
48. Jahn 1965; Elverskog 2010, 145–74; Akasoy 2013, 173–96; Yoeli-Tlalim 2013, 197–211.
49. Canby 1993, 299–310.
50. Jahn 1965, xxxv–lxxv.
51. Jahn 1965, xlviii.
52. Elverskog 2010, 151.
53. In contrast to his precursor Bīrūnī. For Rashīd al-Dīn's reliance on Bīrūnī in the first four chapters on India: Jahn 1965, xiii.
54. Akasoy 2013, 191, 196. Jahn viewed it as the collaborative work between the two: Jahn 1965, xxxiii; Akasoy 2013, 189.
55. Jahn 1965, appendix 51 (facsimile copy of Topkapi Sarayi 940-H. 1654, A.D. 131, f. 328v.). Derived from Greek, *nom* was the Uighur-Mongolian term for law or book. It was also used to translate the Sanskrit *dharma,* and further became the Mongolian designation for "religion." Atwood 2016; Elverskog 2010, 295 n. 53.
56. On the complicated relationship between the two authors: Otsuka 2018, 119–49 (for the India part: 130, 131–34); also: Brack 2016, 322–44. In any case, we should reserve judgment until a full comparison between the two India chapters is completed.
57. Yoeli-Tlalim 2013, 202–4.
58. Jahn 1965, lxxv–lxxvii; Yoeli-Tlalim 2013, 204–11.
59. Jahn 1965, xxxiii, lxx–lxxi; Schopen 1982, 225–35; Elverskog 2010, 157–62.
60. Franke 1951; Calzolaio and Fiaschetti 2019 (parts 1–2).
61. Elverskog 2010, 158; Elverskog 2006/8, 87–124.
62. Yoeli-Tlalim 2013, 207–8.

63. Elverskog 2010, 162.

64. Akasoy 2013, 173–90; Elverskog 2010, 154; Jahn 1965, xliv.

65. Elverskog 2010, 154.

66. Reproductions in Jahn 1980: MS Royal Asiatic Society A 27 (dated 714/1314–15), 2077v; MS Topkapi Sarayi, 940-Hazine 1654 (dated 717/1317), 345r–345v.

67. Rashīd al-Dīn 1993, 2: 1–37; Rashīd al-Dīn 2013, 211–38, 253–301.

68. Pfeiffer 2013, 66–67.

69. For example, Rashīd al-Dīn 2013, 219–20.

70. Rashīd al-Dīn 2013, 282–83.

71. Garrett 1997, 195–209; Assandri 2009, 15–32; Beckwith 2011, 163–75.

72. Sabra 1994, 1–42; Endress 2006, 372–422; Eichner 2009; Belhaj 2016.

73. For example: Rashīd al-Dīn 2008, 353–54, 401–2.

74. According to Rashīd al-Dīn, already under Ghazan, the few Buddhist monks that remained in the Ilkhanate did not even dare to display their "creed or religion" publicly. Rashīd al-Dīn 1994, 2: 1357; Rashīd al-Dīn 1998–99, 3: 676.

75. The enigma appears in the "Questions of Mellinda," a celebrated Pali Buddhist dialogue between a Buddhist sage and the Greek king Menander of Bactria (composed probably between 150 B.C.E. and 100 C.E.). Mendis 1993, 48.

76. On *bakhshī*: Jackson 1988, 535–36.

77. The author refers to Arghun as qa'an, a title reserved for the head of the entire Chinggisid empire (Qubilai at the time), perhaps in attempt to honor the deceased Ilkhan.

78. Rashīd al-Dīn 1976–77, 36–37.

79. Stone 2005, 60.

80. Rashīd al-Dīn 2013, 272–74.

81. Especially seen in Rashīd al-Dīn's responses to questions raised by Shīʿī figures, dominant in Öljeitü's court: Rashīd al-Dīn 2008.

82. Pfeiffer 1999.

83. Rashīd al-Dīn 1976–77, 35–51.

84. DeWeese 2014, 35–76.

85. A similar strategy—claiming the monks' insufficient knowledge of their own tradition—was also applied by Simnānī in the debates: DeWeese 2014, 48–53; Simnānī 1988, 185–88.

86. For example, the vizier's Muslim-like presentation of the Buddha as a "prophet (*nabī*) with a book": Elverskog 2010, 154–56.

87. DeWeese 1994, 244–62.

88. Reimitz 2013, 269.

89. Elverskog 2010, 154.

BIBLIOGRAPHY

Akasoy, Anna. 2013. "The Buddha and the Straight Path. Rashīd al-Dīn's *Life of the Buddha:* Islamic Perspectives." In *Rashīd al-Dīn: Agent and Mediator of Cultural Exchange in Ilkhanid Iran*, ed. Anna Akasoy, Charles Burnett, and Ronit Yoeli-Tlalim, 173–96. London: Warburg Institute.

Allsen, Thomas T. 2001. *Culture and Conquest in Mongol Eurasia*. Cambridge: Cambridge University Press.

Amitai-Preiss, Reuven. 1996. "New Material from the Mamluk Sources for the Biography of Rashid al-Din." In *The Court of the Il-khans, 1290–1340*, ed. Teresa Fitzherbert and Julian Raby, 23–37. Oxford: Oxford University Press.

Amitai, Reuven 2013. "Jews at the Mongol Court in Iran: Cultural Brokers or Minor Actors in a Cultural Bloom?" In *Cultural Brokers at Mediterranean Courts in the Middle Ages*, ed. Marc von der Nöh, Nikolas Jaspert, and Jenny Rahel Oesterle, 33–45. Munich: Wilhelm Fink/Paderborn: Ferdinand Schöningh.

Assandri, Friederike. 2009. "Inter-Religious Debate at the Court of the Early Tang: An Introduction to Daoxuan's *Ji gujin Fo Dao lunheng*." In *From Early Tang Court Debates to China's Peaceful Rise*, ed. Assandri and Dora Martins, 15–32. Amsterdam: Amsterdam University Press.

Atwood, Christopher P. "A Secular Empire? Estates, *Nom*, and Religions in the Mongol Empire." Paper presented at the University of California, Berkeley, September 29, 2016.

Azad, Arezou. 2011. "Three Rock-Cut Cave Sites in Iran and their Ilkhanid Buddhist Aspects Reconsidered." In *Islam and Tibet: Interactions along the Musk Routes*, ed. Anna Akasoy, Charles Burnett, and Ronit Yoeli-Tlalim, 209–30. Farnham, England: Ashgate.

Bar Hebraeus 1932. *The Chronography of Gregory Abû'l Faraj . . . Bar Hebraeus*. Tr. E. A. W. Budge. London: Oxford University Press.

Beckwith, Christopher I. 2011. "The Sarvāstivādin Buddhist Scholastic Method in Medieval Islam and Tibet." In *Islam and Tibet: Interactions along the Musk Routes*, ed. Anna Akasoy, Charles Burnett, and Ronit Yoeli-Tlalim, 163–75. Farnham, England: Ashgate.

Belhaj, Abdessamad. 2016. "*Ādāb al-baḥth wa-al-munāẓara:* The Neglected Art of Disputation in Later Medieval Islam." *Arabic Sciences and Philosophy* 26: 291–307.

Ben Azzouna, Nourane. 2014. "Rashīd al-Dīn Faḍl Allāh al-Hamadhānī's Manuscript Production Project in Tabriz Reconsidered." In *Politics, Patronage, and the Transmission of Knowledge in 13th–15th Century Tabriz*, ed. Judith Pfeiffer, 187–200. Leiden: Brill.

Benjamin of Tudela. 1907. *The Itinerary of Benjamin of Tudela*. Ed. and tr. Marcus N. Adler. New York: Philip Feldheim.

Berlekamp, Persis. 2010. "The Limits of Artistic Exchange in Fourteenth-Century Tabriz: The Paradox of Rashid al-Din's Book on Chinese Medicine, Part I." *Muqarnas* 27: 209–50.

Blair, Sheila S. 2016. S.v. "Rabʿ-e Rašidi." *Encyclopaedia Iranica*. Available at www.iranicaonline.org/articles/rab-e-rashidi (accessed August 16, 2018).

Blochet, Edgard. 1910. *Introduction a l'histoire des mongols de Fadl Allāh Rashid ed-Din*. Leiden: Brill/London: Luzac.

Brack, Jonathan. 2016. "Mediating Sacred Kingship: Conversion and Sovereignty in Mongol Iran." PhD diss., University of Michigan.

———. 2019. "A Jewish Vizier and His Shīʿī Manifesto: Jews, Shīʿīs, and the Politicization of Confessional Identities in Mongol-ruled Iraq and Iran (13th to 14th Centuries)." *Der Islam* 96.2: 374–403.

Buell, Paul D. 2011. "Tibetans, Mongols, and the Fusion of Eurasian Cultures." In *Islam and Tibet: Interactions along the Musk Routes,* ed. Anna Akasoy, Charles Burnett, and Ronit Yoeli-Tlalim, 189–208. Farnham, England: Ashgate.

Canby, Sheila R. 1993. "Depictions of Buddha Sakyamuni in the *Jamiʿ al-Tavarikh* and the *Majmaʿ al-Tavarikh.*" *Muqarnas* 10: 299–310.

Calzolaio, Francesco, and Francesca Fiaschetti. 2019. "Prophets of the East: The Ilkhanid Historian Rashīd al-Dīn on the Buddha, Laozi, and Confucius and the Question of His Chinese Sources." *Iran and the Caucasus* 23.1: 17–34 (part 1); 23.2: 145–66 (part 2).

Chipman, Leigh. 2013. "The ʿAllāma and the Ṭabīb: A Note on Biographies of Two Doctors, Rashīd al-Dīn and Quṭb al-Dīn al-Shīrāzī." In *Rashīd al-Dīn: Agent and Mediator of Cultural Exchange in Ilkhanid Iran,* ed. Anna Akasoy, Charles Burnett, and Ronit Yoeli-Tlalim, 115–26.

DeWeese, Devin. 1994. *Islamization and Native Religion in the Golden Horde: Baba Tükles and Conversion to Islam in Historical and Epic Tradition.* University Park: Pennsylvania State University Press.

———. 2014. "ʿAlāʾ al-Dawla Simnānī's Religious Encounters at the Mongol Court near Tabriz." In *Politics, Patronage, and the Transmission of Knowledge in 13th–15th Century Tabriz,* ed. Judith Pfeiffer, 35–76. Leiden: Brill.

Eichner, Heidrun. 2009. "The Post-Avicennian Philosophical Tradition and Islamic Orthodoxy. Philosophical and Theological *Summae* in Context." Habilitation diss., Martin Luther University of Halle-Wittenberg.

Elverskog, Johan. 2006/8. "The Mongolian Big Dipper Sutra." *Journal of the International Association of Buddhist Studies* 29.1: 87–124.

———. 2010. *Buddhism and Islam on the Silk Road.* Philadelphia: University of Pennsylvania Press.

Endress, Gerhard. 2006. "Reading Avicenna in the Madrasa: Intellectual Genealogies in the Chains of Transmission of Philosophy and the Sciences in the Islamic East." In *Arabic Theology, Arabic Philosophy: From the Many to the One; Essays in Honour of Richard M. Frank,* ed. James E. Montgomery, 372–422. Leuven: Peeters.

Fischel, Walter J. 1969. *Jews in the Economic and Political Life of Medieval Islam.* New York: Ktav.

Franke, Herbert. 1951. "Some Sinological Remarks on Rašîd Ad-Dîn's History of China." *Oriens* 4: 21–26.

Garrett, Mary M. 1997. "Chinese Buddhist Religious Disputation." *Argumentation* 11: 195–209.

Grupper, Samuel M. 2004. "The Buddhist Sanctuary-Vihara of Labnasagut and the Il-Qan Hülegü: An Overview of Il-Qanid Buddhism and Related Matters." *Archivum Eurasiae Medii Aevi* 13: 5–77.

Hoffmann, Birgitt. 2013. "Speaking about Oneself: Autobiographical Statements in the Works of Rashīd al-Dīn." In *Rashīd al-Dīn: Agent and Mediator of Cultural Exchange in Ilkhanid Iran,* ed. Anna Akasoy, Charles Burnett, and Ronit Yoeli-Tlalim, 1–14.

———. 2014. "In Pursuit of *Memoria* and Salvation: Rashīd al-Dīn and his *Rab'-i Rashīdī*." In *Politics, Patronage, and the Transmission of Knowledge in 13th–15th Century Tabriz*, ed. Judith Pfeiffer, 171–85. Leiden: Brill.

Ibn al-Fuwaṭī, Kamāl al-Dīn 'Abd al-Razzāq b. Aḥmad al-Shaybānī. 1995. *Majma' al-ādāb fī mu'jam al-alqāb*. Tehran: Mu'assasat al-ṭibā'a wa'l-nashr, 1416H.

Jackson, Peter. 1988. S.v. "Bakšī," *Encyclopaedia Iranica*. Available at www.iranicaonline.org/articles/baksi-a-buddhist-lama (accessed July 28, 2018).

Jahn, Karl. 1965. *Rashīd al-Dīn's History of India: Collected Essays with Facsimiles and Indices*. The Hague: Mouton.

Kamola, Stephan T. 2013. "Rashīd al-Dīn and the Making of History in Mongol Iran". PhD diss., University of Washington.

Klein-Franke, Felix. 2002. "Rashīd al-Dīn's Self-Defense through his Commenting on al-Ghazālī's 'Reply to the Opponents of the "Proof of Islam": A Philosophical Interpretation of the Koranic Expression 'al-Amāna.'" *Le muséon* 115: 199–214.

Krawulsky, Dorothea. 2011. *The Mongol Īlkhāns and Their Vizier Rashīd al-Dīn*. Frankfurt am Main: Peter Lang.

Lambton, Ann K. S. 1988. *Continuity and Change in Medieval Persia: Aspects of Administrative, Economic and Social History, 11th–14th Century*. Albany: State University of New York.

———. 1998. "The Āthār wa aḥyā' of Rashīd al-Dīn Faḍl Allāh Hamadānī and His Contribution as an Agronomist, Arboriculturalist, and Horticulturalist." In *The Mongol Empire and Its Legacy*, ed. Reuven Amitai-Preiss and David O. Morgan, 126–54. Leiden: Brill.

Lane, George. 2016. "Intellectual Jousting and the Chinggisid Wisdom Bazaars." *Journal of the Royal Asiatic Society* 26: 235–47.

Lo, Vivienne, and Wang Yidan. 2013. "Blood or Qi Circulation? On the Nature of Authority in Rashīd al-Dīn's Tānksūqnāma (The Treasure Book of the Ilkhan on Chinese Science and Techniques)." In *Rashīd al-Dīn: Agent and Mediator of Cultural Exchange in Ilkhanid Iran*, ed. Anna Akasoy, Charles Burnett, and Ronit Yoeli-Tlalim, 127–72.

Mancini-Lander, Derek J. 2019. "Subversive Skylines: Local History and the Rise of the Sayyids in Mongol Yazd." *Bulletin of the School of Oriental and African Studies* 82.1: 1–24.

Melville, Charles. 2008. S.v. "Jāme' al-Tawārik̲." *Encyclopaedia Iranica*. Available at http://www.iranicaonline.org/articles/jame-al-tawarik (accessed June 18, 2018).

Mendis, N. K. G. ed. 1993. *The Questions of King Milinda: An Abridgment of the Milindapañhā*. Intro. Bhikkhu Bodhi. Sri Lanka: Buddhist Publication Society.

Morgan, David O. 1994. S.v. "Rashīd al-Dīn Ṭabīb." *Encyclopaedia of Islam*. 2nd ed. Brill Online available at http://dx.doi.org/10.1163/1573-3912_islam_SIM_6237> (accessed July 7, 2018).

———. 1997. "Rašīd al-Dīn and Gazan Khan." In *L'Iran face a la domination mongole*, ed. Denise Aigle, 179–88. Tehran: Institut français de recherche en Iran.

Morton, Alexander H. 2010. "Qashani and Rashid al-Din on the Seljuqs of Iran." In *Living Islamic History: Studies in Honour of Professor Carole Hillenbrand*, ed. Yasir Suleiman, 166–77. Edinburgh: Edinburgh University Press.

Munshī Kirmānī, Nāṣir al-Dīn. 1959. *Nasā'im al-asḥār min laṭā'im al-akhbār: dar ta'rīkh-i wuzarā'*. Ed. Jalāl al-Dīn Ḥusaynī Muḥaddith. Tehran: Chāpkhānah-yi dānishgāh.

Netzer, Amnon. 1994. "Rashīd al-Dīn and His Jewish Background." *Irano-Judaica* 3: 118–26.

Otsuka, Osamu. 2018. "Qāshānī, the First World Historian: Research on His Uninvestigated Persian General History, *Zubdat al- tawārīkh*." *Studia iranica* 47: 119–49.

Petrushevsky, I.P. 1968. "The Socio-Economic Conditions of Iran under the Īl-*Khā*ns." In *Cambridge History of Iran*. Vol. 5. *The Saljuq and Mongol Periods*, ed. John A. Boyle, 485–537. Cambridge: Cambridge University Press.

Pfeiffer, Judith. 1999. *Twelver Shī'ism as State Religion in Mongol Iran: An Abortive Attempt, Recorded and Remembered*. Istanbul: Orient-Institut der DMG.

———. 2013. "The Canonization of Cultural Memory: Ghazan Khān, Rashīd al-Dīn, and the Construction of the Mongol Past." In *Rashīd al-Dīn: Agent and Mediator of Cultural Exchange in Ilkhanid Iran*, ed. Anna Akasoy, Charles Burnett, and Ronit Yoeli-Tlalim, 57–70.

———. 2016. "Rashīd al-Dīn's *Bayān al-ḥaqā'iq* and its *Sitz im Leben:* A Preliminary Investigation." Introduction to Rashīd al-Dīn's *Bayān al-ḥaqā'iq* (*Beyân'l-Hakâik*) (facsimile of Arabic text), prepared for publication by Judith Pfeiffer, 59–100. Fatih, İstanbul: Türkiye Yazma Eserler Kurumu Başkanlığl.

Prazniak, Roxann. 2014. "Ilkhanid Buddhism: Traces of a Passage in Eurasian History." *Comparative Studies in Society and History* 56: 650–80.

Qāshānī, Abū al-Qāsim 'Abdallāh b. 'Alī b. Muḥammad. 2005. *Ta'rīkh-i ūljāytū*. Ed. Mahīn Hambalī. Tehran: Bungāh-i tarjuma wa nashr-i kitāb, 1384Sh.

Rashīd al-Dīn, Faḍlallāh Abū al-Khayr al-Hamadānī. 1653–54. *Tānksūqnāma-yi Īlkhān dar funūn-i 'ulūm-i Khiṭā'ī*. MS Süleymaniye Kütüphanesi, Aya Sofya 3596.

———. 1957. *Jāmi' al-tawārīkh*. Ed. 'Abd al-Karīm 'Alī Oghlu 'Alī Zādah. 3 vols. Baku, Azerbaijan: Farhangistān-i 'ulūm-i jumhūr-i shurawī-yi sūsīyālistī-yi Adharbāijān.

———. 1976–77. *Laṭā'if al-ḥaqā'iq*. Ed. Ghulām Riḍā Ṭāhir. Tehran: Kitābkhānah-yi markazī wa markaz-i asnād.

———. 1993. *As'ila wa ajwiba-yi Rashīdī*. Ed. R. Sha'bānī. 2 vols. Islamabad: Markaz-i taḥqīqāt-i fārsī-i Irān wa pākistān.

———. 1994. *Jāmi' al-tawārīkh*. Ed. Muḥammad Rawshan and Muṣṭafā Mūsawī. 4 vols. Tehran: Nashr-i Alburz.

———. 1998–99. *Rashīduddin Fazlullah's Jami'u't-Tawarikh: A History of the Mongols*. Tr. Wheeler Thackston. 3 vols. Cambridge, MA: Harvard University, Department of Near Eastern Languages and Civilizations.

———. 2008. *Bayān al-ḥaqā'iq*. Ed. Hāshim Rajabzāda. Tehran: Mīrāth-i maktūb, 1386Sh.

———. 2013. *Majmū'a-yi Rashīdīya*. Facsimile Copy of Manuscript no. 2235, Gulistan Palace Library. Copied in 706 A.H. Tehran: Mīrāth-i maktūb.

Reimitz, Helmut. 2013. "Cultural Brokers of a Common Past: History, Identity, and Ethnicity in Merovingian Historiography." In *Strategies of Identification: Ethnicity and Religion in Early Medieval Europe,* ed. Walter Pohl and Gerda Heydemann, 257–301. Turnhout: Brepols.

Sabra, Adam I. 1994. "Science and Philosophy in Medieval Islamic Theology: The Evidence of the Fourteenth Century." *Zeitschrift fur Geschichte der arabisch-islamischen Wissenschaften* 9: 1–42.

Sachau, Edward C. 1910. *Alberuni's India: An Account of the Religion, Philosophy, Literature, Geography, Chronology, Astronomy, Customs, Laws, and Astrology of India, about* A.D. *1030.* London: Paul, Trench, Trübner.

Samten, Jampa, and Dan Martin. 2014. "Letters to the Khans: Six Tibetan Epistles of Togdugpa Addressed to the Mongol Rulers Hulegu and Khubilai, as well as to the Tibetan Lama Pagpa." In *Trails of the Tibetan Tradition: Papers for Elliot Sperling,* ed. Roberto Vitali, 297–331. Republished in *Revue d'études tibétaines* 31 (2015).

Schopen, Gregory. 1982. "Hīnāya Texts in a 14th Century Persian Chronicle: Notes on Some of Rashīd al-Dīn's Sources." *Central Asiatic Journal* 26: 225–35.

Shabānkāra'ī, Muḥammad. 1984. *Majma' al-ansāb.* Ed. Mir Hashim Muḥaddath. Tehran: Amīr Kabīr, 1363Sh.

Simnānī, 'Alā' al-Dawla. 1988. *'Alā'uddawla Simnānī: Opera minora.* Ed. W.M. Thackston. Cambridge, MA: Harvard University, Office of the University Publisher.

Sperling, Elliot. 1990. "Hülegü and Tibet." *Acta Orientalia Academiae Scientiarum Hungaricae* 44: 145–57.

Stone, Jacqueline I. 2005. "Death." In *Critical Terms for the Study of Buddhism,* ed. Donald S. Lopez, Jr., 56–76. Chicago: University of Chicago Press.

Togan, Zeki Velidi. 1966. "A Document Concerning Cultural Relations between the Ilkhanate and Byzantium." *Islam Tetkikleri Enstitüsü Degrisi* (*Review of the Institute of Islamic Studies*) 3 (1959–60) (printed in Istanbul, 1966), 2–39.

Ṭūsī, Naṣīr al-Dīn. 1964. *The Nasirean Ethics.* Tr. G.M. Wickens. London: Allen & Unwin.

van Ess, Joseph. 1981. *Der Wesir und seine Gelehrten.* Wiesbaden, Germany: Deutsche Morgenländische Gesellschaft; Steiner.

Virani, Shafique N. 2007. *The Ismailis in the Middle Ages: A History of Survival, a Search for Salvation.* Oxford: Oxford University Press.

Yoeli-Tlalim, Ronit. 2013. "Rashīd al-Dīn's *Life of the Buddha.* Some Tibetan Perspectives." In *Rashīd al-Dīn: Agent and Mediator of Cultural Exchange in Ilkhanid Iran,* ed. Anna Akasoy, Charles Burnett, and Ronit Yoeli-Tlalim, 197–211.

CHAPTER 12

Fu Mengzhi

"The Sage of Cathay" in Mongol Iran and Astral Sciences along the Silk Roads

YOICHI ISAHAYA

Among the fields of knowledge, the Mongol conquerors were particularly drawn to and had especially valued the astral sciences.[1] They believed that their universal government depended on the power and will of Heaven (*tengri*). Therefore, the Mongols showed great interest in reading the sky to predict and identify celestial omens, which guided a range of their earthly activities such as detecting auspicious moments for setting on military campaigns or conducting enthronement ceremonies.[2] The Mongols, moreover, appreciated cultural diversity. At their courts, they recruited and collected astronomers and astrologers of varied intellectual and cultural backgrounds. They utilized them along with other diviners to establish consensus and grant legitimation to their policies and decisions.[3]

The account of the Mongol conquest of Baghdad in 1258 is a telling example of the Mongols' appreciation of astral predictions and interest in attaining multiple, often competing, celestial interpretations to support their chosen course of action. Ḥusām al-Dīn was an astrologer in the service of Hülegü (1218–65), the founder of the Ilkhanate (1260–1335), the Mongol successor state centered in Iran. On the eve of the Mongol conquest of Baghdad, Ḥusām al-Dīn warned the future Ilkhan Hülegü of disastrous consequences if Hülegü and his army were to follow the advice of his Mongol commanders and invade the city. After learning of Ḥusām al-Dīn's ominous prediction, Hülegü decided to also seek out the services of his Shīʿī astronomer, Naṣīr al-Dīn Ṭūsī (1201–74), a renowned Muslim polymath.[4] Asking him to consult the stars for an alternative prediction, Hülegü then followed Ṭūsī's counterprediction, according to which, the invasion would turn out favorably for him and his men. When the conquest of Baghdad was completed as Ṭūsī had predicted, the latter found himself admitted into the Mongol ruler's inner circle.[5]

The Mongol appreciation of second opinions, or rather their interest in "celestial insurance," for any course of action, led them to amass at their courts a diverse body of experts, especially those who possessed the more precious esoteric forms of knowledge. Thus, the Mongols directly and indirectly facilitated the movement of professionals along the Silk Roads. Through Mongol encouragement or under Mongol duress, astrologers and astronomers migrated and relocated to other cultural spheres. They often found themselves working side by side with foreign colleagues, who possessed a different set of astral knowledge and skills.[6]

However, even during this period of large-scale Eurasian mobilization, there were only a few cases of actual cross-cultural collaboration between astronomers and astrologers from the western and eastern ends of Eurasia. One reason for this might have been the large, often unbridgeable, differences between the Islamicate and Chinese astronomy. Astronomers from Islamicate western Eurasia represented celestial motions with a series of geometrical diagrams based on the Hellenistic astral tradition (see fig. 12.1), exemplified by the Greco-Roman astronomer Ptolemy's (mid-second century) *Almagest.*[7] This type of geometrical representation of celestial phenomena did not exist in Chinese official astronomical treatises before the later Ming period (1368–1644). Chinese astronomy was based instead on a numerical system. It consisted of a series of values and tables with no geometrical diagrams to represent celestial motions.

In 1259, shortly after Hülegü's victory in Baghdad, a monumental observatory was founded in the nascent Ilkhanate, in the city of Maragha in present-day northwestern Iran, under the initiative of Ṭūsī. Equipped with an impressive library, the observatory functioned as one of the foremost hubs of the new intellectual network in the Mongol-ruled Islamicate world and beyond.[8] Yet, in Maragha, astronomers were primarily focused on revising the Ptolemaic understanding of the universe,[9] a field to which scholars from the east had nothing to contribute. A similar situation seems to have existed under the Yuan dynasty (1271–1368), the Mongol state in China. Although Chinese and Muslim observatories were both established under Yuan rule, the two traditions remained separate. Meaningful collaborations were not pursued and no significant cross-pollination can be found.[10]

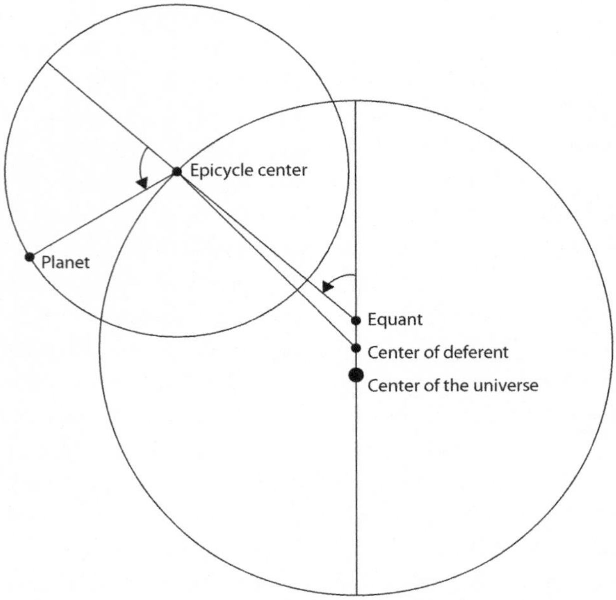

FIGURE 12.1. Ptolemaic celestial model representing planetary motion in geometrical diagram. Drawn by Yoichi Isahaya.

The Ilkhanate, however, also provided the setting for one of the rare exceptions to this situation: an "astronomical dialogue," a collaboration, between Ṭūsī and a Chinese Daoist identified in the Persian accounts as the "sage of Cathay." The work provided the first-ever explication of Chinese astral sciences in the Islamicate world. Ṭūsī moreover situated this explanation of Chinese astronomy alongside Muslim and other calendrical systems, which in itself is a remarkable achievement that attests to the expanding horizons of the Islamicate world during the Mongol era.

Yet, rather than a window onto the potentially unknown integration of Chinese astral knowledge within the Islamicate sciences, the results of this short-lived collaboration between Ṭūsī and his Chinese counterpart speak also to the limits of cultural and scientific commensurability in thirteenth-century Eurasia. This chapter focuses on Ṭūsī's Chinese collaborator and examines his role as an eastern cultural broker in Mongol-ruled Iran. Whereas Ṭūsī's career and works have received considerable scholarly attention, little is known about "the sage of Cathay." Recent studies have identified this individual as Fu Mengzhi, a Daoist court physician who accompanied Hülegü to Iran.

THE "SAGE OF CATHAY" IN THE PERSIAN SOURCES

Rashīd al-Dīn's chapter of Chinese history in the *Compendium of Chronicles* (*Jāmiʿ al-tawārīkh*) provides the most detailed information on the Daoist physician. Rashīd al-Dīn's project, which began during the reign of Ilkhan Ghazan (r. 1295–1304), by compiling the history of the Mongols and other Steppe tribes, was expanded and completed under Ghazan's successor Öljeitü (r. 1304–16). The final product, titled the *Compendium of Chronicles,* encompassed the histories of India, China, Christian Europe, and the Jews, in addition to that of the Mongols and the Muslim world, becoming the first world history in the Islamicate world.[11] In the introduction to his section on China, Rashīd al-Dīn shares his insight on Chinese culture and society. He furthermore depicts there a scene in which Hülegü orders Ṭūsī to study the Chinese astral sciences with a Chinese scholar:

> When the time arrived for Möngke Qa'an [r. 1251–59] to become king and ruler of the earth, he dispatched his brother, Hülegü Khan, son of Tolui Khan, son of Chinggis Khan, to the land of Iran and he [Hülegü] became king of these kingdoms. Philosophers, astronomers,[12] and physicians from Cathay gathered to his service. Since [he] was a king with perfect intellect, ability, and enthusiasm for all the sciences, he ordered. . . . Naṣīr al-Dīn al-Ṭūsī . . . to build an observatory and compile an astronomical handbook (*zīj*) named after his [Hülegü Khan's] majestic name.
>
> Because Hülegü Khan had witnessed their [the Cathayan] astrologers, was informed of the rules of astrology according to their methods, and had become accustomed to it, he ordered Naṣīr al-Dīn [Ṭūsī] to explain their calendar and astrological methods, and incorporate it into the astronomical handbook which he was compiling, so that it would be possible when one calculates to add to our almanacs their calendar and their calculation of the years according to their methods and in their terminology. He [Hülegü] then ordered a Cathay individual named FūMNjī and known as *sīnksīnk*—that is, sage—to explain in detail to Nasīr al-Dīn [Ṭūsī] all that he knew about their calendar and astrology, and to learn from Naṣīr al-Dīn [the Islamicate] astral science. Within two days, Naṣīr al-Dīn learned all that he [the sage FūMNjī] knew in this field, and incorporated it into the *Zīj-i Īlkhānī* [the Ilkhanid Astronomical Handbook] which he compiled.[13]

Rashīd al-Dīn assigns the title *sīnksīnk* to Ṭūsī's Chinese collaborator, whom he names FūMNnjī, and explains it to mean "sage" (*ʿārif*).[14] *Sīnksīnk* is a transcription of the Chinese *xiansheng,* which generally signifies "teacher" or "master,"[15] but in Yuan administrative sources denotes a "Daoist master."[16] Ṭūsī's Daoist informer resurfaces once again in another work of Rashīd al-Dīn, the first-ever Persian translation of medical Chinese treatises. In this work, titled *The Treasure Book of the Ilkhan on the Chinese Arts and Sciences* (*Tānksūqnāma-yi Īlkhān dar funūn-i 'ulūm-i khiṭā'ī*),[17] the vizier writes that the Chinese physician "came with Hülegü from the land of Mongolia (*wilāyat-i mughūlistān*), which is close to the land of Cathay,"[18] implying that FūMNjī likely traveled to Iran in Hülegü's company when he set out west on his expedition in 1253.

FU MENGZHI IN A CHINESE SOURCE

Miya Noriko has recently identified the Daoist FūMNjī in the preface to the Confucian Chinese medical work, the *Rumen shiqin,* or *Duties of Confucians toward Their Parents,* by the famous physician Zhang Zihe (1156?–1228?).[19] The preface was authored by Gao Ming, general administrator of the Zhangde Circuit, which was part of Hülegü's appanage in North China.[20]

The Mongols considered the empire's conquered lands, spoils, and peoples as a shared property, which was to be divided among the members of the Chinggisid family. This understanding is apparent in the Mongol practice of assigning to princes territorial dispensations, or appanages (Ch. *touxia*), which incorporated the lands, but also their properties and inhabitants. This policy both shaped the underlying structure of the empire and functioned as a source of friction and conflict between the Mongol houses, over access and control of the apportioned lands and their rich material and human resources.[21] The fourth qa'an, Möngke (r. 1251–59), had bestowed on his brother Hülegü appanages in North China, possibly already in 1252. The largest of these dispensations was the bulk of 25,065 households in the Zhangde Circuit, around what is today the city of Anyang in Henan province. The reason for this assignment of appanages appears to have been Hülegü's preparations for a long-term military expedition to Iran beginning in 1253, an expedition that resulted in the establishment of the Ilkhanate.[22] The Hülegüid appanages in North China would later play an instrumental role in the cultivation of cross-cultural contact and exchange between the western, Ilkhanid, and eastern, Yuan courts.[23]

The preface to the work describes the 1259 visit of Möngke's emissary, Chang De, the tax collector of the Zhangde Circuit, to Hülegü's court in Iran. The former encountered a Chinese court physician there named Fu Ye:[24] "The Erudite King [Hülegü] as a noble brother [of the qa'an] ruled over the western lands . . . . In the year of Jiwei (1259 C.E.),

FIGURE 12.2. Yuan map of North China (after Chen, 1:48r–v). The two large circles are the capitals of the Yuan dynasty: Shangdu in the north and Dadu (Huangdou Xincheng, "New Imperial Capital") to the south. Zhangde is encircled in a thick line.

Chang De, a fiscal commissioner in the Xiang prefecture [Zhangde Circuit], visited the court [of Hülegü] while the king was resting, and was presented to the king as knowledgeable about the medical science, by an attendant, Wan Gianu,[25] and a court physician Fu Ye."[26] Miya proposes that we identify FūMNjī from Hülegü's court as the Chinese court physician Fu Ye. Her suggestion is based on the potential reconstruction of Fu Ye's style name (*zi*) as Mengzhi.[27]

If indeed the Daoist physician FūMNjī, whom Hülegü had assigned to collaborate with Ṭūsī, and Fu Ye, who is mentioned in the *Rumen shiqin* and whose style name was likely Mengzhi, are identical, it seems further likely that this individual was originally from one of Hülegü's apportioned lands in North China. Since Fu Mengzhi was already aware of the medical expertise of Chang De, who came from the Zhangde Circuit, it is plausible that Fu Mengzhi too came from the same appanage of Hülegü (fig. 12.2).

The physician Fu Mengzhi's affiliation with Daoism is further significant in this encounter between the eastern and western astral sciences.

Under Mongol auspices, Daoism, especially the Quanzhen sect (Complete Truth Daoism), established a strong base in North China. In 1218, Qiu Chuji (1148–1227), the principal Daoist patriarch, known as Changchun (Ever Spring) was summoned by Chinggis Khan, who wanted to inquire about his reputation, especially his expertise in achieving longevity. Meeting Chinggis Khan in Central Asia in 1222, Changchun received considerable favors from the khan, thereby paving the path for the flourishing of Quanzhen Daoism under Mongol rule. Quanzhen Daoists were valued by the Mongols as intellectual technocrats providing knowledge and practice, in particular, in the astral and medical sciences.

The contribution of Quanzhen Daoism also extended to the field of woodblock printing technology. During the reign of Ögödei Qa'an (r. 1229–41), Daoists took on a large-scale project of compiling the Daoist canons (*Daozang*).[28] Significantly represented, especially in the Mongol administrative ranks and educational institutions in China, Quanzhen Daoism further functioned as an intermediary for communication between the Mongol ruling elites and the local literati. Daoism, however, began losing its central position from the start of Qubilai's reign (1260–94). Buddhism replaced Daoist hegemony in the Mongol, and later Yuan, political sphere. Therefore, it was during the final decade of the heyday of Quanzhen Daoism under Mongol rule when, in the early 1250s, Fu Mengzhi, himself probably a Quanzhen Daoist, left for Iran in Hülegü's company.

AN "ASTRONOMICAL DIALOGUE" BETWEEN A SAGE OF CATHAY AND A MUSLIM POLYMATH

The dialogue between the Chinese physician Fu Mengzhi and his Muslim counterpart, the astronomer and polymath Ṭūsī, resulted in the "Cathay calendar" (*tārīkh-i Qitā*) section in the *Ilkhanid Astronomical Handbook* (the *Zīj-i Īlkhānī*), in which Ṭūsī offers a comparative overview of calendrical systems, including not only the "Cathay calendar," but a total of six calendars from distinct cultural backgrounds. These included:[29]

1. the Cathay calendar,
2. the Roman calendar,[30]
3. the Islamic calendar,[31]
4. the Old Persian calendar,[32]
5. the New Persian calendar,[33]
6. the Jewish calendar.[34]

Ṭūsī provides conversions between some of these calendars, which could have been used for a variety of purposes. These included casting horoscopes according to different calendars, assisting in the translation of official documents that needed to be dated according to local calendars, or the compilation of histories such as the *Compendium of Chronicles,* where calendrical variety was integrated into a coherent historical chronology.

Investigations of Ṭūsī's Chinese calendar reveal it to be an amalgam of the official calendar of the eastern part of the Mongol Empire and another, unofficial calendar (*xiaoli*), compiled during the Tang period (618–907).[35] The role of this unofficial calendar in Ṭūsī's "Cathay calendar" sheds a different light on the nature of this "astronomical dialogue" and moreover speaks to the potential limits of cultural and scientific commensurability in thirteenth-century Eurasia.

Chinese dynasties attached great importance to the astral sciences as an apparatus to secure their legitimacy. They devoted substantial resources to employing a retinue of experts skilled in making astronomical instruments and applying necessary computations. When one dynasty was overthrown, the newly established dynasty would embark upon enacting a series of institutional changes and reforms in the government that validated the transfer of the heavenly mandate to a new dynastic formation. Reforming the calendar—or more precisely, the "astronomical system"—was the most significant stage in establishing the legitimacy of the new rulers.[36] Private calendars, however, existed as well, alongside these official dynastic calendars. Further, these unofficial calendars functioned sometimes as conduits for integrating foreign astral features.

The same can be said for the unofficial calendar that was incorporated into the "Cathay calendar." The calendar retained its unsanctioned status since it made use of Western astral science, namely, horoscopic astrology that official dynastic calendars did not incorporate.[37] Horoscopic astrology predicts a person's life on the basis of a diagram of the planetary positions at a particular moment, usually the time of one's birth (see fig. 12.3). Originating in the Mesopotamian and Mediterranean regions, horoscopic astrology arrived in China by the Tang period at the latest, traveling via multiple routes along the Silk Roads. From the Tang period on, horoscopic astrology developed in China in congruence with Western elements and Chinese indigenous celestial divination.[38] Among indigenous religious practices, Daoism especially had a crucial role in what might be termed the naturalization of Western horoscopic astrology in the Chinese sphere.[39] During Mongol rule, there was a strong Daoist astral tradition based on horoscopic astrology.[40]

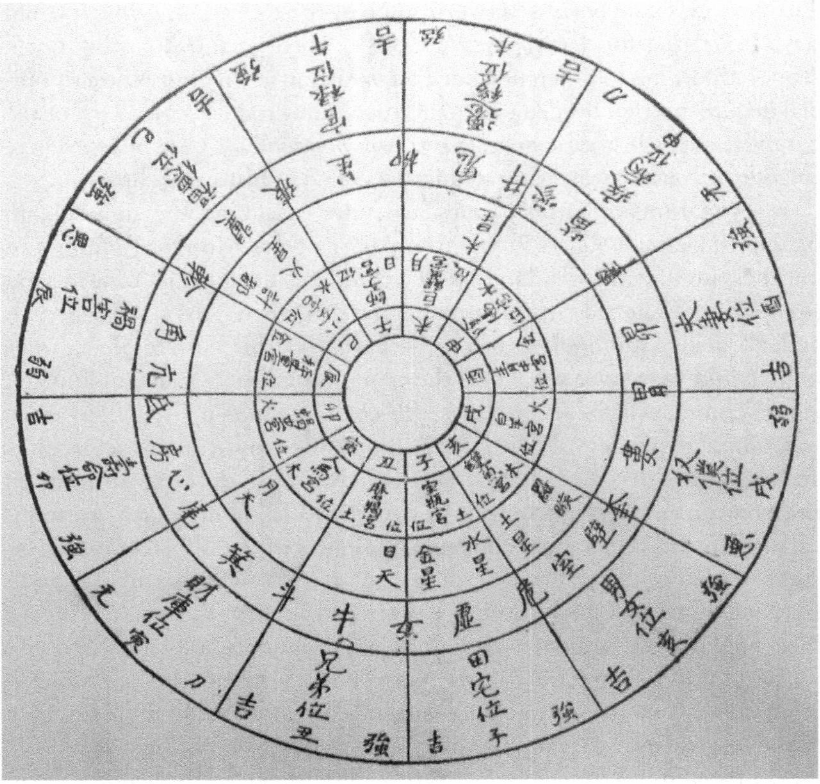

FIGURE 12.3. A Japanese horoscope for the year 1113 C.E., based on the unofficial Tang calendar (Hanawa 1923–28, 31a: 430).

It indeed seems that the conversation between Ṭūsī and Fu Mengzhi revolved around horoscopic astrology. This would explain why the unofficial Tang-era calendar, and not the official dynastic calendar, was chosen for this exchange. Furthermore, in his *History of China,* Rashīd al-Dīn makes the following statement about the exchange between Ṭūsī and Fu Mengzhi: "However, that sage [Fu Mengzhi] did not learn much from Naṣīr al-Dīn [Ṭūsī]. [Although] the said scholar [Fu Mengzhi] had some knowledge about the calculation of the calendar and some astrological rules, he was not quite familiar with the ways to use an astronomical handbook nor did he understand the details of the motion of the stars. It is rare to find a perfect scholar [like Ṭūsī] fully immersed in these kinds of sciences in every region and period."[41] The main usage of astronomical handbooks was to cast horoscopes,[42] and the understanding of planetary motions, too, is a central feature of horoscopic astrology. Rashīd al-Dīn observes, therefore, that Fu Mengzhi's knowledge of horoscopic astrology was insufficient and did not match Ṭūsī's expertise. After mentioning the "astronomical dialogue" between the two masters in his *Tānksūqnāma,* Rashīd al-Dīn then evaluates Fu Mengzhi's level of expertise. He explains that what Ṭūsī included in the *zīj* about Chinese astral science was transmitted to him by the Daoist master: "[Fu Mengzhi's astral knowledge] harmed the reputation of the Cathay scholars since in this land [the Ilkhanate] it is [now] assumed that their astral science is at such a [low] level, and that they are unfamiliar with geometrical astronomy (*ʿilm al-hayʾa*), the *Almagest,* and all that relates to it. What the person [Fu Mengzhi] reported to the late Naṣīr al-Dīn [Ṭūsī] was at such [a low] level that his [Ṭūsī's] knowledge already encompassed it, and the book that this person read was an abridgement that beginners study [in the Islamicate world]."[43] According to this passage, Fu Mengzhi's knowledge of geometrical astronomy, which was common in Islamicate, western Eurasia, and which Ṭūsī had clearly mastered, was insufficient, as it was based on an unofficial Tang calendar that was equivalent to what "beginners" might study in the Islamicate world at this time.

During the Tang period, astral elements, especially horoscopic astrology, were transmitted to China from western Eurasia and incorporated into unsanctioned, nondynastic calendars; however, four centuries later, when the same features and ideas traveled "back" to the Islamicate world within the context of the scientific exchanges orchestrated by the Mongols, they were found to be outdated in comparison to the Islamicate advancements in the astral sciences during the centuries that had passed between these two moments of contact. So long as the terms of exchange were dictated by one side, the Islamic counterpart, the Chinese astral system could not be properly comprehended or evaluated in the Islamicate west. Furthermore, whereas Ṭūsī was by far the greatest Muslim astronomer of this time, Fu Mengzhi was a court physician for whom astronomy was merely an avocation. This asymmetry between the two collaborators certainly did not contribute to a fruitful exchange nor to a proper representation of Chinese astronomical advancements. We might also ask whether this scientific exchange was further limited by the attempt to achieve maximum commensurability,[44] at the expense of an effective exchange between two equally-footed bodies of astral knowledge, or whether this exchange was hindered instead by an innate inability of these two forms of astral knowledge to fully and equally interact.

CONCLUSION

While Fu Mengzhi and Ṭūsī might both be labeled Eurasian cultural brokers, they nevertheless seem to have been unwilling, or simply incapable, of enabling the Chinese and Islamicate astral sciences to fully interact and intermix. Instead of a two-way, cross-Eurasian exchange, Ṭūsī's *Ilkhanid Astronomical Handbook* (*Zīj-i Īlkhānī*) offers a comparative, imperial overview of calendrical systems, separately delineating and explicating six calendars including the "Cathay calendar." The calculation methods and underlying conceptual frameworks behind the calendars are not integrated, but are simply displayed side by side in the *zīj,* although practical conversion of dates among some of the calendars is provided.

As one of the largest landmass empires, the Mongol Empire created on the Silk Roads a "cross-cultural highway" that connected distant cultural zones. Yet, the question of the extent to which these encounters ultimately influenced or informed cultural spheres and local forms of knowledge, leading to Eurasian integration, remains open. When considering this question, we should also take into account the Mongols' attitude to the local forms of knowledge and sciences they encountered and mobilized across their empire.

The Mongols appear more interested in the gathering of what might be termed "second opinions" from each culture, and less in the possible integration of parallel fields of science from different cultures into one unified theory.[45] In Yuan China, Qubilai exhibited the same attitude when he recruited to his service experts in different astral systems, so he might choose from the variety of options of divination and prediction technologies offered by them. He preferred to keep astral knowledges separate, promoting the mobilization of different experts to his court on the one hand, but hindering their cooperation and exchange, on the other.[46]

The same attitude can be observed in the Ilkhanate. The account with which this paper opened, relating Ṭūsī's confrontation with the court astrologer Ḥusām al-Dīn on the eve of the fall of Baghdad and the Muslim polymath's casting of an alternative prediction that supported Hülegü's assault on the city, suggests that Hülegü too was in the habit of searching for alternative celestial forecasts. In the case of the astral sciences, the Mongols held difference more effective and worthwhile than integration. Thus, while the Mongols were ultimately responsible both for the remarkable expansion of Muslim knowledge of Chinese astral sciences, and for China's increasing acquaintance with the Islamicate advancements in the astral sciences, simultaneously, their attitude toward these sciences might also have functioned as an obstacle for a full integration of Eurasian scientific knowledge.

NOTES

1. The astral sciences combine astronomy, which deals with celestial phenomena, and astrology, which considers celestial influences on the terrestrial realm. Whereas nowadays, astrology is dismissed as a pseudoscience, in premodern intellectual traditions, astrology and astronomy were inseparable. North 2013.

2. Baumann 2013, 270.

3. Allsen 2001a, 203–9.

4. Naṣīr al-Dīn Ṭūsī was Hülegü's astronomer and close advisor, as well his supervisor of the Ilkhanate's revenues from the religious endowments (*waqf*, pl. *awqāf*). An influential political figure, Ṭūsī was also the leading intellectual of his age, and a prolific author of more than 150 treatises covering a wide range of fields such as astronomy, philosophy, mathematics, Shīʿī theology, logic, poetry, and ethics. Lane 2003, 217. In mathematical and astral sciences, his main concern was "geometrical astronomy" (*ʿilm al-hayʾa*). He created a mathematical device called the "Ṭūsī couple"—closely related to the Copernican celestial model—aiming to resolve the discrepancy between Ptolemaic astronomy and Aristotelian physics. Ragep 1993; Ragep 2017.

5. Rashīd al-Dīn 1994, 2: 1006–7; Rashīd al-Dīn 1998–99: 2: 492; Lane 2003, 220. Ḥusām al-Dīn was executed.

6. For a general description not confined to astral sciences: Biran 2015a, 541–50.

7. Toomer 1984; Pedersen 2011.

8. Sayılı 1960, 187–223.

9. Saliba 2006; Saliba 2007.

10. Yamada 1980, 100–113; Shi 2014, 49; Yang 2017; Yang 2019.

11. Boyle 1971; Isahaya and Endo 2017, 124; also Brack's contribution in this volume.

12. *Munajjimān*, which also refers to astrologers.

13. Rashīd al-Dīn, MS Topkapı Sarayı, Hazine 1653, 392r; 1654. 252r; Rashīd al-Dīn 2000, 83–84; Rashīd al-Dīn 2006, 5–6; Isahaya 2009, 26.

14. Boyle 1963, 253 n. 4.

15. Jahn 1971, 21–22; Allsen 2001a, 162.

16. Atwood 2016, 281–82.

17. The *Tānksūqnāma* is the main product of Rashīd al-Dīn's "Ilkhanid translation project" from Chinese into Persian. Isahaya 2019.

18. Rashīd al-Dīn, *Tānksūqnāma*, MS Süleymaniye Kütüphanesi, Aya Sofya 3596, 8v; facsimile (intro. Minūwī) 1972, 16.

19. Zhang Zihe (1156?–1228?) was considered the second of the Four Masters of Jin-Yuan medicine. The earliest extant edition, likely the first printed version of the *Rumen shiqin*, was published in 1244, after the Mongol conquest of North China. Shinno 2016, 130.

20. Miya 2016, 28.
21. Allsen 2001b, 172–73.
22. Matsuda 1980.
23. Miya 2016, 24–25.
24. Chang De was appointed a tax collector in the Zhangde Circuit in September 1251, at the latest, when his father passed away (Matsuda 1980, 50). He seems to have been sent at the beginning of 1259 to the Ilkhanate probably to deliver to Hülegü tax revenues from his appanages in Zhangde. Whether Chang De's mission had additional diplomatic purposes is not reported, possibly due to Möngke's death and Qubilai's succession while Chang De was on his way to the Ilkhanate. Chang De's journey across Central Asia was later described in the *Xishiji,* or *Record of the Emissary to the West.* The work also includes descriptions of medical herbs, and Miya suggests that due to his medical knowledge, Chang De might have also been tasked with collecting medical and pharmaceutical information from western and central Eurasia (Miya 2016, 28). On the *Xishiji:* Hodous's article.
25. Wan Gianu is the same Ūnkiyānū or Ankiyānū in the *Jāmiʿ al-Tawārīkh* and Waṣṣāf's history respectively. He was a trusted commander of Hülegü and Abaqa (r. 1265–82), and their governor in Fārs (a province in south-western Iran). Involved later in political intrigue, he was dispatched to Qubilai's court as an emissary, possibly around 1270–71. Rashīd al-Dīn 1994, 2: 1049; Waṣṣāf 1853, 193–95; Āyatī 1967, 111–12; Miya 2016, 29.
26. A photograph of the text is in Miya 2010, 176.
27. Historically, Chinese names consisted of three elements: family name, given name, and style name (*zi*). For example, in the case of Chang De mentioned above, Chang is the family name and De is the given one, respectively. In addition, Chang De's style name is Renqing. The given name was reserved for oneself and one's elders, while the style name would be used by adults of the same generation to refer to each other on formal occasions or in writing. The style name was usually derived from the given name. Miya suggests that Fu Ye's *zi* may have been Mengzhi on the basis of the style name of another renowned figure, the Ming-dynasty literatus Kuang Ye (1385–1449) whose *zi* was Mengzhi. Since in both names the characters denoting the syllable Ye (埜 and 野) are interchangeable, and Ye is the character related to the style name of Mengzhi, it is possible that Fu Ye also had the style name Mengzhi (transcribed FūMNjī in Persian). Miya 2010, 175–80.
28. Miya 2016, 21–24.
29. Ṭūsī, *Zīj-i Īlkhānī,* 5v–20r. For various calendars appearing in *zīj*es, Van Dalen 2000.
30. This refers to the Byzantine or Syrian calendar counted from the reign of Seleucus I (321–281 B.C.E.). It is a solar calendar, and has Tishurīn I (October) as the first month.
31. The Hijrī calendar named after the *hijra* (the Prophet's migration from Mecca to Medina in 622 C.E.). The year in which this event occurred was taken as the starting point for the calendar. The calendar is a lunar one without any intercalation and independent from the seasons.

32. The so-called "Yazdigird calendar," beginning with the year of the accession of the last Sasanian king, Yazdegerd III, in 631 C.E. It consists of twelve thirty-day months with five extra days.

33. The solar Jalālī calendar was introduced in the late eleventh century by the Seljuk sultan Jalāl al-Dīn Malik-Shāh (r. 1072–92). This is a solar calendar, in which the New Year is defined as the day on which the sun reaches the vernal equinox.

34. This is a luni-solar calendar, in which the year starts on the new moon of Tīshrei (September–October).

35. Van Dalen, Kennedy, and Saiyid 1997; Isahaya 2009; Isahaya 2013.

36. Sivin 2009, 38–60.

37. Isahaya and Lin 2017, 163–64.

38. For the Eurasian-scale transmission of horoscopic astrology: e.g., Yano 1997; Mak 2015; Kotyk 2018.

39. For the term "naturalization" in the context of the history of sciences: Sabra 1987, 227–28.

40. Isahaya and Lin 2017, 166–67.

41. Rashīd al-Dīn, MS Topkapı Sarayı, Hazine 1653, 392r; 1654, 252r; Rashīd al-Dīn 2000, 84–85; Rashīd al-Dīn 2006, 6.

42. For Islamicate astronomical handbooks (*zīj*es): King and Samsó 2001, King and Samsó 2002.

43. Rashīd al-Dīn, MS Süleymaniye Kütüphanesi, Aya Sofya 3596, 8v–9r; facsimile (intro. Minūwī) 1972, 16–17.

44. For commensurability in the context of the history of sciences: e.g., Kuhn 1962; Kuhn 1982.

45. Allsen 2001a, 205; Biran 2015b, 5.

46. This is Nathan Sivin's view, a summary of which is provided in Li 2016, 23 n. 6.

BIBLIOGRAPHY

Allsen, Thomas. 2001a. *Culture and Conquest in Mongol Eurasia*. New York: Cambridge University Press.

———. 2001b. "Sharing Out the Empire: Apportioned Lands under the Mongols." In *Nomads in the Sedentary World*, ed. Anatoly Khazanov and André Wink, 172–90. London: Curzon Press.

Atwood, Christopher. 2016. "Buddhists as Natives: Changing Positions in the Religious Ecology of the Mongol Yuan Dynasty." In *The Middle Kingdom and the Dharma Wheel: Aspects of the Relationship between the Buddhist Saṃgha and the State in Chinese History*, ed. Thomas Jülch, 278–321. Leiden: Brill.

Āyatī, ʿAbd Āl-Muḥammad. 1967. *Taḥrīr-i Taʾrīkh-i Waṣṣāf*. Tehran: Bunyād-i farhang-i Īrān. (See also Waṣṣāf.)

Baumann, Brian. 2013. "By the Power of Eternal Heaven: The Meaning of Tenggeri to the Government of the Pre-Buddhist Mongols." *Extrême-Orient Extrême-Occident* 35: 233–84.

Biran, Michal. 2015a. "The Mongol Empire and the Inter-Civilizational Exchange." In *The Cambridge World History*. Vol. 5. *Expanding Webs of Exchange and Conflict, 500 C.E.–1500 C.E.*, ed. Benjamin Kedar and Merry Wiesner-Hanks, 534–58. Cambridge: Cambridge University Press.

———. 2015b. "Introduction: Nomadic Culture." In *Nomads as Agents of Cultural Change: The Mongols and Their Eurasian Predecessors*, ed. Reuven Amitai and Michal Biran, 1–9. Honolulu: University of Hawai'i Press.

Boyle, John. 1963. "The Longer Introduction to the 'Zij-i Ilkhani' of Nasir-ad-Din Tusi." *Journal of Semitic Studies* 8: 244–54.

———. 1971. "Rashīd al-Dīn: The First World Historian." *Iran* 9: 19–26.

Chen Yuanjing 陳元靚. N.d. *Xinbian zuantuzengleiqunshu leiyao shilinguangji* 新編纂圖增類羣書類要事林廣記 [Extensive Records of the Forest of Matters, Newly Compiled, with Illustrations, Expanded Topics, and Categorized Essentials from Many Books]. 8 vols. National Archives of Japan, 別 060–0001.

Hanawa Hokiichi 塙保己一, ed. 1923–28. *Zoku gunsho ruijū* 續群書類從 [Continued Collection of Miscellaneous Books]. Vols. 22–33b. Tokyo: Zoku gunsho ruijū kanseikai.

Isahaya Yoichi. 2009. "History and Provenance of the 'Chinese' Calendar in the *Zīj-i Īlkhānī*." *Tarikh-e Elm* 8: 19–44.

———. 2013. "The *Tārīkh-i Qitā* in the *Zīj-i Īlkhānī:* The Chinese Calendar in Persian." SCIAMVS 14: 149–258.

———. 2019. "Sino-Iranica in Pax Mongolica: The Elusive Participation of Syriac-Rite Christians in the Ilkhanid Translation Project." In *Marco Polo and the Silk Road (10th–14th Centuries)*, ed. Rong Xinjiang and Dang Baohai, 341–62. Beijing: Peking University Press.

Isahaya Yoichi, and Mitsuaki Endo. 2017. "Persian Transcription of Yuan Chinese in the History of China of the *Jāmiʿ al-Tawārīkh* (Ms. Istanbul, Topkapı Sarayı, Hazine 1654)." *Keizai kenkyū* 経済研究 [Economic Review] 9: 123–61.

Isahaya Yoichi, and Jyuh Fuh Lin. 2017. "Entangled Representation of Heaven: A Chinese Divination Text from a Tenth-Century Dunhuang Fragment (P. 4071)." *Historia scientiarum* 26: 153–71.

Jahn, Karl. 1971. *Die Chinageschichte des Rašīd ad-Dīn: Übersetzung, Kommentar, Facsimiletafeln, unter sinologischen Beistand von Herbert Franke*. Vienna: H. Böhlau.

King, David, and Julio Samsó. 2001. "Astronomical Handbooks and Tables from the Islamic World (750–1900): An Interim Report." *Suhayl* 2: 9–105.

———. 2002. S.v. "ZĪDJ." In *Encyclopaedia of Islam*, 2nd ed., 11: 496–508. Leiden: Brill.

Kotyk, Jeffrey. 2018. *The Sinicization of Indo-Iranian Astrology in Medieval China*. Philadelphia: University of Pennsylvania.

Kuhn, Thomas. 1962. *The Structure of Scientific Revolutions*. Chicago: University of Chicago Press.

———. 1982. "Commensurability, Comparability, Communicability." *Proceedings of the 1982 Biennial Meeting of the Philosophy of Science Association*. 2 vols. 2: 669–88. East Lansing, MI: The Association.

Lane, George. 2003. *Early Mongol Rule in Thirteenth-Century Iran: A Persian Renaissance.* London: Routledge.
Li Liang. 2016. "Arabic Astronomical Tables in China: Tabular Layout and Its Implications for the Transmission and Use of the *Huihui Lifa.*" *East Asian Science, Technology, and Medicine* 44: 21–68.
Mak, Bill. 2015. "The Transmission of Buddhist Astral Science from India to East Asia: The Central Asian Connections." *Historia scientiarum* 24: 59–75.
Matsuda Koichi 松田孝一. 1980. "Furagu-ke no tohoryou フラグ家の東方領" [The Eastern Domain of the House of Hülegü]. *Tōyōshi kenkyū* 東洋史研究 [Researches on East Asian History] 39: 35–62.
Miya Noriko 宮紀子. 2010. "Higashikara nishiheno tabibito: Jyo Toku 東から西への旅人: 常徳" [A Traveler from East to West: Chang De]. In *Yurashia chuouikino rekishi kouzu: 13–15 seikino touzai* ユーラシア中央域の歴史構図—13–15 世紀の東西 [Historical Composition in Central Eurasia: East and West during the 13th–15th Centuries], ed. Kubota Jyunpei 窪田順平, 167–90. Kyoto: Research Institute for Humanity and Nature.
———. 2016. "'Knowledge' in East and West during the Mongol Period." *Acta Asiatica* 110: 19–37.
North, John. 2013. "Astronomy and Astrology." In *The Cambridge History of Science.* Vol. 2. *Medieval Science,* ed. David Lindberg and Michael Shank, 456–84. Cambridge: Cambridge University Press.
Pedersen, Olaf. 2011. *A Survey of the Almagest: With Annotation and New Commentary by Alexander Jones.* New York: Springer.
Ragep, Jamil. 1993. *Naṣīr al-Dīn al-Ṭūsī's Memoir on Astronomy: Al-Tadhkira fī ʿilm al-hayʾa.* New York: Springer.
———. 2017. "From Tūn to Turun: The Twists and Turns of the Ṭūsī-Couple." In *Before Copernicus: The Cultures and Contexts of Scientific Learning in the Fifteenth Century,* ed. Rivka Feldhay and Jamil Ragep, 161–97. Montreal: McGill-Queen's University Press.
Rashīd al-Dīn, Faḍl Allāh al-Hamadānī. *Jāmiʿ al-tawārīkh.* MSS Topkapı Sarayı, Hazine 1653 and 1654.
———. *Tānksūqnāma-yi Īlkhān dar funūn-i ʿulūm-i Khiṭāʾī.* MS Süleymaniye Kütüphanesi, Aya Sofya 3596.
———. 1972. *Tānksūqnāma, yā ṭibb-i ahl-i Khitā* (facsimile). Intro. Mujtabā Mīnūwī. Tehran: Intishārāt-i dānishkada-yi adabiyāt wa ʿulūm-i insānī.
———. 1994. *Jāmiʿ al-tawārīkh.* Ed. Muḥammad Rawshan and Muṣṭafā Mūsawī. 4 vols. Tehran: Nashr-i Alburz.
———. 1998–99. *Rashīduddin Fazlullah's Jamiʿu't-Tawarikh: A History of the Mongols.* Tr. Wheeler Thackston. 3 vols. Cambridge, MA: Harvard University, Department of Near Eastern Languages and Civilizations.
———. 2000. *Tārīkh-i Chīn: Az Jāmiʿ al-tawārīkh-i khwāja Rashīd al-Dīn Faḍl Allāh.* Ed. Yidan Wang. Tehran: Markaz-i nashr-i dānishgāhī.
———. 2006. *Jāmiʿ al-tawārīkh: Tārīkh-i aqwām-i pādshāhān-i Khitāy.* Ed. Muḥammad Rawshan. Tehran: Markaz-i pazhūhishī mīrāth-i maktūb.
Sabra, Abdelhamid. 1987. "The Appropriation and Subsequent Naturalization of Greek Science in Medieval Islam." *History of Science* 25: 223–43.

Saliba, George. 2006. “Horoscopes and Planetary Theory: Ilkhanid Patronage of Astronomers.” In *Beyond the Legacy of Genghis Khan*, ed. Linda Komaroff, 357–68. Leiden: Brill.

———. 2007. *Islamic Science and the Making of the European Renaissance.* Cambridge, MA: MIT Press.

Sayılı, Aydın. 1960. *The Observatory in Islam and Its Place in the General History of the Observatory.* Ankara: Türk Tarih Kurumu Basımevi.

Shi Yunli. 2014. “Islamic Astronomy in the Service of Yuan and Ming Monarchs.” *Suhayl* 13: 41–61.

Shinno Reiko. 2016. *The Politics of Chinese Medicine under Mongol Rule.* New York: Routledge.

Sivin, Nathan. 2009. *Granting the Seasons: The Chinese Astronomical Reform of 1280, with a Study of Its Many Dimensions and an Annotated Translation of Its Record.* New York: Springer.

Toomer, Gerald. 1984. *Ptolemy's Almagest.* London: Duckworth.

Ṭūsī, Naṣīr al-Dīn. *Zīj-i Īlkhānī.* MS Bibliothèque nationale de France, Ancien fonds persan 163.

Van Dalen, Benno. 2000. S.v. “Taʾrīkh: I. 2. Era Chronology in Astronomical Handbooks.” *Encyclopaedia of Islam.* 2nd ed., 10: 264–71. Leiden: Brill.

Van Dalen, Benno, Edward Kennedy, and Mustafa Saiyid. 1997. “The Chinese-Uighur Calendar in Ṭūsī's Zīj-i Īlkhānī.” *Zeitschrift für Geschichte der arabisch-islamischen Wissenschaften* 11: 111–52.

Waṣṣāf al-Ḥaḍrat (Sharaf al-Dīn ʿAbdallāh b. Faḍlallāh al-Shīrāzī). 1853. *Tajziyat al-amṣār wa-tazjiyat al-aʿṣār (Taʾrīkh-i Waṣṣāf).* Lithograph. Bombay: Muḥammad Mahdī Iṣfahānī.

Yamada Keiji 山田慶児. 1980. *Jujireki no michi: Chugoku chusei no kagaku to kokka* 授時暦の道: 中国中世の科学と国家 [The Road to the *Shoushi li:* Science and the State in Medieval China]. Tokyo: Misuzu Shobou.

Yang Qiao. 2017. “From the West to the East, from the Sky to the Earth: A Biography of Jamāl al-Dīn.” *Asiatische Studien—Études Asiatiques* 71: 1231–45.

———. 2019. “Like Stars in the Sky: Networks of Astronomers in Mongol Eurasia.” *Journal of the Economic and Social History of the Orient* 62: 388–427.

Yano Michio. 1997. *Kušyār Ibn Labbān's Introduction to Astrology.* Tokyo: Institute for the Study of Languages and Cultures of Asia and Africa.

CHAPTER 13

ʿĪsa Kelemechi

A Translator Turned Envoy between Asia and Europe

HODONG KIM

While the recent surge in popular interest in the Mongol Empire has also drawn attention to the travelers who crossed Mongol-ruled Eurasia, the focus has remained on the eastward travel of Europeans who reached as far as the Mongol court in Mongolia and China, the most famous example being that of Marco Polo (1254–1324). However, several significant Mongol-era Eastern travelers had also set westward, settling or temporarily residing in the Islamic world and even in Europe. Through the studies of Thomas Allsen and Morris Rossabi, we are now better informed on the migration of the Mongol general and cultural broker Bolad (d. 1313),[1] and the travels of the Turkic-Chinese Christian monk and diplomat Rabban Sauma (c. 1220–94), the "Voyager from Xanadu."[2] Still, the case of another Eastern traveler, ʿĪsa Kelemechi ("Jesus the Interpreter," 1227–1308), who reached Iran and Europe, serving the Mongol Empire as an official, interpreter, and diplomat, has remained little known.

ʿĪsa's travels across the Mongol-era Silk Roads, first eastward, and then back to China, matched—if not exceeded—the itineraries of his better-known contemporaries. Born in present-day Azerbaijan or Armenia during the early stages of Mongol expansion into the Islamic world, ʿĪsa was recruited at an early age into Mongol service. Migrating and settling in China, ʿĪsa served in several high-ranking posts in the Yuan government, rising to the position of privy councilor in the Central Secretariat, which was one of the most high-ranking stations in the Yuan government. Dispatched in the 1280s to Ilkhanid Iran as the envoy of

Qubilai Qa'an (r. 1260–94), 'Īsa next represented the entire empire as envoy to the Curia in Rome.

Translator, civil servant, and Mongol diplomat, 'Īsa's meteoric rise and successful career are paradigmatic examples of how human talent was mobilized across Mongol Eurasia. Throughout 'Īsa's career, he was known for his linguistic talents and ability to negotiate diverse cultural spheres enabling him to gain the trust of the ruling elite. Furthermore, through his expertise in medicine and astrology, he contributed to the establishment of Yuan governmental offices and departments dedicated to these fields that facilitated the East-West Eurasian exchange of scientific knowledge.

MIGRATION TO CHINA

'Īsa was born in 1227, probably around the Caucasus region.[3] His grandfather was named *Bar Ali and his father *Bar Lumashi.[4] In the 1240s, the Mongols were consolidating their rule over Central Asia and to this end were recruiting Christians to their service, including members of 'Īsa's extended family. The Mongols enlisted capable individuals from the communities that cooperated with them. Simeon Rabban Ata, a Syrian priest and merchant, was one such Mongol collaborator. Simeon succeeded in securing from Chinggis Khan's heir, Ögödei Qa'an (r. 1229–41), an imperial edict guaranteeing the protection of local Christians under Mongol suzerainty in return for his services.[5] Simeon was also asked by Sorqaqtani Beki (d. 1252), wife of Chinggis Khan's younger son Tolui (1192–1232) and mother to the future qa'ans Möngke (r. 1251–59) and Qubilai, to recommend individuals for her service. When Simeon approached 'Īsa's father, *Bar Lumashi, he sent his son 'Īsa in his place to join Sorqaqtani's service due to his old age. In the mid-1240s, during Güyük Qa'an's reign (1246–48), 'Īsa traveled through Central Asia to the Mongol court in Qaraqurum in Mongolia and joined Sorqaqtani Beki's court. There, 'Īsa married a Mongol of the Kereyit tribe named *Hushinisha. Her baptismal name, Sarah, indicates that like her husband 'Īsa, she too was a Christian, likely of the Church of the East.[6]

We know little about 'Īsa's life during his years in Sorqaqtani's service and up until the early 1260s. During this missing decade, 'Īsa might have been preoccupied with studying languages, eventually earning the title "translator," *kelemechi* (Mong.; Ch. *qielimachi*),[7] and thus also earning his place in the qa'an's imperial guard, the *keshig*.[8]

As *keshig* member, ʿĪsa gained access to, and maintained a close relationship with the qa'an. Moreover, he was not one to shy away from offering his candid advice to the ruler. In 1262, soon after Qubilai proclaimed himself qa'an, ʿĪsa insisted before the ruler that he should cancel a Buddhist ceremonial celebration of the Buddha's birthday. Only one month later, ʿĪsa once again directly criticized Qubilai for planning to spend a night at a Daoist temple outside of the capital. ʿĪsa insisted that the state was in turmoil and the army and people in distress, and thus persuaded Qubilai to change his plans.[9]

ʿĪsa indeed proved himself to be an accurate reader of the political landscape of the empire enabling him to persuade Qubilai. In 1260, following the death of the fourth qa'an, Möngke, his two younger brothers, Qubilai and Arigh Böke, each proclaimed themselves qa'an, leading to a fierce succession struggle that tore apart the United Empire.[10] Qubilai's planned tour furthermore coincided with the rebellion of the Han Chinese general Li Tan (d. 1262) and his briefly occupation of Ji'nan (in present-day Shandong province).

ʿĪsa's rise in the ranks of the Mongol Empire should also be attributed to his expertise in Western astrology and medicine. Aside from his membership in the *keshig*, ʿĪsa's first government office (1263) was his appointment to establish the Medical and Pharmaceutical Office (*jingshi yiyueyuan*, later the Office for Western Medicine [*guanghuisi*]). He was also involved in another governmental office which oversaw astrology and calendar publishing, an office that later became the Astronomical Observatory of Western Knowledge (*huihui sitiantai*).[11] There he closely worked with other experts including another non-Han official, the famous Muslim astronomer Jamāl al-Dīn (d. ca. 1289) who had migrated from Central or West Asia to China and introduced Islamic astronomy, geography, and cartography to Qubilai's court.[12] In the "spirit path inscription" dedicated to ʿĪsa,[13] a commemorative writing composed by the Chinese scholar and official Cheng Jufu (1249–1318), Cheng praised ʿĪsa for his mastery of "various languages, astrology and medical knowledge from the western regions."[14]

Preoccupied with these new governmental posts, ʿĪsa nevertheless continued to cultivate a close relationship with Qubilai. ʿĪsa's great influence over Qubilai and direct involvement in court politics and intrigues are further evident in the year 1276, immediately after the fall of the Song dynasty capital Lin'an (modern-day Hangzhou) to the Mongols. One of the most influential individuals in the Yuan area since the early 1260s was Aḥmad (d. 1282), a Muslim merchant and capable financial advisor who had served as Qubilai's chief financial minister. In 1282, Aḥmad met an unfortunate death, assassinated and posthumously condemned for corruption.[15] In 1276, however, Aḥmad was still at the height of his power and accused the capable military general Bayan (d. 1295), conqueror of the Song capital, of embezzling a jade goblet that had previously belonged to the Song. In fact, Bayan had earlier presented Aḥmad a gift of a jade belt. ʿĪsa advocated for Bayan's innocence, directly challenging Aḥmad's powerful authority. Despite Aḥmad's influence at the court, ʿĪsa had Qubilai's ear and Bayan was exonerated.[16]

Another example of ʿĪsa's involvement in state matters occurred in 1283, when he was appointed to transmit an imperial edict to the officials of the Central Secretariat, the highest-ranking and most powerful office in the Yuan government. The edict ordered the restoration of tax-exemption rights to the *ortaq* (Mong. "partner") merchants, those who worked on behalf of, and often financed by, the Mongol rulers and aristocrats. These commercial agents enjoyed state-sanctioned privileges such as tax breaks and official use of the postal system.[17] Yet, during his tenure as fiscal advisor, Aḥmad introduced a series of aggressive financial reforms, which probably included eliminating the *ortaq* tax privileges. Following Aḥmad's death in 1282, the *ortaq* merchants requested their privileges restored, and Qubilai, who decided to accept their request, assigned ʿĪsa along with *Sarman (Ch. Saliman), another high-ranking official to relay the imperial edict to the Central Secretariat.[18]

To fully comprehend the significance of ʿĪsa's role in this affair, we need to grasp how the Mongols communicated imperial orders. Faithful to their nomadic roots, Yuan emperors were often on the move, migrating between their summer capital Shangdu (modern-day Duolun, Inner Mongolia) and their winter capital Dadu (modern-day Beijing). To accommodate their constant mobility, the Mongol court had to rely on a more fluid system of communication, one based on personal trust and loyalty, as an alternative to adhering to a fixed protocol for the transfer of documents.[19] Thus, in many cases, an official who had earned the qa'an's trust and was also multilingual was charged with the task of delivering edicts. ʿĪsa's appointment to this task reflected not only his ability to communicate across linguistic boundaries, but also his close relationship with Qubilai.

ʿĪsa's alleged role in the famous, so-called "anti-Muslim" edict of 1280, is, however, disputable. As recorded in Chinese, Persian, and

European-language sources,[20] in 1280 Qubilai issued an edict that banned the Muslim (as well as Jewish) manner of circumcision and of slaughtering animals. The edict was issued after a group of Muslim Merchants had refused to eat meat from animals not slaughtered in a *ḥalal* (Muslim) manner. ʿĪsa's name is not mentioned in the two Chinese accounts of this episode. However, the Ilkhanid Persian vizier and historian Rashīd al-Dīn (d. 1318) notes that ʿĪsa took advantage of this opportunity to secure an even stricter edict imposing the death penalty on individuals slaughtering sheep in the *ḥalal* manner, even in the privacy of their homes.[21]

ʿĪsa clearly was influential at the court during this period. Yet, the idea that he maintained such an anti-Muslim attitude and implemented discriminative policies is questionable. First, a comparison of the Chinese and Persian accounts for the Muslim ban indicates that the Chinese version, which refrains from mentioning ʿĪsa's anti-Muslim bias, is more reliable.[22] The Chinese account preserves the full text of the edict, probably a Chinese translation of the original Mongolian document. According to the edict, the prohibition on the Muslim animal slaughter has its historical precedent in Chinggis Khan's reign, and the Mongols considered it a symbolic gesture signifying the Muslim allegiance to Mongol rule. The Persian account, in contrast, claims an overall anti-Muslim sentiment in Qubilai's court, and the following part in the Ilkhanid vizier's history also includes further anecdotes pertaining to Christian plots against Muslims at the Yuan court. Moreover, as seen earlier, ʿĪsa did not seem to have had problems working alongside Muslims. Rashīd al-Dīn's depiction of ʿĪsa's anti-Muslim sentiments more likely reflects the overall anti-Christian attitude prevalent in the Ilkhanid court after Ghazan Khan's (r. 1295–1304) conversion to Islam in the late 1290s—if not even restricted to the vizier's own sentiment toward the Christians. Put differently, the Persian version of this anecdote speaks more to the context in which Rashīd al-Dīn was writing his history in Iran, and less to the actual religious and political atmosphere at the late thirteenth-century Yuan court.

ENVOY OF THE QA'AN: TO IRAN AND EUROPE

The second half of ʿĪsa's life centered on two missions, first, as an envoy to the Ilkhanid court in Iran, and shortly thereafter, when he headed an embassy from the Ilkhanate to the Roman Curia in Europe. In 1283, two months after delivering Qubilai's message to the Central Secretariat, ʿĪsa left the Yuan capital. Together with his son Asutai,[23] ʿĪsa accompanied the famous Bolad Aqa on his westward journey. A Mongol commander well versed in Chinese and Mongol politics, Bolad became an important informant for Rashīd al-Dīn's history after his arrival in the Ilkhanate, and played a leading role as a cultural broker.[24]

While we have ample documentation on Bolad's mission, both in Persian and Chinese sources, we remain ill-informed about the purpose of the mission itself.[25] The political turmoil in the Ilkhanate during the 1280s might explain our lack of information. In 1282, the Ilkhan Abaqa (r. 1265–82) passed away, and a succession struggle between his brother, the Ilkhan Hülegü's oldest surviving son, Tegüder (r. 1282–84), and Abaqa's eldest son, Arghun (r. 1284–91), ensued. Arghun initially conceded to Tegüder and subsequently, Tegüder was enthroned as the next Ilkhan. Two years later, Arghun overthrew and executed his uncle, taking the throne. Scholars suggest that Qubilai sent ʿĪsa and Bolad to exercise his influence over this politically unstable period in the Ilkhanate and ensure that Qubilai's preferred candidate succeed to the throne,[26] but it is similarly possible that Qubilai simply sent Bolad and his company to convey the qa'an's condolences for Abaqa's death and confirm Tegüder's succession. By the time ʿĪsa and Bolad arrived, however, Arghun was already enthroned as the new Ilkhan. Considering the change in the political circumstances, the sources might have preferred to remain silent as to the original purpose of ʿĪsa and Bolad's mission.

ʿĪsa's return to his "homeland" was cut short. Since 1260, when the Mongol advance was halted in Palestine by the forces of the Mamluk Sultanate (1250–1517), the Ilkhans had struggled to find reliable allies to fight against this neighboring Muslim state, making continuous efforts to gain an alliance with European forces. In 1285, soon after his arrival to the Ilkhanate, ʿĪsa embarked on another mission, to Europe, this time as part of the Ilkhan Arghun's embassy to the pope. The letter he carried with him survives today only in Latin and remains in the Vatican archives. According to the letter, Arghun's embassy consisted of Ase *terciman*, Bogagoc, Mengilic, Thomas Banchrinus, and Ugeto *terciman*. Out of these five individuals, Ase *terciman* alone was sent by the *magnus cam* or the Great Khan, clearly referring to Qubilai. Ase seems to reflect ʿĪsa, and *terciman* denotes the Arabic word *tarjumān* meaning "interpreter" or "translator." The remaining four names cannot be identified, though two of them (Bogagoc, Mengilic) are derived from Mongolian and the other two might have been Italians.

In his letter to the pope, Arghun attempted to establish an Ilkhanid-European coalition against the Muslim Mamluks, offering to divide the

"Land of Shām" (Syria and Palestine) after they erase together the "Saracens" (i.e., the Muslims) from the Holy Land.[27] Aside from the names of the delegates, further details on this mission remain unknown. Nothing substantial resulted from it.[28]

By 1286, ʿĪsa was already back at Qubilai's court.[29] His return trip took over a year, mostly due to the political instability in Central Asia arising from the conflict between Qubilai and his Mongolian nemesis, Qaidu (r. 1271–1301).[30] Whereas the Mongol Bolad remained in Iran, ʿĪsa, along with four other unnamed individuals, returned to the China.[31] Qubilai praised ʿĪsa, contrasting his praiseworthy return with Bolad's decision to stay in Iran: "Bolad was born in our homeland and received our support, but he decided to settle over there [in Iran]; ʿĪsa was in fact born over there and still has his home there. Nevertheless, he remains loyal to me! What a difference between these two!"[32]

RETURN TO CHINA AND ʿĪSA'S DESCENDANTS

After his return, ʿĪsa continued to serve in the central government. Qubilai offered him the position of the privy councilor (rank 1B). This position was equivalent to a modern-day minister, outranked only by the senior and junior chief councilors. As a privy councilor, ʿĪsa would have worked within the Central Secretariat. However, ʿĪsa declined the offer and remained assigned to two other offices with which he had been involved prior to leaving for Iran. First, in 1287, ʿĪsa was appointed as the head of the Imperial Library Directorate.[33] The main responsibility of this directorate was managing books on painting, maps, and even prohibited geomantic works. During his tenure in this office, ʿĪsa participated in the compilation of the *Treatise on the Great Unified Realm of the Great Yuan* (*Da Yuan dayi tongzhi*), a geographic work originally intended to cover all regions conquered by the Mongols. ʿĪsa's firsthand experience and knowledge of the western parts of the Mongol empire likely played an important role in the composition of this work.[34] Two years later, in 1289, with the establishment of the Office for Christian Clergy, ʿĪsa became the first to head this new body, taking charge of all affairs related to Christians in the Yuan realm. In 1294, he was also appointed as one of the seven chancellors of the Hanlin and National History Academy.[35] Originally established to serve as an advisory organization to the emperor and assist in the compilation of historical sources, the academy had, by this time, mostly focused on the compilation of the chronicles of the emperor, the so-called Veritable Records.[36]

After Qubilai's death (1294), ʿĪsa received the support of the newly-crowned Temür Qa'an (r. 1294–1307), and remained in his service. By this point, ʿĪsa was already in his late sixties and the new qa'an provided him a dedicated carrier to help him remain mobile.[37]

In 1295, still as the head of the Office for Christians in the Yuan, ʿĪsa became involved in a discussion over taxing Christian churches. On the initiative of Mar Sergis (fl. fourteenth century), a Christian who built numerous churches in South China,[38] ʿĪsa submitted a memorial requesting that the churches be exempted from commercial and land taxes. Despite the qa'an's eventual rejection of this request, the document attests to ʿĪsa's continued efforts on behalf of the Yuan Christian subjects.[39]

In 1297, ʿĪsa agreed to serve as one of the privy councilors of the Central Secretariat, the position he had declined earlier.[40] The Persian sources, too, confirm his new appointment, now adding to ʿĪsa's name the title *finjan* or *pinjan*—the Persian rendering of the Chinese term for privy councilor, *pingzhang zhengshi*.[41]

We know little about ʿĪsa's accomplishments in his new, high-ranking position. His abrupt absence from the historical record might be related to an incident involving bribery, imprisonment, and an official pardon. According to Chinese accounts, in 1302, during his imperial tour to Liulin (in modern-day Hebei), Temür Qa'an became ill. He summoned a Tibetan lama named Danba, and the latter conducted a series of rituals, praying for the qa'an's recovery for over a week. Temür recovered from his illness and eventually pardoned "thirty-eight people in the capital who had committed serious crimes."[42] The Chinese sources do not tell us the identity of the pardoned individuals or the reasons for their initial imprisonment, but Persian sources do provide a more detailed account, albeit with some minor differences.

According to the Persian record, an envoy from Ghazan Khan had arrived in China, and the accompanying merchants sold precious stones to Temür Qa'an at an inflated price. ʿĪsa was among the twelve high-ranking officials who profited from this exchange. Learning of the plot, an enraged Temür imprisoned the entire group, but later released forty individuals, including members of this group.[43] Juxtaposing these two accounts, it seems that ʿĪsa was accused of profiting from manipulating the value of merchandise, and was imprisoned on this charge, but later pardoned and released.

ʿĪsa appears also to have been involved in the succession struggle that ensued with Temür Qa'an's illness and death. He allied himself with the qa'an's nephew, Qaishan (r. 1307–11), in opposition to the empress

Bulughan Khatun (died ca. 1307). In 1303, when Temür Qa'an became ill and his empress, Bulughan, oversaw state affairs, ʿĪsa's relationship with the reigning khatun turned sour. After an earthquake on the eighth month of 1303, Bulughan asked ʿĪsa whether the earthquake could be attributed to the "menial commoners [*xiamin*]," but ʿĪsa answered in the negative. Four years later, in 1307, when Temür passed away, ʿĪsa openly defied the empress's order to provide her with the "secret text" of a calendar stored in the Imperial Library Directorate. When Temür's nephew Qaishan (r. 1307–11) succeeded the crown, the newly enthroned qa'an expressed his gratitude and praised ʿĪsa's loyalty.[44] A year later, in 1308, ʿĪsa passed away. To posthumously celebrate ʿĪsa's accomplishments, Qaishan's brother and successor, Ayurbarwada Qa'an (r. 1311–20), granted the deceased ʿĪsa several honorific titles such as "Grand Preceptor," "Most Honored," and "the Supreme Pillar of the State," in addition to styling him "Prince of Fulin."[45] Furthermore, he conferred on him the posthumous title *Zhongxian* (lit. "Loyal Contribution").

ʿĪsa was survived by six sons, four sons-in-law, and grandchildren. Reconstructing the lives of his descendants is a challenging task, due to their involvement in the political factions in the mid to late Yuan period, often leading to their exile, execution, and disgrace.

ʿĪsa's eldest son, Elijah (Ch. Yeliya), became son-in-law to the powerful, albeit controversial, Temüder (d. 1322), known as the "treacherous minister."[46] Due to his close ties during the 1320s with this powerful official, Elijah was able to retain high-ranking positions and was granted the prestigious title of "the Prince of the State of Qin." Elijah had also advocated for, and eventually secured, the various titles granted to his deceased father by Ayurbarwada.[47] Surviving Temüder's fall from grace in 1322, Elijah continued to serve in positions such as director of the Imperial Academy of Medicine, a position especially fitting for the son of ʿĪsa, who had committed himself to setting up the Yuan medical institutions in the 1270s. During Tuq-Temür's reign (r. 1328–29, 1329–32), he continued to benefit from the emperor's support, even though some high-ranking officials expressed their reservations.[48] In 1330, however, he was executed together with his elder sister *Anasimus on charges of witchcraft and the use of amulets and curses.[49]

According to "the spirit path inscription" dedicated to ʿĪsa, Elijah's five younger brothers, the other five sons of ʿĪsa, were named *Denha (Ch. Tianhe), *Heisi, Giwargis (or "George," Ch. Kuolijisi), Luke (Ch. Luhe) and Johanan (Ch. Yaonan). These appear to have been their Christian baptismal names. Yet, other sources indicate that ʿĪsa had two more

TABLE 13.1 DESCENDANTS OF ʿĪSA AND POSITIONS THEY HELD

Relation to ʿĪsa	Name	Position held
First son	Elijah	Office for Christian Clergy, Imperial Academy of Medicine (*taiyiyuan*)
Second son	*Denha	Hanlin Academy, Imperial Library Directorate
Third son	*Heisi	unknown
Fourth son	Giwargis	Southwest Financial Bureau
Fifth son	Luke	Office for Western Medicine
Sixth son	Johanan	imperial guards
First son-in-law	Unknown	Bureau for Imperial Household Provisions
Second son-in-law	Unknown	Office for Christian Clergy
Third son-in-law	Unknown	Bureau for the Imperial Accessories
Fourth son-in-law	Unknown	imperial guards
Eldest grandson	*Baoge	imperial guards
Grandson	*Xuange	imperial guards
Grandson	Hantun	imperial guards

sons, Asutai (Ch. Ashikedai) and *Bakeshiba, as well as a grandson from Asutai named Möngke Temür. During Qaishan's reign (r. 1307–11), Möngke Temür, ʿĪsa's grandson, became junior chief councilor to the Department of State Affairs. He was involved in a plot to depose the crown prince Ayurbarwada and appoint Qaishan's own son as heir-apparent. This plot failed, and later, after Ayurbarwada became qa'an in 1311, all five conspiring officials were punished. Möngke Temür alone survived the execution and was sent to exile, probably because his uncle Elijah—a close supporter of Temüder—advocated for him and saved him from execution.

As Han Rulin has pointed out,[50] the political fallout from Möngke Temür's disgrace might explain why different sources have different names for ʿĪsa's descendants, making it difficult to cross-reference the names of ʿĪsa's sons. The imperial eulogies for Möngke Temür's father Asutai and uncle *Bakeshiba were written by the famous Confucian scholar Yao Sui (1239–1314) in the 1310s, before Asutai's son, Möngke Temür, was embroiled in the plot. However, when Cheng Jufu (1249–1318) wrote the spirit path inscription for ʿĪsa in 1318, Möngke Temür had already fallen from grace. Cheng Jufu likely used the Christian names of ʿĪsa's sons and grandsons alone to avoid mentioning the names of the once influential, but now disgraced individuals.[51]

As for ʿĪsa's other sons, few details of their lives are known beyond the list of the positions they held in the Yuan government (see Table 13.1, above). Their Christian and sometimes even Mongol names indicate that ʿĪsa's descendants continued, at least for several generations, to maintain their Christian faith in Yuan China. Although some Christians and Muslims followed a more Han Chinese lifestyle and adopted Han Chinese names,[52] the ruling Mongols continued to respect the religions of groups and individuals. The list, furthermore, shows that the family retained its hold on positions in the central government, especially posts related to ʿĪsa's accomplishments, including the Office for Christian Clergy, offices related to medicine, and offices related to documents and translation such as the Imperial Library Directorate and the Hanlin Academy. Their continuity with ʿĪsa is furthermore attested through their ongoing affiliation with the imperial guard: ʿĪsa's grandsons all started their careers as members of the imperial guard.

CONCLUSION

The life and career of ʿĪsa demonstrates the unprecedented degree of exchange and mobility along the Silk Roads, enabled and promoted by the Mongol Empire. Born in the Middle East, ʿĪsa migrated along the trade routes to China, where he proved himself competent in astrology, medicine, and languages. Achieving high-ranking positions within the Yuan government, ʿĪsa then traveled back, once again along the Silk Roads, to Iran and later continued westward to Europe, where he served as the Mongols' ambassador to the pope.

ʿĪsa's story demonstrates some of the key aspects of Mongol imperial rule: the importance of service in the imperial guard (*keshig*) and language skills to advancement in the official ranks; the promotion of highly competent individuals; the recruitment of intellectual experts whose skills covered fields favored by the Mongols such as medicine, astronomy, and linguistics; and the mobility of Mongol administrators across Eurasia. ʿĪsa traveled through and beyond the empire, further even than the better-known travelers of his era, and eventually returned to Yuan China, which became a permanent home for him and his descendants. With his mastery of various languages, and profound knowledge of astrology and medicine, he served primarily as an intellectual of the empire, an expert versed in Mongolian, in addition to Western and East Asian cultures. His career, moreover, is an example for the often-overlooked contribution of Western migrants to the intellectual life of Yuan China.

NOTES

This chapter is an edited and shortened version of Kim 2006 (in Korean) and Kim 2015 (in Chinese), following the editorial direction of this volume. Dr. Wonhee Cho (Academy of Korean Studies) translated and edited the article.

1. Allsen 1996.

2. Rossabi 2010.

3. According to the Chinese accounts, ʿĪsa came from "the land of Qin" or "Fulin," which broadly refer to Rome, Anatolia, or the Seljuk realm. Since Rabban Ata and his contemporaries established contacts with the Mongols in Tabriz in Azerbaijan, it seems likely that ʿĪsa too came from this area.

4. No other biographical information on these figures is known aside from their names, which are recorded in Chinese. "Bar," reconstructed from the Chinese characters *bu* or *bo*, was a common denomination among Syrians, equivalent to the "Ben" or "Ibn," namely son, among Jewish and Arabs: Yao 2011, 37–38.

5. Kirakos 1986, 237–40; Pelliot 1923, 29–65. Simeon Rabban Ata is identical with **Liebian Ada* in the Chinese sources: Cheng 2009, 57.

6. Han 1982, 93–108. For the Church of the East, previously known as the Nestorian church: Brock 1996; Malek and Hofrichter 2006, 12–13.

7. Wang and Shang 1992, 32, 54, 69, 74. ʿĪsa presumably spoke Persian, and probably Mongolian, considering he served as a translator and member of the *keshig*.

8. Xiao 1996 argues that the *kelemechi* too consisted one of the functionaries in the *keshig*, though this is not stated in the Chinese sources.

9. Cheng 2009, 57.

10. Kim 2006.

11. Song 1976, 134: 3249. On these offices: Farquhar 1990, 134.

12. On Jamāl al-Dīn: Yang 2017.

13. Spirit-path inscriptions (*shendaobei wen*) were commemorative writings carved on steles that were erected on the path leading to the tomb of individuals. Although the steles themselves might have been lost, their content is often preserved in the collective writings of their authors.

14. Cheng 2009, 57.

15. Franke 1993.

16. Song 1976, 134: 3249, 127: 3113.

17. On the *ortaqs:* Endicott-West 1989; and Gill's chapter in this book.

18. Chen Gaohua et al. 2011, 989.

19. Li 2003, 5–58.

20. Togan 2013; Cleaves 1992.

21. Franke 1993, 293–94.

22. For the Chinese: Chen Gaohua et al. 2011, 1893–94; for the Persian: Rashīd al-Dīn 1998–99, 3: 446.

23. Yao 2011, 39; Cheng 2009, 57–58.

24. Allsen 1996.

25. Rashīd al-Dīn 1998, 565–66; Cheng 2009, 57–58.

26. Allsen 2001, 27–28.

27. Lupprian 1981, 78.
28. Jackson 2005, 169–70.
29. Wang and Shang 1992, 54, 74.
30. Biran 1997.
31. Yao et al. 1959, 8: 7202.
32. Cheng 2009, 58.
33. Song 1976, 134: 3249; Wang and Shang 1992, 9: 163. The *haixue* here in the Chinese text is obviously a misprint for *aixue,* ʿĪsa.
34. Wang and Shang 1992, 54, 74.
35. Song 1976, 134: 3249–50.
36. Farquhar 1990, 127–29. The Veritable Records (*shilu*) were the basis for the compiling of the dynasty's official history, completed after the dynasty's fall by its successors.
37. Cheng 2009, 58.
38. Tang 2011, 112–19.
39. Fang 2001, 29: 720–21.
40. Song 1976, 134: 3249–50.
41. Rashīd al-Dīn 1994, 959; Āyatī 1967, 284.
42. Song 1976, 20: 440; Nianchang 1988, 22: 725/11; Franke 1993.
43. Unlike the Chinese account, the Persian version does not provide exact dates for the incident. The Ilkhanid historian Waṣṣāf has another version of the incident, according to which ʿĪsa was arrested for illegally confiscating the merchants' goods. Waṣṣāf's version confuses the dates, situating the incident two years later, in 1304. Āyatī 1967, 284.
44. Cheng 2009, 58; Song 1976, 134: 3250.
45. On Fulin: note 3 above.
46. On Temüder: Cho 2017.
47. Han 1982, 93–101.
48. Song 1976, 32: 715.
49. Song 1976, 34:761–62. Chen Gaohua et al. 2011, 1422.
50. Han 1982, 93–101.
51. With the lack of information available, it is impossible to know which of the five sons named in this way were Asutai or *Bakeshiba.
52. Multiple examples in Chen 1923.

BIBLIOGRAPHY

Allsen, Thomas T. 1996. "Biography of a Cultural Broker: Bolad Ch'eng-Hsiang in China and Iran." In *The Court of the Il-Khans, 1290–1340*, ed. Julian Raby and Teresa Fitzherbert, 7–22. Oxford: Oxford University Press.

———. 2001. *Culture and Conquest in Mongol Eurasia.* Cambridge: Cambridge University Press.

Āyatī, ʿAbd Āl-Muḥammad. 1967. *Taḥrīr-i taʾrīkh-i Waṣṣāf.* Tehran: Bunyād-i farhang-i Īrān.

Biran, Michal. 1997. *Qaidu and the Rise of the Independent Mongol State in Central Asia.* Richmond, Surrey: Curzon.

Brock, S.P. 1996. "The 'Nestorian' Church: A Lamentable Misnomer." *Bulletin of the John Rylands Library* 78: 23–35.

Cho Wonhee. 2017. "From Military Leaders to Administrative Experts: The Biography of the 'Treacherous Minister' Temüder and his Ancestors." *Asiatische Studien—Études Asiatiques* 71: 1213–30.

Chen Gaohua 陳高華, et al., eds. 2011. *Yuan dian zhang: Da Yuan sheng zheng guochao dianzhang* 元典章: 大元聖政國朝典章 [Institutions of the Yuan Dynasty: Compendium of Statutes and Substatutes of the Sagely Administration of the Great Yuan Dynasty]. Tianjin: Tianjin guji chubanshe.

Chen Yuan. 1923. *Western and Central Asians in China under the Mongols: Their Transformation into Chinese*. Monumenta Serica Monograph Series 15. Nettetal, Germany: Steyler Verlag.

Cheng Jufu 程鉅夫. 2009. *Cheng Jufu ji* 程鉅夫集 [Collected Works of Cheng Jufu]. Ed. Zhang Wenshu 張文澍. Chengdu, China: Jilin wenshi chubanshe.

Cleaves, Francis W. 1992. "The Rescript of Qubilai Prohibiting the Slaughtering of Animals by Slitting the Throat." *Journal of Turkish Studies* 16: 67–89.

Endicott-West, Elizabeth. 1989. "Merchant Associations in Yüan China: The 'Ortoɣ.'" *Asia Major* 2: 127–54.

Fang Linggui 方齡貴, ed. 2001. *Tongzhi tiaoge jiaozhu* 通制條格校注 [Comprehensive Regulations and Statues of the Yuan: Collated and Annotated]. Beijing: Zhonghua shuju.

Farquhar, David. 1990. *The Government of China under Mongolian Rule: A Reference Guide*. Stuttgart: Steiner.

Franke, Herbert. 1993. "Aḥmad." In *In the Service of the Khan: Eminent Personalities of the Early Mongol-Yüan Period (1200–1300)*, ed. Igor de Rachewiltz et al., 539–57. Wiesbaden, Germany: Harrassowitz.

Han Rulin 韓儒林. 1982. "Aixue zhi zai tantao 愛薛之再探討 [A Re-Examination of ʿĪsa]." In *Qionglu ji: Yuanshi ji xibei minzhu shi yanjiu* 穹廬集: 元史及西北民族研究 [Collected Works from the Yurt: Research on the History of the Yuan and the Northwestern Minorities], 93–108. Shanghai: Shanghai renmin chubanshe.

Jackson, Peter. 2005. *The Mongols and the West, 1221–1410*. Harlow, Essex: Pearson Longman.

Kim Hodong 김호동. 2006. "Mongwŏnchekukki han saekmokin kwansaŭi ch'osang isa k'ellemich'iŭi saengaewa hwaltong 몽원제국기(蒙元帝國期) 한 색목인(色目人) 관사의 초상—이사 켈레메치의 생애와 활동 [A Portrait of a Christian Official in China under the Mongol Rule—The Life and Career of ʿIsa Kelemechi (1227–1308)]." *Chungang Ashia Yŏngu* 11: 75–114.

———. 2015. "Mengyuan diguo shiqi de yiwei semu guanli Aixue qielimachi (Isa Kelemechi, 1277–1308 nian) de shengya yu huodong 蒙元帝國時期一位色目官吏爱薛怯里馬赤 (Isa Kelemechi, 1227–1308 年) 的生涯與活動 [A Portrait of a Christian Official in China under the Mongol Rule—The Life and Career of ʿIsa Kelemechi (1227–1308)]." Tr. Li Huazi 李華子. *Ouya Yicong* 歐亞譯叢 [Collected Translations on Eurasia], 1: 224–63. Beijing: Shangwu yinshuguan.

Kirakos, Gandzakets'i. 1986. *Kirakos Gandzakets'i's History of the Armenians*. Tr. Robert Bedrosian. New York: Sources of the Armenian Tradition.

Li Zhian 李治安. 2003. *Yuandai zhengzhi zhidu yanjiu* 元代政治制度研究 [A Study on the Political Institutions of the Yuan]. Beijing: Renmin chubanshe.

Lupprian, Karl-Ernst. 1981. *Die Beziehungen der Päpste zu islamischen und mongolischen Herrschern im 13. Jahrhundert anhand ihres Briefwechsels.* Studi e testi (Biblioteca apostolica vaticana) 291. Vatican: Biblioteca apostolica vaticana.

Malek, Roman, and Peter Hofrichter, eds. 2006. *Jingjiao: The Church of the East in China and Central Asia.* Sankt Augustin, Germany: Institut Monumenta Serica.

Nianchang 念常. 1988. "Fozu lidai tongzai" 佛祖歷代通載 [Comprehensive Record of the Buddhist Patriarchs]. In *Beijing tushuguan guji zhenben congkan* 北京圖書館古籍珍本叢刊 [Collection of Rare Editions of Manuscripts from the Peking National Library]. Vol. 77. Beijing: Shumu wenxian chubanshe.

Pelliot, Paul. 1923. *Les Mongols et la papauté.* Paris: Picard.

Rashīd al-Dīn, Fadlallāh al-Hamadānī. 1994. *Jāmiʿ al-tawārīkh.* Ed. Muḥammad Rawshan and Muṣṭafā Mūsawī. 4 vols. Tehran: Nashr-i Alburz.

———. 1998–99. *Rashiduddin Fazlullah's Jamiʿuʾt-Tawarikh: Compendium of Chronicles: A History of the Mongols.* Tr. Wheeler M. Thackston. 3 vols. Cambridge, MA.: Harvard University, Department of Near Eastern Languages and Civilizations.

Rossabi, Morris. 2010. *Voyager from Xanadu: Rabban Sauma and the First Journey from China to the West.* Berkeley: University of California Press.

Song Lian 宋濂. 1976. *Yuanshi* 元史 [The Official History of the Yuan]. Beijing: Zhonghua shuju.

Tang, Li. 2011. *East Syriac Christianity in Mongol-Yuan China.* Wiesbaden, Germany: Harrassowitz.

Togan, Isenbike. 2013. "Variations in the Perception of Jasagh." In *History of Central Asia in Modern Medieval Studies (In Memoriam of Professor Roziya Mukminova),* 67–101. Tashkent, Uzbekistan: Yangi Nashr.

Wang Shidian 王士點 and Shang Qiweng 商企翁. 1992. *Mishujian zhi* 秘書監志 [Records of the Imperial Library Directorate]. Ed. Gao Rongsheng 高榮盛. Hangzhou, China: Zhenjiang guji chubanshe.

Xiao Qiqing 蕭啓慶. 1996. "Yuandai de tongshi yu yishi 元代的通事與譯史 [Translators and Interpreters in the Yuan]." In *Yuanshi luncong* 元史論叢 [Collected Essays on Yuan history], Ed. Zhongguo Yuanshi yanjiuhui 中國元史研究會, 6: 24–51. Beijing: Zhongguo shehui kexue chubanshe.

Yang Qiao. 2017. "From the West to the East, from the Sky to the Earth: A Biography of Jamāl al-Dīn." *Asiatische Studien—Études Asiatiques* 71: 1231–45.

Yao Guangxiao 姚廣孝 et al. 1959. *Yongle dadian* 永樂大典 [Great Compendium of the Yongle Era]. Beijing: Zhonghua shuju.

Yao Sui 姚燧. 2011. *Yao Sui ji* 姚燧集 [Collected Works of Yao Sui]. Ed. Cha Hongde 查洪德. Beijing: Renmin wenxue chubanshe.

CHAPTER 14

Pādshāh Khatun

An Example of Architectural, Religious, and Literary Patronage in Ilkhanid Iran

BRUNO DE NICOLA

In comparison to sedentary societies, women in the Turkic-Mongol nomadic and seminomadic societies showed greater involvement in the political sphere, enjoyed a greater measure of financial autonomy, and generally had the freedom to choose their religious affiliations.[1] Some women advanced to positions of immense power and wealth, even appointed as regent-empresses for the entire empire or regional khanates. Such examples included Töregene Khatun (r. 1242–46), Oghul Qaimish (r. 1248–50), and Orghina Khatun (r. 1251–59).[2] Other women such as Qutui Khatun (d. 1284) in Mongol-ruled Iran accumulated great wealth from war booty, trade investment, and the allocation of tax revenues from the newly conquered territories.[3]

Through their unique prominence in the empire's socio-economic system, elite women had an active role in financially supporting and protecting cultural and religious agents. Our understanding of the impact that Chinggisid women had on the flourishing of cultural life in the empire as a whole, and in the Ilkhanate of greater Iran in particular, remains poor, however. The historical record tells us little about the role that Chinggisid female members played as patrons of religious and cultural life, especially when comparted to the relative wealth of references to female influence in the political and economic arenas. However, abundant accounts show that female elite members from the local Turkic-Mongol dynasties who ruled as vassals for the Mongols, or had been incorporated into the ranks of the ruling Chinggisid household through marriage, played a pivotal role as cultural and religious patrons. Doing so, they indirectly contributed to the empire's religious and intellectual life, and in some instances, were further directly involved in the cultural activities of the societies they were ruling.[4]

The female patronage of religious institutions and clergy was especially prominent in the case of the Turkic-Mongol dynasties that ruled as Ilkhanid vassals, on the peripheries of Ilkhanid Iran, in Fārs, Kirmān, or Anatolia.[5] This chapter provides an overview of the life of Pādshāh Khatun (1256–95), a prominent lady of the Qutlughkhanid line of rulers. Despite being born in Kirmān, on the periphery of the Ilkhanate, she played an active role in Ilkhanid politics during the second half of the thirteenth century. Furthermore, her life and patronage activities open a window into the architectural, literary, and religious patronage of royal women in the Ilkhanate, and more broadly, the Mongol Empire.

FROM CENTRAL ASIA TO KIRMĀN: THE ESTABLISHMENT OF THE QUTLUGHKHANID DYNASTY IN SOUTHERN IRAN

Pādshāh Khatun belonged to the Qutlughkhanid line that ruled Kirmān in southern Iran (1222–1306) under the Mongol and, later, Ilkhanid aegis. The dynasty owed its emergence, first, to the historical turmoil that ensued from the Mongol conquests in Central Asia, and later, to the establishment of Mongol rule in Iran. The founder of the Qutlughkhanids, Baraq Ḥājib (Baraq the Chamberlain, r. 1222–35), was a scion of the ruling house of the Qara Khitai. The Qara Khitai were Khitan fugitives from North China who ruled in Central Asia in the century that preceded the rise of the Mongols (1124–1218).[6] Despite ruling over a majority-Muslim population in Central Asia, the nomadic Qara Khitai did not convert to Islam maintaining instead their Chinese trappings and mainly, their Buddhist affiliation.[7] However, their policy of religious tolerance, and the security and prosperity that Qara Khitai rule brought to the region, guaranteed the cooperation of their Muslim subjects. In addition to their religious policies, the Qara Khitai were also distinguished for the prominent position they attributed to female members of the ruling line. Out of the five Qara Khitai emperors, two were empresses. These empresses ruled in their own right, not as temporary regents for their underage male offspring or until a succession struggle was resolved.[8]

This relative peace and prosperity in Central Asia abruptly ended in the early thirteenth century, when Qara Khitai rule was afflicted with political crisis. Their former vassal, the Muslim Khwārazmshāh Muḥammad (r. 1200–1220), who would become Chinggis Khan's main opponent in Central Asia and the Middle East, seized this opportunity, and in 1210 conquered Transoxiana (mostly in modern-day Uzbekistan), the Qara Khitai's richest province and main source of revenue.

During the battle between the Qara Khitai and the Khwārazmshāh, Baraq Ḥājib, Pādshāh Khatun's great-uncle, was either taken captive or detained prior to the battle in Khwārazm. Impressed by his talents, the Khwārazmshāh appointed him as a chamberlain (*ḥājib*) and assigned him to the service of his son Ghiyāth al-Dīn, who had ruled central Iran. Baraq then converted to Islam. Ghiyāth al-Dīn appointed him governor of the city of Isfahan (in central Iran) and perhaps of Kirmān as well.[9] According to a different version, Baraq was heading to the Delhi Sultanate (1206–1526) when he defeated the local governor of Kirmān and decided to settle there.[10]

Baraq's decision was probably also influenced by the Chinggisid conquest and expansion, first to the heart of the Qara Khitai realm (1218), and soon thereafter, through most of the Khwārizmian domain (1219–20). In 1224, the Khwārazmshāh Jālal al-Dīn (r. 1220–31), now a fugitive fleeing the Mongol forces, confirmed Baraq's position as governor of Kirmān, conferring upon him the title Qutlugh Khan (Turk. "the fortunate khan"). Witnessing, however, the Khwārazmian Empire's collapse in the 1220s, Baraq sought to guarantee his new dominion initially through the blessing of the ʿAbbasid caliph, who invested him with the title of Qutlugh Sultan. Subsequently, in 1232, he also approached the new rising force of the Mongols, who too confirmed his position in Kirmān and his title Qutlugh Khan.[11] Baraq Ḥājib's new Qara Khitai state in southern Iran maintained some characteristics of its Central Asian predecessors, including the elevated position of women. However, Baraq's new polity was now ruled by a Muslim dynasty reigning under Mongol aegis.

After the establishment of the Ilkhanate in the second half of the thirteenth century, the Qutlughkhanid kingdom of Kirmān played a prominent role in Ilkhanid trade networks, and especially in the vibrant intra-Asian commercial trade. Strategically situated along the road connecting Europe, Asia Minor, and West Asia to India, Kirmān also benefited from its location between the Ilkhanate's thriving cities in northern Iran and the strait of Hormuz, the Ilkhanate's main gateway to the Persian Gulf, which connected the maritime trade routes from Iran to India and the Far East.[12] The city of Kirmān was itself a center of production, both for raw materials and manufactured goods. The famous Italian merchant

Marco Polo mentions the importance of mining activity in the region, with turquoise and iron produced in great quantities, as well as "exquisite needlework in the embroidery of silk stuff in different colours, with figures of beasts and birds, trees and flowers, and a variety of other patterns . . . for the use of noblemen so deftly that they are marvels to see, as well as cushions, pillows, quilts and all sort of things."[13]

As rulers of the region, the Qutlughkhanids controlled trade in the area. They received revenue from the taxation of the population and the land, as well as from the traffic in trade commodities through their territories. As with the Mongol ruling house, female members of the Turkic-Mongol elites that ruled under the Ilkhans too shared in the economic surplus of their houses.[14] In the Mongol Empire, women were free to accumulate and invest considerable wealth, based on revenues from their share in booty, land and tax allocations, and the usufruct of the livestock and the population under their rule, in addition to the trade revenues. Women became important financial investors in religious and cultural life, a tradition that continued under the Mongols' successors—the Muzaffarids (r. 1314–93), the Timurids (r. 1370–1507), and the Safavids (r. 1501–1736).[15]

THE LIFE OF PĀDSHĀH KHATUN: A TURKIC-QARA KHITAI WOMAN IN MONGOL IRAN

Pādshāh Khatun was among a select group of women who, despite her lack of Mongol roots, achieved elevated political status at the Ilkhanid court. Born in 1256 at the Qutlughkhanid court, Pādshāh was the daughter of Quṭb al-Dīn Muḥammad (r. 1236, 1252–57), nephew and heir to Baraq Ḥājib, the founder of the Qutlughkhanid kingdom in Kirmān, and Terken Qutlugh Khatun (r. 1257–82), a noble Qara Khitai and Baraq's widow (see fig. 14.1).[16] When Quṭb al-Dīn, her father, died shortly after her birth, Pādshāh's mother, Terken Qutlugh, assumed control over large parts of southern Iran receiving Mongol consent. She ruled first as a regent for her minor son, and later in her own right, governing Kirmān for over twenty years.[17] Terken Qutlugh initially resisted her Muslim daughter's marriage to the infidel Ilkhan Abaqa (r. 1265–82); the latter requested Pādshāh's hand shortly after his ascension. According to a later account, Pādshāh was even raised as a male named "Ḥasan Shāh" so she could avoid being made to marry the "infidel" Mongol.[18] Yet in 1271–72, when Pādshāh was sixteen years old, the marriage took place.[19]

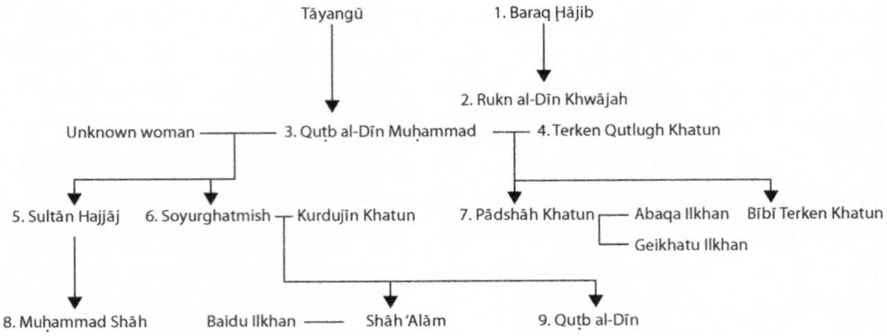

FIGURE 14.1. The Qutlughkhanids of Kirmān.

Despite Terken Qutlugh's initial resistance, the marriage appears to have been mutually beneficial. The Qutlughkhanids in Kirmān further solidified their political alliance with the Ilkhans, gaining a foothold at the Mongol court as well. Through the marriage alliance, Terken Qutlugh guaranteed Ilkhanid military protection and political recognition of the vassal status of Kirmān.[20] The Ilkhanid court, on the other hand, used the marriage to further secure its control and to guarantee the flow of economic tribute from the rich province of Kirmān. Kirmān itself could not sustain the permanent presence of a Mongol nomadic regiment, and therefore, the Ilkhans used the Qutlughkhanids to indirectly rule the province. The Qutlughkhanids were further required to provide the Ilkhan with military support during times of need. During the Battle of Herat (1270), where the Ilkhan Abaqa faced, and eventually defeated, the Chaghadaid Khan Baraq (r. 1266–71), the Qutlughkhanids, indeed, provided important military assistance, warding off the Chaghadaid military encroachment from Central Asia.[21] Pādshāh Khatun's marriage provided the Ilkhans with further guarantee of Qutlughkhanid loyalty .

Following her marriage, Pādshāh Khatun was incorporated into Abaqa's court and given the *ordo* (camp, mobile court) of her husband's mother, Yesünjin. The latter died a few months after the marriage.[22] Pādshāh was not the sole, nor the main wife of the Mongol ruler. Yet through her marriage, she secured herself an influential position at the court. There she was able to advance her mother's interests vis-à-vis the Mongol overlords, and became an effective political actor. In 1282, Abaqa died, and while Pādshāh remained at the Mongol court, the new Ilkhan Aḥmad Tegüder (r. 1282–84) made different plans for the Qutlughkhanid dynasty. He removed Pādshāh's mother, Terken Qutlugh, from her position as ruler of Kirmān and enthroned in her place her stepson, Soyurghatmish.[23] Pādshāh firmly opposed her half-brother's appointment to no avail. Nevertheless, she maintained her loyalty to her mother. When Terken Qutlugh's health deteriorated, likely due to old age, Pādshāh Khatun and her sister Bībī Terken traveled from the court to Siyāh Kūh (possibly in the region of Gīlān, near the Caspian shores), to meet their mother there, offering their support for her claim to the throne. When Terken Qutlugh died shortly afterward, in 1283, Pādshāh sent her sister Bībī to Kirmān with their mother's body, but also with a secret plan to remove Soyurghatmish from office.[24] Pādshāh's plot to take over her homeland and reestablish her influence in the region, however, failed, mainly because the Ilkhan Aḥmad Tegüder remained supportive of her half-brother.

Fortunately for Pādshāh, Tegüder's reign did not last. Two years only after his ascension, his nephew, Arghun, backed by prominent Mongol commanders, orchestrated a coup that placed him on the throne in 1284. Political alliances in Iran shifted once again. The new Ilkhan ordered that Pādshāh Khatun and her brother share in Kirmān's government. Pādshāh Khatun did not hesitate to complain to the Ilkhan about his decision, publicly rejecting this Solomonic solution. Her courageous move backfired: her complaints were interpreted as rebellious and her claim for rulership over Kirmān did not gain any sympathy with the Ilkhanid elite.[25] The Mongol commander Boqa (d. 1289), who was instrumental in promoting Arghun to the throne and was subsequently appointed vizier, decided to remove Pādshāh from the center of power by forcing her to remarry.[26] She was given in marriage to Arghun's brother, Geikhatu (r. 1291–95). Whereas levirate, the widow's marriage to her husband's male relative, often a younger sibling or a son (from another mother), was common in Mongol and Qara Khitai societies, it was not sanctioned from a Muslim standpoint. Despite her expressed devotion to Islam (see below), Pādshāh Khatun had married two non-Muslim Mongol partners, one of whom was the son (Geikhatu) of her late husband. This suggests a level of compromise and rapprochement between the Mongol traditions and the Muslim faith, perhaps alluding to some form of religious syncretism, to which the Turkic Muslims in Mongol service were accustomed.[27]

After her marriage to Geikhatu, Pādshāh accompanied him to Rūm (Anatolia), where he was appointed governor.[28] Pādshāh Khatun remained there between 1286 and 1291. During this period, she remained far from the Ilkhanid political scene. Instead of politics, she devoted her time in Rūm to literary activity and architectural patronage (see below). This intermezzo ended with Arghun's death in 1291 and her husband Geikhatu's ascension to the throne, which allowed Pādshāh to return to Iran. As soon as she set foot in the Mongol court, she reclaimed control over her homeland. Indeed, immediately after securing the throne, Geikhatu granted Kirmān to Pādshāh Khatun, summoning her brother Soyurghatmish to the court. She triumphantly returned to Kirmān as the new Qutlughkhanid ruler. Furthermore, Geikhatu granted her custody of her brother. Initially locking him behind bars, she executed him in August 1294.[29]

During her husband's reign, Pādshāh extended the influence of Kirmān's government over the regions of Yazd (north), Shabānkārah (east), and Hormuz (south).[30] However, after Geikhatu's death and Baidu's (r. 1295) ascension, a new succession struggle broke out in the Ilkhanate. Pādshāh opposed the new Ilkhan, but managed to remain in Kirmān despite the desertion of many of her supporters. Eventually, the remaining forces were defeated by the Mongol troops, and she was forced to surrender. Kurdujīn Khatun, the widow of Pādshāh Khatun's half-brother Soyurghatmish, was now at play as well. Kurdujīn claimed Kirmān for herself, and sent Pādshāh as a prisoner to the court. Pādshāh never made it to Baidu's court; she was killed near the city of Mishkin (northwestern Iran) in June/July 1295, where she was initially buried.[31] In time, her remains were transferred to Kirmān and she was reburied in the madrasa of Qubbat Sabz, which her mother Terken Qutlugh had founded.[32]

WOMEN'S ARCHITECTURAL PATRONAGE IN ILKHANID IRAN

Despite the havoc and disruption the Mongol conquests caused, some practices, including patterns of court patronage of Islamic institutions, remained largely unchanged. Since the eleventh century, local rulers, officials, and aristocratic families, especially female elite members, had carried out the traditional role of architectural patrons.[33] In the twelfth century, noblewomen from regional and imperial Turkic dynasties such as the Seljuk Empire vigorously promoted construction activity and financed diverse religious buildings, including mosques, mausoleums, and hospices (*khānqāh*), throughout Iran, for example, in Yazd, Mashhad, and Shirāz.[34] This female patronage activity continued in the early thirteenth century as well, and especially under the Seljuk branch in Anatolia.[35]

The practice of elite female patronage of religious institutions and leaders was familiar among the Mongols as well. Shortly after Chinggis Khan (r. 1206–27) started to expand and consolidate his empire, Mongol elite women began performing acts of patronage. During the empire's first decades, most female patronage was directed at the religions the Mongols had initially encountered. Daoists, Buddhists, and Eastern Christians (mainly Nestorians) were the first to benefit from their patronage. Although Islam was not included in this group,[36] there are early examples of Mongol women contributing to the construction of Muslim sites of education and worship. For example, Sorqaqtani Beki (d. 1251), Chinggis Khan's daughter-in-law and mother of his son Tolui's (d. c. 1232/3) four main sons,[37] donated a thousand dinars to the famous Kubrawī Sufi master Sayf al-Dīn al-Bakhārzī (d. 1261),[38] for the construction of a madrasa and a *khānqāh* in Bukhara in the 1240s; and she did this despite being a confessed Christian.[39]

While the Mongols brought with them their own tradition of female patronage, their expansion into the Muslim world of the thirteenth century also brought into their fold local expressions of female patronage by members of Muslim dynasties of Central Asian origin. Terken Khatun (d. 1264), the wife of Atabeg Saʿd II (d. 1262) of the Salghurids of Fārs (r. 1148–1282), another Mongol vassal dynasty in southern Iran, directly ruled over this region during the mid-thirteenth century.[40] She used her political influence and the resources at her disposal to promote and finance the construction of a mosque inside the Atabeg's palace in central Shiraz.[41] Similarly, her niece, namesake, and Pādshāh's mother, Terken Qutlugh, established several pious foundations (*waqf*, pl. *awqāf*), providing funds to support the construction of colleges (madrasas), a hospital, and mosques in Kirmān.[42] Pādshāh Khatun was likely influenced by her mother's philanthropic activity, and followed her example once she became a political actor in the Ilkhanid court.

Pādshāh Khatun, however, outdid her female relatives, expanding her patronage activity beyond southern Iran, and representing its transregional nature. Her name is connected with the construction of the dome of the famous "Çifte Minaret" madrasa (also known as Hatiniye Madrasesi) in the modern Turkish city of Erzurum (see fig. 14.2).[43] It is uncertain whether she directly participated in financing the dome. Yet, she seems to have donated to this madrasa when she resided in Anatolia in the late 1280s.[44] We know little about her activity as an architectural patron once she returned to Kirmān in 1291, although she appears to have continued to support Islamic institutions. A contemporary source mentions that she

FIGURE 14.2. The dome of the mausoleum at the "Çifte Minaret" madrasa, Erzurum, Turkey, the building of which was paid for by Pādshāh Khatun. Photo by Patricia Blessing.

"gave many pensions and allowances to scholars and she ordered [the construction] of extraordinary madrasas and mosques."[45]

WOMEN AS PATRONS OF RELIGIOUS PERSONALITIES

Noblewomen's involvement in financing and supporting religious institutions in medieval Turkic-Mongol societies often proceeded from an earlier relationship with a charismatic religious leader, mostly a leading figure in the institution. Such interactions, between Turkic female elite members and religious leaders, largely predated the Mongol invasions.[46] Mongol elite women, too, maintained close ties with charismatic figures following the expansion of the empire, establishing direct patronage relationships with personalities of different backgrounds and religious creeds such as Christian priests (Armenians, Nestorians, or Catholics), Buddhist and Daoist monks, Muslim shaykhs, and shamans (both male and female), all of whom frequented the *ordo*s of Mongol women.[47]

Muslim scholars, and especially Sufi shaykhs, were also quick to receive the protection and financial patronage of noble Mongol women. Donations to Islamic institutions by Turkic-Mongol women were generally accompanied by provisions for the shaykhs, scholars, and imams attached to the financed *madrasa* or *khānqāh*. Sorqaqtani Beki's support for the mystic Sayf al-Dīn al-Bākharzī in the early years of the empire (above) was not an isolated case. Sufi literature, especially lives of saints (hagiographies), contains multiple references to Mongol and Turkish women in greater Iran before and during the Ilkhanid period.[48] Different hagiographic accounts of Mongol-ruled Anatolia recall numerous examples of upper-class Turkic women with close contacts with Sufi masters such as Awḥad al-Dīn Kirmānī (d. 1238), the famous mystic and poet Jalāl al-Dīn Rūmī (d. 1273), and his son and successor Sultān Walad (d. 1312).[49]

Pādshāh Khatun, too, might have associated with Sufi shaykhs in the period she spent in Anatolia. Shams al-Dīn Aḥmad Aflākī included in his fourteenth-century hagiography of the mystical poet Rūmī and his offspring an anecdote depicting the close relationship between Pādshāh Khatun and ʿĀrif Chalabī (d. 1320), Rūmī's grandson. According to one such anecdote,[50] which contains some chronological inconsistencies, Pādshāh was a supporter of Mawlānā's family. The account mentions that Pādshāh Khatun was so fond of ʿĀrif Chalabī that she would not release him from her presence in Erzurum even after receiving numerous letters from ʿĀrif's father, Sultan Walad (d. 1312), the Sufi family's head, beseeching her to let his son return to Konya. The hagiographical account continues with ʿĀrif Chalabī leaving after a significant period of time at the khatun's side due to a dispute. Upon his arrival in Konya, ʿĀrif fasted in silence for three straight days until he announced to his followers that Pādshāh Khatun had died, a detail that was confirmed by a letter ʿĀrif immediately received. The grieving shaykh returned to Erzurum to pay his respects to Pādshāh; afflicted he lay over her body, pardoned her offenses, and recited some quatrains in her honor. The purpose of these hagiographic accounts is to highlight the miraculous abilities of the shaykh (in this case his anticipation of the khatun's death). Even if the details are exaggerated and inaccurate (for one, Pādshāh did not die in Erzurum), the anecdote still is an important indication of Pādshāh's cultivation of a close relationship with Ārif (or any other member of the Sufi family).

Pādshāh seems to have also fostered relationships with non-Muslim religious figures. According to the Venetian merchant Marco Polo, when he met with her during one of his famous journeys, he noticed a Nestorian priest in her service.[51] Her mother, Terken Qutlugh, made the region of Kirmān a safe haven for merchants, and especially for Muslim scholars and shaykhs, many of whom had migrated from Central Asia in search of patronage and a sanctuary.[52] There is no indication that the policy of welcoming religious leaders that started under Terken Qutlugh diminished once Pādshāh Khatun became ruler of Kirmān. This continuous interaction between women and shaykhs comprised both devotional affiliations and economic and political patronage and benefits, and religious leaders appear to have competed for the favor of influential women. Scholars have concluded that Sufis had a less significant role in the conversion of the Mongols to Islam than had been previously suggested. Still, Sufi masters certainly played a role in making Islamic practices more familiar to the new rulers and their wives.[53]

The incorporation of female members of the Muslim vassal dynasties into the Ilkhanid court through marriage from the 1270s onward was also an avenue for advancing the gradual Islamization of the Mongols. The marriage of Ilkhanid rulers and princes (Abaqa, Geikhatu, and Möngke Temür) with Muslim Turkic women did not induce them to convert to Islam; yet, as scholars note, the years during which these marriages largely took place, the 1270s through the 1280s, marked a turning point in the slow but steady Islamization process of the Mongols.[54] Women such as Padshāh Khatun remained active in supporting Muslim communities in Iran after their marriages to the Ilkhans. Bringing Muslim practices and patronage patterns into the Mongol court environment, the new wives further facilitated the cultural rapprochement between the Mongol overlords and the Muslim communities they ruled.

LITERARY PATRONAGE AND WOMEN'S CULTURAL ACTIVITY

While the role of women as patrons of buildings, institutions, and religious leaders is often recorded, female involvement in the patronage of cultural activities is less evident. Many surviving Islamic manuscripts, especially in Iranian and Central Asian collections, remain unexplored. However, some evidence suggests that these women were directly or indirectly involved in what some scholars have termed the "renaissance" of Persian literature—the increase in literary and manuscript production in the thirteenth- and fourteenth-century Persianate world. One of the few clearly documented examples of the direct patronage of literature is found during the reign of the Salghurid dynasty of Fārs in Shiraz.[55] The famous poet Saʿdī (d. c. 1292) dedicated two of his most famous works to different rulers of Fārs, and highlighted the "pious and generous" character of one of the ruler's wives, the above-mentioned Salghurid Terken Khatun (d. 1264), praising her support for literary production.[56]

In addition to poetry, local chronicles and histories too blossomed during the period alongside the major Ilkhanid historical compositions, authored by historians like Rashīd al-Dīn, Juwaynī, and Mustawfī.[57] The writing of two local histories of Kirmān was closely connected to Pādshāh's patronage activities. The first of these works is the incomplete and anonymous *History of the Qara Khitai Kings of Kirmān* (*Tārīkh-i shāhī Qarā-Khitāʾīyān-i Kirmān*), which appears to have been commissioned by Pādshāh Khatun in the second half of the thirteenth century.[58] The work was intended as the official history of the Qutlughkhanid dynasty, highlighting the deeds of Pādshāh's mother, Terken Qutlugh, during what was considered the golden age of medieval Kirmān.[59] The other work, *Simṭ al-ʿulā li'l-ḥaḍra al-ʿulyā* (The Sublime Necklace for her Great Majesty), was written by Nāṣir al-Dīn Munshī Kirmānī (d. after 1316). While the work was composed two decades after Pādshāh Khatun's death and was dedicated to the Mongol general Isan Qutlugh Noyan (d. 1337–38),[60] in the early stages of his career, the author, Kirmānī, served as a court official in the chancellery of Pādshāh Khatun's court, and became one of the most powerful courtiers in the Qutlughkhanid administration.[61]

Due to the symbolic meaning the Quran holds for Muslims, women often sought to patronize lavish copies of the sacred text. A manuscript containing the details of a *waqf* (charitable endowment) dated Safar 1, 786 (March 25, 1384) mentions that Bībī Terken, Pādshāh's sister, donated a gold-plated Quran to be kept at her parents' tomb in the Qubbat Sabz *madrasa*.[62] There are no records of a specific donation of copies of the Quran by Pādshāh. However, that she would support the reproduction of the text is plausible considering her long-standing patronage record. A passing reference in an early fourteenth-century chronicle does in fact state that, while she was in Anatolia, Pādshāh dedicated part of her time to writing a commentary on the Quran.[63] Unfortunately, we know nothing else of this commentary, but the chronicler mentions that "she herself was a good scholar,"[64] highlighting that she was responsible for the composition of different literary works.

This is an important statement that sets Pādshāh Khatun apart from other women. She was one of the few Turkic-Mongol women who directly contributed to cultural production in the Ilkhanate.[65] Further she was a skillful calligrapher and composed several short poems that were reproduced in medieval works.[66] Contemporary male scholars recognized her poems, and not only the local chroniclers copied them, but also Ilkhanid court historians such as Ḥamd Allāh Mustawfī Qazwīnī.[67] One poem composed possibly in Anatolia exemplifies the self-reflective nature of her poetry and her longing for her hometown in Kirmān:

> Although I am the child of a mighty sultan
> and the fruit of the garden that is the hearth of the Turks
> I laugh at fate and prosperity
> but I cry at this endless exile.[68]

That Pādshāh Khatun chose to write her poetry under different pseudonyms—the female pseudonym Lāla Khatun, or the male Ḥasan Shāh—is unique as well.[69] Outspoken woman that she was, it seems unlikely that she felt compelled to hide her poetry. Scholars have suggested that she used pseudonyms in the hope that it would help the dissemination and acceptance of her poetry.[70] "Ḥasan Shāh" might have also been the name under which Pādshāh was raised to avoid her having to marry a Mongol prince. In any case, hidden behind her pseudonyms, Pādshāh managed to leave a literary legacy and open the field for other women. In the mid-fourteenth century, almost fifty years after her death, Jahān Khatun (d. 1382),[71] a granddaughter of the Persian vizier and historian Rashīd al-Dīn (d. 1317), mentions Pādshāh in the introduction to her *dīwān* (poetry collection). In this work, Pādshāh is described as one of a small group of Muslim women (together with Fāṭima, daughter of the Prophet Muḥammad, Qutlughshāh Khatun,[72] and ʿĀʾisha Muqrīya),[73] who had contributed to the field of poetry. This enabled Jahān Khatun to legitimize her own status as a Muslim poet.[74] In doing so, a new generation of noblewomen in Iran acknowledged Pādshāh Khatun as a pioneer, who not only promoted culture as a ruler, but also actively contributed to the intellectual production of medieval Iran.

CONCLUSION

Pādshāh Khatun is an example of the politically active, economically autonomous, and culturally involved Turkic-Mongol noblewomen of her time; but, fusing Steppe vigor and Islamic piety, she was also an exceptional character who defied cultural norms. She was involved, like many of her contemporaries, in the internal political struggles that were common in the unstable Ilkhanate. She succeeded in accumulating political influence and economic wealth as the wife of infidel Mongol rulers, and as the daughter of a Muslim ruler of Kirmān, and during her last years, even ruled her native province under the Mongol aegis. Similar to other Turkic-Mongol elite women, she was involved in the patronage of Islamic institutions and scholars at the Mongol court, as the governor's wife in Anatolia, and then as the ruler of Kirmān. Her contributions, however, to the Islamic sciences and Persian poetry further elevate her beyond her female contemporaries.

NOTES

The research leading to these results has received funding from the Institute of Iranian Studies (ÖEAW) as part of the project Centre and Periphery in Ilkhanid Iran: The Qutlughkhanids of Kerman (1222–1307).

1. Ratchnevsky 1976; Rossabi 1979; De Nicola 2017a; Broadbridge 2018.
2. For Turco-Mongol women in the political sphere: De Nicola 2017a, 65–89; De Nicola 2016b, 107–20; Broadbridge 2018, 164–224.
3. De Nicola 2016a, 91–94.
4. Patronage activity was not restricted to Mongol women in the medieval Islamic world. For example, Ayyubid Damascus: Chamberlain 1994.
5. Lambton 1988, 258–96; De Nicola 2014a.
6. Originally ruling in North China and Mongolia as the Liao dynasty (907–1125), the Qara Khitai (also known as the Western Liao) escaped westward to Central Asia after the Manchurian Jurchen people, founders of the Jin dynasty (1124–1234) took over North China (Biran 2005b).
7. Biran 2005a.
8. Biran 2005b, 160–68.
9. Biran 2005b, 87–88.
10. Munshī Kirmānī 1983–84, 22; also, Juwaynī 1997, 476; Biran 2005b, 88.
11. Biran 2005b, 88.
12. On the trade routes: Aubin 1953, and Gill's chapter in this volume.
13. Polo 1903, 1: 86.
14. Yazd was another region where the local elites were greatly involved in patronage projects. Aubin 1975, 107–18.
15. Thys-Şenocak 2006; Bates 1993; Newman 2009, 108; Soucek 1998.
16. Munshī Kirmānī 1983–84, 35. There is no comprehensive narrative account of the Qutlughkhanid dynasty available in English. For a general

account in German: Quade-Reutter 2003, 53–234. For brief accounts on the Qutlughkhanid women: Lambton 1988, 276–87; Lane 2003, 96–99.

17. For Terken Qutlugh: Lane 2006, 248–50; Quade-Reutter 2015.

18. Minorsky 2012, quoting Mīrkhwānd, *Rawḍat al-ṣafā'*.

19. Lambton 1988, 280–81.

20. The territories of the Qutlughkhanids roughly included the present borders of the province of Kirmān in the modern Islamic Republic of Iran, including the cities of Bam and Sīrjān.

21. Shabānkāra'ī 1984, 198–99; on the battle: Biran 2002.

22. She died in Jumada II/January of that year (1272): Rashīd al-Dīn 2: 1098; Rashīd al-Dīn 1998, 536.

23. Shabānkāra'ī 1984, 200; Khwāndāmīr 1954, 3: 269; Khwāndāmīr 1994, 155.

24. Munshī Kirmānī 1983–84, 54–55.

25. De Nicola 2017a, 108–9.

26. Melville 2009, 1: 75.

27. Ratchnevsky 1976, 517; Holmgren 1986; Ratchnevsky 1968.

28. Al-Aqsarā'ī 1944, 145–46; Anonymous 1976, 112–13.

29. Rashīd al-Dīn 1994, 2: 935; Rashīd al-Dīn 1971, 306; Munshī Kirmānī 1983–84, 73; Spuler 1943, 154.

30. Quade-Reutter 2016; Munshī Kirmānī 1983–84, 75.

31. Quade-Reutter 2016.

32. Munshī Kirmānī 1983–84, 76; Mustawfī Qazwīnī 2008–9, 1: 537; Rashīd al-Dīn 1994, 2: 935; Rashīd al-Dīn 1971, 306.

33. E.g., Grabar 1968, 626–58; Blair 1994, 5–20; Pfeiffer 2013, 136–37.

34. De Nicola 2014a, 146–47; De Nicola 2017a, 228.

35. Yalman 2017; Redford 2015.

36. De Nicola 2017a, 210–16.

37. On Sorqaqtani: De Nicola 2017a, 72–76; Broadbridge 2018, 195–224.

38. Sayf al-Dīn Bākharzī was a prominent disciple of Najm al-Dīn Kubrā (d. 1221), founder of the Kubrawiyya Sufi order. He is famous for converting Berke Khan (r. 1257–67), the first royal Chinggisid convert: Algar 2012. On the Kubrawiyya: DeWeese 1988.

39. Rashīd al-Dīn 1994, 2: 823; Rashīd al-Dīn 1998, 2: 400; Juwaynī 1912–37, 3: 8–9; Juwaynī 1997, 552–53; Banākatī 2000, 400.

40. De Nicola 2017a, 110–12.

41. Limbert 2007, 16, 63.

42. Bāstānī Pārīzī 1991, 55–68.

43. De Nicola 2014a, 148. On the controversy about her involvement in the dome's construction: Rogers 1976, 76–77.

44. Quade-Reutter 2016, quoting Karamağalı n.d.

45. Shabānkāra'ī 1984, 202.

46. De Nicola 2017a, 208.

47. Khazanov 1994, 12; De Nicola 2017a, 186–88. Dawson 1955, 165–66; William of Rubruck 2009, 195–99; Rossabi 1989, 41

48. The "propagandistic" nature of the hagiographies raises questions regarding the authenticity of their accounts. Yet, even if the interactions of Sufi shaykhs

with Turco-Mongol women are exaggerated, they still offer unique insight on these women's contacts with religious circles. De Nicola 2014b, 134–35; Paul 1990.

49. De Nicola 2014b.

50. Aflākī 1959–61, 2: 889–91; Aflākī 2002, 621–23.

51. Marco Polo 1903, 1: 92.

52. Quade-Reutter 2015.

53. DeWeese 2009; De Nicola 2017b, 353–76.

54. Pfeiffer 2006, 369–89; De Nicola 2017b, 362–64.

55. On the Salghurids: Aigle 2005.

56. Brookshaw 2005, 187–88; De Nicola 2017a, 110–11.

57. Melville 2000.

58. Anonymous 1976.

59. Aigle 2005, 63–64; Fahīmī 2013, 111–13.

60. Īsan Qutlugh was active in Iran during the early decades of the fourteenth century. He served as amir for Ilkhan Öljeitü (r. 1304–16) and remained an important figure during the reign of the last Ilkhan Abū Saʿīd (r. 1316–35). He was executed soon after Abū Saʿīd's death, due to his involvement in a rebellion in 1337–38. Ḥāfiẓ Abrū 1972, 65, 131–37, 200–201; Wing 2016, 85.

61. Aigle 2005, 64.

62. A reproduction of the original *waqf* written in Arabic can be seen at Asnad.org (Philipps Universität Marburg), www.asnad.org/en/document/514 (accessed August 28, 2018).

63. Shabānkāraʾī 1984, 201.

64. Shabānkāraʾī 1984, 201.

65. On her patronage of scholars, Quade-Reutter 2015, quoting Munshī Kirmānī 1983–84, 73; Waṣṣāf 1853, 292.

66. Quade-Reutter 2015.

67. Munshī Kirmānī 1983–84, 70; Anonymous 1976, 61; Mustawfī 2008–9, 533.

68. Translation in Lane 2006, 246; Lane 2003, 110 (for the full poem).

69. Quade-Reutter 2015; Ṣadaqiāni 1991, 244.

70. Ingenito 2018, 195.

71. On Jahān Khātūn: Ṣafā 1984, 2: 1045–56.

72. Qutlughshāh Khatun was Öljeitü's wife and daughter of Amir Irinjn. She inherited the *ordo* of Doquz Khatun, Hülegü's wife. De Nicola 2017a, 157; Qāshānī 2005, 8.

73. Ingenito 2018, 195.

74. Ingenito 2018, 195.

BIBLIOGRAPHY

Aflākī, Shams al-Dīn. 1959–61. *Manāqib al-ʿārifīn*. Ed. Tahsin Yazıcı. 2 vols. Ankara: Chāpkhānah-yi anjuman-i tārīkh-i Turk.

———. 2002. *The Feats of the Knowers of God: Manāqeb al-ʿārefīn*. Tr. John O'Kane. Leiden: Brill.

Aigle, Denise. 2005. *Le Fārs sous la domination mongole : Politique et fiscalité, XIIIe-XIVe s.* Paris: Association pour l'avancement des études iraniennes.

Algar, Hamid. 2012. S.v. "Sayf al-Dīn Bāk͟harzī." *Encyclopaedia of Islam*. 2nd ed. Available at http://dx.doi.org/10.1163/1573-3912_islam_SIM_6683 (accessed August 28, 2018).

Amitai, Reuven. 1999. "Sufis and Shamans: Some Remarks on the Islamization of the Mongols in the Ilkhanate." *Journal of the Economic and Social History of the Orient* 42: 27–46.

Anonymous. 1976. *Tārīkh-i shāhī Qarākhitā'īyān-i Kirmān*. Ed. Muḥammad Ibrāhīm Bāstānī Pārīzī. Tehran: Bunyād-i farhang-i Īrān.

al-Aqsarā'ī, Karīm al-Dīn Maḥmūd. 1944. *Müsâmeret ül-ahbâr*. Ed. Osman Turan. Ankara: Türk tarih kurumu basımevi.

Aubin, Jean. 1953. "Les princes d'Ormuz du Xiii au Xv siècle." *Journal asiatique* 241: 77–137.

———. 1975. "Le *patronage culturel* en Iran sous les Ilkhans: Une grande famille de Yazd." *Le Monde iranien et l'Islam: Sociétés et cultures* 3: 107–18.

Banākatī, Fakhr al-Dīn Dāwūd. 2000. *Tārīkh-i Banākatī: Rawḍat ūli'l-albāb fī ma'rifat al-tawārīkh wa'l-ansāb*. Ed. Ja'far Shi'ār. Tehran: Anjuman-i āthār wa mafākhir-i farhangī.

Bāstānī Pārīzī, Muḥammad Ibrāhīm. 1991. "Madrasa-yi Tirkān Saljūqī wa Tirkān Khatāyi dar Kirmān." In *Kirmān dar qalamraw-i taḥqiqāt-i īrāni*, ed. Muḥammad Rasūl Daryāgasht, 55–68. Kirmān, Iran: Markaz-i Kirmānshināsī.

Bates, Ü. 1993. "The Architectural Patronage of Ottoman Women." *Asian Art* 6: 50–65.

Biran, Michal. 2002. "The Battle of Herat (1270): A Case of Inter-Mongol Warfare." In *Warfare in Inner Asia*, ed. Nicola Di Cosmo, 175–219. Leiden: Brill.

———. 2005a. "True to Their Ways: Why the Qara Khitai Did Not Convert to Islam?" In *Mongols, Turks, and Others: Eurasian Nomads and the Sedentary World*, ed. Reuven Amitai and Michal Biran, 175–199. Leiden: Brill.

———. 2005b. *The Empire of the Qara Khitai in Eurasian History: Between China and the Islamic World*. Cambridge: Cambridge University Press.

Blair, Sheila S. 1994. "Architecture in Iran and Central Asia under the Il-khanids and Their Successors." In *The Art and Architecture of Islam 1250–1800*, ed. Sheila S. Blair, 5–20. New Haven, CT: Yale University Press.

Broadbridge, Anne F. 2018. *Women and the Making of the Mongol Empire*. Cambridge: Cambridge University Press.

Brookshaw, Dominic P. 2005. "Odes of a Poet-Princess: The Ghazals of Jahān-Malik Khatun." *Iran* 43: 173–95.

Chamberlain, Michael. 1994. *Knowledge and Social Practice in Medieval Damascus, 1190- 1350*. Cambridge: Cambridge University Press.

Dawson, Christopher. 1955. *The Mongol Mission: Narratives and Letters of the Franciscan Missionaries in Mongolia and China in the Thirteenth and Fourteenth Centuries*. London: Sheed and Ward.

De Nicola, Bruno. 2014a. "Patrons or Murids? Mongol Women and Shaykhs in Ilkhanid Iran and Anatolia." *Iran: Journal of the British Institute of Persian Studies* 52: 143–56.

———. 2014b. "The Ladies of Rūm: A Hagiographic View on Women in Thirteenth- and Fourteenth-Century Anatolia." *Journal of Sufi Studies* 3: 132–56.

———. 2016a. "The Economic Role of Mongol Women: Continuity and Transformation from Mongolia to Iran." In *The Mongols' Middle East: Continuity and Transformation in Ilkhanid Iran*, ed. Bruno De Nicola and Charles Melville, 79–105. Leiden: Brill.

———. 2016b. "The Queen of the Chaghatayids: Orghīna Khatun and the Rule of Central Asia." *Journal of the Royal Asiatic Society* 26: 107–20.

———. 2017a. *Women in Mongol Iran: The Khātūns, 1206–1335*. Edinburgh: Edinburgh University Press.

———. 2017b. "The Role of the Domestic Sphere in the Islamisation of the Mongols." In *Islamisation: Comparative Perspectives from History*, ed. A. C. S. Peacock, 353–76. Edinburgh: Edinburgh University Press.

DeWeese, Devin. 1988. "The Eclipse of the Kubravīyah in Central Asia." *Iranian Studies* 21: 45–83.

———. 2009. "Islamization in the Mongol Empire." In *The Cambridge History of Inner Asia: The Chinggisid Age*, ed. Nicola Di Cosmo, Allen J. Frank, and Peter B. Golden, 120- 34. Cambridge: Cambridge University Press.

Fahīmī, Mahīn. 2013. "Ta'rīkh-i Shāhī." In *Historical Sources of the Islamic World: Selected Entries from Encyclopaedia of the World of Islam*, ed. Gholamali Haddad Adel, Mohammad Jafar Elmi, and Hassan Taromi-Rad, 111–13. London: EWI Press.

Grabar, Oleg. 1968. "The Visual Arts, 105–1350." In *The Cambridge History of Iran*, ed. John A. Boyle, 5: 626–58. Cambridge: Cambridge University Press.

Ḥāfiẓ Abrū. 1972. *Dhayl-i jāmi' al-tawārīkh-i Rashīdī, shāmil-i waqā'i' (703–781) Hijrī Qamarī*. Ed. Khānbābā Bayānī. Tehran: Intishārāt-i anjuman-i athār-i millī.

Holmgren, Jennifer. 1986. "Observations on Marriage and Inheritances in Early Mongol Yüan Society, with Particular Reference to the Levirate." *Journal of Asian History* 20: 127–92.

Ingenito, Domenico. 2018. "Jahān Malik Khatun: Gender, Canon, and Persona in the Poems of a Premodern Persian Princess." In *The Beloved in Middle Eastern Literatures: The Culture of Love and Languishing*, ed. Alireza Korangy, Hanadi al-Samman, and Michael C. Beard, 177–212. London: I. B. Tauris.

Juwaynī, 'Alā' al-Dīn 'Atā Malik. 1912–37. *Tarīkh-i jahān-gushā*. Vol. 3. Ed. M. Qazwīnī. Leiden: Brill.

———. 1997. *Genghis Khan: The History of the World Conqueror*. Tr. John A. Boyle. Manchester: Manchester University Press.

Karamağalı, Halûk. n.d. "Erzerum'daki Hatuniye Medresenin tarihi ve bânisi hakkında baz mülâhazalar." *Selçuklu Araştırmalar Dergisi* 3: 209–47.

Khazanov, Anatoly M. 1994. "The Spread of World Religions in Medieval Nomadic Societies of the Eurasian Steppes." *Toronto Studies in Central and Inner Asia* 1: 11–33.

Khwāndāmīr, Ghiyāth al-Dīn. 1954. *Tārīkh-i ḥabīb al-siyar*. 4 vols. Tehran: Kitābkhāna-yi Khayyām.

———. 1994. *Habibu's-Siyar: The Reign of the Mongol and the Turk*. Tr. W. M. Thackston. Cambridge, MA: Harvard University, Department of Near Eastern Languages and Civilizations.

Lambton, Anne K. S. 1988. *Continuity and Change in Medieval Persia: Aspects of Administrative, Economic and Social History*. New York: Columbia University Press.

Lane, George. 2003. *Early Mongol Rule in Thirteenth-Century Iran: A Persian Renaissance*. London: RoutledgeCurzon.

———. 2006. *Daily Life in the Mongol Empire*. Westport, CT: Greenwood Press.

Limbert, John W. 2007. *Shiraz in the Age of Hafez: The Glory of a Medieval Persian City*. Seattle: University of Washington Press.

Melville, Charles. 1990. "Pādshāh-i Islām: The Conversion of Sultan Mahmud Ghazan Khan." *Pembroke Papers* 1: 159–77.

———. 2000. "Persian Local Histories: Views from the Wings." *Iranian Studies* 33: 7- 14.

———. 2009. "The Mongols in Anatolia." In *The Cambridge History of Turkey*, ed. Kate Fleet, 1: 51–101. Cambridge: Cambridge University Press.

Minorsky, Vladimir. 2012. S.v. "Ḳutlug̲h̲-K̲h̲ānids." *Encyclopaedia of Islam*. 2nd ed.. Available at http://dx.doi.org/10.1163/1573-3912_islam_SIM_4588 (accessed August 28, 2018).

Munshī Kirmānī, Nāṣir al-Dīn. 1983–84. *Simṭ al-ʿulā li'l-ḥaḍra al-ʿulyā: Tārīkh-i Qarā-Khitāʾīyān -i Kirmān*. Tehran: Asāṭīr, 1362.

Mustawfī Qazwīnī, Ḥamd Allāh. 2008–9. *Taʾrīkh-i guzīdah*. Ed. ʿAbd al-Ḥusayn Nawāʾī. Tehran, Iran: Amīr Kabīr, 1387.

Newman, Andrew. 2009. *Safavid Iran: Rebirth of a Persian Empire*. London: I. B. Tauris.

Paul, Jürgen. 1990. "Hagiographische Texte als historische Quelle." *Saeculum* 41: 17–43.

Pfeiffer, Judith. 2006. "Reflections on a 'Double Rapprochement': Conversion to Islam among the Mongol Elite during the Early Ilkhanate." In *Beyond the Legacy of Genghis Khan*, ed. Linda Komaroff, 369–89. Leiden, Brill.

———. 2013. "Confessional Ambiguity vs. Confessional Polarization." In *Politics, Patronage, and the Transmission of Knowledge in 13th–15th Century Tabriz*, ed. Judith Pfeiffer, 129–68. Leiden: Brill.

Polo, Marco, 1903. *The Book of Ser Marco Polo, the Venetian: Concerning the Kingdoms and Marvels of the East*. Tr. Henry Yule. 2 vols. London: John Murray.

Quade-Reutter, Karin. 2003. "Denn Sie Haben einen unvollkommenen Verstand—Herrschaftliche Damen im Grossraum Iran in der Mongolen- und Timuridenzeit (ca. 1250–1507)." PhD diss., Albert-Ludwig Universität, Freiburg.

———. 2015. S.v. "Qotloḡ Tarkān Ḳātun." *Encyclopædia Iranica*. Available at www.iranicaonline.org/articles/qotlogh-tarkan-khatun (accessed August 28, 2018).

———. 2016. S.v. "Pādšāh Ḳātun." *Encyclopædia Iranica*. Available at www.iranicaonline.org/articles/padshah-khatun (accessed April 18,2016).

Rashīd al-Dīn. 1971. *The Successors of Genghis Khan*. Tr. John Andrew Boyle. New York: Columbia University Press.

———.1994. *Jāmiʿ al-tawārīkh*. Ed. Muḥammad Rawshan and Muṣṭafā Mūsawī. 4 vols. Tehran: Nashr-i Alburz, 1373.

———. 1998–99. Rashiduddin Fazlullah's *Jami'u't-tawarikh: Compendium of Chronicles*. Tr. Wheeler M. Thackston. 3 vols. Cambridge, MA: Harvard University, Department of Near Eastern Languages and Civilizations.

Ratchnevsky, Paul. 1968. "The Levirate in the Legislation of the Yuan Dynasty." In *Asiatic Studies in Honour of Dr. Jitsuzo Tamura*, 45–62. Kyoto: n.p.

———1976. "La condition de la femme mongole au 12e/13e siècle." In *Tractata Altaica: Denis Sinor sexagenario optime de rebus altaicis merito dedícate*, ed. G. Doerfer et al., 509–30. Wiesbaden, Germany: Harrassowitz.

Redford, Scott. 2015. "The Rape of Anatolia." In *Islam and Christianity in Medieval Anatolia*, ed. Andrew C. S. Peacock, Bruno De Nicola, and Sara N. Yıldız, 107–16. Farnham, VT: Ashgate.

Rogers, J. M. 1976. "Waqf and Patronage in Seljuk Anatolia: The Epigraphic Evidence." *Anatolian Studies* 2: 60–103.

Rossabi, Morris. 1979. "Khubilai Khan and the Women in his Family." In *Studia Sino- Mongolica: Festschrift Fur Herbert Franke*, ed. W. Bauer, 153–80. Wiesbaden, Germany: Steiner.

———. 1989. *Khubilai Khan: His Life and Times*. Berkeley: University of California Press.

Ṣadaqiāni, Nayyera Aqdas. 1991. "Ṣafwat al-Dīn bānu-i shā'ir-i Kirmāni." In *Kirmān dar qalamraw-i taḥqiqāt-i īrāni*, ed. Muḥammad Rasūl Daryāgasht, 241–47. Kirmān, Iran: Markaz-i Kirmānshināsī.

Ṣafā, Dhabīḥ Allāh. 1984. *Ta'rīkh-i adabiyyāt dar Īrān*. 8 vols. Tehran: Firdaws.

Shabānkāra'ī, Muḥammad Ibn 'Alī. 1984. *Majma' al-ansāb*. Ed. Hāshim Muḥaddith. Tehran: Mu'assasah-yi intishārāt-i Amīr Kabīr, 1363.

Spuler, Bertold. 1943. *Die Goldene Horde: Die Mongolen in Russland, 1223–1502*. Leipzig: Harrassowitz.

Soucek, Priscila. 1998. "Timurid Women: A Cultural Perspective." In *Women in the Medieval Islamic World: Patronage and Piety*, ed. Gavin R. Hambly, 199–226. New York: St. Martin's Press.

Thys-Şenocak, Lucienne. 2006. *Ottoman Women Builders: The Architectural Patronage of Hadice Turhan Sultan*. New York: Ashgate.

Waṣṣāf, Sharaf-al-Dīn 'Abd Allāh. 1853. *Tajziat al-amṣār wa tazjiat al-a'ṣār*. Ed. M. M. Iṣfahāni. Lithograph Printing. Bombay: Muḥammad Mahdī Iṣfahānī, 1269/1853. Reprint, Tehran: Ibn Sīnā, 1338/1959.

William of Rubruck. 2009. *The Mission of Friar William of Rubruck: His Journey to the Court of the Great Khan Möngke, 1253–1255*. Tr. Peter Jackson. Indianapolis: Hackett.

Wing, Patrick. 2016. *The Jalayirids: Dynastic State Formation in the Mongol Middle East*. Edinburgh: Edinburgh University Press.

Wittfogel, Karl August, and Chia-sheng Feng. 1949. *History of Chinese Society: Liao (907–1225)*. Philadelphia: American Philosophical Society.

Yalman, Suzan. 2017. "The 'Dual Identity' of Mahperi Khatun: Piety, Patronage, and Marriage across Frontiers in Seljuk Anatolia." In *Architecture and Landscape in Medieval Anatolia, 1100–1500*, ed. Patricia Blessing and Rachel Goshgarian, 224–52. Edinburgh: Edinburgh University Press.

CHAPTER 15

Islamic Learning on the Silk Roads

The Career of Jalāl al-Dīn al-Akhawī

OR AMIR

In 1341, the Muslim Central Asian scholar Jalāl al-Dīn al-Akhawī began a twenty-five-year journey that would carry him from Samarqand, in modern-day Uzbekistan, through the Volga Region in Russia and the Muslim centers of Damascus and Baghdad, ending up in Medina in Arabia. There, al-Akhawī would spend the last decades of his life teaching and writing. Al-Akhawī's journey offers an important account for the flourishing of Muslim intellectual life in the long-standing Central Asian centers of Samarqand, Bukhara, and Khwārazm, during a period of Mongol rule which generally lacks documentation. His expansive travels also speak to the founding of new Muslim centers of learning and the flourishing of Muslim intellectual exchanges under the rule of the Mongol state of the Golden Horde, and, more broadly, to the formation of new and the continuity of old patterns of Muslim scholarly mobility in fourteenth-century Mongol Eurasia.

Throughout his journey, al-Akhawī followed a trade route that, to a large degree, was shaped by a number of historical processes taking place in the Mongol period. On the political and economic levels, al-Akhawī's path was influenced, first, by the stability and safety offered by the Golden Horde's rule over a vast area, stretching from Khwārazm to the Crimea during the first half of the fourteenth century; and second, by the flourishing slave trade between the Golden Horde and the Mamluk Sultanate in Egypt.

In scholarly and religious terms, al-Akhawī's movement was influenced by the strong relations between those two states, and mainly, by their common leaning toward the Ḥanafī school of Muslim jurisprudence. This leaning was expressed in the growth in opportunities of patronage and material support for Ḥanafī scholars in both the Golden Horde and the Mamluk realm. Whereas Central Asian Ḥanafī scholars had first immigrated to Egypt and Syria seeking refuge from the Mongol onslaught in Central Asia during the first half of the thirteenth century, they continued to travel to Syria and Egypt later in large numbers due to the increasing support offered to them by the Mamluk elite in the numerous newly founded learning institutions.[1] While al-Akhawī himself, for reasons we cannot fully ascertain, never made it to Egypt as did many of his peers and teachers, he clearly followed the westward direction that contemporary eastern Ḥanafī scholars undertook since the early thirteenth century, and in greater numbers since the second half of the fourteenth century. His journey thus shows the impact of the political climate on scholars, on the one hand, while on the other, it demonstrates how intellectual and religious networks during this period often transcended the political boundaries.

First tracing al-Akhawī's journey, as it is accounted for in the biographical collection of the Egyptian scholar Shams al-Dīn al-Sakhāwī (d. 1497),[2] this chapter outlines and analyzes the Central Asian scholar's travels and his experiences after finally settling in Medina. The chapter then offers some insights on al-Akhawī's legacy and related historiographical aspects.

FROM CHILDHOOD IN TRANSOXANIA TO SETTLING DOWN IN MEDINA: THE LIFE TRAJECTORY OF A MUSLIM SCHOLAR

Jalāl al-Dīn Aḥmad b. Muḥammad al-Khujandī al-Akhawī, hereafter al-Akhawī,[3] was born in 1319 in the Central Asian town of Khujand in today's Tajikistan, on the banks of the middle Sir Darya, between Farghana and Samarqand.[4] He probably belonged to a family of religious scholars (*'ulamā'*).[5] Starting at the age of six or seven, his early education followed the typical path for a Ḥanafī scholar from this region, and included some of the classic works on jurisprudence (*fiqh*) and the basic auxiliary sciences such as grammar, linguistics, poetry, and prose.[6] Al-Akhawī's early years in Khujand suggest that the town

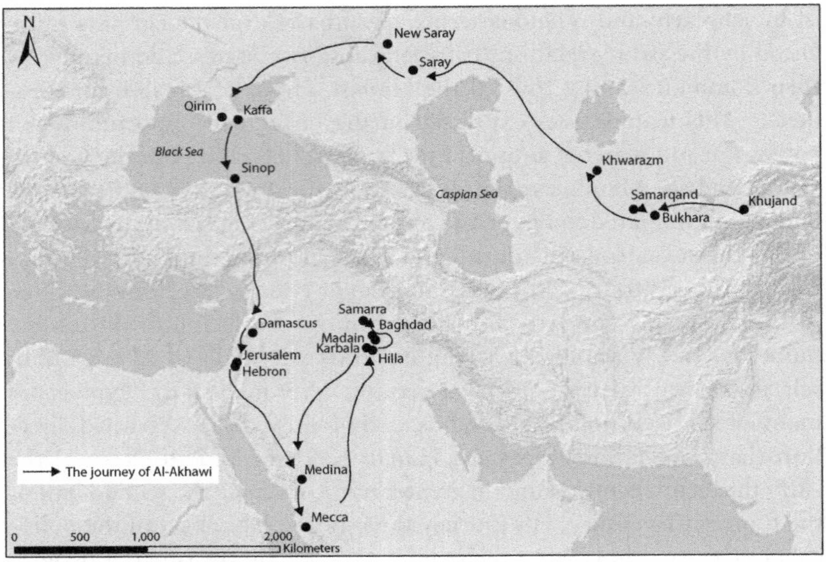

MAP 15.1. Al-Akhawī's Route.

was a respectable, albeit minor, center of Islamic learning. It was during these years that al-Akhawī's primary identity as a Ḥanafī scholar was formed, and this background would play a major role in his later journey and career.

In 1341, at the age of twenty-two, al-Akhawī left his hometown and started a journey that would last some twenty-five years, on and off, ending with his settlement in the faraway city of Medina (see map 15.1).

Al-Akhawī's journey fits the Muslim ideal of travel "in search of knowledge."[7] The notion of traveling for the sake of training and knowledge over vast geographical distances, even "as far as China," as a famous Arabic proverb states, was a common ethos for Muslim scholarly communities since the first centuries of Islam.[8] This travel "in search of knowledge" was less focused on *what* one learned, and more on *from whom* one learned. That is, the movement of students and scholars was dictated more by the search for prestigious scholarly authorities, and less so, by the search for specific teachings.

Samarqand, one of the main urban centers of Transoxania, which, like Khujand, lay in the domains of the Chaghadaid Khanate, the Mongol state in Central Asia, was the first stop in al-Akhawī's journey. The journey's original aim seems to have been to study in Samarqand with leading Ḥanafī scholars. His visit there, however, does not seem to have lasted long, and al-Sakhāwī briefly mentions only two or three teachers with whom al-Akhawī studied, and none of the books he learnt there. Al-Akhawī did, however, make pilgrimage (*ziyāra*) to some of the shrines that bore witness to Samarqand's glorious past as an important Islamic—mainly Ḥanafī—learning center.[9]

The pious visitation of tombs and holy shrines is one of the main themes in al-Akhawī's journey. Pilgrimage (*ziyāra*) was among the central expressions of piety in the Islamic later Middle Ages, and was practiced throughout the Muslim world by all classes of society. This practice was motivated by the wish to attain spiritual blessing (*baraka*) from Muslim shrines and living and deceased saints. Even if it was not the raison d'être of such voyages, *ziyāra* nonetheless became an important facet of scholarly journeys. Furthermore, shrines and pilgrimage played a major role in the popularization and dissemination of Sufism, the Muslim mystical tradition, and in the shaping of Central Asia's Islamic landscape.[10]

Returning to our voyager: from Samarqand, al-Akhawī continued to his next and first major stop, Bukhara, where he stayed for some sixteen months. While in Bukhara, al-Akhawī resided in two Muslim colleges (madrasas), the first being the Khān Madrasa—founded by the Mongol royal lady Sorqaqtani Beki (1198–1252)[11]—and the second, a madrasa located in the nearby town of Vābkent (see fig. 15.1), which hosted about eighty students.[12]

Besides their obvious role as learning institutions, madrasas as well as other institutions of learning such as Sufi hospices (*khānqāh*s, *ribāṭ*s) played a major part in accommodating visiting scholars, and thus facilitated mobility on both the regional and transregional levels. Al-Akhawī, for example, resided in such institutions also in Khwārazm, Damascus, Jerusalem, Baghdad, and Medina. Many of the institutions had special endowments dedicated for hosting visiting scholars, and some were even founded with this specific aim in mind.

Bukhara was blessed by the presence of many great scholars—both past and present[13]—and al-Akhawī took his time to exploit both worlds. He studied there with eight teachers, including the renowned Ṣadr al-Sharīʿa al-Maḥbūbī (d. 1347/8).[14] The content of his studies remained mainly Ḥanafī jurisprudence and the auxiliary sciences, but now also included theology (*kalām*).[15] In Bukhara, al-Akhawī was also able to gain access to relatively recently authored works, for example, a work on rhetoric titled *The Resumé to the Key* (*Talkhīṣ al-miftāḥ*). Its author, the Damascene scholar ʿAbd al-Raḥmān al-Qazwīnī (d. 1338), had died

FIGURE 15.1. The Minaret of Vabkent, near the madrasa where al-Akhawī studied.

less than five years before al-Akhawī studied his book in Bukhara, indicating the high rate of scientific and scholarly exchanges among Muslim intellectual communities throughout the fourteenth-century Islamic world.[16] As he had done beforehand in Samarqand, al-Akhawī did not neglect the glorious deceased scholars who had "blessed Bukhara with their presence," and visited at least six shrines assigned to local Ḥanafī and Sufi scholars.[17]

From Bukhara, al-Akhawī continued to Khwārazm (nowadays Urgench), essentially following the same route that the famous traveler Ibn Baṭṭūṭa had undertaken some twenty years earlier, albeit eastward, that is, in the opposite direction. While departing Khujand westward for Samarqand and then Bukhara seems to have been the most obvious choice of a young Central Asian scholar such as al-Akhawī in search for authoritative masters, his break northward, toward Khwārazm, had a major impact on the rest of his journey. We cannot know if al-Akhawī had any long-term plans when he left Khujand, but from Khwārazm his route would naturally take him northward, that is, the northern trade route,[18] toward Sarai, capital of the Golden Horde,[19] and so, al-Akhawī would end up bypassing Iran, whereas had he continued southwest from Bukhara, he would have reached the heart of Khurasan and its great centers of Islamic learning.

How do we explain al-Akhawī's decision to head north, to Khwārazm, rather then the more obvious, traditional, option of the southwest route to Khurasan? His choice possibly indicates the growing prestige of the teachers residing in Khwārazm, but it can also be ascribed to contemporaneous political and economic factors, namely, the safe passage and favorable conditions afforded by the northern route, which peaked under the Muslim convert Özbek Khan (r. 1313–41),[20] and the flourishing economic and intellectual life in the Golden Horde, which stood in contrast to the ongoing instability in the Chaghadaid Khanate in Central Asia at this time.[21]

Khwārazm was a central stop for al-Akhawī. He studied there for over twelve years, residing at least for part of this period in the city's Tanakiyya Madrasa. Al-Sakhāwī praises the Khwārazmian scholarly scene, which, he states, included about a thousand students and numerous scholars.[22] This short description of the city by the Egyptian al-Sakhāwī, along with the subsequent list he provides of the teachers and books al-Akhawī encountered there, is an important testimony to the city's thriving Islamic intellectual life. It is also in line with Ibn Baṭṭūṭa's enthusiastic description of Khwārazm's learning institutions, especially in comparison with his somewhat depressing impressions of Bukhara's intellectual community.[23]

Unfortunately, we have additional information only for three out of al-Akhawī's fifteen Khwārazmian teachers, and even there, we have only brief accounts. ʿAbdallāh al-Sabʿa al-Khwārazmī (d. 1359) is the sole teacher of al-Akhawī to receive his own entry in the Mamluk-Arabic biographical compendiums. He was an expert in the variant readings of the Quran (*qirāʾāt*) who traveled from Khwārazm to Damascus.[24]

This lack of detail on the Khwārazmian intellectual scene in the rich Arabic biographical collections probably says more of the prejudice of the Mamluk writers toward the Khwārazmian scholarly community, than about its actual state. For instance, al-Akhawī's main teacher in Khwārazm was the *sayyid* (a descendant of the Prophet Muḥammad)

FIGURE 15.2. Mausoleum of Najm al-Dīn Kubrā, Urgench, Uzbekistan. Photo by Sheila Blair and Jonathan Bloom.

Jalāl al-Dīn al-Kurlānī (d. 1365/6).[25] Al-Akhawī studied with him for a total of eleven years, mainly working on Ḥanafī jurisprudence but also other Islamic sciences such as Quran commentary (*tafsīr*) and hadith.[26] Al-Kurlānī was an extremely prolific scholar, and manuscripts of his works are still extant in various libraries. Yet, despite his successful career, al-Kurlānī's name is not mentioned in any of the biographical dictionaries from the Mamluk Sultanate.[27]

The curriculum to which al-Akhawī was exposed while in Khwārazm was far more diverse than his earlier training, also featuring Shāfiʿī jurisprudence and the rational sciences, including classic works by Ibn Sīnā (Avicenna, d. 1037) and Naṣīr al-Dīn al-Ṭūsī (d. 1274).[28] Nevertheless, his focus remained Ḥanafī jurisprudence, the region's specialization.[29] Of course, the stay in Khwārazm would not have been complete without the customary visits to local shrines, this time featuring two major sites situated outside the town—the tombs of the Sufi shaykh Najm al-Dīn Kubrā (d. 1220) (see fig. 15.2), and the twelfth-century Muʿtazilī scholar al-Zamakhsharī (d. 1144), both of which were also visited by Ibn Baṭṭūṭa.[30]

From Khwārazm al-Akhawī continued northwest to the city of "Sarai Berke," probably referring to Old Sarai, the former capital of the Golden Horde.[31] There seems to be a mistake in the itinerary at this point:

al-Sakhāwī writes that al-Akhawī first traveled to Sarai Berke and then continued to Aq Ṣarāy,[32] the name of a town in central Anatolia. This makes no sense, considering al-Akhawī's next stop, the town of Qirim (i.e., Solkhat in the Crimea). Furthermore, in Sarai Berke, al-Akhawī met with one scholar and visited several tombs of past "celebrities," two of whom—al-Shihāb al-Sāʾil and al-Shaykh Nuʿmān[33]—might be identified as scholars active in Özbek Khān's court, whom Ibn Baṭṭūṭa had supposedly encountered as well twenty years earlier.[34] Meanwhile, in "Aq Ṣarāy," al-Akhawī studied with two exceptional scholars: Saʿd al-Dīn al-Taftāzānī (1322–90) and Quṭb al-Dīn al-Rāzī (d. 1365), both known to have resided at this time in New Sarai, the newly founded capital of the Golden Horde, about 125 kilometers to the north of the Old Sarai.[35] Considering this along with the northerly travel route al-Akhawī was traversing and moreover, the confusion of Mamluk writers regarding the two towns,[36] it seems safe to assume that al-Akhawī, in fact, moved between the two Sarais.

Qirim was al-Akhawī's next stop. The town featured Islamic institutions, a mosque and a madrasa built during Özbek's reign,[37] and was one of the Golden Horde's developing regional centers of Islamic learning. Al-Akhawī is said to have traveled from Qirim to the nearby Black Sea port town of Kaffa, and from there to Sinope, on the southern Black Sea coast. Then he returned to Qirim, where he stayed for two more years, although this period might refer to the length of his entire stay in Crimea.

Through the nearby port of Caffa, Qirim was the main slave (*mamālīk*) market for the Mamluks in Egypt and Syria.[38] The governor of Qirim maintained close diplomatic relations with Cairo and merchants frequently traveled between the Mamluk Sultanate and Qirim. It is, therefore, not surprising that al-Akhawī should meet in Qirim a disciple of the Alexandrian Shādhilī shaykh Yāqūt al-ʿArshī (d. 1307).[39] The Shādhilī Sufi order was mainly present in Egypt and North Africa, and to a lesser extent, in Syria as well. Ibn Baṭṭūṭa, too, attests to the presence of Egyptian scholars in the Golden Horde, which was probably also due to the long-lasting diplomatic and mercantile connections between the Horde and the Mamluk Sultanate.[40]

These strong mercantile connections between Crimea and the sultanate may also explain al-Akhawī's next destination, Damascus. He probably traveled to Syria by sea, perhaps joining one of the trading ships heading south.[41] In Damascus, al-Akhawī was introduced to a whole new culture, Arabic in speech and predominantly Shāfiʿī in its juridical affiliation (*madhhab*). Yet, al-Akhawī's visit to Damascus is reported in a dry tone, surprisingly so, especially considering the fact that it was by far the grandest Islamic center he visited up to this point. He learned there from seven teachers—the most notable was the Sufi scholar Walī al-Dīn al-Manfalūṭī (d. 1372).[42] However, unlike the accounts of his earlier stops, al-Sakhāwī does not mention al-Akhawī visiting any of the shrines scattered around the metropolis.[43] This might be due to the familiarity of al-Sakhāwī and his readers with Damascus making the mention of such visitations redundant, but might also indicate that al-Akhawī's stay in the city was cut short.

From Damascus, al-Akhawī joined the hajj caravan to the Hijaz, visiting the Prophet's grave in Medina and performing the pilgrimage to Mecca. Then, he returned to Medina and thought, for the first time, of settling there. This was the beginning of his deep attachment to the city, which was destined to become his home several years later. But at this stage, al-Akhawī was advised to return to Syria (al-Shām). Joining the caravan back to Damascus, al-Akhawī made a detour to visit the holy sanctuaries of Hebron and Jerusalem once the caravan had stopped at Maʿān, in modern Jordan.

The pilgrimage routes leading to the Hijaz were another important facilitator of mobility, one which al-Akhawī and many other scholars exploited. These routes provided infrastructure for pilgrims and the pilgrimage caravan offered relative security for mobile scholars.

After a visit to Abraham's tomb in Hebron, al-Akhawī spent six weeks in Jerusalem. Here, for the first time since he left Khwārazm, we get a detailed account of the books he studied. In Jerusalem—probably already in Damascus—the emphasis on Ḥanafī jurisprudence turned to hadith-oriented studies. Al-Akhawī's main teacher in Jerusalem was the great traditionalist Khalīl b. Kaykaldī al-ʿAlāʾī (d. 1359), whose lessons he attended at al-Ṣalāḥiyya and al-Karīmiyya madrasas.[44]

From Jerusalem, al-Akhawī returned to Damascus, where he stayed at the Sumaysāṭiyya *khānqāh,* before setting out again with the hajj caravan to the Hijaz. After performing the hajj, al-Akhawī again considered settling in Medina, but was once again advised, this time through a dream-vision, to continue traveling.[45] He now made his way to Baghdad, ruled by the Jalayirid dynasty (c. 1336–1412).[46] Overall, he spent about three years there, visiting important Muslim shrines throughout Iraq and associating with the local religious scholars, mainly Ḥanafīs. He spent four months at the shrine of Abū Ḥanīfa and, later, two and a half years in the Mustanṣiriyya madrasa, Baghdad's leading college. During this period, the bulk of his studies still focused on hadith.[47]

Through al-Akhawī's stay in Baghdad, we are informed of another aspect of his religious life, his initiation into, and practice of Sufism. The combination of what might be seen as more "traditional" juridical studies with Sufism, which Vincent Cornell refers to as "juridical Sufis," was not uncommon during this period.[48] Al-Akhawī moreover appears to have been already involved with Sufi masters in Khwārazm, Qirim, Mecca, and Jerusalem.[49] However, it is only in the description of his stay in Baghdad that we get the first meaningful details of the kind of Sufism he practiced.[50]

In Baghdad, al-Akhawī was initiated into the Sufi path by Nūr al-Dīn Zādah al-Isfarāyīnī,[51] who taught him his methods of performing the Sufi *dhikr* ritual,[52] and the solitary retreat (*khalwa*). He further authorized him to initiate new novices.[53] Al-Isfarāyīnī also introduced al-Akhawī to one of his own shaykhs, Khālid al-Kurdistānī, who in turn, initiated al-Akhawī in the same rites and gave him his cap (*taqiya*). Then al-Akhawī started practicing solitary retreats during the three middle days of the lunar month (*al-ayyām al-bīḍ*), at the Shūnīziyya cemetery of Baghdad, a habit he maintained for two years.[54] Al-Akhawī next joined the hajj caravan for the third and final time, and after visiting Mecca, he arrived in Medina once again, this time for good. He settled there in 1364/5 and remained there until his death thirty-five years later.

SETTLING DOWN AND ESTABLISHING AUTHORITY

The first years that al-Akhawī spent in Medina marked the culmination of his previous education and his maturation into an authority in the religious sciences. During this period, he studied with several important shaykhs, including two of Medina's greatest contemporaneous authorities, ʿAbdallāh al-Yāfiʿī (1298–1367) and ʿAbdallāh al-Maṭarī (1299–1364). Meanwhile, al-Akhawī also established himself, at least locally, as an authority in his own right. He started to teach others and held paid positions. His arrival in Medina coincided with a reinforcement of the Ḥanafī presence in the city driven by support from the Mamluk state.[55] This was carried out notably through the creation of new teaching positions designated for Ḥanafī scholars,[56] and the installation of Ḥanafī prayer leaders (imams) and judges (qadis), both in Mecca and Medina.[57]

Al-Akhawī, too, benefited from the Mamluks' support for Ḥanafīs, attaining positions such as Ḥanafī professor of law (*mudarris*) and the first Ḥanafī imam in the Prophet's sanctuary (*al-rawḍa al-sharīfa*), a post he retained until death, passing it on to his son. This position further remained in al-Akhawī's family: his descendants, known as the Khujandī clan (*bayt al-Khujandī*), held it for about 350 years after his death.[58] Attaining a key position in Medina and retaining his Central Asian *nisba,* al-Akhawī and his successors demonstrate the prestige the older centers of Ḥanafīsm in Central Asia would continue to hold in the Arabic-speaking Middle East.

During his Medina days, al-Akhawī also authored various works in fields such as hadith, theology (*kalām*), Sufism, jurisprudence, and the panegyrics of the Prophet (*madā'iḥ nabawiyya*).[59] Unfortunately, it seems that only one of his works survived.[60] Judging from the scarcity of information on him in the Arabic biographical literature, his writings were probably not very well circulated.[61]

The Medinese period was also marked by al-Akhawī's successful efforts to put down roots and establish a family and legacy in the city. He married into the local elite and all of his children were born in Medina, thus establishing himself both socially and economically. Although he was an immigrant and probably not an outstanding religious authority, al-Akhawī managed to establish a household that held a key position in Medinese society, accumulating both cultural and material capital over many generations.[62] Al-Akhawī spent his lifetime acquiring cultural capital,[63] which was then translated into creating an enduring elite household in a new locality, thousands of miles away from his hometown. This capital was acquired first through travel in search of knowledge, and no less importantly, in search of authority—manifested in the accumulation of licenses to teach (*ijāzāt*) and Sufi initiations (*khirqa; taqiya*). This was followed by more "mundane" maneuvers such as marrying into families distinguished for their scholarship, if not also for their financial wealth.[64]

AL-AKHAWĪ AS A SUFI SCHOLAR

Recent scholarship has made it clear that we should resist the traditional dichotomy between Sufi and *faqīh* (jurisprudent).[65] Throughout his travels, in different intellectual and cultural climates (Persianate/Arabic, Ḥanafī/Shāfiʿī, etc.), al-Akhawī moved through overlapping circles that more often than not combined moderate Sufism with traditional learning. Like many of his contemporaries, al-Akhawī did not adhere to a specific Sufi order (*ṭarīqa*), but participated in networks of "shariʿa-minded" Sufis who emphasized strict adherence to the prescriptions of the Sacred Law and to the ideal of "knowledge before action."[66] Several of the main Sufi networks in this period, including the Kubrawiyya, Suhrawardiyya, Shādhiliyya and Qādiriyya, and their shaykhs complied with these lines.[67] Being initiated into the Kubrawiyya path in Baghdad and having studied with shaykhs related to the other networks, al-Akhawī appears to have also been an advocate of "shariʿa-minded" Sufism.

Furthermore, in his early years in Medina, al-Akhawī associated with two of the city's leading scholars, who both exemplified the scholar-Sufi ideal of his time. Al-Yāfiʿī and al-Maṭarī were great authorities in both the traditional Islamic sciences and the path to spiritual perfection (i.e., Sufism). They represented what Aaron Spevack has recently termed "the Archetypal Sunni Scholar," who embodies mastery in Islamic law, theology, and mysticism.[68] The two masters exemplify, therefore, al-Akhawī's scholarly and religious milieu and persona.

Al-Akhawī first encountered al-Maṭarī in his penultimate (second) visit to Medina in 1362/3. He studied with him the *Ṣaḥīḥ Muslim*—a classical collection of hadiths—and also received from him a Sufi cloak (*khirqa*).[69] But al-Maṭarī passed away just prior to al-Akhawī's final return to Medina, and therefore, al-Yāfiʿī probably had a greater influence on the latter.

ʿAbdallāh al-Yāfiʿī was a prolific scholar, and embodied the scholar-Sufi ideal.[70] Born and raised in Yemen, he spent the last decades of his life in Mecca, acquiring great prestige as an authority in hadith, *fiqh*, and Sufism. A lengthy anecdote in al-Akhawī's biography speaks to his special teacher-student or master-disciple relationship with al-Yāfiʿī and the cultivation of al-Akhawī's own persona as scholar-Sufi. Upon his arrival for settlement in Medina, al-Akhawī approached the old shaykh and asked to study with him. Al-Yāfiʿī requested him, however, to patiently wait until the right time, and when that came, he ordered al-Akhawī to gather the six canonical collections of hadith, along with the other works he wanted to study, and head to the Prophet's sanctuary, where the two read the works together.

Al-Akhawī then received from al-Yāfiʿī the license (*ijāza*) to teach the works in a series of sessions (*majālis*) in the Prophet's sanctuary that were attended by the religious scholars of the city. The list of titles that al-Akhawī chose to read in the sessions also speaks to his scholarly identity: besides the Six Books and al-Yāfiʿī's own works, it names seventeen other titles, encompassing classic works of Islamic thought in fields such as Sufism and jurisprudence.[71] This fusion of hadith, jurisprudence, and Sufism in a series of scholarly sessions in one of the holiest Muslim sanctuaries emerges as the climax of al-Akhawī's education and his twenty-five-year journey in search of knowledge. It is, furthermore, a telling moment for the ongoing and gradual integration of Sufi practice and culture into mainstream Sunni Islam.

To what extent, however, is this biographical portrayal of al-Akhawī a true representation of his religious and scholarly learnings? Or rather, is it the product of its medium, the literary corpus, in which it is conveyed? Let us compare the representation of another contemporary Sufi-scholar, Jalāl al-Dīn al-Bukhārī (d. 1384), who shared much of al-Akhawī's scholarly background. A native of present-day Pakistan, al-Bukhārī, like al-Akhawī, was a Ḥanafī *faqīh,* but is nevertheless largely renowned as a Sufi shaykh. Residing for several years during the 1340s in the Hijaz, he learned with some of the same teachers as al-Akhawī, especially his two Medinese teachers, al-Maṭarī and al-Yāfiʿī. Al-Bukhārī, furthermore, studied roughly the same works with them, and was also blessed by them with Sufi cloaks. In her study of al-Bukhārī's life and career, Amina Steinfels notes that, in blurring the boundaries between a Sufi shaykh and a scholar (*ʿālim*), al-Bukhārī resembles more the Sufis and scholars with whom he associated in the Hijaz, than his Persian-writing Sufi masters in the Indian subcontinent.[72]

Thus, while al-Bukhārī is depicted in later accounts largely as a Sufi shaykh, a close reading of his oeuvre reveals the image of an *ʿālim,* a scholar of the more traditional ilk. Al-Akhawī, on the other hand, is indeed portrayed as such a *faqīh,* a more traditional scholar, although his Sufi training dominated throughout his life, career, and writings. As is the case with al-Bukhārī, al-Akhawī's image is shaped by the sources at our disposal. Whereas the accounts on al-Bukhārī composed in Persian at the Indian subcontinent place a greater emphasis on the Sufi and hagiographic aspects of his life, the Arabic Middle Eastern biographical literature treated Akhawī's career in a far more hadith/*fiqh*-oriented manner.[73]

However, can al-Akhawī's writings and his collection of *khirqa*s, *ijāzāt,* and so on, tell us something about his personal inclinations not covered by his historical representation?[74] While only one of his works is still extant,[75] the inventory of his works, available in al-Sakhāwī's biography and reproduced in later bibliographical collections, provides a general idea of his scholarly interests. The titles indicate that he authored a range of works on hadith, *fiqh, kalām,* Sufism, and the life and panegyrics of the Prophet. Seemingly full of contradictions, the list is very diverse, showing the fluidity of Islamic learning at the time.[76] It presents a scholar whose persona combined a Ḥanafī background, Shāfiʿī education, hadith expertise, and Sufi tendencies.

Like the Central Asian émigré al-Akhawī, al-Bukhārī, who came from the Indian subcontinent, al-Yāfiʿī with whom al-Akhawī and al-Bukhārī both studied in the Hijaz, and al-Isfarāyīnī,[77] with whom al-Akhawī studied in Baghdad, all shared similar ideas about the relationship between Sufism and *fiqh*. These Sufi-scholars formed a broader network of mainstream Sunni-Muslim scholars that was characterized by its widespread mobility and dispersal across Eurasia.[78]

POST-MORTEM: AL-AKHAWĪ'S LEGACY, THE FAMILY AND THE HISTORIOGRAPHICAL PROCESS

Al-Akhawī's legacy was mainly posthumously shaped through his family's hagiographic enterprise. The family's efforts came to fruition in the generous biographical entry that al-Sakhāwī devoted to al-Akhawī. In other contemporaneous and later biographical collections, however, we find meager details about al-Akhawī. He is mentioned only very briefly by his contemporaries Ibn Ḥajar and al-Fāsī,[79] and moreover, not at all by Ibn Taghrī Birdī. The three wrote extensive biographical dictionaries of Muslim notables during the fifteenth century. The sixteenth-century Damascene historian Ibn Ṭūlūn mentions him in his biographical dictionary devoted to Ḥanafī scholars, even adding some minor details to al-Sakhāwī's biography.[80] However, later authors such as the seventeenth-century al-Ghazzī and Ibn al-ʿImād had entirely relied on Ibn Ḥajar's brief entry, while ignoring al-Sakhāwī's.[81] Succinct and generic, these notices bear no sign of al-Akhawī's extensive journey or his Sufi background, portraying him merely as another, seemingly average, scholar from the holy city of Medina.

How and why, then, did the Egyptian biographer al-Sakhāwī come to devote an extensive biography to the Central Asian scholar? A simple explanation can be found in al-Sakhāwī's personal ties to al-Akhawī's offspring. Al-Sakhāwī, who completed his work about a hundred years after al-Akhawī's death, included several biographies of the latter's descendants as well. Moreover, al-Sakhāwī himself was a teacher to two of al-Akhawī's great-grandsons and two great-great-grandsons, all four of whom received dedicated notices in his biographical compendium.[82] Furthermore, he indicates that he received his information regarding al-Akhawī from the latter's descendants, perhaps even in the form of a written document that preserved their ancestor's biography.[83]

Yet, why would the great-grandsons and great-great-grandsons of the Central Asian migrant-scholar go to the effort to include their ancestor's biography and moreover, his journey in search of teachers, in a biographical dictionary? This brings us to consider the social function of the genre of Arabic biographical dictionaries such as al-Sakhāwī's. Drawing on Michael Chamberlain's groundbreaking study, Konrad Hirschler suggests viewing such biographical dictionaries as fulfilling the same functions that documentary sources carried out in European societies during the same time period, that is, to record, present, and narrate what was considered worthy of remembrance, with the intention of securing the future of a certain individual or group.[84] These functions are especially evident when authors recorded the biographies of their own ancestors and teachers, but also in biographical entries of individuals that were based on what their descendants deemed worthy of remembrance.

Several anecdotes in al-Akhawī's biography give the reader the impression that al-Akhawī had a metaphysical connection to the Prophet's persona and final resting place (see fig. 15.3). Thus, al-Akhawī is led to Medina after being instructed to do so throughout his journey in mysterious ways, including in a vision of the Prophet himself. Al-Akhawī's appointment as the Ḥanafī imam in the Prophet's sanctuary, a position that would be firmly held by his descendants, is accompanied in the biography by several accounts where the Prophet appears in visions and declares his satisfaction with the scholar. Finally, the works that al-Akhawī is mentioned to have studied in Medina, and some of the works he is claimed to have authored there, include the genre of panegyrics to the Prophet. Indeed, a later biographical collection, an eighteenth-century work on notable Medinese clans that also relied on al-Sakhāwī's biography of al-Akhawī, highlights exactly the same passages in al-Sakhāwī's work that stress his metaphysical connection to the Prophet. Al-Sakhāwī's biography of al-Akhawī was "harvested" by the eighteenth-century author to further reinforce the family's Medinese status. Anecdotes about an individual's special linkage to the Prophet via dreams, visions, or genealogy are not uncommon in biographical collections. However, al-Sakhāwī's biographical notice on al-Akhawī, as well as its later adaptations, appear to be particularly geared toward supporting al-Akhawī's appointment as Ḥanafī imam of the Prophet's sanctuary, and moreover, the appointment of his descendants over the next three and a half centuries.

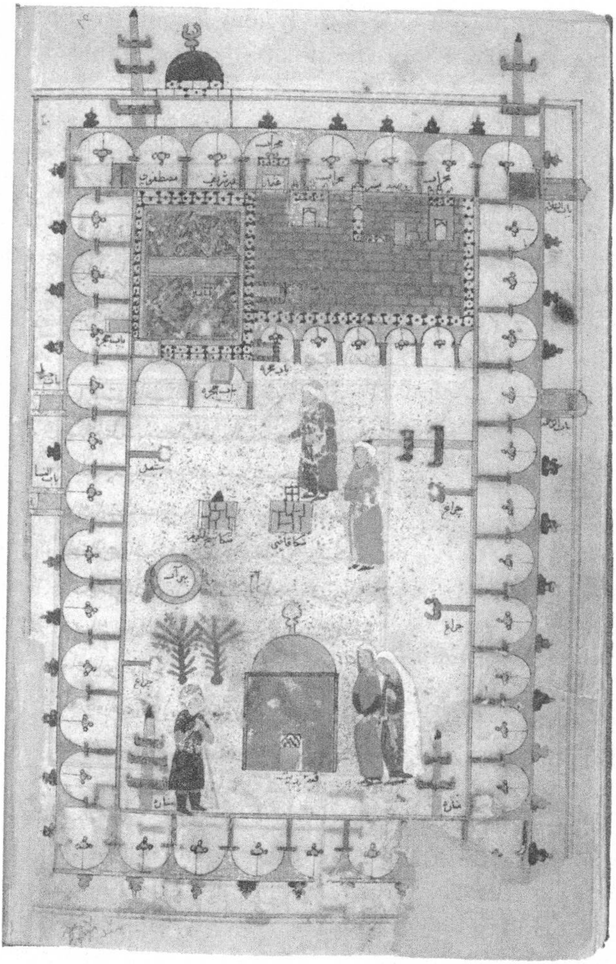

FIGURE 15.3. Illustration of the Prophet's grave and mosque in Medina, from the mid-sixteenth-century copy of Muḥyī al-Dīn Lārī's pilgrimage guidebook, Description of the Holy Cities (*Futūḥ al-ḥaramayn*), MS 32.131, fo. 41v, the Metropolitan Museum of Art (Rogers Fund, 1932).

CONCLUSIONS: AL-AKHAWĪ AND THE EURASIAN NETWORK OF SUNNI SCHOLARS

Jalāl al-Dīn al-Akhawī's twenty-five-year long journey from Khujand to Medina left little impression on his contemporaries. Travel in search of knowledge was a common practice for Muslim scholars, and while al-Akhawī's might have been relatively longer and lengthier, his journey, nevertheless, did not draw the attention of the Arabic authors, save al-Sakhāwī.

However, for modern-day historians, al-Akhawī's biography is a rare source, mainly due to the relatively detailed account of his journey and studies in the Chaghadaid Khanate and the Golden Horde. It offers a glimpse into the intellectual milieu of the fourteenth-century Mongol-Muslim world. It testifies to the flourishing, yet little documented, Islamic learning scene of Khwārazm, just over a hundred years after its conquest and devastation by the Mongols, and to the ongoing importance of recent and ancient shrines in the itineraries of pious Muslims. In the absence of meaningful local narratives, these scattered references offer us the best opportunity for reconstructing a picture of Islamic learning in the Chaghadaid Khanate and the Golden Horde.

Al-Akhawī's "travelogue" should be considered, then, alongside sources such as Ibn Baṭṭūṭa's diary or the earlier account of Jamāl Qarshī (d. ca. 1301). These all point to the continuation of Islamic culture and learning after the Mongol conquest,[85] but also to the emergence of new prospering Muslim centers along the northern trade routes, in the territories of the Golden Horde.[86] Furthermore, an analysis of the list of authorities from whom al-Akhawī learned, along with the relatively detailed list of titles he studied, sheds light on the otherwise elusive subject of what the curriculum of Islamic learning was in certain periods and regions.[87] Al-Akhawī's long journey reveals, for one, the specializations of different regions in the Muslim world. For example, we can identify along with al-Akhawī's advance further southwest, toward the Arabic-speaking centers of learning, a gradual shift in his studies and interests from Ḥanafī law to hadith.

Al-Akhawī's biography also attests to the role of the trade routes in facilitating the mobility of scholars and the dissemination of Islamic learning across Eurasia. Al-Akhawī traveled along an important trade route—the product of the specific political climate of his time—linking Samarkand and Bukhara to Khwārazm, Sarai, and the Crimea, and continuing from there along the maritime routes to Egypt, Syria, and Mecca and Medina. Al-Akhawī encountered along his path caravansaries and post stations, but also learning institutions which hosted visiting scholars. It was considered the duty of the pious Muslim ruler—and certainly some Mongol khans such as Özbek wished to be portrayed as such—to facilitate the mobility of scholars and promote Muslim scholarship in their lands.[88]

Finally, al-Akhawī's journey was facilitated by the "Ḥanafī Moment," when the majority of the Muslim world—from Egypt in the southwest to Tranoxiana in the northeast and the Crimea in the north—was ruled by Turkish-Mongol dynasties that particularly supported scholars of the Ḥanafī School of Law. This climate offered Ḥanafī scholars more patronage opportunities than ever before and surely encouraged their mobility across Eurasia. This was especially relevant for scholars from Transoxania such as al-Akhawī, who, after receiving their initial training in Ḥanafī law, might have had extra motivation to move away from the volatile political situation prevailing in the Chaghadaid Khanate to the prospering centers in the Golden Horde and the Middle East, which were also abundant in patronage opportunities. As Carl F. Petry remarked, those scholars, traveling between the far-flung regions of the Muslim world, provide the most concrete evidence for the kind of contacts that unified the Abode of Islam in the Middle Ages.[89]

NOTES

This research has received funding from the European Research Council under the European Union's Seventh Framework Programme (FP/2007–13) / ERC grant Agreement n. 312397. This paper was mostly written when I stayed at the University of Bonn. I thank Judith Pfeiffer, Giovanni Maria Martini, and Walter Edward Young for their hospitality and insights; Undine Ott for inviting me to present an early draft at the University of Göttingen; and Reuven Amitai and Hermann Landolt for their valuable comments.

1. The Ḥanafī school of Muslim jurisprudence, one of the four principle schools of Sunni Islam, was especially widespread in Central Asia and among Turkish-speaking populations.

2. Al-Sakhāwī dedicated a biographical entry to al-Akhawī in two of his biographical compendiums. The two are nearly identical. The first appears in his monumental dictionary of notable Muslims who lived in the ninth *hijri* century (roughly corresponding to the fifteenth century C.E.), and the second in a collection dedicated to scholars from Medina. Al-Sakhāwī 1934, 2: 194–201; al-Sakhāwī 1993, 1: 147–53.

3. The adjective of relation (*nisba*) al-Akhawī (literaly, fraternal or brotherly) was given to him since one of his ancestors had married his half-sister (from his mother's side). Al-Sakhāwī 1934, 2: 194.

4. Bosworth 1986, 45.

5. Al-Sakhāwī 1934, 2: 197, 201.

6. Al-Sakhāwī 1934, 2: 195.

7. This journey is narrated in al-Akhawī's biographical entry as one long sequence, which suggests a continuous journey, even though he spent years in some of the stations en route. Despite the occasional descriptive impression, it is not a diary or travelogue.

8. Touati 2010.

9. Those were the popular mausoleum of Qutham b. al-ʿAbbās (d. 677), a companion and relative of the Prophet (also visited by Ibn Baṭṭūṭa, see: Ibn Baṭṭūṭa 1971, 3: 568); and "the scholars and shaykhs buried at the Jākardīza cemetery" in Samarqand, notably four outstanding Ḥanafī scholars: Abū Manṣūr al-Māturīdī (d. 940s), Fakhr al-Islām al-Bazdawī (d. 1089), Abu Ḥafṣ ʿUmar al-Nasafī (d. 1142), and Burhān al-Dīn al-Marghīnānī (d. 1197).

10. On this phenomenon see: Taylor 1999.

11. Juwaynī 1997, 108–9.

12. Vābkent featured a grand mosque, erected in 1198/9, known mainly for its splendid minaret, which still stands. I found no other evidence for the presence of a madrasa there. See: O'Kane 1994.

13. Subtelny 2001; Biran 2015.

14. On him: Muʿīn al-Fuqarāʾ 1960, 23–25.

15. Al-Sakhāwī 1934, 2: 195.

16. Al-Musawi 2015.

17. Those are the shrines of Abū Ḥafṣ al-Kabīr (ninth century), Abū Bakr al-Kalābādhī (d. 990), Shams al-Aʾimma al-Ḥalwānī (d. 1056), Shams al-Aʾimma al-Kardarī (d. 1240), Ḥāfiẓ al-Dīn al-Kabīr (d. 1294), Sayf al-Dīn al-Bākharzī (d. 1261), as well as "the others worthy of visitation." Al-Sakhāwī 1934, 2: 195–96.

18. On this route, connecting Khwārazm to Sarai and Kaffa: Ciocîltan 2012, 96–114.

19. On the close ties between Khwārazm and Sarai: Bosworth 1978, 1064.

20. Ciocîltan 2012, 111–14.

21. Biran 2009, 54–60.

22. Al-Sakhāwī 1934, 2: 196.

23. Ibn Baṭṭūṭa 1971, 2: 541–44, 550–51.

24. Ibn al-Jazarī 1932, 1: 465. Al-Khwārazmī's biographical notice appears only in a compendium specifically devoted to experts in the field of variant Quran readings.

25. DeWeese 2012, 221–22.

26. Al-Sakhāwī 1934, 2: 196.

27. He is mentioned in a sixteenth-century biographical dictionary of Ḥanafī scholars. Al-Kafawī 2017, 3: 469–72.

28. Al-Sakhāwī 1934, 2: 196–97. Ibn Sīnā (in the West, known as Avicenna) and Ṭūsī were two of the major polymaths of the premodern Muslim world. Ibn Sīnā was famous mainly for his medical works and Ṭūsī for his astronomical compilations. See also Isahaya's article in this volume.

29. Ahmed 2000, 42.

30. Ibn Baṭṭūṭa 1971, 3: 542–43.

31. Allsen 1997, 41–42.

32. Al-Sakhāwī 1934, 2: 197.

33. Al-Sakhāwī 1934, 2: 197.

34. Ibn Baṭṭūṭa mentions a judge named Shihāb al-Dīn al-Sāʾilī (Ibn Baṭṭūṭa 1971, 2: 493). Regarding the shaykh Nuʿmān, who might be identified as Nuʿmān al-Khwārazmī, see DeWeese 1994b, 125–30.

35. Madelung 2000, 88; Ibn ʿArabshāh 1817, 116.
36. Allsen 1997, 42.
37. Spuler 1986, 136; Kramarovsky 2008, 74–75.
38. Amitai 2008; Ciocîltan 2012, 89–95.
39. Al-Sakhāwī 1934, 2: 197.
40. Ibn Baṭṭūṭa 1971, 2: 516; al-Dhahabī 1987–2004, 57: 191.
41. On this sea route: Ciocîltan 2012, 89–95.
42. Ibn Ḥajar 1966, 3: 306–7.
43. Al-Sakhāwī 1934, 2: 197.
44. Al-Sakhāwī 1934, 2: 197.
45. Al-Sakhāwī 1934, 2: 198.
46. Wing 2016, 107–10.
47. Al-Sakhāwī 1934, 2: 198.
48. Cornell 1998, 67.
49. In Khwārazm, he was given a cap (*taqiya*) by his teacher ʿAlāʾ al-Din al-Sighnāqī, which might be a Sufi initiation; and while nothing is said about this, his aforementioned teacher there, al-Kurlānī, is associated in later genealogies with Sufi lineages (DeWeese 2012, 221–22). In Mecca, he met with a certain Ḥaydar, who is described as "one of the Sufis," and who might have been a disciple of al-Isfarāyīnī (Landolt 1972, 8); in Jerusalem he studied with Jalāl al-Dīn al-Bisṭāmī, perhaps from the local Bisṭāmiyya Sufi sect.
50. Since we have only one source to rely on for al-Akhawī's life and career, it might be misleading to interpret his focus on Sufi practice in Baghdad as marking a shift in his interests. Possibly, in Baghdad, he associated with a more authoritative shaykh, or at least, one who was deemed more significant for readers from the Mamluk Sultanate, and therefore, we are only given information on al-Akhawī's Sufi affiliation at this later point in his biography.
51. He is probably Nūr al-Dīn ʿAbd al-Raḥmān al-Thānī (the second) who directed his grandfather's *khānqāh*. Al-Isfarāyinī 1986, 30–31, 93, notes 72–73. He was the grandson of the great Kubrawī shaykh ʿAbd al-Raḥmān (d. 1317). Landolt 1972, 7–9.
52. The *dhikr* (lit. to remind oneself) is a ritual which consists of tireless repetition of the names of God, or another litany, and which became one of the central features of Sufi devotion. Different Sufi masters or orders formed their own versions of this ritual, one being ʿAbd al-Raḥmān al-Isfarāyīnī, the grandfather of the shaykh Nūr al-Dīn, who evidently taught al-Akhawī that same version.
53. While we have no concrete information about earlier association with Kubrawī shaykhs, al-Akhawī came from the area where this tradition emerged and was still clearly present during the fourteenth century. DeWeese 1994b.
54. Al-Sakhāwī 1934, 2: 198. ʿAbd al-Raḥmān al-Isfarāyīnī and his renowned disciple ʿAlāʾ al-Dawla al-Simnānī also performed solitary retreats at this celebrated location, where the great early Sufi masters al-Junayd (d. 910) and Sarī al-Saqaṭī (d. 865) performed their devotions. Landolt 1972, 8, 18; Martini 2018, 60.
55. The Mamluks exerted partial sovereignty over Mecca and Medina, through the brokerage of the local *ashrāf*: Meloy 2015, 11–38.

56. Al-Fāsī 1998, 2: 399; al-Maqrīzī 2002, 3: 168.
57. Al-Sakhāwī 1993, 1: 32; Ibn Ḥajar 1966, 3: 217.
58. Al-Anṣārī 1970, 208.
59. Al-Sakhāwī 1934, 2: 200; al-Baghdādī 1951, 1: 117–18.
60. This is a commentary on *al-Burda* ("The Mantle"), extent in a single manuscript at Topkapi Saray in Istanbul (al-Ziriklī 1980, 1: 226). *Al-Burda* is a celebrated Arabic poem in praise of the Prophet, composed by the Egyptian poet al-Buṣīrī (d. 1294–97). Basset 1986.
61. The only reference to his works I was able to trace comes from a work on the virtues of the third caliph ʿAlī, written in the fifteenth century. Al-Ījī 2007, 212.
62. Al-Anṣārī 1970, 207–8.
63. Chamberlain 1994, 21–25.
64. Al-Sakhāwī 1993, 1: 140, 2: 117; al-Sakhāwī 1934, 2: 199.
65. Steinfels 2012, 75–77.
66. According to this ideal, a novice aspiring to spiritual perfection first attains religious knowledge (i.e., of the Quran, hadith, etc.) as the basis for his spiritual or mystical journey. Steinfels 2012, 66–80.
67. See, e.g., Martini 2018, 74–80.
68. Spevack 2014.
69. Al-Fāsī 1990, 1: 400; al-Sakhāwī 1934, 2: 199; al-Sakhāwī 1993, 1: 152.
70. Geoffroy 2002, 236; Pouzet 1991, 233.
71. It included works by such scholars as al-Ghazālī, al-Nawawī, al-Tirmidhī, and al-Qushayrī, as well as al-Suhrawardī's *ʿAwārif al-maʿārif,* one of the most influential and widely-circulated Sufi manuals at the time. Al-Sakhāwī 1993, 1: 151–52.
72. Steinfels 2012, 36.
73. Steinfels 2012, 44.
74. At the same time we often get different images of the very same individual, intended for different audiences and functions. Ohlander 2008, 136–38; Paul 2008, 309–10.
75. See note 61 above.
76. Al-Sakhāwī 1934, 2: 200. It incorporates esoteric topics, such as the Names of God (*asmāʾ allāh*), alongside a collection of traditions on *jihād* (holy war); a commentary on Ibn al-Fāriḍ's highly controversial wine ode, next to a commentary on al-Nawawī's "traditional" *Forty Hadiths;* and a gloss (*ḥāshiya*) on the famous Quran commentary *al-Kashshāf,* in which al-Akhawī "showed Muʿtazilī inclinations," despite learning this work from—among others—a supposedly fiercely anti-Muʿtazilī shaykh (al-Yāfiʿī). Geoffroy 2002, 236. On the wine ode, see Homerin 2005, introduction.
77. For al-Isfarāyīnī teaching *Ṣaḥīḥ al-Bukhārī,* see al-Sakhāwī 1934, 3: 109.
78. Steinfels 2012, 56.
79. Ibn Ḥajar 1992, 83–84; al-Fāsī 1990, 1: 400.
80. Ibn Ṭūlūn 1924, 61–62.
81. Even though al-Ghazzī at least was well aware of the position al-Akhawī's descendants kept in Medina. Al-Ghazzī 1983–89, 2: 87; Ibn al-ʿImād 1986, 9: 30.

82. Al-Sakhāwī 1993, 1: 83, 2: 415–17, 2: 430–31.

83. In a biography devoted to one of al-Akhawī's teachers, al-Sakhāwī writes in passing (1993, 2: 86) that, "I saw in the biography of al-Jalāl Aḥmad b. Muḥammad b. al-Khujandī, as narrated by his sons." Furthermore, in the entry devoted to al-Akhawī's son Ṭāhir, al-Sakhāwī notes that he saw the latter's date of birth written in his father's handwriting: al-Sakhāwī 1934, 4: 2. Al-Akhawī might have written the document down on his own, or it was written by one of them. Reynolds 2001, 59–68.

84. Hirschler 2013, 175.

85. Biran 2009, 63–66.

86. DeWeese 2009, 133.

87. Al-Akhawī's list can be analyzed alongside documents such as *ijāzāt* (licenses to transmit a work) or *mashyakha*s (list of teachers) of other Muslim scholars: Ahmed 2000, 42; Subtelny and Khalidov 1995, 214–15, 224. On Islamic curriculum: Makdisi 1981, 80–91.

88. Petry 1985, 73.

89. Petry 1985, 73.

BIBLIOGRAPHY

Ahmed, Shahab. 2000. "Mapping the World of a Scholar in Sixth/Twelth Century Bukhāra: Regional Tradition in Medieval Islamic Scholarship as Reflected in a Bibliography." *Journal of the American Oriental Society* 120: 24–43.

Allsen, Thomas T. 1997. S.v. "Saray." *Encyclopaedia of Islam*. 2nd ed. Ed. P. Bearman et al. 9: 40–45. Leiden: Brill.

Amitai, Reuven. 2008. "Diplomacy and the Slave Trade in the Eastern Mediterranean: A Re-Examination of the Mamluk-Byzantine-Genoese Triangle in the Late Thirteenth Century in Light of the Existing Early Correspondence." *Oriente moderno* 88: 349–68.

al-Anṣārī, ʿAbd al-Raḥmān. 1970. *Tuḥfat al-muḥibbīn wa'l-aṣḥāb fī maʿrifat mā lil-madaniyyīn min al-ansāb*. Ed. Muḥammad al-ʿArūsī al-Maṭwī. Tunis: Al-Maktaba al-ʿatīqa.

al-Baghdādī, Ismāʿīl Bāshā b. Muḥammad. 1951. *Hadiyyat al-ʿārifīn: Asmāʾ al-muʾallifīn wa-āthār al-muṣannifīn*. 2 vols. Istanbul: Milli Egitim basimevi.

Basset, René. 1986. S.v. "Burda." *Encyclopaedia of Islam*. 2nd ed. Ed. P. Bearman et al. 1: 1314–15. Leiden: Brill.

Biran, Michal. 2002. "The Chaghadaids and Islam: The Conversion of Tarmashirin Khan (1331–34). *Journal of the American Oriental Society* 122: 742–52.

———. 2009. "The Mongols in Central Asia from Chinggis Khan's Invasion to the Rise of Temür: The Ögödeied and Chaghadaid Realms." In *The Cambridge History of Inner Asia: The Chinggisid Age*, ed. Nicola Di Cosmo, Allen J. Frank, and Peter B. Golden, 46–66. Cambridge: Cambridge University Press.

———. 2015. "The Mental Maps of Mongol Central Asia as Seen from the Mamluk Sultanate." *Journal of Asian History* 49: 31–51.

Bosworth, Clifford E. 1978. S.v. "Khwārazm." *Encyclopaedia of Islam.* 2nd ed. Ed. P. Bearman et al. 4: 1060–65. Leiden: Brill.

———. 1986. S.v. "Khudjand(a)." *Encyclopaedia of Islam.* 2nd ed. Ed. P. Bearman et al. 5: 45–46. Leiden: Brill.

Chamberlain, Michael. 1994. *Knowledge and Social Practice in Medieval Damascus, 1190–1350.* Cambridge: Cambridge University Press.

Ciocîltan, Virgil. 2012. *The Mongols and the Black Sea Trade in the Thirteenth and Fourteenth Centuries.* Tr. Samuel Willcocks. Leiden: Brill.

Cornell, Vincent J. 1998. *Realm of the Saint: Power and Authority in Moroccan Sufism.* Austin: University of Texas Press.

DeWeese, Devin A. 1994a. "Bābā Kamāl Jandī and the Kubravī Tradition among the Turks of Central Asia." *Der Islam* 71: 58–94.

———. 1994b. *Islamization and Native Religion in the Golden Horde: Baba Tükles and Conversion to Islam in Historical and Epic Tradition.* University Park: Pennsylvania State University Press.

———. 2009. "Islamization in the Mongol Empire." In *The Cambridge History of Inner Asia: The Chinggisid Age,* ed. Nicola Di Cosmo, Allen J. Frank, and Peter B. Golden, 120–34. Cambridge: Cambridge University Press.

———. 2012. "Sacred Descent and Sufi Legitimation in a Genealogical Text from Eighteenth-Century Central Asia: The Sharaf Atā'ī Tradition in Khwārazm." In *Sayyids and Sharifs in Muslim Societies: The Living Links to the Prophet,* ed. Morimoto Kazuo, 210–30. London: Routledge.

al-Dhahabī, Muḥammad b. Aḥmad. 1987–2004. *Ta'rīkh al-islām wa-wafayāt al-mashāhīr wa'l-a'yān.* Ed. 'Umar 'Abd al-Salām al-Tadmurī. 61 vols. Beirut: Dār al-kitāb al-'arabī.

al-Fāsī, Taqī al-Dīn Muḥammad b. Aḥmad. 1990. *Dhayl al-taqyīd fī ruwāt al-sunan wa'l-asānīd.* Ed. Kamāl Yūsuf al-Ḥūt. 2 vols. Beirut: Dār al-kutub al-'ilmiyya.

———. 1998. *Al-'Iqd al-thamīn fī ta'rīkh al-balad al-amīn.* Ed. Muḥammad 'Abd al-Qādir Aḥmad 'Aṭā. 7 vols. Beirut: Dār al-kutub al-'ilmiyya.

Geoffroy, Eric. 2002. S.v. "Yāfi'ī." *Encyclopaedia of Islam.* 2nd ed. Ed. P. Bearman et al. 11: 236. Leiden: Brill.

al-Ghazzī, Taqī al-Dīn b. 'Abd al-Qādir. 1983–89. *Al-Ṭabaqāt al-saniyya fī tarājim al-Ḥanafiyya.* Ed. 'Abd al-Fattāḥ Muḥammad al-Ḥilū. 4 vols. Riyadh, Saudi Arabia: Dār al-Rifā'ī.

Hirschler, Konrad. 2013. "Studying Mamluk Historiography. From Source-Criticism to the Cultural Turn." In *Ubi sumus? Quo vademus? Mamluk Studies—State of the Art,* ed. Stephan Conermann, 159–86. Göttingen: V&R Unipress; Bonn University Press.

Homerin, Th. Emil. 2005. *The Wine of Love and Life: Ibn al-Fāriḍ's* al-Khamrīyah *and al-Qayṣarī's Quest for Meaning.* Chicago: Middle East Documentation Center.

Ibn 'Arabshāh, Aḥmad b. Muḥammad. 1817. *'Ajā'ib al-maqdūr fī akhbār Tīmūr.* Kolkata: Dār al-'imāra.

———. 1986. *'Ajā'ib al-maqdūr fī akhbār Tīmūr.* Ed. Aḥmad Fā'z al-Ḥimṣī. Beirut: Mu'assasat al-risāla.

Ibn Baṭṭūṭa, Muḥammad b. ʿAbdallāh. 1958–2000. *The Travels of Ibn Baṭṭūṭa A.D. 1325–1354*. Tr. H. A. R. Gibb and Charles Buckingham. 5 vols. Cambridge: Hakluyt Society.

Ibn Ḥajar al-ʿAsqalānī, Aḥmad b. ʿAlī. 1966. *Al-Durar al-kāmina fī aʿyān al-miʾa al-thāmina*. Ed. Muḥammad Sayyid Jād al-Ḥaqq. 5 vols. Cairo: Dār al-kutub al-ḥadītha.

———. 1992. *Dhayl al-Durar al-kāmina*. Ed. ʿAdnān Darwīsh. Cairo: Maʿhad al-makhṭūṭāt al-ʿarabiyya.

Ibn al-ʿImād, ʿAbd al-Ḥayy b. Aḥmad. 1986. *Shadharāt al-dhahab fī akhbār man dhahab*. Ed. Maḥmūd al-Arnāʾūṭ. 11 vols. Damascus: Dār Ibn Kathīr.

Ibn al-Jazarī, Muḥammad b. Muḥammad. 1932. *Ghāyat al-nihāya fī ṭabaqāt al-qurrāʾ*. Ed. G. Bergstraesser. 3 vols. Cairo: Maktabat al-Khānjī.

Ibn Ṭūlūn, Muḥammad b. ʿAlī. 1924. *Al-Ghuraf al-ʿaliyya fī tarājim muta'akhkhirī al-ḥanafiyya*. Süleymaniye Library MS Şehid Paşa.

al-Ījī, Shihāb al-Dīn Aḥmad. 2007. *Faḍāʾil al-thaqalayn min kitāb tawḍīḥ al-dalāʾil 'alā tarjīḥ al-faḍāʾil*. Ed. Ḥusayn al-Ḥasanī al-Bīrjandī. Teheran: Al-Majmaʿ al-ʿālamī lil-taqrīb bayn al-madhāhib al-islāmiyya.

al-Isfarāyinī, ʿAbd al-Raḥmān. 1986. *Le Révélateur des mystères*. Tr. Hermann Landolt. Lagrasse, France: Verdier.

Juwaynī, ʿAlāʾ al-Dīn ʿAṭāʾ Malik. 1997. *The History of the World-Conquerer*. Tr. John A. Boyle. 2nd ed. Manchester: Manchester University.

al-Kafawī, Maḥmūd b. Sulaymān. 2017. *Katāʾib aʿlām al-akhyār min fuqahāʾ madhhab al-nuʿmān al-mukhtār*. Ed. Ṣafwat Kūsā et al. 4 vols. Istanbul: Maktabat al-irshād.

Kramarovsky, Mark G. 2008. "Solkhat (Crimea) in the 13th and 14th Centuries: People, Culture, and Handicraft Traditions." In *Islamic Art and Architecture in the European Periphery: Crimea, Caucasus, and the Volga-Ural Region*, ed. Barbara Kellner-Heinkele, Joachim Gierlichs, and Brigitte Heuer, 73–82. Wiesbaden, Germany: Harrassowitz Verlag.

Landolt, Hermann, ed. 1972. *Correspondance spirituelle échangée entre Nuroddin Esfarayeni (ob. 717/1317) et son disciple 'Alaoddawleh Semnani (ob. 736/1336)*. Teheran: Département d'iranologie de l'Institut franco-iranien de recherche/Paris: Librairie d'amérique et d'orient Adrian Maisonneuve.

Madelung, Wilferd. 2000. S.v. "Al-Taftāzānī." *Encyclopaedia of Islam*. 2nd ed. Ed. P. Bearman et al. 10: 88–89. Leiden: Brill.

Makdisi, George. 1981. *The Rise of Colleges: Institutions of Learning in Islam and the West*. Edinburgh: Edinburgh University Press.

al-Maqrīzī, Aḥmad b. ʿAlī. 2002. *Durar al-ʿuqūd al-farīda fī tarājim al-aʿyān al-mufīda*. 4 vols. Beirut: Dār al-gharb al-islāmī.

Martini, Giovanni M. 2018. *ʿAlāʾ al-Dawla al-Simnānī between Spiritual Authority and Political Power: A Persian Lord and Intellectual in the Heart of the Ilkhanate*. Leiden: Brill.

Meloy, John L. 2015. *Imperial Power and Maritime Trade: Mecca and Cairo in the Later Middle Ages*. Chicago: Middle East Documentation Center.

Muʿīn al-Fuqarāʾ, Aḥmad b. Muḥammad. 1960. *Kitāb-i Mullāzādah (Mazārāt-i Bukhārā)*. Tehran: Kitābfurūshī-i Ibn Sīnā.

al-Musawi, Muhsin J. 2015. *The Medieval Islamic Republic of Letters: Arabic Knowledge Construction.* Notre Dame, IN: University of Notre Dame Press.

Ohlander, Erik S. 2008. *Sufism in an Age of Transition: ʿUmar al-Suhrawardī and the Rise of the Islamic Mystical Brotherhoods.* Leiden: Brill.

O'Kane, Bernard. 1994. "The Minaret of Vābkent." In *The Art of the Saljūqs in Iran and Anatolia,* ed. Robert Hillenbrand, 46–58. Costa Mesa, CA: Mazda.

Paul, Jürgen. 2008. "Islamizing Sufis in Pre-Mongol Central Asia." In *Islamisation de l'Asie centrale: Processus locaux d'acculturation du VIIe au XIe siècle,* ed. Étienne de la Vaissière, 297–318. Paris: Association pour l'avancement des études iraniennes.

Petry, Carl F. 1985. "Travel Patterns of Medieval Notables in the Near East." *Studia Islamica* 62: 53–87.

Pouzet, Louis. 1991. *Damas au VIIe/XIIIe s. Vie et structures religieuses dans une métropole islamique.* Beirut: Dar el-Machreq. Second ed.

al-Qurashī, ʿAbd al-Qādir b. Muḥammad. 1993. *Al-Jawāhir al-muḍiyya fī ṭabaqāt al-Ḥanafiyya.* 5 vols. Cairo: Hajar.

Reynolds, Dwight F., ed. 2001. *Interpreting the Self: Autobiography in the Arabic Literary Tradition.* Berkeley: University of California Press.

al-Sakhāwī, Muḥammad b. ʿAbd al-Raḥmān. 1934. *Al-Ḍawʾ al-lāmiʿ li-ahl al-qarn al-tāsiʿ.* 12 vols. Cairo: Maktabat al-Quds.

———. 1993. *Al-Tuḥfa al-laṭīfa fī taʾrīkh al-madīna al-sharīfa.* 2 vols. Beirut: Dār al-kutub al-ʿilmiyya.

Spevack, Aaron. 2014. *The Archetypal Sunnī Scholar: Law, Theology, and Mysticism in the Synthesis of al-Bājūrī.* Albany: State University of New York Press.

Spuler, Bertold. 1986. S.v. "Ḳīrīm." *Encyclopaedia of Islam.* 2nd ed. Ed. P. Bearman et al. 5: 136–43. Leiden: Brill.

Steinfels, Amina M. 2012. *Knowledge before Action: Islamic Learning and Sufi Practice in the Life of Sayyid Jalāl al-dīn Bukhārī Makhdūm-i Jahāniyān.* Columbia: University of South Carolina Press.

Subtelny, Maria E. 2001. "The Making of *Bukhārā-yi Sharīf:* Scholars and Libraries in Medieval Bukhara (The Library of Khwāja Muḥammad Pārsā)." In *Studies on Central Asian History in Honor of Yuri Bregel,* ed. Devin A. DeWeese, 79–111. Bloomington: Indiana University Press.

Subtelny, Maria E., and Anas B. Khalidov. 1995. "The Curriculum of Islamic Higher Learning in Timurid Iran in the Light of the Sunni Revival under Shāh-Rukh." *Journal of the American Oriental Society* 115: 210–36.

Taylor, Christopher S. 1999. *In the Vicinity of the Righteous: Ziyāra and the Veneration of Muslim Saints in Late Medieval Egypt.* Leiden: Brill.

Touati, Houari. 2010. *Islam and Travel in the Middle Ages.* Chicago: University of Chicago Press.

Wing, Patrick. 2016. *The Jalayirids: Dynastic State Formation in the Mongol Middle East.* Edinburgh: Edinburgh University Press.

al-Ziriklī, Khayr al-Dīn. 1980. *Al-Aʿlām: Qāmūs tarājim li-ashhar al-rijāl wa'l-nisāʾ min al-ʿArab wa'l-mustaʿribīn wa'l-mustashriqīn.* 8 vols. 5th ed. Beirut: Dār al-ʿilm lil-malāyīn.

Glossary

A (Arabic); C (Chinese); M (Mongolian); P (Persian); T (Turkic)

AL TAMGHA (M) red (imperial) seal
ʿĀLIM (PL. *ʿULAMĀʾ*) (A) scholar
AMĪR (A) commander, amir (also prince)
BAGHATUR (M); *BAHĀDŪR* (P) lit. "hero," title of a military officer
BASQAQ (M); *BASKAK* (T) governor (see also darughachi, shiḥna)
BAKHSHĪ (M) Buddhist monk; shaman
BARAKA (A) spiritual blessing
BA'URCHI (M) cook (member of the guard)
CHINGSANG (C) chancellor
DARUGHACHI (M) lit. "the one who presses the seal," governor, representative of the khan (see also *shiḥna, baskak*)
DAWĀDĀR (A); *DAWĀTDĀR* (P) lit. "bearer of the inkstand," one of the caliph's leading officials
ELCHI (M); *ĪLCHĪ* (P); *YILICHI* (C) envoy, emissary
FAQĪH (A) jurist
FIQH (A) jurisprudence
GÜREGEN (M) son-in-law
ḤĀJIB (A) chamberlain
ḤAJJ (A) pilgrimage to Mecca
HIZĀRA, HAZĀRA (P) myriarchy; military unit of one thousand
IJĀZĀ (A) teaching permission
JAM (M); *YAM* (T) post or relay station; the Mongol postal system
JARGHUCHI (M); *YARGHUCHI* (T) judge
JARLIG (M) see *yarligh*

JASAQ (M) order, regulation, law; the law code ascribed to Chinggis Khan, see *Yasa*
KHATUN (T) noble lady, queen
KELEMECHI (M) translator
KESHIG (M) bodyguard, imperial guard
KHĀNQĀH (A) Sufi hospice
KHUSHDĀSH (T) brother-in-arms
KALĀM (A) Islamic theology
MADRASA (A) Muslim college
MAMLŪK (A) military slave
NOYAN (M) military commander, also "nobleman"
NÖKÖR (M) companion or bondsman of a higher ranking individual
ORDO (M) encampment, mobile court
ORTAQ (T) "partner," merchant trading with the capital of a Mongol dignitary
QA'AN (M) Great Khan, supreme ruler of the empire
QĀḌĪ (A) Muslim judge
QORCHI (M) quiver bearer (member in the guard)
QORUQ (M) Mongol royal tomb
QURILTAI (M) assembly; gathering of nomadic leaders to select a new ruler or make major decisions such as heading for war
SAYYID (A) descendant of the Prophet Muḥammad
SEMUREN (C) lit. "people of various categories," non-Mongol, non-Chinese individuals
SHIḤNA (SHAḤNA) (P) military governor; Persian equivalent of Mongol *darughachi* and Turkic *baskak*
SHUMIYUAN (C) Bureau of Military Affairs
TAMMA (M) garrison troops
TENGRI, TENGGERI (M) Heaven, Sky God
TOUXIA (C) appanages
TÜMEN (M) ten thousand; Myrarchy; army unit of ten thousand soldiers (theoretically); the administrative territory that provides support for a *tümen*
ṬARĪQA (A) Sufi order
ULUS (M) people subject to a certain lord; by extension, nation or state
WAQF (A) Muslim religious endowment
WAQFIYYA endowment deed
WANG (C) king, Prince
WANHUFU (C) myriarchy; military unit of one thousand; see also *tümen*
YAM (T) see *jam*
YARLIGH (T) edict, decree, see *jarlig*
YASA (T) see *jasaq*
YEKE MONGGHOL ULUS Great Mongolian Nation; the appellation of the Mongol Empire, usually applied to the United Mongol Empire (1206–59), but used after 1260 as the Mongol name denoting the realm of the Great Khan
ZĪJ (P) astronomical handbook

Chronology

1162? (1167?)	Temüjin's (Chinggis Khan) birth
1202	Temüjin's defeat of the Tatars
1203	The Baljuna covenant; Temüjin's conquest of the Kereyit tribe
1204	Capture of Constantinople by the army of the Fourth Crusade; Temüjin defeats the Naiman tribe
1206	Great *quriltai* (assembly) and the proclamation of Temüjin as Chinggis Khan, supreme ruler of the tribes in Mongolia
1209	Submission of the Uighur to the Mongols; Chinggis Khan's victory over the Xi Xia (Northwest China)
1211	Submission of the Qarluqs to the Mongols; the Mongols' first attack on the Jin dynasty (North China)
1215	Second Mongol siege of the Jin capital of Zhongdu and conquest of the city
1218	The Qara Khitai fall to the Mongol forces
1218–19	The massacre of Chinggis Khan's trade delegation by the Khwārazmian governor of Utrār (Central Asia)
1220–21	Conquest of the Khwārazmian empire (Central Asia and Eastern Iran)
1223	Battle of the Kalka River: Defeat of the Russians and Qipchaqs by the Mongol generals Sübe'etei and Jebe
1227	Chinggis Khan's conquest of the Xi Xia (Northwest China); Chinggis Khan's death

1229	Ögödei's succession
1231	Jalāl al-Dīn Khwārazmshāh's death
1234	Mongol final conquest of the Jin
1235	Mongol capital of Qaraqorum established by Ögödei in central Mongolia
1236	Beginning of the Mongols' European campaign led by Batu; the Qipchaqs' submission
1239–41	Batu's forces' attack on Kiev and conquest of Russia, and Mongol armies' attack on Poland and Hungary (up to eastern Germany)
1241	Ögödei's death
1243	Battle of Kösedağ: defeat the Seljuks of Anatolia by the forces led by the Mongol general Baiju
1246	Güyük's succession as qa'an; the arrival of Plano Carpini, papal envoy, in Qaraqorum
1246	The summoning of the Council of Lyons by Pope Innocent IV (r. 1243–54)
1248	Güyük Qa'an's death
1250s	The voyage of the pearl merchant Jamāl al-Dīn al-Ṭībī to China
1251	(The Toluid) Möngke's election as qa'an; Toluid coup d'état and massacre of the Ögödeids
1251/2	Baldwin of Hainaut's departure from Constantinople for Qaraqorum
1253	The start of Hülegü's march to the west, as ordered by Möngke
1253–5	The journey of William of Rubruck to Qaraqorum
1254	Qubilai's conquest of Dali in Yunnan
1256	The Battle of Aksarai, the second Mongol conquest of Anatolia; Hülegü defeats the Assassins
1258	Hülegü's conquest of Baghdad and execution of the last ʿAbbasid caliph
1259	Möngke's death during his campaign against the Song; establishment of the Maragha (present-day northwestern Iran) observatory under the supervision of the Muslim astronomer Naṣīr al-Dīn Ṭūsī and by the order of the Hülegü
1260	Qubilai's election as qa'an; beginning of the conflict with his brother Arigh Böke; victory of the Mamluks of Egypt

	and Syria over the Mongols in the Battle of ʿAyn Jālūt; beginning of the Ilkhanate; dissolution of the United Empire
1262	Conflict between the Golden Horde and the Ilkhanate over Tabriz
1264	Ariq Böke's surrender to Qubilai Qa'an
1270	The Battle of Herat, between the Ilkhan Abaqa and Chaghadaid Khan Baraq
1271	Qaidu's self-declaration as the Ögödeid Khan; resurrection the Ögödeid *ulus*
1271	Renaming the Mongol regime in China as the Yuan dynasty
1271–2	The marriage of Pādshāh Khatun of the Qutlughkhanid rulers of Kirmān to the Mongol Ilkhan Abaqa
1274	Qubilai's move to the new capital of Dadu (modern Beijing); first invasion to Japan
1276	Surrender of the Song court; Mongol conquest of the Song capital of Lin'an (Hangzhou)
1277	Battle of Abulustayn (Elbistan, in modern South Turkey) between the Mongols and Mamluks
1279	Drowning of the Song emperor: final Mongol conquest of South China; Mongol invasion of Burma
1280	Qubilai's anti-Muslim edict forbidding the Muslim slaughtering (*halal*)
1280	Yang Tingbi's first maritime embassy to Maʿbar and Kūlam in India
1281	Mongol general Sogatu's punitive expedition against Champa (Central and Southern Vietnam)
1281	Destruction of the Mongol fleet in a typhoon in front of the coast of Japan
1281	Yang Tingbi's second maritime voyage to Kūlam
1283	Beginning of ʿĪsa Kelemechi's mission westward, to the Ilkhanate, on a mission from Qubilai
1285	ʿĪsa Kelemechi's second embassy, from the Ilkhanate to the pope and the Vatican
1294	Qubilai's death; Temür Öljeitü's ascension to the Yuan throne
1295	Ghazan Khan's conversion to Islam
1299–1300	Ilkhanid victory in the Battle of Wādī al-Khaznadār (north of Homs, Syria) over the Mamluks, and five-week long Mongol occupation of Damascus and Syria

1301	Qaidu's death
1301	Fakhr al-Dīn Ṭībī's voyage to Yuan China on an embassy from the Ilkhan Ghazan
1304	The announcement of an all-inclusive peace between the four Mongol khanates
1305–6	Completion of the *Compendium of Chronicles* of the Ilkhanid vizier Rashid al-Din
1308–9	Ilkhan Öljeitü's conversion to Shiʿism
1310	The submission of Chapar, Qaidu's son and heir, to Qubilai's great-grandson Qaishan
1313	Özbek's enthronement in the Golden Horde; the beginning of his Islamization policies; reestablishment of Confucian examination system in Yuan China
1323	Peace agreement between the Mamluks and the Ilkhans; surrender of the Chaghadaid Khan Kebek to the Yuan, thereby completing the khanates' acknowledgment of the qa'an's superiority.
1328	Yesün Temür's death in the Yuan summer capital Shangdu; "The War of the Two Capitals" succession struggle; enthronement of Tuq Temür
1331	Tarmashirin's appointment as khan of the Chaghadaid Khanate; Islamization of Transoxania
1333	Enthronement of Toghon Temür, the last Yuan emperor
1335	Disintegration of the Ilkhanate following the death of Abū Sa'īd
1346	Spread of the Black Death to Sarai and the Crimea
1347	Dissolution of the Chaghadaid Khanate to western and eastern parts
1357	The invasion of Janibeg, ruler of the Golden Horde, into Azerbaijan and occupation of Tabriz
1360	The overthrowing of the last of the Batuid line of the Golden Horde by the Shaibanid Khizr
1368	Fall of the Yuan; beginning of the Ming dynasty

Contributors

OR AMIR is a PhD candidate in the Department of Islamic and Middle Eastern Studies at the Hebrew University of Jerusalem.

MICHAL BIRAN is the Max and Sophie Mydans Foundation Professor in the Departments of Islamic and Middle Eastern Studies and Asian Studies at the Hebrew University of Jerusalem.

JONATHAN BRACK is Assistant Professor in the Department of Middle East Studies at Ben-Gurion University of the Negev.

FRANCESCA FIASCHETTI is University Assistant in the History Department and the Institute for Austrian Historical Research at University of Vienna.

JOHN GIEBFRIED is Assistant Professor of History at East Georgia State College.

MATANYA GILL is a PhD candidate in the Department of Islamic and Middle Eastern Studies at the Hebrew University of Jerusalem.

FLORENCE HODOUS is a Postdoctoral Fellow at Renmin University, School of Chinese Classics.

YOICHI ISAHAYA is Assistant Professor in the Department of Slavic-Eurasian Research Center, Hokkaido University.

SZILVIA KOVÁCS is Senior Lecturer in the Department of Medieval History at the University of Szeged.

HODONG KIM is the Distinguished Professor in the Department of Asian History at Seoul National University.

AMIR MAZOR is a Research Fellow in the Department of Israel Studies at the University of Haifa.

MASAKI MUKAI is Associate Professor in the Faculty of Global and Regional Studies at Doshisha University.

BRUNO DE NICOLA is Lecturer in the History of the Middle East at Goldsmiths University of London, and a Research Fellow at the Austrian Academy of Sciences.

YIHAO QIU is Associate Professor in the Department of History at Fudan University.

VERED SHURANY is a PhD candidate in Department of Asian Studies at the Hebrew University of Jerusalem.

SARA NUR YILDIZ is a Research Scholar at the Max Planck Institute for the History of Science.

Index

Founded in 1893,
UNIVERSITY OF CALIFORNIA PRESS
publishes bold, progressive books and journals on topics in the arts, humanities, social sciences, and natural sciences—with a focus on social justice issues—that inspire thought and action among readers worldwide.

The UC PRESS FOUNDATION
raises funds to uphold the press's vital role as an independent, nonprofit publisher, and receives philanthropic support from a wide range of individuals and institutions—and from committed readers like you. To learn more, visit ucpress.edu/supportus.

Made in the USA
Las Vegas, NV
14 May 2021

23020982R00208